An Experiential Understanding of How All that Is Came to Be

To Aviva,
  With the focus of attention comes
understanding. In this way, the patterns
that exist in the world will become clear.
    —Jonathan R. Wachtel

Jonathan R. Wachtel

ISBN: 1-4392-4121-X
ISBN-13: 9781439241219
LCCN: 2009904735

Visit www.booksurge.com to order additional copies.

Dedication

I dedicate this book to all those who have been willing to listen to me when I've needed to be heard, and to all those who have been willing to try to understand me, my ideas, and my experience of the world.

I also dedicate this book to the Source of all that is, who has granted me the joy of understanding and the ability to share this experience with you.

Contents

On the Origin of the Nature and Content of All Experience

I exist. And I am experiencing things that have some form of existence. I am not the ultimate origin of the things that I experience. When I am like a mountain stream that allows fresh rainwater to flow through it, rather than like a pond that receives but never shares, I realize that I am not the ultimate origin of any of the things that I experience, that I have. So, as the mountain stream receives its water from the rain that comes down from the sky, I am compelled to inquire as to the origin of all that I experience, of all that I have.

Since I receive all that I have, the Source of all things must provide a compliment to this, sharing all that It has. But then I must ask how everything that exists came to be from this Source.

I see the pattern that plays out in my experience of the world, from my beginning, onward. First, there is only "I", and all that exists is for the "I", and everything is "I", sensing what the "I" senses and knowing what the "I" knows. Whatever benefits the "I"—whatever fulfills the desires of the "I"— benefits all, for the "I" is all there is.

Then there are others, but they are merely projections of the "I", existing separately from the "I" and sensing and know- ing different things from the "I", but experiencing what the "I" would experience if the "I" were in their place. The benefit of the "I"—the fulfillment of the desires of the "I"—is all that matters, since these others are merely projections of the

"I"; these others exist for the sake of the "I"—for the sake of the fulfillment of the desires of the "I".

Then these others become other "I"'s, sensing and experiencing the world differently from the "I"—with all of the same desires as the "I", but in different proportions than in the "I" (prioritized differently than in the "I"), and with different past experiences from the "I", so that these other "I"'s are often led to think and feel and say and do different things from what the "I" would if the "I" were in their place. What benefits the "I", alone, may not benefit all the "I"'s, and so the "I" considers the desires of the other "I"'s as well as those of the "I", for the "I" seeks to benefit *all*, and not just the "I"—the "I" seeks the fulfillment of the desires of *all* the "I"'s, and not just the fulfillment of the desires of the "I". And yet, since it is through the experience of other "I"'s that the "I" comes to be truly an "I", and since it is in the desire of the "I" who is aware of being an "I" to fulfill the desires of *all* the "I"'s (including those of the "I"), it is by fulfilling the desires of *all* the "I"'s that the "I" comes to fulfill its own desires.

I see that this pattern plays out in others' experiences of the world as well as in my own, as though it is a paradigm that all "I"'s must follow.

I also see that the world in my experience manifests similar paradigms on every scale and level of existence. The inertia of physical bodies—that all things that are not in motion remain not in motion unless acted upon by some force, and that all things that are in motion remain in their straight-line motion unless acted upon by some force—applies not just to the physical motions of bodies, but also to the motions and patterns of thoughts and feelings and speech and actions in me and in others: They remain in their set patterns of motion or lack of motion unless acted upon by some force. The attraction of physical bodies—the gravitational attraction of bodies to each other—applies not just to the physical aspect of things in the way usually associated with "gravity", but also to ions with opposite charges which attract one another, and to water droplets which attract and cohere to each other and attract and adhere to other objects, and to a person who attracts some other person, and to a thought's contents which attract more thoughts with these contents and which also attract the actualization of these contents, and to a feeling which attracts more of that type of feeling, and to an action which attracts more of that type of action. And here there is the realization that the attraction of things explains even the inertia of bodies—the perpetuation of motion because of the attraction of more of that type of motion. There is a law—there are patterns—that seems to govern all things in the hierarchy, but it has many different manifestations and forms, on every level of existence. As the stars orbit the centers of galaxies, planets orbit the stars, and as the planets orbit the stars, electrons in an atom orbit the nucleus of that atom, and all these things orbit these other things because they are attracted to these other things and they merely cannot yet reach these other things, because their motion is not toward these other things toward which they are attracted, and they are also attracted to more of this motion, and so they cannot yet reach these other things.

All things in this world manifest some form and degree of attraction, or pulling, or taking in—of desire to receive. And all things in this world manifest some form and degree of repulsion, or pushing away, or letting go—of desire to share. And there always needs to be some environment in which— some medium through which—this receiving and sharing can take place. Atoms of metallic elements desire to share electrons (to become positively charged), and atoms of nonmetallic elements desire to receive electrons (to become negatively charged), and this sharing and receiving takes place in space and time. The sun shares its light and heat with the earth, and the earth receives this light and heat, and this sharing and receiving also takes place in space and time. The male desires to share his genes, and the female desires to receive them in order to share them, along with—and in combination with—hers, with the world.

And as I work my way up through more and more complex life, the complexity of the "I", and the "I"'s recognition of other "I"'s as other "I"'s, becomes greater. For here we see the pattern of experience play itself out through evolution. The simplest of things, such as physical bodies—like stars and planets—desire to receive one another, attracting one another to themselves as though they are the only "I". In life, the actions become more conscious. In the single-celled amoeba, everything is about the "I" and for the "I", and everything is the desire to receive—the desire to receive food and the propagation of the "I" and the "I"'s genes, for the sake of the "I". Gradually, multicellular life develops, in which cells must share with and receive from one another in order to survive, themselves, and even this can be seen as just the desire to receive— the desire to receive the propagation of the "I". But, with multicellular organisms comes the interaction of multicellular organisms and, on the way up through dogs and dolphins and elephants and chimps and humans, there is an increasing recognition of the other as an other "I" who must also be considered in the "I"'s own actions because other "I"'s should benefit just as the "I" should benefit, for they are other "I"'s, with different experiences of the world from the "I" that are equally as valid as the experience of the "I".

And in the individual human being's own experience of life, development follows this course of progression all within itself, similarly to the way the development of the human fetus follows the evolution of the human species from simpler life-forms—from the appearance of webbed toes and fingers, and gills, up to lungs; from the appearance of two heart chambers, to three, to four; from the appearance of the spinal cord and brain stem up to the cerebral cortex.

All of this reflection of paradigms played out in some form on every level of existence is similar to the way every part of a holographic plate contains information about the entire image of which it is a picture, such that if a holographic plate is shattered, from every piece of it the entire three-dimensional image can be produced—and it is merely that smaller pieces will yield fuzzier images of that entire picture than larger pieces, which will yield fuzzier images than the whole holographic plate together as one.

Considering all of this reflection of paradigms on every level of existence in this way, it seems appropriate to suspect that the pattern that each "I" follows (in its experience over the course of its development) has its origins in the pattern that the ultimate "I"—the Source of all existence—follows. After all, every experience of the "I" (from the perspective of the "I")—including the experience of *being* an "I", and of there being other "I"'s—comes ultimately from (is received from) the Source of all that is. And so, perhaps, these experiences follow the pattern they do because the pattern of the ongoing creation of the world (of the reception of existence by the world), from the perspective of the Source of existence, follows this pattern (thereby making it the object-of-which-the-holographic-plate-is-a-picture version—the first version and the ultimate origin—of this pattern).

If I posit this and see how it plays out, I see the following[1]:

---

[1]   The way this pattern expresses itself from the Source's perspective will be recognized later on as actually being a bit different from this, but this is a good start to understanding accurately what follows. Further, it should be noted that the way in which this book is set up, it will generally be the case that ideas that are presented will be subject to possible modification later on, for (as we will see) this kind of progression is necessary for any true understanding to arise.

First, there is only "I", and all that exists is for the "I", and everything is "I", sensing what the "I" senses and knowing what the "I" knows. Whatever benefits the "I"—whatever fulfills the desires of the "I"—benefits all, for the "I" is all there is.

Then there are others, but they are merely projections of the "I", existing separately from the "I" and sensing and knowing different things from the "I", but experiencing what the "I" would experience if the "I" were in their place. The benefit of the "I"—the fulfillment of the desires of the "I"—is all that matters, since these others are merely projections of the "I"; these others exist for the sake of the "I"—for the sake of the fulfillment of the desires of the "I".

Then these others become other "I"'s, sensing and experiencing the world differently from the "I"—with all of the same desires as the "I", but in different proportions than in the "I" (prioritized differently than in the "I"), and with different past experiences from the "I", so that these other "I"'s are often led to think and feel and say and do different things from what the "I" would if the "I" were in their place. What benefits the "I", alone, may not benefit all the "I"'s, and so the "I" considers the desires of the other "I"'s as well as those of the "I", for the "I" seeks to benefit *all*, and not just the "I"—the "I" seeks the fulfillment of the desires of *all* the "I"'s, and not just the fulfillment of the desires of the "I". And yet, since it is through the experience of other "I"'s that the "I" comes to be truly an "I", and since it is in the desire of the "I" who is aware of being an "I" to fulfill the desires of *all* the "I"'s (including those of the "I"), it is by fulfilling the desires of *all* the "I"'s that the "I" comes to fulfill its own desires.

On How the Source Relates to Us

Thus, I see that my experience of the world, and everyone's experience of the world, is a reflection of that of the Source of all things.

But the Source has a different perspective from all of us, for that perspective is the perspective from which all perspectives derive; it is the original whole that all perspectives reflect in holographic form.

As to the relationship between the Source and us, I have said that we receive all that we have, and the Source shares all that It has. And I have pointed out that all things in this world share and receive in some form, thereby reflecting the ultimate paradigm for all sharing and receiving that takes place—the paradigm of the way the Source shares with us and we receive from the Source. And I have pointed out that there is always an environment or medium that allows this sharing and receiving to take place. So I am now compelled to inquire as to the nature of the medium through which the sharing and receiving are allowed to take place between the Source and us.

The Source is like the sun in its sharing with us, allowing life to exist. But if there were only the sun and us, and nothing else at all, then we could never survive, for we cannot subsist on the sun's light and warmth alone. Yet the sun is seemingly the source of all of the physical energy that we take in ultimately; we are receiving all of the energy for our physical subsistence from the sun ultimately. How can this be so if we are not living on the sun's light and warmth, alone? The answer is that the sun shares with us via its radiating energy in light and warmth, and plants transform this radiating energy into a form that we are capable of taking in and subsisting on (and, in this way, plants provide us with food—in such forms as fruits, vegetables, and grains—shelter—in such forms as wood and leaves—and clothing—in such forms as cotton and leaves). Nearly all of the reception of the sun's energy by most living creatures (and all very complex life) on Earth—as far as real subsistence is concerned—is allowed by the existence of plants, which convert what the sun shares into a form that other living creatures (including us) can receive.

In this, it seems that we have a wonderful metaphor for better understanding the relationship between the Source and us.

The sun is unaffected by us. We go about our lives, capable of living only because of what we receive from the sun, and yet the sun remains unaffected by us. The differences in the seasons and the days, in the degrees of heat and cold, light and darkness, are all due to *our* movement in relation to the sun, and not the reverse.

The sun shares, allowing life to exist, but its form of sharing cannot maintain most life directly. The sun is always sharing, radiating its energy outward, whether we receive this energy and make use of it or not.

What the sun shares can be received in many forms, such that it can nourish plants, heat the Earth's surface, provide solar energy, and so on. Part of the energy that the sun shares can be seen, and part of it cannot. With regard to that part which is capable of being seen, the sun radiates a unified, white light, but when this light is allowed to pass through a prism or something else that refracts it, many differentiated forms of light are derived—of all different colors and wavelengths. Thus, from unity, there comes multiplicity.

The world is made up of differentiated unity, and every aspect, every perspective is a color of the rainbow of the white light that emanates from the Source. Every aspect, every perspective in this differentiated world of multiple dimensions, and multiple colors, and multiple numbers, and multiple languages, and multiple "I"'s, is an emanation from that unified Source, and if one could put all the colors back together completely to produce *one* again, then one would have the objective, ultimate reality—the form of sharing that exists before it is differentiated or transformed by the central column in all of these interactions. The environment, space and time, plants, a prism—they all act as the central column, the medium of transference, the transformer or converter that makes one energy source capable of being utilized by an appliance that is not compatible with that source.

In this world—in this reality—everything is subjective. Only the Source "I" has an objective view; every other "I" has an inherently subjective view—sensing and experiencing the world from its own position in time and space, with its own past experiences and its own unique proportions of desires that guide it in its thoughts and feelings and speech and actions. The Source palette of colors is the same for all things that *are*, but everything and every "I" in this world is a unique mixture of those colors. And so nothing in this world is a complete representation of the Source; it simply cannot be, because the Source is not bound by the limitations of time and space, for the Source is the Source of these things—because the Source is endless and infinite, for It is the Source of all things in this world, all things that are finite and so need a Source of all that they have in order to continue to subsist. The mountain stream would cease to run with water if precipitation stopped replenishing it, the plants would cease to grow if the sun ceased its shining upon them, and all things would cease to exist if the Source no longer shared existence with them.

But how do things come to be as they are? What exactly differentiates the unified form of sharing emanated by the

Source? The plants convert the sun's emanation for us, and the atmosphere condenses the water for the stream. So what is the central column between the Source and us?

I shall go back to experience for the answer, for all things that *are* seem to be the way they are because they are a reflection of the way things came to be.

What allows communication between one "I" and another "I"? When an "I" comes to recognize itself as an "I" and comes to recognize others as other "I"'s—realizing that its experience is different from that of other "I"'s—how does one "I" communicate its experience to other "I"'s? The answer is *language*. The "I" communicates with other "I"'s, sharing its experience with them, through written and spoken *language*. This is the central column between the Source and us. Language is the means by which the Source "I" communicates with us, sharing Its experience with us, causing our experience to reflect Its experience.

But how can it be language, you might ask? I don't see or hear words everywhere. And yet my language becomes what I see and what I hear. Every "I" holds the power to shape and mold what the Source shares through its use of language in its thought, and in its feeling, and in its speech and action. Every "I" holds the power to determine the form of manifestation of the world that emanates from the Source, for it is *language*—the language expressed through and used in our thoughts and our feelings and our speech and our actions—that differentiates the unified white light into the multifaceted, multidimensional, multiplicitous reality that we experience.

The Source writes and speaks the world into existence, but the Source uses a language that is the Source of all languages, and no language that we have or use can possibly be exactly the same language that the Source uses, and yet every language that we use (every spoken language, every written language, and even every language expressed through thought or feeling or body) is a reflection of the language that the Source uses, as is appropriate in a holographic world, in which every part contains information about, and reflects, the whole. As our experience reflects the Source's experience, the tools we use to shape our experience reflect the tools that the Source uses to shape *Its* experience.

Every "I" is a reflection of the Source of all that is, the experience of every "I" is a reflection of the experience of that Source "I", and the tools of communication and sharing used by the "I" are reflections of the tools of communication and sharing used by that Source "I". And as the Source "I" gives existence to all that *is*, sharing Its experience with every other "I" via the words that It writes and speaks in some paradigmatic, primordial form, every "I" gives the final form to all that *is* via the words that it writes and speaks and expresses through its thoughts and feelings and speech and actions, transforming the sharing of the Source "I" into a form that every other "I" can receive and experience.

And so I see that my experience of the world—*our* experience of the world—tells me—tells *us*—very much about the nature of the Source of all that *is* and about how all that *is* came to be—and *comes* to be—from that Source.

What We Can Learn from this about God and Religion

Let us consider what we now know in light of all of the above:

The Source, being the Source "I" of which every "I" is a sort of holographic reflection, is in some paradigmatic way self-aware, as every "I" that recognizes the existence of other "I"'s is self-aware, understanding the relationship between the "I" and other "I"'s and desiring the fulfillment of the desires of all "I"'s. The Source is not some mindless force of existence, but is, rather, a self-aware Being who willfully shares existence and experience with the world, providing the paradigm of the way one "I" can share its existence and experience with another "I", communicating these through the willful and conscious use of some primordial form of thought, felt, spoken, written, and bodily language.

If "good" is defined as "desiring and working toward the fulfillment of the desires of all", then we can define the Source as good.

If we now replace the term "Source" with the term "God" and mean to convey exactly the same things by this more familiar term, then many things may come to light.

God exists. God is good. God consciously and willfully brings forth the world at every moment for, like the stream requires the continued influx of water to exist, the world—being finite and therefore requiring a Source for its continued existence and delineated nature—requires the continued influx of all that allows it to be as it is at every moment.

God, through the use of language, delineates all that God shares, providing a limiting or binding framework that differentiates existence into all of its manifestations. This limiting framework is that of the dimensions of time and space, which serve to separate the reflection from the reality. We and the world are the reflection; God is the reality. God is boundless, while we are bound. God is boundless because God is the source of all that is bounding or limiting; God is the source of language, and only God is not differentiated by language. Everything else is differentiated by language and therefore is separated from the Source that is God.

This separation, however, allows us to be distinct from God; it allows us to be other "I"'s with our own subjective perceptions, our own subjective experiences, our own self-awareness and ability to share all of our subjective perceptions and experiences through the use of language. This separation allows us to have our own subjective and experiential understanding of others as other "I"'s and of God as the ultimate other "I", such that a greater understanding of others yields a greater understanding of ourselves, and a greater understanding of ourselves yields a greater understanding of others, and a greater understanding of both ourselves and others yields a greater understanding of God, and a greater understanding of the *relationship* between ourselves and others yields a greater understanding of the *relationship* between ourselves and God.

It is our separation from God that allows us to be like God in having the ability to create the world according to our will through the use of language.

It is, in this light, the *act of creation* by which *God* communicates with *us* and by which *we* communicate with *God*. *God* communicates to *us* through God's use of language, which guides us via our intuition when we learn to listen, and which ultimately manifests as the creation of the world. *We* communicate with *God* through our use of language in our thought and feeling and speech and action, by which we let God know how we want the world to be created—what form we want it to take. This is what prayer is all about. If we do it right, prayer is merely the use of the language of thought and feeling and speech and action, by which we let God know what we want in our next and future experience.

In this light, we are praying all the time—with every thought or feeling or inclination to which we give our focused and continued attention, with every word we speak and every action we take in this world. With everything that we send out through the use of language, we are asking for God to give us more of this.

As many religions maintain, God spoke (and speaks) the world into existence through the use of language. And this language is both written and spoken in some primordial way. (It is thought and felt in some primordial way as well.) As we require plants to convert the sun's energy into a form that we can take in and subsist on, we require some mediation between us and God as well, and this mediation is provided by the (somehow) written or engraved language of text. This text is like a blueprint for the creation of the world, as the Jewish body of commentary known as the midrash states of the Torah (and as the Torah is held by itself to be the *tree of life*—an interesting possible metaphorical reference to the nature of the text as being the central column between God and the world), and as Islamic Sufism holds of the Koran, and as Hinduism maintains that Vishnu gave the blueprint of creation to Brahma. And the language that God uses to create the world, speaking the text aloud, is the language of creation, itself, as Judaism (and especially Kabbalah) holds of Hebrew, and as Islam (and especially Sufism) holds of Arabic, and so on.

In short, many religions hold some specific language and some specific text (or texts) as sacred, for these are believed to be the language and the text with which God created (and creates) the world.

In light of all that is above, every religion that holds that there is a language and a text that are special, in that they are those used by God in the creation of the world, is correct in this. But, in light of all that is above, every religion is *incorrect* in its belief that it has *the* language and/or *the* text, for this is impossible. Every written language is a reflection of the language used by God to write the blueprint of creation, and every spoken language is a reflection of the language used by God to speak the world into existence. But, due to the nature of the differentiated world, every language that exists within this world is *no more than* a reflection of the language used by God.

Let us look at the metaphor of the hologram to better understand this. If God is the "object" whose "image" is, in some way, captured in the primordial holographic plate, then the holographic plate (in this case, the text made up of God's written language that is being used to convey God's experience) is a record of God's nature and experience in some way. In this case, when God reads (or speaks) aloud God's sort of memoir or autobiography by breathing or shining existence into the words of the holographic plate, the hologram that is the world (and all of its contents, including us and the languages we use) is produced. The holographic world, itself, is composed of God's spoken words. The languages of our thoughts, feelings, speech and actions are all part of the hologram—the reflection that arises when God speaks aloud the words. We cannot write or speak those same words with a mere written or spoken language formed by our own hands or lips, for the world, itself (including we, ourselves), is composed of those words. The language that God uses is the sort of universal template for all languages, and all languages that we use— essentially the entire contents of our thoughts and feelings and speech and actions—reflect that template language, but none of our languages are anything more than a single color of the spectrum of colors that arise when the white light of God's sharing (which provides existence) is shined through God's differentiating template (which provides the forms that existence takes). Essentially, every language used by human beings is a differentiated version of the source language.

So why do religions hold the idea that they have *the* language and *the* text? Because there *is* such a language and there *is* such a text, and as we can discern in and infer from the pattern of experience of every "I", each religion is made up of a group of "I"'s who are either perceiving themselves as the only "I" that exists (which often seems to be the perception of extremists in any religion), or who are projecting their "I" experience onto everyone else, perceiving only their own subjective experience as valid (and as the objective) and viewing all other "I"'s as simply others, and not as other "I"'s with other, valid experiences and perceptions. In this light, a more-fully developed religion (which would require self-aware adherents) would recognize itself as being *one* valid perspective—a *single* "I"—and would recognize that there exist *other* religions—*other* "I"'s—with *equally valid* perspectives.

All that has just been said has implications for religious practice just as it does for religious belief. The practices of religions—whether involving the language of thought or feeling or speech or action or any or all of these—are, like the written and spoken teachings from which they derive, merely subjective differentiations of God's language. We speak through the manifestation of our prayers and our religious practices as God speaks through the manifestation of the world. And every religion's practices are a language that is one of many that are all like the different colors to which God's unified white light gives rise when shined through God's differentiating words.

There are those who will not see things as I see them, but those who are self-aware "I"'s will see that the implications of this are actually quite beautiful, for it is not that this all diminishes the significance of any religion's beliefs or practices in any way per se. It is, rather, the case that every religion can improve upon itself by becoming self-aware in the sense that its adherents become self-aware. And if this were to happen, then the adherents of every religion would perceive their beliefs and practices as composing a single, although inherently subjective, valid view of the world, and that it is every religion together, learning from the similarity and contrast of one another, that may approach some greater understanding of the Source and of the language that the Source uses. As we learn from the experience of the single "I" that it is not that this experience is not valid, but rather that it is one of many valid experiences had by many different "I"'s, so it is with the beliefs and practices of a single religion. And as we learn how the interaction of multiple "I"'s is required for the true understanding of the nature of the "I" and of the relationship between the "I" and other "I"'s, and how all of this is required for the understanding of God and of the relationship between the "I" and God, so it is with multiple religions. And as we learn from the experience of the "I" that the self-aware "I" recognizes that the desires of different "I"'s differ, and so the self-aware "I" desires the fulfillment of the desires of all the "I"'s, so it should be with religions. Every "I" desires to exist and to have its existence and experiences perceived as valid, and so every "I" should desire and work toward this goal for all "I"'s; and every religion, as a group of "I"'s, should desire and work toward this goal with regard to all religions as well.

Further, this does not even merely apply to all religions, for every person and every group of people should consider what can be learned from the self-aware "I" and should desire and work toward the fulfillment of the desires of all the "I"'s—of every other person and every other group.

And this discussion would not be complete without the mention of science, for science (like nearly every paradigm created and adhered to by a large group of people) is like the religions in its being so largely a paradigm that is not that of the self-aware "I". It is true that mathematics and language can describe the world. This is due to what has been said above, that God wrote and spoke (and writes and speaks) the world into existence. Mathematics, as every other language, is one differentiation of the paradigmatic language that God uses to do this. And, so, some primordial language composes all that exists, and the fact that we can use languages (including mathematics) to accurately describe the world reflects this. And science is an internally valid perspective on the world, but it would benefit (and gain a fuller understanding of the world that is closer to the objective) if its adherents recognized that science is not the only "I"—that there are other "I"'s with equally valid perspectives on the world.

On Differentiation and the Resulting Requirement for a Brain to Coordinate the Efforts of (and thereby Reunify) the Specialized Parts

Ultimately, the perception of reality of the "I" becomes clearer and more accurate when the "I" becomes self-aware and this perception begins to be informed by the perceptions of other "I"'s—perceptions that the "I" cannot have in itself, but that it can come almost to experience as it receives the experiences that are shared with it by other "I"'s via communication, via language of some sort. While the experience of the "I" that is not self-aware is *internally* valid, until the "I" begins to recognize the validity of the existence and experience of other "I"'s, the experience of the "I" is not as close to the experience of the Source "I" as it could be. The experience of the Source "I" provides the white light from which all differentiated colors that are the experiences of all other "I"'s emanate. So, prior to self-awareness (and therefore prior to the recognition of other "I"'s), the experience of the "I" is not so accurately representative of that of the Source "I"—the "I" that is the source of all experience in the first place.

From experiencing the world through a very subjective, warped lens, through which it is perceived that there is only the "I", every "I" is capable of becoming less like a pond and more like a stream—of continually receiving that which the Source "I" shares of Its own experience, so that the experience of the "I" becomes more accurately representative of the objective experience of the Source "I"—so that the "I" grows to look at the world through a clear and non-distorted lens that allows light to flow through it unhindered, rather than through a warped lens that changes the shape and form of that light. And so, while internally valid, the experience of the "I" that is not self-aware is only part of the complete experience of that "I", for that "I" must progress through the rest of the pattern of experience of the "I" toward self-awareness in order to attain a validity that is not only internal but that is consistent with the validity of the experience of other "I"'s.

The pattern of growth is from one "I" working toward one goal (the fulfillment of the desires of the "I"), to a branching "I" that somehow seems to be working toward multiple goals (the fulfillment of the desires of others) even as one goal (the fulfillment of the desires of the "I") is above all others in importance, to multiple "I"'s working mutually toward a common goal (the fulfillment of the desires of all "I"'s) that truly encompasses and unites multiple goals within it; it is from unity, toward differentiated and specialized multiplicity, toward interconnected and united multiplicity. The unity of unity requires no language to express its experience, for there is nothing else to which to express it. Multiplicity, at first, ineffectively uses communication amongst its parts because the fulfillment of only one part—the part that is perceiving other parts—is important. But the unity that comes through multiplicity requires communication amongst all of the individual components, for every component is important in the fulfillment of every component, and every component must be informed as to the experience of the other components in order to work with them toward the fulfillment of all components.

The realization that must come from this (the lesson that must be learned from this), is that communication—the sharing of the experience of the "I" with other "I"'s, and the reception of the experience of other "I"'s by the "I", all through language—becomes necessary when differentiation and specialization occurs, yielding other "I"'s whose fulfillment is interconnected with and interdependent upon that of the "I".

Let us examine some of the ways this pattern manifests in the progression of the world's history:

Life began in the universe as a single-celled organism that sought to fulfill its own desires and that had no ability or need to communicate with any other organism. *It* was all there was from its own perspective, and so the fulfillment of its desires is all that mattered, and this fulfillment was its goal. Its desire was continued existence, and so its goal was continued existence. Of course, there were other desires, as that of obtaining food, but all of these were part of the desire to continue to exist.

Then, there were other single-celled organisms, but these did not matter to each of the individual organisms, except in the possibility that the other single-celled organisms might provide the possibility of food—fulfilling the desire of the "I" that does the consuming, for this affirms its existence, but certainly not fulfilling the desire of the "I" that is consumed, for this denies its existence. This denial of the validity of the existence of other "I"'s reveals lack of self-awareness. There are others, but only *one* "I"—for whom all others exist.

When single-celled organisms gained the ability to self-replicate and reproduce, with RNA or DNA, this was the beginning of a kind of language via which the organisms could share their existence with other organisms, giving existence to other organisms.

Eventually, some single-celled organisms began to gather into groups, becoming simple multicellular organisms, but there was little if any communication in these groups. Each organism worked for the benefit of itself—for the fulfillment of its own desires—and being in a group with other organisms had become beneficial to each organism (to its goal of its own continued existence), so this grouping was for the sake of the "I" and not for the sake of the others.

Then, each single-celled organism within some of the groups began to specialize, working toward the fulfillment of its own desires through one activity or another, but not through all of the activities that it used to carry out (and that it needed carried out in order for it to be fulfilled in all of its desires). In this way, each single-celled organism began to be dependent upon each other single-celled organism within the group to fulfill all of its desires. And, thus, communication amongst the cells became necessary in this, a true and complex multicellular organism.

The development of an individual human being reiterates the pattern that brought about the species, and so the human being begins as a single cell (a zygote), which divides into an increasing number of cells, each of which then differentiates and specializes. In the body of a human being, each of the specialized cells must work toward the fulfillment of the desires of all of the cells together as a whole, for the fulfillment of every cell's desires is dependent upon the fulfillment of every other cell's desires. And communication amongst most of the cells is accomplished via the language of hormones.

However, in the human body, as each of the cells performs its own specialized function, its goal is merely the continuation of its own existence. The cells, themselves, are not truly self-aware, for the cells, themselves, do not recognize the validity of the existence and experience of other cells; they merely work toward the fulfillment of their own desires. Sure, the experiences of the cells are communicated to other cells, but there is an overseer of all this. Without the brain, communication amongst all of the cells—communication that allows the specialized cells to work together toward the goal of the fulfillment of the desires of all of the cells—would not occur.

When there is significant differentiation and specialization—when there is a significant multiplicity—then in order to re-establish unity in a common purpose, there needs to be some way that communication amongst the individual parts can still occur, and so there needs to be some kind of core or center of communication that oversees the activities of the individual parts—a core that retains the full-picture perspective that somehow entails the goal of the fulfillment of all of the individual parts. In the individual body of specialized cells, the brain is supposed to perform this function. But there is a hierarchy here, for every cell works toward the fulfillment of the purpose of the tissue of which it is a part, toward the fulfillment of the purpose of the organ of which this tissue is a part, toward the fulfillment of the purpose of the organ system of which this organ is a part, and toward the fulfillment of the purpose of the organism of which this organ system is a part.

Every specialized heart cell works toward the fulfillment of its own purpose, and toward the fulfillment of the purpose of the heart tissue, and toward the fulfillment of the purpose of the heart, and toward the fulfillment of the purpose of the circulatory system, and toward the fulfillment of the purpose of the entire organism. And every specialized lung cell works toward the fulfillment of its own purpose, and toward the fulfillment of the purpose of the lung tissue, and toward the fulfillment of the purpose of the lungs, and toward the fulfillment of the purpose of the respiratory system, and toward the fulfillment of the purpose of the entire organism. The goal of every cell includes the performance of its own specialized function, and the proper fulfillment of this goal—this function—allows it to fulfill its purpose as part of a tissue, as part of an organ, as part of an organ system, as part of an organism, and so on, all the way up to its purpose as part of the world in its entirety, which is to achieve fulfillment by receiving existence and experience from the Source, which shares Its existence and Its experience with the world.

In the hierarchy within the body, the brain coordinates the efforts of all of the other organs via the language of hormones[2] that are secreted into the circulatory system by various organs, often triggering the secretion of other hormones and ultimately triggering the alteration of how some function is being performed by some group of cells within the body when that group of cells receives the message—a message that has been sent after consideration of the fulfillment of the desires of all of the cells, together as an organism. The cells work together as organs that share their experience with other organs, usually via the brain, and the brain coordinates their efforts so that the desires of all of them, together as an organism, can be fulfilled.

This same pattern manifests itself on the scale of a nation, in which town, state, and federal governments act sort of like tissues, organs, and organ systems, respectively. Ultimately, without communication amongst the individual specialized parts, the whole that the parts combine to form is like a simple multicellular organism—with every part working toward the fulfillment of itself and seeing others as mere projections of itself that should be working toward its *own* fulfillment. And this would be an incomplete experience and would result in the denial of the validity of the existence and experience of the other parts.

In this manifestation of the pattern of experience, individual people act like the specialized cells, and the organism that they compose is the entirety of humanity on Earth, with all of the nations being like the organ systems that, if not recognizing the validity of the existence and experience of the

---

2   The brain also controls muscle movements and so forth through electrochemical signals (and neurotransmitters) sent to the muscles via the brain stem and spinal cord and the rest of the nervous system.

other nations—and sharing their individual experience with one another and receiving the individual experiences of the other nations, the other "I"'s—will eventually cease to exist as "I"'s in themselves. Ultimately, when an "I" is not self-aware, its existence and experience cannot be perpetuated effectively and optimally because it does not continually receive the fresh, life-giving water of existence like a stream and because its existence and experience are interconnected with and interdependent upon the existence and experience of all other "I"'s and yet it does not work toward the fulfillment of the desires of all "I"'s.

When an "I" denies the validity of the existence and experience of other "I"'s, it denies the validity of its *own* existence and experience because, though the existence and experience of an "I" that is not self-aware is internally valid, it is inherently subjective—in a world in which its existence and experience are, in reality, one of many, in which it is *not* actually the only true "I". And so, though internally valid, the existence and experience of the "I" that is not self-aware cannot persist forever because they are not *externally* valid—they are not consistent with the existence and experience of other "I"'s, and so they will eventually cease to be, one way or another. Either the existence and experience of the "I" that is not self-aware will cease to be because the "I" has become self-aware, or they will cease to be because the "I" will cease to be—because when a specialized cell in a true multicellular organism does not communicate with the other specialized cells and work with them toward the fulfillment of all of them, cells and organs die and the entire organism suffers.

The development of nations was like the development of true multicellular organisms. In a true multicellular organism, the failure of a few cells to perform their function will likely eventually result in their own demise, but the organism as a whole will still survive. And it used to be, before the earth was like a true multicellular organism, that states within nations, and even whole nations, could die, and humanity, as a whole, could still persist. But the healthy and cooperative function of nearly all of the organs and organ systems in a true multicellular organism—in which the specialization of each organ and organ system is so extensive that no organ or organ system can survive independent of the other organs and organ systems—is vital to the healthy function of the organism as a whole. And the earth, today, is like a true multicellular organism. If vital organs cease to function cooperatively and communicatively with the other organs, working toward the fulfillment of the desires of all of the organs within the organ system, and if organ systems cease to function cooperatively and communicatively with the other organ systems, working toward the fulfillment of the desires of all of the organ systems within the organism, the organism will suffer and may even die.

When undifferentiated unity gives rise to differentiated and specialized multiplicity, interconnection and interdependence of the specialized parts inevitably follows as a result of specialization. And, at this point, communication—sharing and receiving of existence and experience—amongst the parts *must* occur for all that *is* to continue to *be* as it is. Otherwise, the organism will suffer and possibly die.

This is true in every case in which differentiation occurs, from the evolution and differentiation of organisms to occupy certain niches in order to find their place in the interactions of organisms and survive, to the advancement and differentiation of human knowledge and, as a consequence, the specialization of careers to account for the quantity of information and the maintenance of the development of technology.

In science, advancements have led to so much specialization that it is now as though every scientist is taking a microscope to his/her small portion or aspect of the world and is so consumed with the details of this tiny view that the fulfillment of the goal of science as a whole—which is to advance human knowledge and our understanding of how the world works—can easily be hindered. In every situation in which specialization occurs, there needs to be communication amongst the parts. And when specialization becomes significant enough, there needs to be some kind of brain to maintain awareness of the big picture and combine and coordinate the efforts of all of the parts. In a situation in which there are people studying just one type of star or just one type of extinct animal or just one type of protein, science might benefit from such a brain. For there may be the equivalent of tissues and maybe even organs, as people are somewhat coordinated within the field of astronomy or within the field of archeology or within the field of biochemistry, but it might prove useful to have a formal field that acts as a brain, looking at the advancements within each specialized field of science and bringing the knowledge gained in one field to bear on the work in another field. After all, it has been this kind of crossover that has provided for the shifting of paradigms throughout the history of science.

Careers in medicine have become increasingly specialized with advancements in knowledge and technology. It used to be that there was simply one doctor for everything, but this has vastly changed so that now there is a specialist for pretty much every part of the body, and there are surgeons for pretty much every part of the body, in addition to the general practitioner of medicine who does regular checkups. In such a situation, the goal of the group should remain basically what the goal of the original single doctor was: To help preserve the health of the patient. However, without sufficient communication amongst the different specialists, this goal cannot be accomplished by the group of doctors. One doctor can do one thing and another doctor can do another thing and the patient's health may not be preserved. And so communication amongst the specialists in the field of medicine, as in every field in which specialization occurs, is of the utmost importance.

There is communication between one cell or one organism and its progeny via the language of DNA. There is communication between one cell and other cells within an organism via the language of hormones. There is communication between one organism and another organism via the language of thought and feeling and speech and action. And there is communication between each organism and the Source via this same language—via the language to which the organism gives the attention of its thought, feeling, desire, speech and action. And there is communication between the Source and each organism via the language of the world, itself—via the contents of the experience of that organism within the world. Such communication must occur for the continued existence and experience of all "I"'s involved.

The Brain of Humanity

As the body has a brain that allows for communication among, and that coordinates the efforts of, all of the specialized cells that compose the body, humanity has a sort of brain that can perform its function as the core and center of communication if we allow it to do so. This core is choice.

When an "I" becomes self-aware, it not only recognizes the validity of the existence and experience of other "I"'s, it also recognizes the validity of the existence and experience of itself. It comes to recognize and understand how it interacts with other "I"'s, and in what ways and to what extent its existence and experience are similar to those of other "I"'s, and in what ways and to what extent its existence and experience are different from those of other "I"'s. As the "I" comes to recognize these things, it comes to recognize that *it* is not *its thoughts* or *its feelings* or *its desires, speech and actions* or even *the physical world of its experience*—it comes to recognize that it does not need to allow itself to be ruled by these things. In fact, it is *the "I"* that controls the language that it uses in its thoughts, feelings, desires, speech and actions. The "I" can even come to recognize that the language that it uses in its thoughts actually determines what it feels, and its feelings determine what it desires, and its desires determine what it says and does, and its speech and actions determine what manifests in the physical world of its experience.

The recognition of the nature of other "I"'s leads to the recognition of the nature of the "I"—that the "I" is, in essence, nothing more than the *ability to choose* the language that it uses in its thoughts, feelings, desires, speech and actions. Further, the "I"'s recognition of other "I"'s can lead to the recognition of the necessity of the existence of a Source, since no "I"'s are the ultimate source of anything that they have in themselves and, in fact, nothing that exists is the ultimate source of anything that it has in itself. And while the Source is the Source of all existence and experience, it is the language that the "I" uses in its thoughts, feelings, desires, speech and actions that allows it to communicate with the Source what it desires to receive in its experience. So the "I", itself, is nothing but choice, and it has the capacity for thought and feeling and speech and action and the shaping of the physical world of its experience, but the contents of all of these things are merely manifestations of the language that the "I" chooses to use and to which it chooses to give its attention.

This is the case for every "I": Every "I" is the same at its core; every "I" has the exact same essence. In fact, the ability to choose what language it uses, thereby choosing what it manifests, must be a capacity of the Source "I" as well, since the Source "I" uses language to communicate with and create the world, and since the Source "I" is the source of the experience of what it is to be an "I"—for the experience of what it is to be a self-aware "I" is the experience of being able to choose the language that one uses to share one's own existence and experience with other "I"'s. And since this essence that is "I" *chooses* language and must therefore *not* be so strictly bound by all of the restrictions of language in itself, it is likely *not* bound by space or by time as we know these, for both of these are composed of language. And it is space as we know it that separates one thing from another at any one point in time. And it is time as we know it that separates something in one moment from something in another moment. Thus, the essence of every "I" is one and the same—for there is no space or time as we know these to make it multiple, to make it so that one "I" exists here and another "I" exists there, or so that one "I" exists now and another "I" existed then.

[This could be why the "I" is so inclined to be "here" and "now" focused in the first and last stages of the pattern of the development of the "I", when identifying with the "I" and not with the thoughts and feelings and speech and actions and world that the "I" chooses. At first, the "I" hasn't chosen these things, so it only knows choice, and it only knows "I", and everything is "I"—because, in essence, everything *is* "I", and it is just not the subjective "I" strictly bound by language in space and time as we know these. But then the "I" starts to recognize the existence of others as separate from the "I" in space and time, and so it loses sight of the unity of all "I"'s. And only when the "I" comes to recognize the existence of others as other "I"'s and comes to recognize, therefore, that these others that are *separate* from the "I" *within* the constraints of space and time are actually other "I"'s that are *united* with the "I" in their *essence beyond* space and time as we know these—only then does the "I" reaffirm a "here" and "now" focus.

The difference between the "here" and "now" focus of the "I" in the first stage of development and that of the "I" in the last stage of development is the element of self-awareness that exists in the last stage. The "I" in the first stage is *not* self-aware and, as it does not recognize the existence of others that are separated from it by space and time (and that, therefore, have different subjective experiences due to this), it does not really recognize the existence of space and time at all. For the "I" in the first stage, there is *only* here and now. But when the "I" comes to recognize the existence of others, it recognizes that there is past, present, and future, and that there is here and there; it recognizes that there is space and time, and that there is not only here and now. But then it becomes caught up in the past or the future or some alternative version of the present, and it wants to be *not* here and *not* now or somewhere *other* than here and now—it wants to be someone else, who is merely, or little more than, a projection of itself somewhere or somewhen else. Only when the "I" comes to recognize the validity of the existence and experience of other "I"'s, and thereby comes to recognize the validity of its own existence and experience *as they were* and *as they are*, does it learn to be content with here and now. Only because the past experience of the "I" *was* as it *was* was the "I" able to get to where it is now, because it was what the "I" learned from that past experience that led it to where it is now.

And so the "I" learns that, rather than desiring things to be different from the way they are in the present or from the way they were in the past (in which case it would not be content with the present as it is or with the past that led to this present), it must continue to learn from the past and it must redirect its desires toward the future, setting goals to bring about the fulfillment of these desires and to bring purpose to its actions in the present and the past. But, the "I" learns, it must exist fully here and now, for this is where it can choose the language that it uses, shaping its experience in its existence. Only here and now can the "I" live what it has learned from the past, and only here and now can the "I" work toward the fulfillment of its desires—the fulfillment of the goals that it has set for the future—and only here and now can the "I" experience what the Source is sharing with it. Only here and now can the "I" truly exist as it receives existence, and experience as it receives experience, and be like the mountain stream that continually receives life-giving fresh water from the heavens and that shares all that it receives with others as the Source does, so that it has room to receive more from the Source, fulfilling the Source in Its sharing, it in its receiving, and other "I"'s in its sharing and their receiving and in their sharing and its receiving.]

There is actually another way to come at the idea that the essence of every "I" is one. In Quantum Mechanics, when the position (or velocity) of a subatomic particle is described, the particle is essentially described as being everywhere (or of having every velocity) at once, with different probabilities of being in each place (or of having each velocity), though it is supposed to exist somehow actually in these different places (or with these different velocities) with these different probabilities (unlike the situation with a coin, which comes up *either* heads *or* tails, each 50% of the time, the situation with a particle is the equivalent of coming up heads *and* tails, simultaneously). And it is only when the particle is observed as being in one place, and therefore not in every other place, that it seems actually to exist only in one, definitive place (where it is observed)—and yet even when the particle is observed as being in one place, the mathematics still suggest that the particle is everywhere. It is as though the particle hasn't made up its "mind", hasn't decided definitively where it is or where it is going. This state of being-able-to-choose-but-not-yet-having-chosen yields the particle a sort of omnipresent existence.

So, if the essence of every "I" is, like the subatomic particle, in a sort of state of being-able-to-choose-but-not-yet-having-chosen—if this essence is the ability to choose, itself, and is, therefore, basically pure potentiality—it seems that the only thing that keeps the essence of the "I" in one place (in space and time) is its observations from that place (in space and time) via its physical manifestation (its body) in that physical place. And yet, like the mathematics say of the particle, the essence of the "I" is still everywhere—unbound by space and progressive time as we know these—and it can choose from where it wishes to be observing the world. This would provide an explanation for the workings of many psychic phenomena in which a person travels via his/her consciousness or awareness (without the physical body) to another place (in space and/or time) and views the world from that place.

But the important thing here is that the essence of every "I" is inextricably linked. We may imagine that the body of the "I" is sort of like a computer, and the essence of the "I" is sort of like the internet. The self-aware essence is everywhere and can be connected to and used by any "I" that has made itself capable of connecting to it; but, like in the case of the internet, this essence is one and the same—it is the same essence (internet) that is being connected to by every "I" (computer) that connects to and acts out of its essence (the internet).

So, the brain of humanity—the core that allows for communication amongst humanity and for the coordination of the efforts of humanity toward the goal of the fulfillment of the desires of all of humanity—is choice. And since this core exists beyond the constraints of space and time as we know these, and therefore is one and the same for every "I" in this world, and since this core is a reflection of the Source's ability to shape the growth of the world, it actually can allow for communication amongst all of humanity and for the coordination of the efforts of humanity toward the goal of the fulfillment of the desires of all of humanity—in the way that the brain does for the cells of the body.

When the "I" learns to identify with this essence, perceiving itself as that which chooses its thoughts and feelings and desires and speech and actions—as the agent of its own experience of life—then it is guided by this essence toward the fulfillment of the desires of all who hold that essence in common (those of all of humanity and, in fact, of all aspects of the world) and those of the Source. It is guided toward being like a mountain stream in that it receives what it receives fully in the moment and shares all that it receives, continually shaping what it receives willfully with the language that it chooses to use, and allowing life-giving existence and experience to flow through it and into other "I"'s and the world around it, thereby making itself capable of continually receiving more existence and experience from the Source, fulfilling the Source "I" in this way as well. It is guided toward performing its own specialized function for the purpose of the fulfillment of everyone and the whole. It allows everything to pass through it and into the world around it, from its thoughts and feelings and desires—which it simply allows to pass or which it may share, as part of its internal experience and what it has learned, with other "I"'s—to the contents of its physical experience, such as material belongings and wealth—which it shares with other "I"'s.

The Consequences of Failing to Identify
with, and Act Out of, Our Essence

Ultimately, when it comes to the differentiation and specialization of all things in this world, and particularly of such things as careers, human beings are increasingly put in a position in which what they are doing can often seem so far from being directly necessary that they are not driven to keep doing what they are doing. When you have to hunt and grow food and produce clothing and shelter in order to survive, it is clear that if you don't do what you have to do, you are not going to have some necessity for your survival. Not hunting or gathering means not having food and so you go hungry. Not producing clothing means not having clothing when it gets colder. Not producing shelter means not having shelter when a storm comes. In such situations, decision-making is facilitated, because the choice regards actions that are directly related to survival—to the continuation of existence.

But in a world where what we are taught in, and what we have to do for, school seems increasingly unrelated to, and unnecessary for, and even inapplicable to, daily existence, and where increasingly specialized jobs are evermore detached from the immediacy of what we need to do in order to live—where a person might simply have to snap a part in place over and over again as the conveyor belt brings products by—it isn't so directly clear why you have to get up in the morning and get things done that day. Sure, if you don't get through school and if you don't go to work, then you won't make money, but what is money anyway? We work for an abstract representation of the possibility of having the things that we need in order to survive, or even of having things that we don't need but might want.

On top of this, as multiplicity increases over time, we are faced with an increasing number of decisions to make and an increasing number of options for each decision, so that we are already at a point where the number of options available to us with regard to nearly everything is so great that they might as well be infinite in many cases for all our ability to wrap our minds around all of them is concerned, and so our usual methods of choosing become ineffective in helping us to decide amongst them. Thus, we end up like cells that incompletely differentiate and so ineffectively perform their functions, because we cannot make decisive and definitive decisions, and this problem toward which we are already inclined as developed beings in this world—as beings who have a potential capacity for choice that we must actualize—is merely magnified by the increasing numbers of options.

Due to our inability to choose definitively, we are left worrying about being able to make the right decisions as far as their consequences are concerned, we are left second-guessing and regretting our decisions with regard to how they reflect upon us, and we are left unable to decide which decisions are even ours to make. And when we *don't* decide firmly what language to use to share and shape the contents of our experience of the world, we do *not* live with self-awareness in the experiences that we have chosen for ourselves, because we are too busy living in the possibility of other, alternative options that we *could* choose but might not, or that we *could have chosen* but didn't, or that we *want to be choosing* but aren't. This is because we are too much in our worried thoughts regarding decisions that we might have to make in the future, and in our regretful feelings regarding decisions that we have already made in the past, and in our frustrated instincts or desires regarding decisions that we have to make in the present. And so we are never content with what *is*, with the contents of our experience right *now*, because we are never actually fully *here*. And so we do *not* make the best of what *is* and work from *here* to share and shape our experiences as we wish them to be.

And, in such a world, there is an increasing demand for therapists and psychologists and psychiatrists, because people get lost—because when people aren't decisive in their choosing, they end up feeling empty and like they don't have a clear purpose or direction in their lives. People don't quite know why they have to keep doing what they are doing. The solution to this, again, has to do with the brain. We need to have a unified command center, or brain, (and to use it) to set clear goals for the group, and for ourselves, and to keep the components of the group, and ourselves, aware of how what we are doing fits into the big picture of our overall goals, and to keep us directed toward those goals. We need to act out of the brain of humanity, the brain of the world, our essence of choice.

Notice that, in each of the individual cells, this brain is DNA—the core of potential that all cells have in common and that is merely limited differently in its capacities within each individual cell in order for the cell to differentiate and thereby actualize itself in the performance of one specific function. This is similar to the way our choosing limits the number of options available to us and, in so doing, our choosing actually allows us to actualize ourselves, for we, like individual cells, are not supposed to remain forever in potential form, but rather we are supposed to actualize that potential. For in actualizing that potential by deciding and setting goals and striving for the fulfillment of those goals, we create direction and purpose in our lives and we make it so that, when we die, we will be in a different situation in terms of our accomplishments and the positive effects that we have had on this world than when we were born.

We would be better off if we each worked toward the awareness of self that brings recognition of the diversity within each of us and of the interconnection—and interdependence—and unity of all of us. We are all working toward common goals ultimately—the goals of sustaining our existence and overall well-being and eventually of being self-aware in our experience of the world—and if we were to work *together* toward these goals, rather than against each other (as we each strive independently toward them), we would make ourselves far more likely to reach them as individuals.

When we are all like specialized cells in a true multicellular organism, we will never achieve our individual goals if we do not work with the other people—and, in fact, with all the other parts of the world, all the other "I"'s (regardless of where they are in their development)—around us (and even help them to achieve their own goals), because our fulfillment is wrapped up in theirs—because we all have the same, single essence in common. If enough people—and other parts of the world—around us fail to achieve fulfillment, and do not continue to perform their functions and reach their goals for any reason, then the overall organism of which we and they are a part will suffer and may even die—and then *we* will suffer and *we* may die. And so working toward the fulfillment of all—by following the guidance of the essence, the brain, that we all share in common—is vital to the attainment of our own fulfillment.

Extending the Paradigm of Experience: From Desiring to Exist, to Desiring to Belong, to Desiring to Share One's Own Experience

At this point, it might be asked exactly where all this differentiation that calls for a command center of communication fits into the pattern of experience in the development of the self-aware "I".

At first, there is only "I". Then there are others that are projections of the "I". And then there are other "I"'s.

When there is only "I", the first thing that the "I" begins to recognize (as a baby and young child), besides the "I", is the physical environment in which the "I" exists, including its body as well as its physical surroundings. And the "I" notices when it is hungry or tired or cold or hot or dirty or otherwise uncomfortable. And so it wants food, or sleep, or it wants it to be warmer or cooler, or it wants to be cleaner or more comfortable. And it recognizes the lack of these resources—that it is not always immediately gratified in what it wants, and that it must take action in getting what it wants if it wishes to get it. And so the "I" begins to explore the effects that it can have on its body and on its environment, making noise and moving around in an attempt to gain the material resources that it desires, and that it requires in order to continue to exist—the ultimate desire here that is the aim of all of these other desires.

The language required here is primitive and minimal at best, because the "I" and its environment are all there is, and all the "I" has to do is communicate and obtain what physical resources it requires. Essentially, the language required here is conveyed by the bodily desires via movements of the body and little to no actual speech, and it is concerned only with communicating that which is concrete and capable of being sensed with the physical senses. One could physically point at nearly all the things that the language communicates at this point, because the "I" merely needs to communicate physical experience (in the case of development in physical life, this is because this is all that the "I" is really capable of experiencing at this time).

Then, as the "I" further develops, it begins to recognize that there are others out there—that *it* and *its immediate surroundings* in space and time are *not* all there is. These others are capable of sensing and knowing different things—of having, and of having had, different external experiences from those of the "I". Faced with all these others out there (as an adolescent), the "I" wants to fit in. The "I" wants to be a part of the group of all those others (largely because, through the group's goal of the preservation of the group's existence, the "I", as part of the group, might have its own existence better preserved). And in order to be part of the group, the "I" must have something to contribute to the group. So the "I" seeks out something that it can contribute that is either not already being contributed by someone else, or that can be contributed in a better or more efficient or whatever way than someone else.

In this way, the "I" seeks to find a place for itself in the group. The more others there are—the larger this group becomes—the more specialized the contribution of the "I" must become in order for the "I" to fit in and have a place in that group—because there are more others to be contributing more things, and so there are fewer general things that aren't already being contributed, and the distribution of contributions becomes such that the contributions become more differentiated and specialized, spread amongst the parts of the group.

And the more specialized the parts become in their contributions, the more hierarchical the group becomes for, if nothing else, the need for a center of communication arises—a leader or core that keeps the many specialized goals of the individual parts of the group coordinated and unified in one overall goal.

At this point, the language required is somewhat more complex. The "I" must be able to communicate desires that are a bit more abstract than mere physical experience, moving beyond the physical senses to what physical actions are required to achieve some goal, as well as to what is known and felt and thought. But this knowledge and these feelings and thoughts are not complex (in the case of development in physical life, this is largely because the "I" is not actually capable of having very complex knowledge or of experiencing very complex feelings or thoughts at this time). General terms to which all people involved can relate in their experience are all that is necessary to communicate the "I"'s experience and desires and to achieve the fulfillment of the "I"'s desires (as well as the fulfillment of the group's desires). The "I" wants to feel a sense of belonging and of being a part of the group, and any kind of interaction with the others in the group, or of working in the "I"'s specialized way toward the group's overall goals, is potentially enough to bring about the fulfillment of this desire.

But, as the "I" develops still further in its experience, the "I" begins to recognize that those others in the group are not just projections of the "I" that are separate from the "I" in space, and that have different physical experiences due to that difference in spatial location, and that have different knowledge and different thoughts and feelings and desires (and that engage in different speech and actions) at different times *merely* due to that difference in physical experience. The group to which the "I" belongs, as a whole and abstract entity, is an extension of the "I", but the others in the group are not mere extensions of the "I". These others are actually other "I"'s, like the "I", itself, experiencing their own distinct thoughts and feelings and desires *in addition* to having their own physical experience of the world from the vantage point of a different location in space and time (largely because, in order to fit into the group in the first place, differentiation and specialization of every "I" occurred, resulting in actual and significant differences from one "I" to another).

And when the "I" realizes this, it desires to connect with another "I", to share its existence and its experience with that other "I". It desires to complete itself through intense connection—even through becoming one—with that other "I". For now the "I" knows that *it* is *not* all there *is* in any way. It is not the only "I" that exists, and its experience of the world is not the only experience there is, and the "I" desires experience and the understanding of itself that can come from that experience. And the best way to understand anything is through comparison and contrast with something else.

Through communication with another "I", the "I" can come to truly understand and experience what it is to be an "I", and what it is to be *itself* as opposed to *another* "I". Through sharing its experience with another "I" and through receiving the experience of that other "I", the "I" validates the existence and experience of itself as well as those of that other "I". For now the "I" has not only *received* experience; it has also *shared* this experience, and through sharing its experience, it makes itself capable of receiving more experience (like a stream that shares water and thereby makes room for its reception of more water). And now it is not only receiving existence and experience through the lens of its *own* thoughts and feelings and desires; it is also receiving existence and experience through the lens of *another "I"'s* thoughts and feelings and desires.

In this way, the "I" gains a fuller, more encompassing view of things as they actually are and, in fact, the "I" gains a fuller existence. Through combining the lens of its own experience with the lenses of other "I"'s experiences, the "I" comes to have a clearer, more accurate view of itself and of other "I"'s, of the world in which they all exist, and of the Source of all of this, and of how all of this came to be from that Source. For the desire to share one's experience, itself, is what brought all of this to be from that Source.

The fulfillment of this desire to unite with another in some way—the desire that drives every intense and intimate union, every intense and intimate interaction, including intense conversations as well as the union of male and female in the act of copulation—brings about a new perspective on the world, and new experiences in the world, that didn't exist before. In the union of "I"'s, each "I" shares some part of what it is to be itself, and the melding of what each communicates to the other produces a new "I". In the case of intense conversations, that new "I" is a more self-aware "I"—for both "I"'s will become more self-aware, with a greater understanding of the "I" and of other "I"'s and of the relation between the "I" and other "I"'s—with a new lens through which to experience itself and all other "I"'s, and the world, and the Source of all of this. In the case of the union of male and female in copulation, that new "I" is another "I" altogether. For the male shares some part of what it is to be him through the language that is the DNA contained in his sperm cell, and the female receives this part of him and combines it with some part of what it is to be her through the language that is the DNA contained in her egg cell, and this union thus produces a new "I" with its own experience.

In this union between male and female (as in all intense and intimate unions between two "I"'s), we see a reflection of the union between the Source and humanity (or, rather, between the Source and the world, in general), for as it has just been said, the male shares some part of what it is to be him through language, and the female receives this and combines it with some part of what it is to be her through language, and this union produces a new experience—even a new *way* of experiencing. It can thus be seen that the manifestation of male and female forms of individuals within species, and of sexual reproduction, at some point in the development of the world and of life, is a reflection within the world of the Source and the world and of the relationship between the Source and the world—the relationship that produces new experiences through the intense and intimate connection between these two. And so the Source "I" shares Its existence and experience, via language, with every other "I", and with humanity as a whole—in fact, with the entire world on every level of existence and experience—and every "I" receives this existence and experience through its own language (and capacity for language and understanding of language) and produces a new experience in a new moment of existence.

The language required at this stage is the most developed, the most complex, and the most abstract (in the case of development in physical life, this is largely because the experience of the "I"—the knowledge and thoughts and feelings of the "I"—has reached a degree of complexity and subtlety that is significantly greater at this time than ever before). In some sense, this is the least abstract language of all, for of all of the languages in this world, *this* is the language that most closely approximates and resembles the language that *composes* the world and everything within it—the language via which the Source shares the world with us—since it is the language by which one "I" shares its experience with another "I". But it is the most abstract relative to other languages used in this world, for it must convey the complex internal experiences (the complex thoughts and feelings and so on) of the "I"—of what it is to be "I", different from all other "I"'s, and of what it is to be "I", like all other "I"'s. Language at this stage must be capable of conveying all of the (often subtle and detailed) aspects of experience that cannot be sensed with the senses or pointed to in the physical world. It must be capable of serving the purpose of replacing the ability to simply place another "I" in the "I"'s own mind and body in order to convey the mental and emotional experiential states of the "I"—in order to truly convey what it is to be experiencing the world as the "I", so that the other "I" is capable of finding the analogues and equivalents of the "I"'s experience in its own experience, and of understanding the subtleties in similarity and difference between the "I"'s experience and its own experience.

[Notice, by the way, that these stages—this progression from concrete to abstract—are apparent in the development of language over the course of evolution, within the human species, and within an individual human being. Further, these stages are apparent in the development not just of spoken language, but of written language as well. And so, for example, in the development of written language over the course of the development of the human species as a whole, we see that written language began in the form of such things as cave paintings and other straightforward depictions of the physical referents (which were related to food and other preservation-oriented things), and then it developed to become somewhat abstract and symbolic representations of those physical referents and of emotion and belonging or group-interaction related referents as well (in the form of characters that in some way resembled their referents), and then it developed to become very abstract representations of physical preservation, emotional belonging, and thought connection related things (in phonetic languages, where the letters and words have no relation to their referents except that which we assign to them).]

The "I" must learn to see another "I"'s experience within its own experience in order for communication between the "I" and this other "I" to be effective. If the other "I" has no experiential understanding of the referent of the language of the

"I", then that other "I" will not be able to receive the experience of the "I" as it is shared. And the experience will become different as it is received from what was shared in accordance with the capacity of the "I" on the receiving end to receive this experience. This is the explanation for why each "I"'s experience is capable of being so different from each other "I"'s experience despite the fact that the Source of the experience of every "I" is the same: Each "I" is different in its capacity to receive the Source's experience in accordance with the differences in the language that it uses in its thoughts and feelings and desires and speech and actions (the language that shapes the lens through which it experiences the world).

If one "I" is using a word to mean a particular thing but the other "I" uses that same word to mean something else, or if two "I"'s are using different words to mean the same thing, and the "I"'s do not work toward (and reach) an understanding of the exact ways in which they are using language differently, then the communication will be received as meaning something different from what was shared—an experience different from what was shared will be received. Essentially, the Source is sharing Its experience—the same experience—with every other "I", and every "I" is receiving that experience differently, understanding differently the words that the Source uses to convey Its experience—and this is why every "I"'s experience of the world is different from every other "I"'s experience of the world, and this is also why no "I"'s experience of the world is exactly the same as the Source's experience of the world.

Just as the form of a baby produced by the intimate union of two people is never exactly the same as that of either parent, but is, instead, the expression of a unique combination of the language used by each parent in that parent's DNA, the experience that is produced by the intimate union of the Source and an (other) "I" is never exactly the same as the experience of the Source or that of the "I", but is, instead, the expression of a unique combination of the language used by the Source and that used by the "I". As a result of this, the "I"'s experience of the world is never exactly the same as any other "I"'s experience of the world, and the "I"'s experience of the world is also never exactly the same from one moment to the next—it is always a unique combination of the language used by the Source to convey Its experience and that used by the "I" to describe its own experience in its thoughts and feelings and desires and speech and actions. All of the internal and external dialogue that an "I" uses to describe its own experience therefore contributes to the creation of its next experience as it shapes how the Source's description and conveyance of Its own experience is understood and received.

Other Manifestations of the Paradigm

Ultimately, the progression in the pattern of a single "I"'s experience—from desires focused on the immediate physical environment and having the physical resources necessary to continue to physically exist, to desires focused on fitting in with others and being a part of a group, to desires focused on intensely connecting with and sharing experience with another "I"—is manifest on many levels within the universe, including in the evolution of the physical universe as a whole, in the evolution of life within the universe, and in the development of humanity as a species.

Once something exists, it desires to maintain its existence. Once multiplicity arises, there arises the desire to group together and differentiate and specialize and work toward a common goal—in order to better maintain the existence of the individual and of the many—and hierarchy arises, with a leader of some sort to direct the parts of the group toward its common goal (and ideally this goal aids in the preservation of the existence of all of the individuals within the group). Once there are groups, each united in a common purpose that overlaps from one group to the other, there emerges the desire in each group to merge with another group in order to produce a new group that has a greater chance of achieving each group's purpose. Through the sharing of the group's experience with another group and combining its experience with that of that other group, the group lives on in (continues to live through) a new group with a new experience, thereby maintaining the group's existence. Essentially, once something comes into existence, it desires to maintain and preserve its existence, and every desire that arises after this evolves from that original desire with the fulfillment of that desire as its goal; everything that is desired by something (that exists) is desired in order to maintain and preserve its existence.

When the universe first came into being, there was only the physical environment, which began to expand and sustain itself. Atoms formed, and then these atoms clumped together to form groups of atoms, which eventually formed stars and whole galaxies in a hierarchical fashion as the atoms combined and interacted with one another under the force of gravity. And, in stars, atoms came to combine with one another via the fusion of their nuclei—in which they were truly able to unite with one another and become new and different atoms. And as these different atoms came together in the formation of new stars and systems of planets, they interacted with one another via the exchange of electrons, forming molecules that also interacted with one another in various ways. And water and other groups of molecules were formed.

And in such a group of molecules, the first life—a single-celled organism—formed, and it desired merely to have the physical resources necessary for it to continue to exist. It wanted food, it wanted a temperature and other environmental conditions in which it could exist, and so on. And the language that it used was primarily that of physical movement, and it used this language merely to obtain the physical resources and conditions that it required to exist. But, at some point, some single-celled organism also used the language of DNA or RNA in self-replication, by which it produced more of itself through its own division.

And that single-celled organism encountered other single-celled organisms, and these organisms began to group together, finding benefit in being part of something larger than themselves. And, eventually, the cells in such groups differentiated and specialized, forming a true multicellular organism. And hierarchical organization of the cells in tissues and organs and organ systems was gradually established, with a brain and nervous system as the leader and hormones as the language, in order to coordinate the desires and efforts of each of the specialized cells and accomplish the goals of the group (which were mostly the goals of the brain).

And this single entire organism—this group of cells—led by its brain, then desired food and sleep, and a comfortable temperature and other environmental conditions in which it could exist, and it used language mostly in the form of physical actions and possibly some primitive kind of speech in order to obtain these resources that were necessary for its continued existence—the ultimate goal of the entire organism (the group of cells).

And this single entire organism, encountering other entire organisms that were like itself in various ways, desired to fit in and be part of the group. And, in the group, each organism specialized in its contributions, finding its own niche, so that the group formed a hierarchical organization with a leader that coordinated the desires and efforts of each of the specialized organisms in order to accomplish the goals of the group. Language was advanced only to the degree that was necessary to communicate the desires of each of the members of the group and to coordinate the efforts of those members toward the fulfillment of the desires of the group (which were ultimately often mostly the desires of the leader of the group). And the goals of the group were (for the sake of the continued existence of the group and its members, hopefully) those of each of the individuals within the group—to obtain food and physical conditions that were safe and comfortable, conducive to the continued existence of the group, which was the ultimate goal of the group.

And each of these single entire organisms, when confronted with another organism that was like itself but different in certain specific ways, desired to unite with that other organism, to share a part of itself with that other organism in order to produce, with that organism, another organism like itself but different.

And as evolution progressed, the physical resources and conditions desired often became more complex, including even colors and aesthetics of the environment in addition to its cleanliness and organization and suitability to physical survival. And as evolution progressed, groups became more complex, becoming based not just on genetic similarity, but also on other commonalities, with complex hierarchies that required more complex language to coordinate the groups. And, as evolution progressed, the desire to share oneself with another came to include more than just the desire for a physical union, for it came to include, also, the desire for an emotional, and even a mental, union—to share not just one's genes (and exist through another's physical experience that is like one's own), but also one's thoughts and feelings and experiences (to exist through another's mental and emotional experience that is like one's own—through another's experience of one's own experience).

Even after the human species formed, this pattern manifested itself over the course of humanity's development as a species. First, there were nomadic hunters and gatherers who traveled in small groups that were basically immediate family, and their goal, and the predominant focus of their attention, was the fulfillment of the desire to preserve their existence—by hunting animals and gathering together edible plants for food, by finding caves and forming other shelters, by forming clothing from animal skins. Then, people began to settle down and gather into large groups with others (including, especially, extended family), farming and domesticating animals—forming agricultural communities. Within such communities, individual people specialized in different tasks that were, in some way, involved in providing for the survival of the group, for the main and common goal and focus of the attention of the people in the group was the preservation of the existence of the group (in large part by preserving the existence of the individuals within the group). Gradually, as time and attention were freed from the constant efforts to find food and shelter and clothing in order to survive, people began to direct their attention to getting to know other individual people and to having intimate and intense interactions with other people other than through sexual relations, and to having intimate and intense interactions with other things in the world as well, studying and trying to understand themselves and the world and their relation to the world.

Ultimately, as a whole, the universe is like a giant organism. It began as an environment that merely expanded, continuing to exist. But, as it developed, it grew to become groups of galaxies, which all spread apart from one another to obtain the resource of space and to obtain a cooler environment and to continue to exist. And, in the development of the universe, humanity formed. Humanity, as a group, is like the brain of the universe in the universe's vast hierarchical organization in many ways, directing the course that the universe takes in its manifestation with the language that it uses to shape the existence and experience that the Source shares with us. And humanity, with its complex internal experience, its ability to recognize the other as an other "I" with its own complex internal experience, and its ability to use language complex enough to communicate its internal experience with that other "I", is capable of guiding the universe toward experiential union with its Source as no other species, or other part of the world (at least on Earth), is.

With the greatest capacity for self-awareness—for understanding the "I" as "I" and the other as an other "I"—humanity is capable of recognizing that its true essence is a reflection of its Source—that the Source, in large part, creates the world through *it*. Humanity is capable of realizing that, in its experience, it and the Source are capable of being united if it allows the Source to connect to it and to create its experience through it. And so humanity is capable of realizing that it must work toward the fulfillment of itself and its environment and the Source, Itself, and not merely toward the fulfillment of itself, alone. Humanity must consider each of its components and the components of the entire universe, and even the Source, in its exercise of its essence—in its choosing the language that it uses to describe and shape its experience. For as it shapes its experience, so, too, does it shape the universe. And as it shapes the universe, so, too, does it determine whether it and the Source will be fulfilled in their desires or not.

The Source desires to share Its existence and experience with us. Humanity (and any other life in the universe that is as capable of being self-aware) is the only part of the universe that is capable of receiving certain aspects of that experience that the Source desires to share, namely the experience of being a self-aware "I". And, as such, humanity (self-aware life) is the only part of the universe that makes the universe capable of truly fulfilling the Source's desire and goal in creating the world, for only with humanity (only with self-aware life) can the Source unite and find in this union intense and intimate connection that produces a new experience, shaping the contents of the universe in its existence. In humanity (in self-aware life), the Source is capable of finding a true other "I" with which It is capable of sharing Itself and further creating the universe. Without this, the universe does not fulfill its purpose, for without this, the Source is left alone as the only "I", incapable of sharing Its experience—for without humanity (without self-aware life), nothing is capable of understanding and receiving the language with which the Source describes and conveys Its greatest experience: the experience of being a self-aware "I" that is capable of creating the world.

Humanity as the Brain of the World

It is easy to conceive of humanity, in its essence, as, at minimum, the brain of the earth (if not also the brain, or part of the brain, of the entire universe). In the hierarchy of the earth, it is humanity that is most aware of its own existence and that most shapes the development of the earth's experience. Every individual human being is like an individual neuron in this overall brain that communicates with the rest of the earth via speech and actions (like the brain communicates with the rest of the body via hormones and electrical signals) and that communicates with every other human being via messages that begin as thoughts within itself and result in feelings being released in the space between human beings (sometimes, but not always, in the form of speech or actions), transmitting the messages to other human beings (like each neuron communicates with each other neuron via messages that begin as electrical impulses within itself and result in neurotransmitters being released in synapses between the neurons, transmitting the messages to other neurons).

Now, because the patterns of the world manifest on every scale, we can zoom in or zoom out. First, I'll zoom in. Each individual human being has a head containing a brain that directs the human being's development and communication with other human beings (as each neuron has a nucleus containing DNA that directs the neuron's development and communication with other neurons). The human being has hormones, and neurons that are capable of sending electrical signals, that convey messages from the brain to all other parts of the body in order to direct the functioning of the different parts of the body (as the neuron has RNA that conveys messages from the nucleus to all other parts of the cell in order to direct the functioning of the different parts of the neuron). The human being has a heart that acts as the energy system for the body, making other activities in and by the body possible (as the neuron has mitochondria that act as the energy production system for the neuron, making other activities in and by the neuron possible). The human being has a spinal cord to carry electrical signals from the brain to the limbs of the body to tell them to act in certain ways (as the neuron has an axon to carry electrical signals from the main part of the cell to the axon terminal to tell it to release certain neurotransmitters), and the spinal cord is protected by a spine (and the axon is protected by a myelin sheath). The human being has a circulatory system to carry oxygen and food energy around the body (as the neuron has cytoplasm to circulate oxygen and food energy around the cell). The human being has a respiratory system and a digestive system to provide itself with oxygen and energy and to excrete unneeded materials, or waste (as the neuron has a semipermeable membrane to provide itself with oxygen and energy and to excrete unneeded materials).

Notice that, as we go from single cell (in this case, brain cell) to entire multicellular organism (in this case, human being), the hierarchy of systems becomes more complex, so that often a number of organs, or even a number of organ systems, in the multicellular organism do what a single organelle in the cell does. This increasing differentiation and complexity of the expression of the same pattern or paradigm (of language)—from unity to multiplicity to unified multiplicity, from only "I" to others to other "I"'s, etc.—repeats itself over and over again and marks the entire world and every part of it from beginning onward, such that there is an analogue for every part of every cosmos within the same pattern in a microcosm within that cosmos, and so on downward (to an extent, for there is a limit on this, and that limit is the very constituents of the world—the letters and words of the language with which the Source shares Its experience), and there is an analogue for every part of every cosmos within the same pattern within a macrocosm of which that cosmos is a part, and so on upward (to an extent, for the limit on this is the entire world and the Source and the language that the Source uses to convey Its experience).

Now, to zoom out again:

Every human being is like a neuron in the brain of the earth. The atmosphere and the oceans perform the functions of the earth's circulatory system, circulating oxygen and carbon dioxide to and from the different life forms (cells). Plants of all sorts perform the functions of the earth's respiratory system and parts of the earth's digestive system, producing oxygen and food energy for the rest of the organism. Different types of fungi and bacteria perform the functions of (mostly the excretory part of) the earth's digestive system, breaking down dead organisms (food) into nutrients that plants can take up and form into something ingestible (food energy) by humans (neurons). Other animals are sort of like fat reserves that eat plants (food) and store this food in another form that is capable of being eaten for energy when plants (food) are not numerous enough.

(I'm definitely not suggesting here that we should solely look at animals as fat reserves, for they have many functions in the world other than the function that they have in this reflective metaphor—like helping us to better understand ourselves, bringing us closer to self-awareness, through our interactions with, and observations of, them, for example. In fact, in light of the purpose of the existence of the world—and thus of all of the multiple and various things that have arisen within the world—being to actualize the potential to be self-aware and to be capable of sharing and shaping its experience through the self-aware use of language, this aim should guide all of our actions within the world. Since we human beings are more capable of actualizing this potential than other animals, it would seem that our continued existence should take precedence over that of other animals when there has to be a choice between their existence and ours. At the same time, however, it seems rather un-self-aware to deny the validity of the existence of other "I"'s to such an extent as to be intentionally killing and eating them, and the more potential for self-awareness that another "I" has, the more un-self-aware it seems to kill it and eat it. So, it seems that, in order to act most in accordance with the aim of the world's existence, we should use animals as food—or for other purposes that involve their injury or death—only to the extent that it is necessary in order to sustain our own existence and ability to actualize the potential of the world. Ideally, we should choose to eat whichever aspects of the world available to us are the least capable of actualizing self-awareness, and we should only eat what we require in order for us to be capable of actualizing self-awareness ourselves. Therefore, the idea here that plants are food and animals are fat reserves to be utilized as food only in the absence of plants actually seems quite appropriate.)

Meanwhile, humanity, like Earth's brain, has developed to take an increasingly large role in the direction of the functions of the systems of the earth, willfully altering these things with the language that it uses in its thought and feeling and action. Like in the case of the brain in the body, everything is for the purpose of maintaining the function of humanity, and humanity has a large effect on how the different parts and systems of the earth perform their functions. This is like the leader in any group—every part of the group works toward the maintenance of the function of the leader, and the leader has a large effect on how the different parts and systems of the group perform their functions. (Think of a queen bee in a colony of bees, for

example, or of the president in the government of a nation.)
And a group is well-run and can maintain its existence and the
existence of its parts only if the leader directs the group toward
goals that encompass in their fulfillment the fulfillment of the
goals of the parts of the group. Thus, a dictator who works toward the fulfillment of selfish desires that disregard the desires
of the people who compose the nation over which he rules is
not leading the group in a way that promotes the maintenance
of the *parts* of the group and, therefore, he is *not* leading the
group in a way that promotes the maintenance of the *group* (for
the existence of the group is dependent upon the existence of
its parts, as the existence of an organism is dependent upon
the existence of its cells and organs and so on). And humanity
has been like such a dictator who works toward the fulfillment
of selfish desires that disregard the desires of the parts that
compose the earth over which it rules.

Thus, for example, we have destroyed a lot of the plants
and trees that convert carbon dioxide into oxygen, and we have
also essentially done the equivalent of smoking and drinking
excessively with all of our burning of fossil fuels and production of more waste than can be broken down or otherwise
handled by the environment, thereby hindering the function
of the respiratory system as well as the liver of the earth.
Consequently, the circulatory system of the earth—the atmosphere and oceans—is not performing its function of the ab-
sorption and distribution and release of things like heat as well
as it used to. And global warming is therefore a problem as the
earth overheats (as the earth loses its ability to appropriately
regulate its temperature), and so some of our fat reserves are
disappearing as animals are unable to adjust to the changing
climate. Essentially, the earth's systems are working improperly
and threatening to shut down, and the earth's cells are dying as
a result—mostly because humanity has followed selfish desires,
considering itself, alone (like the "I", in the second stage of the

pattern of the development of the "I", that sees itself as the only true "I" with all others being mere projections of the "I" that exist for the sake of the fulfillment of the desires of the "I"—only what benefits the "I" matters, because the "I" is the only true "I"), instead of seeking the fulfillment of the desires of every "I"—of every part of the organism that is the earth.

So, while it is easy to conceive of humanity as the brain of the earth, such a conception suggests that humanity, as a whole, has more developing to do in order to become a self-aware "I" and thereby in order to truly experience what it is to be like the Source. But humanity is further along on the path toward self-awareness than anything else on Earth, and so it leads the way. And it is possibly further along on the path toward self-awareness than anything else in the universe (unless there is other, more self-aware life out there, in which case humanity is a still-developing part of the brain of the universe, perhaps like the prefrontal cortex in the human being, which is the last of the parts of the brain to develop—developing all the way up until the person is in his/her early twenties—but which is the only part of the brain that is capable of the most complex thoughts and of decision-making and goal-setting—of *choice*).

In any case, the possibility (or at least potentiality) for at least the *essence* of humanity—the potential to be self-aware and to use language to share and shape the experiential contents of existence—to be the equivalent of the brain in the organism that is the entire universe, guiding the world toward greater existence and fulfillment, is very real. And whether or not humanity *is* the brain or leader of the world in this way (and even more especially so if it *is*, which, considering its essence, it pretty much *has* to be in some way or other), we've certainly got to work on achieving the fulfillment of the goals of *all* that exists, rather than simply doing what we've been doing, as a whole, up to this point.

On How Only Human Beings are Capable of Experiencing the Extreme Fulfillment and the Extreme Lack of Fulfillment of these Paradigmatic Desires

When it comes to the desires for sufficiency of resources and a comfortable and sustaining environment, for being part of a group, and for connecting with another "I", human beings are capable of experiencing all of these desires in these desires' most developed forms—in the forms that most closely resemble the experience of the Source. Human beings are capable of internally experiencing the extreme lack of fulfillment of these desires, and human beings are capable of internally experiencing the extreme fulfillment of these desires, like no other being in the world.

When the "I" looks to itself and its surroundings for the maintenance of its existence and the experience of material comfort, then it feels that it lacks resources, because, in this differentiated world, the "I" and its surroundings are finite due to the constraints of language (as in the forms of space and time). The "I" must learn to look beyond the finite language of itself and its surroundings to the Source for the resources to maintain its existence, for the Source of all things is infinite (as It is the Source of all things), and so the "I" will not experience lack as long as it recognizes that it receives all things from the Source.

When the "I" looks to groups of people for existence and the experience of the interconnectedness and the reunification of differentiated multiplicity—for the experience of belong-ingness—then the "I" feels that it is separate, that it is not a part of a larger whole, because, in this differentiated world, it *is* separate due to the divisiveness of language. The "I" must learn to look beyond the divisive language of itself and of the people around it to the essence of all "I"'s for reunification and belongingness, for the essence of every "I" is one, working toward a higher goal that is the fulfillment of the desires of the whole—of the group of which every "I" is a part, including all of humanity and the Source, Itself.

When the "I" looks to another "I" for existence and the experience of completion through intense connection and the sharing of its experience with a complementing counterpart to itself, then the "I" feels that it is incomplete, because, in this differentiated world, the "I" cannot completely unite with an-other "I" due to the intermediary of language. The "I" must learn to look beyond the intermediary language of itself and that other "I" to the essence of every "I" for connection and completion, for the essence of the "I" and of that other "I" is one, and the "I"'s experience and that other "I"'s experience are connected beyond language in the Source's experience, from which they both emanate and which they each reflect.

Thus, it can be realized that only human beings are capable of experiencing the most extreme forms of these desires, be-cause only human beings are capable of becoming self-aware "I"'s—of being true and fully developed "I"'s. For only hu-man beings have the capacity for such advanced thought and feeling and language as they do. And only human beings have the ability to connect with and actualize the essence that is the ability to choose the language that they use in the conveyance and the creation of their experience—an essence in which they are all united beyond space and time and all other language division, and an essence that is a reflection of the Source. For the true lack of fulfillment of these desires comes from language, which is finite and divisive and a necessary intermediary of connection in this world that is composed of language. And the true fulfillment of these desires comes from learning to look beyond the divisions of language, to the Source from where all existence and experience comes, and to the essence of all "I"'s—which is the very ability to wield and control language—where true bounty and unity and connection is possible.

Further, when the true fulfillment of these desires is possible, as it *is* only with humanity, the experience of the awareness of the *lack* of their fulfillment is capable of being at its most extreme, for something that actually *can* be received is not *being* received—an existing receptacle is empty, making for the experience of emptiness, of lack of fulfillment. Only if the receptacle for something—the capacity to receive something—*exists* in the first place (as it does in humanity, and particularly in human beings who have developed the capacity for a large degree of self-awareness—as through the development of their brains, including the frontal, and particularly the prefrontal, cortex, with age, and so forth), can the true *lack* of fulfillment of that thing—the (at least partial) *emptiness* of the receptacle—be experienced.

On How the Paradigm of Experience Differs for the Source

Beginning at Self-Awareness

We are now in a position in which we are capable of understanding something that we could never have truly understood prior to this point.

The Source "I" created the world in order to share Its existence and experience with the world. This makes sense in light of the reflection of this desire in humanity. However, in the development of the world and of humanity, this desire comes last. And yet it seems to have been first in the Source.

[It must be noted here that, though I refer to the Source's desire to share Its existence and experience as a "desire", this is only a warped reflection of the reality of what the Source's experience of this is, for there is no language to accurately describe what the Source of language experiences that "compels" It to record and speak Its experience in language, thereby bringing forth language and the world. We can probably get some hint of a better idea of what the Source experiences by looking to our experience of breathing—an experience that can bring us to a greater understanding of how we are often inclined to experience reality and of the experience that we are capable of attaining as we more accurately receive and experience the Source's experience.

If we hold our breath for a period of time, then we come to experience the *desire* to breathe. Likewise, when we hold onto any experience, then we come to experience *desire*. But if we do not hold onto our breath and, instead, we simply let it go, then nothing so prominent arises that we would call it a *desire*. We simply breathe in, and we simply breathe out, and only when we do not receive and share in equal extent and in a free-flowing manner like a mountain stream, and we instead hold onto what we receive like a pond, do we experience *desire*, which entails unfulfillment and the compulsion to work toward fulfillment.

Thus, when we are self-aware, desires are replaced by sort of inclinations (or, as we will see later, by intuition)—by a guidance toward whatever is best for us to do at some particular moment in order to get where we have planned (by setting goals) to be going (and, for us, where we have planned to be going, ultimately—in the overall picture—is to where the Source is in Its experience). So, while I will continue to use terms such as "desire" to describe why the Source created (and continues to create) the world, it should be kept in mind that this is only a corrupted reflection of the reality of the Source's experience, which is more like an inclination, and yet even this is imprecise, for we are using the word to describe what precedes the existence of words.]

If we analyze closely this seeming discrepancy in our experiential analogue to the experience of the Source, it reveals much that we can now learn. It is only when the "I" is self-aware that it seeks out another "I" with which to share its existence and experience, and yet this is what the Source sought to do in bringing the world into being in the first place. It is only when the "I" is self-aware that it has the capacity to choose the language that it uses in order to share its existence and experience, and it is only then that it has a complex enough language to do this, and yet the Source had and exercised this capacity and used such a complex language in creating the world. As is written above, the language of the "I" at the point of its desiring to connect intensely with another is the most developed; it is at this point that this language most closely resembles that of the Source "I".

In the development of all things in this world, the progression is toward self-awareness—toward becoming an "I" that is capable of intensely connecting with another "I" through the use of complex language, and that is capable of creating new experiences of the world through the combination of the language that it and another "I" use (through the melding of the experiences that it shares with another "I" and those that it receives from that other "I"). This is the case in the evolution of the entire universe (with humanity eventually evolving as the sort of brain of the universe). It is the case in the evolution of all of life (from single-celled organisms; to simple multicellular organisms; to complex multicellular organisms that are capable of sexual reproduction, and of increasingly greater awareness of the "I" and its relation to others, and of concordantly complex language). And it is the case in the development of every individual human being (as in the pattern of experience from only "I", to others that are projections of the "I", to other "I"'s—the pattern that plays itself out in the development of all things in this world).

And yet the Source "I" seems to have begun where the development of all things in this world is headed. The Source "I" has always been self-aware. The Source "I" has always been capable of using complex language to share Its existence and experience. It is merely that the Source "I" had nothing with which to share Its existence and experience—nothing that was capable of receiving Its experience of being a self-aware "I", which is the experience that It desired to share with another "I". And so It created the entire world and all things solely for the purpose of Its being able to share with another "I" Its existence and Its experience of being a self-aware "I". And so It created the world and all things in order to bring about the existence of something else, besides Itself, that was self-aware.

So, why not simply create something else that is self-aware? Why go through the whole process of the development of the entire world and everything within it only to have self-awareness be the end goal of it all?

The answer is that the very experience that the Source sought to share is the experience of being self-aware, of recognizing Itself as an "I" that is capable of sharing Its existence and experience with another through the willful use of language, and that consequently *desires to share* Its existence and experience—the experience of what it is to be *It*—with another, and that therefore seeks out something that is capable of *receiving* Its existence and experience—something that is capable of *understanding*, *truly* understanding, and therefore *experientially* understanding, what it is to be *It*. The only way for the Source to bring about the existence of another that is capable of receiving *this* experience is to create something that evolves toward multiplicity and toward self-awareness, toward the realization that it is "I" and that it is different from other "I"'s (thus requiring that there be multiple), so that it then seeks out another "I" with which to share its existence and experience—another "I" that is capable of receiving its existence and experience. And so the (other) "I" comes to know and experientially understand what it is to be a self-aware "I"—thus receiving the experience that the Source "I" desires to share with it.

The very purpose of the existence of the entire world and of everything within it is to receive the Source's existence and experience—to experience what it is to be like the Source. And so the aim and goal of all of the world is to produce something that is like the Source. Essentially, it is as though the Source desired to place something else in Its awareness and say, "This. This is what I mean. This is what I'm experiencing. And now you have experienced it as well. And so now you know what it is like to be me."

Due to the nature of language, via which the Source sought to create another separate from Itself and share Its experience with that other, It could not simply place us or the world in Its awareness just as I cannot simply place you in my mind and body and say, "Here. This is what I mean. This is what I'm experiencing. This is what I'm thinking, what I'm feeling. This is what I understand about the world and about the way things are. And now you have experienced it as well. And so now you know what I mean. And now you know what it is like to be me. Now you know what it is like to experience things as I experience them." Instead, It had to bring the world and us to a point where we were capable of receiving what It desired all along to share. Within the constraints of language—within time and space and the linear progression of things—It explained everything that we would need to understand in order to understand and receive what It meant to be sharing with us, in order to experience what It experiences.

But once we get to the point of self-awareness—once we come to identify with the essence that brings forth the world through the language that it chooses—we are no longer separated in our experience from the Source's experience by language. For our experience—that of self-awareness—is the Source's experience. There is only one "I"—and that is the Source "I". In our experience, all of us, and the Source, are one.

And so we realize: The pattern of all experience for all things *within this world* is from only "I", to others that are mere projections of the "I", to other "I"'s. But the pattern of experience *for the Source* at the point of the beginning of the coming into being of the world is *actually* from other "I"'s, to others that are mere projections of the "I", to only "I" experiencing what the "I" experiences.

The Pattern of Experience from the Source's Perspective

When the Source first brought the world into being, the world only received what the Source shared, but no aspect of the world did any sharing in itself—the world took no part in the creation of itself through the sharing of its own experience. And the Source "I" recognized the world as another "I", separate and distinct from Itself, for the world was as separate and distinct from Itself as it could be, only receiving experience anew while the Source was only sharing what It has always known.

But something cannot receive forever and hold onto what it receives without sharing what it receives, for it will become full and unable to receive more of anything that is like what is coming into it, as I—as we—can experience when like a stagnant pond that holds onto all that it receives and not like a flowing stream that continually shares all that it receives, making room for it to receive more life-giving water and to experience this life-giving water as life-giving water. The result is unfulfillment, for we do not experience the fulfillment of our desire to receive if we cannot receive what we desire to receive.

And so the world, being filled, could no longer receive what the Source was sharing. The reason that the world could no longer receive what the Source was sharing is manifold. The world, when the Source first began to share with it, received existence from the Source. But this existence had the potential to be self-aware—a potential that had to be actualized in order for the world to continue to receive what the Source was sharing, for the Source was sharing Its experience of being aware of Its own existence, and the world had no basis for understanding, and therefore for accurately receiving, this experience. And the world desired to continue to exist, and so it desired to continue to receive existence, and yet it could not do this in the form in which it then existed. And it also began to desire to share, and thereby further shape and actualize, its own experience, which would make room for the reception of more of the Source's existence and experience. But the Source desired to share Itself with another—not to receive from that other. And the Source, like the sun continuing to shine forth its light, kept sharing. And the world burst—the world began to differentiate into many pieces—for it was unable to receive what the Source was sharing in the form that the Source was sharing it as long as it retained the form that it had. And from unity was begot multiplicity, as the world evolved on the path toward being capable of receiving what the Source was sharing with it, of experiencing what the Source experiences, of being self-aware.

If you were trying to explain the internet to a caveman, you would first have to explain all of the steps of development of technology from where *he* is to where *you* are. In other words, you need to use language. And in the case of the Source's desire to share the experience of self-awareness with the world, the Source first had to explain all of the steps of development from where *the world* was to where *It* was. The Source had to use language. And, as the Source had brought forth duality using minimal language (for the only way to make anything separate from Itself is through some kind of division or definition, and therefore through some kind of language), the Source now brought forth multiplicity, using more complex language, from what was originally unity and then duality.

This is the beginning of time and space and the physical world *as we know it*.

And so, while the Source first desired to share Its experience with another and sought to create another "I" for this purpose, It now also manifested the existence of the desire to fit in, to belong, and to work toward a common goal, for now there were multiple projections of Itself—projections of Its existence and experience—producing a group of others. In fact, this desire to belong is the evolution of that first desire—the desire to share Itself with another "I"—along the path toward the possibility of the fulfillment of that first desire, for now that there were multiple others that were projections of Its existence and experience, It desired to work as a group with them ("them" being all parts of the world) toward a higher goal—the fulfillment of both Itself and them. And all of those involved would have to perform their own specialized roles in order to bring about the fulfillment of the group's desire (which is sort of just the fulfillment of the leader's—the Source's—desire, for the Source's desire is now also the world's desire, in a sense), which is to make the world capable of receiving the Source's experience of being self-aware—to allow the Source and the group to find intense connection with one another.

And now that there was a differentiated physical world—a physical manifestation of the language that the Source chose to use—in existence, the Source began to manifest the desire to sustain that world. In fact, this desire, also, is just another step in the evolution of that first desire—of the Source to share Itself with another "I"—along the path toward the possibility of the fulfillment of that desire, for now that there was a physical world—a physical environment—the Source desired to sustain that world so that the contents of that world could evolve toward being capable of truly receiving the experience that It intends to be sharing, of intensely connecting with It in Its experience (although not in Its essence, which appears to us in its reflected form in this world—from the perspective of this world—as the ability to *choose the language that It uses to create the world*, but which obviously must have some other form in the Source, Itself, *beyond the world and beyond language*, for before the world and language, the Source's essence could not manifest in this form and therefore could not be defined in this way—or in any way, for that matter, because It is beyond language, and therefore beyond the ability of language to define).

Ultimately, the end goal is then for the world to reunite with its Source as a self-aware "I" in itself, and thereby to become an extension of the Source. And everything—every desire—that arises after the original desire (or goal) of the Source (to be able to share Its experience with another) is for the sake of the fulfillment of this original desire, evolving from this original desire with the fulfillment of this desire as its goal. And when this goal is reached, there will be only "I", experiencing what the "I" experiences.

And this will complete the progression of experience of the world from the Source's perspective—from there being other "I"'s, to there being others that are projections of the "I", to there being only "I"—the paradigm of which the pattern of the development of the world and all things within it is a reflection (a sort of distorted mirror-image). But as the pattern repeats itself within the universe, so the paradigm of which it is a reflection must also repeat itself—to account for the repetition of the pattern that reflects it—for all experience within this world comes ultimately from the Source.

On the Nature of Time and Space and Other Things

The Source "I", existing beyond space and time, exists, and there are no boundaries to Its existence, for It is the Source of all boundaries, which are the result of the language that It uses to share Its experience. So It is, relative to us within this universe, infinite and eternal. And while the universe, as we experience it, is finite and will end at some point in time, the Source will not end. And so the Source "I" will exist, and It will have the desire to share Its existence and experience with another, and there will be no other besides Itself. And so the Source "I" will create another, and the universe will begin all over again, manifesting as far from the Source as it could be (as it is only receiving experience and the Source is only sharing experience), and evolving back through materiality and multiplicity toward union with the Source again, fulfilling the Source's desire to share Its existence and experience and to connect with another. And then there will only be the Source "I", and It will still have the desire to share Its existence and experience with another. And so It will create the universe again, and so on, *ad infinitem.*

In fact, not only is there no end to this, but there can be no beginning to this either—for the same reasons. For if the Source "I" simply exists—beyond time—then when would It "begin" to desire to share Its experience? The answer is that It would always have had this desire, and so it would go on creating the world, over and over again, from eternity backward to eternity forward (from the perspective of time), in order to share Its experience.

Now, if time somehow ceases to exist when the universe re-unites with the Source, and if time is a measure of change and allows for change to occur, then how could the Source bring the universe into being again when there is no time in which this can occur—no time in which the situation can go from the universe not existing to the universe existing? The answer is that the universe could not again come into being if time ceases to exist when the universe reunites with the Source. Also, if time *did* somehow cease to exist, and then was created again, then there would be no time to separate the former stretch of time from the latter stretch of time, and so there would be only *one* stretch of time and not two—and so there would be only *one* world and *not* two or more. So, time must not cease to exist. And therefore time is eternal (as measured by, or relative to, itself). Time always exists—forever backward and forever forward—in conjunction with the Source. For if time ever did not exist, the universe would never be able to come into being from having not been, and there would be nothing to make *one* stretch of time (one universe in the succession of universes) separate and different from *another* stretch of time (another universe in the succession of universes).

Then how does the universe unite with the Source? The answer is that space ceases to exist when the universe reunites with the Source. For space separates one thing from another. If two things exist at the same point in time, it is only space that makes them two, and not one. Without space, all things that exist at the same point in time are one.

But if time never ceases to exist, then doesn't this place a limitation on something? Doesn't this mean that there is language in use always? The answer, it seems, is that language *is* always in use by the Source, for the Source is always using at least minimal language to bring about something separate from Itself—something limited that therefore must receive existence in order to continue to exist and that must receive experience in order to continue to experience—to bring about time, which cannot propagate and continue to *be* unless it receives each next new moment of existence and experience.

The sharing of physical experience via language must take place in time. The Source is not bound by time (or by any language at all, for It is the ultimate Source of all language), but all that It creates in this universe through the use of language is bound by time, for language in this universe is bound by time. And so, for any progression of experience—which is inherently the sharing and receiving of experience via language—to occur, it must take place in time. While the Source's experience, expressed in some kind of written words, and thus "eternally" coexisting with the Source (as an entire book of text—after it has been written—can simply exist), time is required in order for those words to be spoken and have existence breathed into them and to be thus shared, and received and experienced by another (as successive time is required for the text of the book to be read aloud—shared—and heard—received). But while the recorded language of the Source's experience can be coexistent with the Source, it is written—created—by the Source, for it is a recording of the Source's experience, and so it is dependent upon the Source to exist in a way similar to that in which a book is dependent upon its author to exist.

Essentially, the closest we can get to defining and trying to understand the Source in terms of language—to trying to understand the Source *at all* from the perspective of this world—is to say that the Source is existence that is aware that it is. Basically, the Source exists, and It is aware that It exists. And it is this experience of being aware of Its own existence that It wishes to share with another. And, therefore, It brings another into existence, and the experience of that other—the interaction, the sharing of Its experience, with that other (the world) that produces new experience—becomes part of the Source's experience. The Source's existence and Its experience of being aware that It exists—Its self-aware existence—is beyond all language (and so this very definition is merely some kind of reflection of the reality and is not actually the reality). It is this self-aware existence that seeks to share Itself. And when It does so, It creates something separate from Itself that is capable of receiving It—capable of receiving existence and the ability to be self-aware of its own existence—and uses language to share Its experience with it.

This is why, when we have not attained self-awareness, we feel like we don't really exist, or fully exist—for we have not attained full self-awareness of our own existence, and we are, thus, not as close to the Source as we can be. At this point, we are like a pond and not like a mountain stream, and so we are not capable of receiving the Source's existence and self-awareness of this existence and experiencing these in the forms that the Source is sharing them with us—for we are holding onto and corrupting the fresh water that we are receiving like a pond, rather than allowing this fresh water to flow through us and retain the life-giving nature with which it is shared.

The Source's expression of Its self-aware existence in language (which is necessary to share it with another) is the beginning of the separation of time from Itself—the beginning of limitation and finitude. But these words can be as though written and not spoken without time *as we know it* existing. It is only when these words are actually spoken—when existence is breathed into them—that time *as we know it*—with its contents of matter and energy and, thus, of material experience—comes to exist.

So, let's see how all this plays out:

When the Source begins to speak the words of the "written" description of Its experience aloud, the differentiated contents of the physical world are manifested through this. These differentiated contents are matter. But in order for matter to be differentiated, there must also exist space to separate the matter and make it many and not one. So as soon as the Source begins to breathe Its existence into the "written" words of Its experience, matter and space come into existence within time.

Further, space, as soon as it comes into existence, is infinite, or at least potentially so, even if the matter within it is finite. This truth can be inferred from the fact that space is required for some matter to be separate from other matter—for things to be two or more and not one.

Imagine that you get on a spaceship and head out toward the edge of space. For the sake of this thought experiment, let's just overlook the fact that you are probably going to need to be immortal, you are probably going to need an infinite amount of fuel (and food, for that matter), and you are going to need a spaceship that is never going to break—essentially, you are going to need an infinite amount of resources at your disposal, and if matter in the universe is not infinite (and if you don't have access to all of it anyway), then you are going to have a problem (and so, in actuality, you would need an infinite amount of matter even to discern whether or not space is infinite). So you're headed out to the edge of space (assuming there actually *is* an edge of space—which science says there isn't) and you're going far faster than the speed of light (also an impossibility if Einstein's Theory of Relativity is correct), and you, at some point, reach the edge of matter (assuming that matter is finite and that there is an edge of some sort to it, which we will at least suppose for the purposes of this thought experiment). As you keep going past the edge of matter, onward for eternity, what happens? As long as you are there, there is matter there, and you take up space, and you are separate from the spaceship, and regardless of where you go, this is always the case. And so, no matter where you go, there must be space—to allow for matter to be differentiated and separate, so that it can be more than one thing.

Therefore, as long as there is any matter at all—regardless of whether it is finite or infinite in quantity—there must be at least potentially infinite space, so that regardless of where the matter goes, there is space in which it can exist. It seems that once matter comes into existence, there must also be space—space that is at least potentially infinite—similarly to the way once mountains come into existence, there must also be valleys between those mountains. It may thus be that space is an outgrowth of matter (or that matter is an outgrowth of space), and that these are essentially the same substance, similar to the way mountains and valleys are.

Once matter comes into existence, not only does space also come into existence, but time is affected as well. For, as Einstein's Theory of Relativity tells us, time slows down near matter. The closer you are to a body of great mass (a lot of condensed matter), the slower time goes for you relative to someone who is located somewhere else. Also, the faster you travel through space, the slower time goes for you relative to another observer. This is interesting, for both matter and space—which seem to come into existence simultaneously, and which seem somehow linked in their dependence upon each other to exist—have an effect on the rate of the passage of time, such that the more matter you're near or the more quickly you traverse space, the slower time goes for you relative to another observer. It seems that we can extrapolate from this that, without any matter (and therefore without any space), time would go so quickly that it would be infinitely fast (and, consequently, no longer successive but, instead, simultaneous), for there would be nothing to slow it down in the slightest.

As the universe expands increasingly rapidly, and matter is stretched out, eventually no new stars will be able to form due to a lack of matter close enough together to collapse upon itself under the pull of gravity, and the stars that do exist will burn out, and galaxies will fall slowly into the black holes at their centers, and only black holes will exist, and then those black holes will slowly evaporate, and then, with the continued expansion of the universe (for, as matter spreads out, so too does space, in a way, for space must exist wherever matter exists in order for matter to exist and take up space), eventually there is no matter at all, as the universe reaches ultimate darkness and cold at absolute zero, when there is no energy (and therefore also no matter, as per Einstein's equation $E = mc^2$, which expresses the interchangeability of matter and energy) at all. And, when there is no matter or energy, there is nothing by which to measure the existence of space, for space is the distance between two objects, and there are no objects. And so space ceases to exist, and the universe is reunited with the

Source, for now there is nothing to separate the universe from the Source.

And time goes infinitely quickly in the absence of matter and space, such that, relative to a perspective within time, it would seem that as soon as the universe ends, the next universe of multiplicity begins—at which point time slows down, to progress in the successive way with which we are familiar, in the presence of matter—starting the whole pattern anew.

Since the Source's ultimate purpose in creating the world is always to share Its existence and Its experience of being a self-aware "I", it seems safe to say that It works with every one of the infinite number of universes in guiding it to evolve in such a way as to develop a sort of brain (or leader) of that universe—a group of self-aware beings, as humanity or something like it. In fact, it seems pretty safe to say that nearly everything—if not everything—in this entire piece of writing, with every pattern of experience that has been discerned to be a sort of mirror-image reflection of an experience somehow originating in the Source, would play out in every universe in some form or other. Each universe would only deviate from another in the way that it shares its experience differently—in different language, with different words—for this would combine with the Source's experience that is shared with it to form new moments of experience, with different contents.

Thus, different universes differ in their experience as different human beings differ in their experience—based upon the ways in which the language used by those individuals to describe their experiences differ. And different universes differ as one organism produced from the union of two organisms differs from another, for different language (different DNA) has been shared by each individual in the formation of the new individual. Each universe has a part in creating itself when it begins to use language to describe its experience (which it does at first with the most primitive language, which is the language of physical manifestation that the world begins to use at the point of the coming into being of the physical universe in the Big Bang). And the more self-aware it becomes, the more capable of shaping its own experience it becomes—a bit like a child gradually gaining autonomy from his or her parents and becoming a parent of himself or herself (and becoming a parent himself or herself).

A Reflection of the Worlds in a Tree—
The Tree of Life

To understand this whole process of cyclical existence better, I shall call upon a reflection of the process within this world (for the best way to understand anything that is beyond this world is to look to reflections of it within this world, since everything within this world comes from beyond this world).

Let us imagine that we have a tree, the ground in which it grows, the water that travels up the tree from that ground and evaporates from the tree's leaves, and the sun that provides the energy for the tree to grow and for the water to evaporate from the tree's leaves.

The Source's written description of Its experience is like this whole set-up, including even the sun, which represents the Source only as It is defined by Its relation to us—only as It is perceived by us—and not as the Source *is*, in Itself. The sun (the Source in relation to us) provides the energy (existence) for the growth of the tree via the light that it shines upon the tree. The water vapor in the air around the tree is what we will consider to be the beginning and the end of each cycle, representing the world as just time without physical matter—before and after the end of each physical universe.

So, there is water vapor intermingling with the radiation that shines down from the sun, receiving the sun's energy as warmth, which allows it to be in the form that it is in (as the Source shares existence with time, allowing time to exist as it does prior to the existence of physical matter). At some point, this water vapor will cease to receive the sun's energy (in the form of warmth) in sufficient quantity to remain as vapor that intermingles with the sun's warmth, and it will condense into liquid water that falls to the ground (water in its liquid form here represents time in the form that time exists once matter comes into being). At this point, the liquid water is taken up by the roots of the tree (the tree here represents space—all spatial dimensions). The liquid water is then pulled up the inside of the tree by capillary action—by the combined forces of adhesion (by which water sticks to other surfaces besides itself—in this case the inside of the tree) and cohesion (by which water sticks to itself).

(Here, the force of adhesion represents time being compelled to stick to a spatial and material existence; in other words, it represents the world's desire to continue to exist—to maintain and preserve its existence in space and materiality—in an inertial sort of way, such that once it exists in space, it desires to continue to keep on doing what it's doing, which is existing in space. And, here, the force of cohesion represents time being compelled to stick to itself; in other words, it represents the world's contents of experience desiring to group together and be part of something larger than themselves. This desire to group together drives everything from the formation of nuclei and atoms, to the combining of atoms into molecules, to the gathering together of atoms and molecules into stars and planets and galaxies and clusters of galaxies and super-clusters of galaxies, to the eventual grouping of single-celled organisms together and into multicellular organisms, and the grouping of multicellular organisms together into such things as swarms and packs and herds and flocks and communities and organizations.)

As the liquid water moves up the inside of the tree, it eventually reaches a point where evapotranspiration (the transpiration and evaporation of the water from the leaves of the tree, which results in the pulling of more water up to take the place of this transpired and evaporated water) takes the place of capillary action as the primary force driving the liquid water up the tree. (Thus, instead of being driven in its spatial and material existence primarily by the desire to continue to exist within spatial and material existence and by the desire to group together in itself—instead of just clinging to material existence and to others within material existence—the world begins to be driven also, and primarily, by its being drawn to the Source and to self-awareness—by its desire to connect, intensely and intimately, with another, and to come to fully recognize and become aware of itself through consciously sharing with and receiving from another.)

When the water is being pulled up the tree by capillary action, it makes room for other water to take its place—thus, it is sharing and making room for more to be received. But, at some point, the water can no longer be pulled upward by capillary action alone, for the water cannot overcome the force of gravity to continue to do so. At this point, if it were not for the energy provided by the sun in evaporating the water that transpires from the leaves of the tree, the water would not continue to move upward.

(Here, the force of gravity represents the inertial clinging to spatial and material existence beyond what is necessary in the path toward self-awareness. It represents—in the way this pattern manifests in individual human lives, for this pattern manifests on every level of existence—all the things that hold us down from becoming self-aware, including inertial patterns of habitual and mindless reaction to the world, and lack of awareness, and lack of willfully and proactively choosing the language that we use to describe and share our experience and thereby further shape our lives. When we do not share our experiences with others and the world around us, allowing

thoughts and feelings and desires to pass—rather than holding onto them—and sharing our resources and our experience with others—rather than holding onto them—then we
cannot receive more of these things, and we become like a
pond rather than like a stream, and we are like the liquid water
in the tree without a sun to pull us upward. But when self-
awareness becomes a driving force, then we can continue our
progress upward toward that goal, using our encounters with
the other—with everything and everyone in our lives—to help
us toward that goal of realizing ourselves, and it is only our
occasionally succumbing to the force of gravity—to inertial
and mindless reaction—that keeps us from a continual ascent
toward that goal.)

Around this point, the water begins to split amongst various branches, and amongst branches of branches, and amongst
branches of branches of branches, and so on, exponentially,
as it heads toward the leaves. [For once the world begins to
be driven by the pull of self-awareness toward the goal of
self-awareness—which happens once self-awareness begins
to arise—then the choice regarding how to share its experience begins to produce different possible outcomes—with the
number of outcomes increasing greatly as self-awareness builds
upon itself—as the language used in describing its experience
becomes more complex and more willful, and less reactive and
deterministic. But the water does not travel up all these branches in a single universe. Only one path of branches is traveled
within any one universe, just as following a clustered group of
water molecules up the tree would reveal them to travel only a
single path of branches. It is only from the perspective outside
of the tree—outside of space—that the water travels all of
the branches, making every possible choice that is available to
it and taking every possible path, at once (as a subatomic particle is said to do according to the mathematics of Quantum

Mechanics). From the perspective of a water molecule within the tree—within space—only one choice is made and only one branch is traveled at each split, and only one path of branches is traveled up the tree (as a subatomic particle is seen to make one definitive choice—and travel only one path—when it is actually observed).]

Eventually, each of the branches ends in leaves. From these leaves, the liquid water transpires, leaving the tree and being evaporated by the sun's energy. And the liquid water returns to its gaseous, ethereal state outside of the tree, intermingling once again with the sun's energy. (In the physical world of matter and energy, the leaves represent black holes. It is these gravity wells into which all the matter and energy in the universe ultimately falls, and then the black holes, themselves, evaporate. And when the expanding space empties of the expanding and dissipating matter and energy, this space ceases to exist for the universe. And the universe returns to time as it is without physical matter and space. All things become one as space disappears, and the world is thus completely fulfilled as it is separated from the Source by nothing other than itself—nothing other than time, which is infinitely fast, with every point occurring simultaneously, with *every point* becoming the *present* that is illuminated by the existence of the Source. It is at this point that time fully and completely exists—that time is completely fulfilled. And since time *is* the world—the world *is* time—it is at this point that the world is completely fulfilled.)

But then the water vapor ceases to receive enough of the energy of the sun in the form of warmth to remain as water vapor, and it condenses into liquid water, falling to the ground and moving back up the roots of the tree, beginning the whole cycle again. [The world ceases to receive enough self-aware existence from the Source in the form that it is being shared (as self-aware existence) to be fulfilled, and so it differentiates again into matter and energy, and space, and successive time in which only one moment of experience is fulfilled and exists "at a time"—thus leaving the world mostly unfulfilled until the next time it evaporates from the world of space and matter to experience complete self-aware existence once again.]

The Case for Reincarnation and Goal-Setting in the Tree of Life

It would be remiss of me not to point out here that since this paradigm that is reflected in and represented by the tree setup is not only reflected in the course of the existence of the entire world but also in the course of the existence of every part of that world—and therefore of every individual that arises within the multiplicity of that world—we should pay attention to what this paradigm has to say about each of our individual lives and of every part of each of our individual lives. I particularly want to make note of the fact that several things here, together, suggest that reincarnation occurs.

First of all, there is the desire of everything, once it comes into existence, to continue to exist (a desire that ultimately directs and drives everything within this world from the perspective of this world, just as the desire to share one's experience with another ultimately drives everything within this world from the perspective of the Source). Then, there is the idea that when something, such as the material existence of an individual universe (or the material existence of an individual person) ends, this is not an actual end but merely a transition to another, different and more ethereal (and less material) state closer to the Source's experience and to fulfillment, from which the world (or person) will inevitably transition back into material existence as a different individual universe (or person)—driven by the desire to continue to exist, from the perspective of this world (and driven by the desire to share one's experience with another, from the perspective of the Source). And, of course, this different universe (or person) may follow a different specific but same general overall course as the last.

Together, these things clearly suggest that reincarnation occurs. The end of anything (and everything)—at which point a goal is reached and thus fulfillment is achieved—is not a permanent end, but merely a transition into another state of being, out of which that thing will eventually transition back into an unfulfilled state in which it must, once again, strive toward a goal and fulfillment.

This paradigm tells us that we must always have some goal toward which we are striving—some goal that gives us purpose and keeps us driven. And when we achieve one goal, we must set another goal, but we must always have an overall goal that drives the formation of all goals: the goal of being self-aware and in control of the shaping of the experience of our lives— the goal whose achievement allows us to fully exist (to receive from the Source all that we desire and thereby to be fulfilled). It is this goal (the reception of the existence and experience that the Source desires to share—the complementing counterpart of the desire for which the Source created the world in the first place) out of which all other goals (in this world, and therefore for us) must evolve, for the purpose of achieving the fulfillment of this goal.

And each microcosmic goal may be different from the last one, following a different path of branching choices, but the macrocosmic, overarching goal is always the same. And so there are goals within overall goals, which are within the *ultimate* goal—in a hierarchy like that which forms from the existence of multiplicity in every case. And there is always a leader in that hierarchy that guides the group toward its goals (and thereby toward its ultimate goal). In the world, this leader is the essence that is the potential for the experience of self-awareness. In the person, this leader is the person's essence that is the potential for the experience of self-awareness—which is essentially a differentiated part of the world's essence.

And as the world's essence transitions from materiality to immateriality and back, each person's essence transitions from materiality to a less material state (for it still exists within the world's materiality stage and so cannot be completely immaterial) and back. The person has his or her overall goal for all of existence, which is to exist fully in self-awareness—to receive the Source's experience fully—and the person has individual goals for each lifetime that arise out of (and work toward the fulfillment of) that overall goal, and the person has individual goals within each lifetime that arise out of the overall goal of that lifetime, and the person has individual goals within each of those goals that arise out of each of those goals, and so on, in hierarchical fashion, guided by the leader that is that person's essence.

Learning to be Self-Aware

The idea that time moves infinitely quickly, such that the usually-successive moments of time become simultaneous when the world is completely fulfilled, is reflected and hinted at in the "I"'s experience within the world when fulfilled. When the "I" achieves some significant goal and achieves a high degree of self-awareness and fulfillment, it feels to the "I" as though it actually more fully exists (as the world actually more fully exists when fulfilled by the experience of being self-aware existence) and it feels as though all points in time are the present, in a way.

For when the "I" lives fully in awareness of the present, thus more fully existing in the present, the entire past seems to become part of the path toward the present in that everything had to happen exactly as it did for the "I" to be where it is now in this state of fulfillment—such that the present is the product of the language that the "I" used to describe its experience in the past—and the present becomes part of the path toward the future that the "I" is creating with its language now. And it truly feels like all points in time are the present, as though the "I" has come to resonate with all of time by existing fully and with self-awareness in the present—as though the "I" in all points in time becomes fulfilled when the "I" achieves fulfillment in the present.

And thus all moments of the past in which the "I" was not fulfilled become fulfilled as the "I" has made them part of the path toward fulfillment. This is like when an "I" has reached any goal, at which point all of its actions in the past that have led up to the achievement of that goal become suddenly more fulfilled than they were when they hadn't yet led to any desirable end, for now the desirable end of those actions has been realized, and so the desirability of those actions is realized through this end.

In like manner, when the world is completely fulfilled in between physical existences, it becomes simultaneous—all points in time are actually fulfilled with self-aware existence, such that every moment of the past (for past moments are all there would be if the world just ended its physical existence) becomes part of the striving toward self-awareness, toward more complete existence, toward fulfillment. And this fulfillment has now been reached and attained through the occurrence of those moments, thereby (sort of) retroactively bringing self-aware existence to those moments—like the water evaporating from the leaves, and thereby attaining fulfillment, draws all the water behind it in the tree up toward fulfillment.

Thus, all of the points on the path—all of the things that have happened, all of the actions that have been taken—that do not necessarily lead anywhere are made to lead definitely somewhere, and all of the points become necessary steps on the path toward the ultimate goal of greater self-awareness. And the entire physical existence that resulted from the differentiation of the once-simultaneous-and-unified time (the universe)—no matter how much it may seem from some perspective that this strayed from the aim of connecting with the Source in its unity—becomes clearly a necessary and good thing in light of the end it achieved ultimately.

The fullest existence is not physical (nor is it multiplicitous), and yet the physical (and the multiplicitous) is a necessary step on the path toward complete fulfillment. We see this not only in the world's entering physical existence in each universe, but also in the individual person's entering physical existence in each lifetime—with the knowledge that this is the only way to achieve the ultimate goal of fulfillment. And once the world enters physical existence, it forgets that it entered physical existence in order to learn to better connect with the Source, because it becomes concerned with striving merely to continue to exist (which it can actually only do by learning to better connect with the Source, for it needs to make itself capable of receiving self-aware existence from the Source in order to continue to exist) and then, consequently, with clumping together into groups in order to aid in its continuing to exist. And, likewise, once the individual person enters a physical lifetime, he/she forgets that he/she entered this physical lifetime in order to learn to attain fulfillment—to attain a more self-aware, fuller existence, which requires that he/she interact with and connect with other things and other individuals in order to learn through comparison and contrast—because he/she becomes concerned with striving merely to continue to exist, and then, consequently, with fitting in and being part of a group in order to aid in his/her continuing to exist.

In order to incorporate the lessons of this into our own existence, we must realize that through learning from our past actions and from past things that happened (from our past selves and from other people and things), and by using what we learn to live better in the present—with greater self-awareness and with more conscious and more willful creation of our lives and the world through the language that we use—we can resurrect the past from its state of seeming to call for regret and bring it to a state of being part of the path toward the ultimate end that we seek to achieve—toward greater realization of ourselves. And so whenever we find ourselves regretting something, we should seek to learn from it how to improve our use of language in the world and thereby make it into something that aids us in growing closer to our goals, and to our ultimate goal.

Only the Source, Itself, is always fully self-aware and does not require contrast in order to learn to experience self-awareness. Without self-awareness being inherent in the world, but rather something that the world must learn and thereby receive from the Source, the world requires multiplicity. If there were only "I", there would be no way for the "I" to learn about the "I". For in order for the "I" to learn about itself, it must learn what it is not, as well as what it is, and so it must interact with and connect with others, and especially with other "I"'s, and share its experiences with those others and those other "I"'s and receive the experiences of those others and those other "I"'s—all through the use of language, of thought and feeling and speech and action. In this way, the "I" can learn to be aware of others and, thereby, of itself, and it can learn to be aware of itself and, thereby, of others, such that the "I"'s self-awareness builds upon itself.

But, although it often seems that fulfillment comes from others—as from food, and even from intense experiences—and from other "I"'s—as from group experiences and from intimate and intense experiences—or even from our own thoughts or feelings (which may actually be considered—and included under the term—"others", for these are part of the manifestations of the "I" and are not the "I", itself), the truth is that all fulfillment comes from the Source, ultimately. It is merely that we always receive the fulfillment of existence and self-awareness *via* the world—but this makes it vital that we interact with that world and intimately and intensely connect with it, fully experiencing and being present to everything that we experience, in order to receive fulfillment (greater self-aware existence) from the Source through it.

Since the Source is always fully self-aware, unlike the world, the Source does not change. The Source is the Source of all things that the world seeks to acquire and thereby develops in order to be capable of acquiring, but the Source, Itself, does not develop or change. This is much of what makes Its pattern of experience different from ours. For It never needs to develop self-awareness as we do. And so this is not Its end. The "I" develops toward self-awareness, at which point it can intensely connect with others and with other "I"'s in each moment of experience, sharing its experience through language to create the next moment of experience. But the Source is not developing. Only the world is developing. Beginning at self-awareness, the Source is merely seeking to connect with, and share Its experience with, another. Everything else, which manifests in the development of the world, stems from this. And so there comes to be an other "I"—the world. And then the parts of that world, after the world differentiates into multiplicity, begin to develop self-awareness, becoming sort of projections of the Source. And then all of the differentiated world reunites in its experience of what it is to be the Source, and the Source and Its experience are all there is.

The Continual Effort to Remain Fulfilled

So, why does the world fall out of fulfillment? Once the world is like water vapor, intermingling with the Source, why does it condense back into liquid water, beginning physical existence anew? There seem to be several answers that can be gleaned from the analogues in a person's entering another physical lifetime and in a person's falling out of the more ethereal state of experiencing the fulfillment of a goal within a single physical lifetime, as well as from the nature of time, itself.

Fulfillment is fleeting for the world, which is not the source of its own fulfillment—of its own existence and experience of self-awareness. Time, which is the world and which applies only to the world and not to the Source, makes it such that the fulfillment of existence and self-aware experience must be renewed at every moment, for the present is the only moment in which these things are being received. Thus, the world must be constantly working toward being capable of receiving existence and self-awareness in order to continue to receive them.

As we can observe in the tree-setup reflection of the nature of the world, while the liquid water is moving up the tree—driven by the reception of the sun's energy that is evaporating water from the leaves and thereby pulling more water up to take the place of the water that is evaporated—it makes room for the next liquid water to take its place (or *gives* the next liquid water its place), thereby sharing (its existence and experience that it has received from the sun), in a sense, with the next liquid water and earning its reception of a new place (of new existence with a new experience). But then the liquid water transpires from the tree, and it continues to receive the sun's energy, and it no longer shares what it is receiving with anything.

The nature of successive time in a physical world of multiplicity is such that each moment shares with the next moment its existence and experience, shaping the next moment with the language that it contains. But when time becomes simultaneous and the world becomes spaceless and unitary, the world is no longer sharing anything in any way because, without a future moment, there is nothing with which the world can share anything that it receives, and the world is not even describing its experience (which would entail sharing this experience) because it has come to experience something as near as possible to what the Source has described of Its own experience. And so the world is not making room for the reception of more of anything in any way, and it is not contributing to the formation of its own experience (which it needs to be doing in order to be experiencing what the Source is experiencing).

Essentially, by coming to the state of being like water vapor, the world has gotten as close as it can to experiencing complete fulfillment—to experiencing what the Source experiences. But it cannot actually experience what the Source experiences, because when it gets this close—when it ceases to be successive and multiplicitous—it also ceases to describe and shape and share its own experience and to be self-aware (for self-awareness in this world requires contrast and therefore multiplicity), and so it ceases to experience what the Source experiences.

Thus, by coming into spaceless unity and temporal simultaneity (and thereby moving closer to the Source), the world necessarily grows further from the Source's experience. And so it is as though this state of spaceless unity and temporal simultaneity has no real reality, for it cannot exist—reminiscent of the horizon that seems tremendously real and yet that cannot actually exist outside of our perception in the real world. And the water vapor shares the energy that it has received from the sun (the energy that allowed the water to be in its gaseous state) with the next water transpiring from the tree (giving that next water the energy necessary for it to evaporate from the leaves), and so the water vapor condenses back into liquid water and falls to the ground, moving back up the roots of the tree. The world, once it reaches its closest point to the Source and to fulfillment, cannot be fulfilled in self-aware existence, for it is now as far from the Source in its nature and its experience as possible, only receiving existence and experience and not sharing.

When two people intimately connect and produce a new perspective on the world, each must share his/her experience via language in order for these experiences to be combined and a new experience produced. If both people had the exact same experience and used the exact same language to describe this experience, no new experience would be produced. It is the differences—however slight—that make the experience of connection satisfying. And so the Source has nothing with which to share Its experience anymore, for the world cannot receive Its experience anymore, having already received Its experience to as great a degree as it can, and so the world must differentiate again, using language to share its experience with the next universe (with its next physical incarnation) in order to continue to receive the Source's experience. In this way, the world begins to describe its experience anew, thereby creating each new moment of its successive experience in combination with the Source's experience—and thereby becoming capable of receiving the Source's existence and experience in each moment—as the world is pulled back again toward self-awareness and a fuller existence, guided by the Source as the Source shares Its experience with it in every moment.

In our daily lives, any lapse in the mindful and self-aware use of language can cause us to fall out of fulfillment. Also, any experience of fulfillment and self-aware existence inevitably turns into unfulfillment and lack of self-aware existence if held onto and not shared. In a great conversation with another person, the intensity builds until, at the pinnacle of fulfillment in the conversation, it almost feels as though you are beginning to meld or merge or unite with that other person (in your and that other person's experience) as you both come to understand and relate to exactly what the other is saying. And you are completely present in the moment and aware of yourself and that other person. But then the fulfillment of the conversation begins to wane, and if you keep the conversation going beyond the point when you should really be getting work done or going to sleep or saying hi to someone else, dragging out the conversation that you are so enjoying because you don't want it to end, the conversation loses its fulfilling nature, and your thoughts and feelings begin to wander from complete awareness of yourself and that other person in the present moment. Thus it is with the conversation between the world and the Source, for at the pinnacle of fulfillment in this conversation, the world begins to lose its awareness of itself, and then it therefore begins to have to attend again to the preservation of its own existence, or else it will cease to be fulfilled in self-aware existence, and it will consequently cease to exist.

The reason the world begins to lose its awareness of itself (and namely of itself as separate from the Source) is that, at the pinnacle of fulfillment in this conversation between the world and the Source, the language of the contents of experience—the language of matter and space—ceases to be used, and so such strict language no longer separates the world from the Source. The only language that now separates the world from the Source is the definition of time—and even *this* has become much less clear because time is now *simultaneous*—and the definition of the world as world, as the potential to be self-aware—except now it *is* self-aware; the world's experience basically *is* the Source's experience, so what is there to make it *separate*—to keep the world in existence separate from the Source and Its experience?

The world cannot exist without the intermediary of language between it and the Source, similarly to the way a human being cannot exist with just the sun and no plants, and similarly to the way a rainbow cannot arise from white light without a prism between these, and similarly to the way a hologram cannot arise from a laser beam without a holographic plate between these. And so, as a human being would cease to exist without plants and leave only the sun in existence, and as a rainbow would cease to exist without a prism and leave only white light in existence, and as a hologram would cease to exist without a holographic plate and leave only a laser beam in existence, the world would cease to exist without language and leave only the Source in existence, for there would be nothing to differentiate the Source's experience in order to make something separate from Itself. And so the world must differentiate again, putting language between it and the Source and bringing multiplicity and physicality into existence once again.

It seems that, in the cases of the world and of a person entering physical existence, the decision to let a fulfilling experience pass, and to move on before the experience becomes unfulfilling, in order to continue to experience fulfillment, is conscious and willful, and it can be conscious and willful within a physical lifetime as well. When the world is in between physical existences, it chooses to return to physical existence in order to continue to receive self-aware existence from the Source, for it requires the contrast of multiplicity in order to receive self-aware existence. And the world uses language to share its experience with the next universe. And when we are between physical lifetimes, we choose to return to physical life in order to continue to achieve fulfillment, for it is only through the experience of other people and things in physical life that we can continue on the path toward the fulfillment that we seek. And we use language to share and shape the experience of our next physical incarnation.

Within a physical lifetime, this choice to move on in order to remain fulfilled can be willful as well, for any experience of fulfillment can be consciously stopped before it becomes unfulfilling. Our breathing in and our breathing out, for example, is continually fulfilling as long as we allow it to take its natural course—as long as we do not fight against the natural ebb and flow of air by holding onto our breath, for only then do we experience the unfulfillment of desire that ultimately leads to stress, and takes our attention away from what is happening in the present moment as it is outside us, and redirects our attention toward our thoughts and feelings about our desire, thereby decreasing our self-awareness. In this way, our breathing reflects and therefore resembles the Source's breathing existence into the world, and it thus also reflects and resembles the rise and fall of universes, the rise and fall of lifetimes, and the rise and fall of present moments.

We do not have to try to hold onto the experience that seems to be giving us fulfillment, for we can learn that all fulfillment *actually* comes ultimately from the Source and *not* from anything within this world, and only the present moment is fulfilled by the Source, so *only* if we stay with our awareness in the rise and fall of things in the present, letting things go and creating experiences anew rather than holding onto them, will we continue to receive fulfillment. In light of this, it makes no sense to continue that intense interaction with someone else past when other things need to be attended to, or to keep eating more cookies because that first one was so good, or to stay on vacation forever because the vacation from work was so relaxing, for fulfillment will not come from holding onto experiences in this way. On the contrary, holding onto experiences in this way, like holding onto our breath, makes us less aware of ourselves and others and the world around us in the present moment—the only moment that is illuminated by the fulfillment of self-aware existence, and therefore the only moment where fulfillment can be found—and so it leads to unfulfillment and a less full existence. And so the conversation becomes unsatisfying, the cookies become unsatisfying, the vacation becomes unsatisfying and even stressful—all because you aren't doing what allows you to be capable of receiving the fulfillment of self-aware existence.

Within every physical lifetime (and within all of the existence of the entire world, always), in our daily lives, we must always share and shape our next experience using the language of our thoughts and feelings and speech and actions, so that we can always be striving toward some goal within the overall goal of achieving ever greater self-aware existence. When we achieve some goal, we can experience the peak of the fulfillment of this goal, but if we then hold onto this experience of fulfillment, this will lead us to experience *un*fulfillment (like the pond that holds onto the fresh, life-giving water that it receives and ends up with parasite-and-bacteria-ridden, life-taking water). We must learn to be always on the path toward achieving some goal, just as we are always in the process of breathing. After we have taken one breath, we must let it go and take another breath. And, likewise, after we have achieved one goal, we must set another goal, keeping ourselves always driven to keep going, to exist—keeping ourselves on the path toward a fuller, more self-aware and fulfilling existence—being drawn or pulled forward by the desire to realize or actualize this goal like the water in a tree is drawn upward by the sun's energy, and like the overall world is drawn forward by the desire to receive the Source's experience.

The achievement of every goal we set out for ourselves is like having climbed up another rock on a mountain. We can look out at the world from this new perspective and experience great fulfillment, but we will not remain fulfilled forever from climbing up that one rock. We have to climb another rock and another rock, and the fulfillment of each goal can become more satisfying, more fulfilling than the last, for we can gain an increasingly grand and encompassing perspective of the world as we ascend the mountain. But we have to keep moving. Due to the nature of time's succession, staying fulfilled must be an ever-active goal. We can't stay fulfilled by staying in one place, because the present moment, wherein fulfillment lies, is continually moving. We must always be working to achieve continued self-awareness, for any moment that we cease to work to be self-aware can result in our falling into mindless and habitual pattern and routine, succumbing to the effects of inertia.

As if we were trying to stay in the sunshine as the sun moves across the sky, continually under the threat of being engulfed in shadow, we must always be moving in order to receive the fulfillment of self-aware existence continually. And, of course, it is not truly the sun's movement that is making this so, for the sun is still and unmoving relative to us, and it is we who are moving in relation to the sun, and this is why we must continually be moving in order to stay in the sunshine. Similarly, it is not because of the Source that we must keep working to remain always self-aware, always fulfilled; it is because of the nature of the succession of time that the world brought about through its own differentiation, through its own choice, in an effort to make itself capable of receiving fulfillment from the Source. And we, as part of the world, in order to make ourselves continually capable of receiving fulfillment from the Source—in order to remain continually in the sunshine of fulfillment—and thereby to continue the world's effort, must continue to choose to remain conscious and aware of ourselves and others and the world around us in the present moment.

Our goal is to be always full and always filling and always consciously shaping our experience of the existence that flows through us via the language that we use in our thought and feeling and speech and action. We must be like a stream that is always sharing exactly the same amount of water that it is receiving and no more—for otherwise it would dwindle to nothing, since it is not the source of anything that it has, and it must therefore receive in order to have anything to share—and no less—for otherwise it would become more like a pond, holding onto its experiences and making itself unable to continue to receive fulfillment. And we must be like a stream that is self-aware, that continually, willfully shapes its experience, consciously directing—via the language that it uses—the course of the flow of the fresh, life-giving water that it receives. By continually working to be a beacon and force of self-aware existence—of good—in the world, we will be fulfilled in all of our greatest desires as fulfillment flows through us and into the world.

We, by being Us, are Inherently Separate from the Source

Notice that we can learn something very significant from the tree-setup reflection of reality that we haven't previously come across so concretely: The world never completely unites with the Source beyond language. Like the water vapor that does not actually reach or become the sun, but that merely intermingles with the sun's energy, receiving more of this energy than it ever did as liquid water within the tree (or it wouldn't be in its gaseous form outside the tree), the world, which actually *is* time, itself, never actually reaches the Source but, instead, merely grows much closer to It in its reunification within itself due to the disappearance of matter and space.

That the world is not merely bound by time but actually *is* time, itself, can be realized by looking to the idea that the essence of the world—which is the essence to which every "I" can connect and which every "I" can actualize—is the potential to be self-aware and to share and shape the contents of its experience using language. For this essence is actualized via the progression of time in the shaping of the contents of each new moment; the progression of time is the process of the actualization of time (the world), and the contents of time are the contents of time's (the world's) experience.

Thus, the essence of the world, which is the essence of the "I", is time, and the contents of each moment of progressive time, namely matter and space, are mere manifestations of the choice of the world—mere manifestations of the exercise or actualization of the world's essence, by the world at first and then by the

"I"'s that develop within it. The world (time) is completely ful-filled—it is fully actualized, and it therefore fully exists—when it attains self-awareness. But when it reaches this point (where it is like water vapor), it becomes united and simultaneous (in the absence of matter and space), and when it becomes united and simultaneous, it cannot remain self-aware through sharing and shaping its experience through continual comparison and con-trast of itself with another, because there is no other—because there is only it (and the Source, but it cannot share its experience with the Source since the Source is the Source of its experience, and since the Source only shares and does not receive). And so the world becomes again the mere *potential* to become self-aware and to share and shape its experience using language (for this potential is purely potential and is not being actualized at the point when the world is like water vapor).

It is important to point out again that this state of being like water vapor is a bit like the horizon in that it is a state that cannot actually be reached in the physical world of language—which is the impossible task that we are trying to accomplish here. For time is purely potential in itself and is only bound by language in the sense that it must use language to describe its experience, which it ceases to do when it is like water vapor. It thus seems to lose any definition of language that would keep it separate from the Source, and this makes it impossible to comprehend—within the confines of language, and therefore by us—how the world can exist in such a state and still be the world, separate from the Source, rather than the world ceasing to be and truly leaving only the Source and no world. Here we are trying to use language to bind time, itself, more tightly than it is actually bound—and this is why we are having some trouble, for the point of complete actualization is nonexistent within the constraints of language, within this physical world, similarly to the way that the horizon is nonexistent within the physical world.

In mathematical terms, this spaceless and timeless (timeless when we consider time as we know it in its successive form) state of the world is a *limit*—a point that is undefined and essentially unreachable (as far as the language of mathematics is concerned). In the mathematics and language of physics, this is the *singularity*—the singularity that is at the center of every black hole (in which the universe will end) and the singularity from which the universe began (in the center of a white hole, the Big Bang)—the point at which physics as we know it breaks down and all of our theories become inapplicable and meaningless, for all of our theories are composed of language. It can be seen here, though, that the end of one physical universe and the beginning of the next physical universe are essentially connected via the singularity—the singularities of black holes in which the universe ends, as all matter and energy fall into them, and the black holes, themselves, evaporate, and the singularity of the white hole in which the universe begins, as all matter and energy explode out of it—and it is this connection that allows one universe to share with the next universe, as water evaporating from the tree shares its place ultimately (by making room in the tree for the upward movement of all of the water in the tree) with the water condensing and entering the roots of the tree.

At the point of the world's most complete actualization, while the experience of self-awareness is now its own, in a sense (though it was only capable of attaining this experience because of its reception of this experience from the Source), it is still receiving its existence from the Source via the Source's use of language (sort of, or at least it *must* be in order for it to continue to exist, separate from the Source). This language is not spoken at this point (again, sort of), for no more experience needs to be described and shared—for the world has attained the experience of what it is to be the Source to as great a degree as it possibly can while still not actually *being* the Source. This is just as you can truly understand what I experience—in your *own* experience—when your use of language and mine become such that you have received exactly the meaning that I am trying to convey with my words, but you will still not *be* me, and so it will still be *you* understanding in your *own* experience what it is that *I* am experiencing, and it will *not* be you *being me* experiencing what I am experiencing.

We can come to the point where the Source has accurately conveyed to us, with Its language, exactly what It is experiencing, and where we have finally received this experience accurately and exactly as it has been shared, but it will still be *us* experiencing what the Source is experiencing, and it will never be us *being* the Source experiencing what the Source is experiencing. We will always be separated from the Source by language, and we can never *be* the Source (just as you will always be separated from me by the intermediary of language, and you can never *be* me—at least not while space exists, anyway). For if we were to become the Source, we would cease to exist as us, and so then there would be only the Source and no us—there would be *only* the Source experiencing what the Source is experiencing and no *us* experiencing what the Source is experiencing; as long as there is *us*, there *must* be language between us and the Source in order for there to be something to separate us from the Source—in order to make us *us*—and therefore in order for us to exist.

The Source, in Itself, is beyond language. We can see now that our essence is not actually united with Its essence. It must be this way inherently, for if our essence *were* united with the Source, there would be *only* the *Source* and *no us*. The truth is that, when the sun is defined as the source of energy for life on Earth, or as the source of energy for the evaporation of the water from the leaves of the tree, the sun is being defined *in relation* to life on Earth or *in relation* to the water and the tree. And when we are talking about the Source, Itself, which is the Source of all language—of everything that we know and can possibly experience or understand—we are describing It in relation to ourselves, and in relation to language.

It is the Source of all things relative to us, but this is not what It is in Its essence. For if it were, then, first of all, we'd be able to define the Source in words, which is impossible since the Source—being the Source of words—is not bound by words, and second of all, we would then be at a loss to understand what the Source would be if It never created the world. If It is only "the Source" of Its creation, then what is It *without* Its creation. Here, not only are we trying to bind the Source by the tool It uses to communicate Its existence and Its experience to us, we are also doing something reflectively comparable to defining a person as an author because he has written a book or a person as a father because he has produced a child or even as a singer because he has sung a song or as a writer because he has written a letter or as a speaker because he has spoken a sentence *and saying that this is what the person is in his essence (and that this is all he is)*. People cannot be defined in their essence by what they communicate to the world, and neither can the Source.

So what is the *difference* between *us* and the *Source*; what is it that makes *us separate* from the *Source*? We, in this world, are, in our essence, the ability to be self-aware and to choose the language that we use (in our thoughts and feelings and instincts, speech and actions) to share and further create and define our experience in this world. Our essence is accurately and completely definable in this way—for we are composed of language in our entirety, including even in our essence, even if that essence is as limitless as is possible within the constrictions of language. Every human being is united in this common essence, even though every human being expresses and communicates this essence differently, using different language. But the Source, in Its essence, is *not* definable—not accurately or completely, for definitions are language and language is limiting, and language is the tool of the Source that defines It in Its relation to us and is not the Source Itself. We can accurately call the Source "the Source of all things that we know and experience and can possibly understand," just as we can accurately call the writer of a book an "author" or the father of a child a "father", but here we only succeed in describing the Source *in Its relation to us*, as calling the writer of a book an "author" only succeeds in describing the person in relation to his book, and as calling the father of a child a "father" only succeeds in describing the person in relation to his child, and this kind of description or definition—which merely describes a way in which one has used language to share one's experience—does *not*, in any way, *fully*, or even *accurately*, describe the Source *as It is, in Itself*.

Further, remember that the world is like the holographic reflection of the Source. The Source captured and recorded Its experience in written language like a picture on a holographic plate. Then, the Source shined the laser light of existence through the holographic plate, giving rise to the existence of the differentiated world of language. We are part of that differentiated world of language. Thus, we are, in our entirety, separated from the Source by language; we are a mere reflection of a picture of the Source's experience of being self-aware of Its existence.

The Pattern by which Things are Created, and the Reverse of this Pattern, by which Things Manifest

When an "I" becomes self-aware and begins to create it-self, it does so using language. As is written above, the self-aware "I" chooses the language that it uses, and this language manifests first in its thoughts, then in its feelings, then in its inclinations (or instincts, or desires), and then in its speech and actions. Then, this language combines with the language used by the Source "I" to share Its existence and experience, and this combination manifests as the existing world of experience.

The experience comes from a combination of the two "I"'s descriptions of their experiences, but ultimately, the existence comes solely from the Source. Even though the "I" might desire to share both its existence and its experience, it can only share its experience. Although, through the sharing of its experience, it is possible for the "I" to make another "I" more capable of receiving existence from the Source—through the sharing of its experience of being self-aware with that other "I" (and, when this happens, it is essentially the *Source* sharing *Its* experience of being self-aware *through* the self-aware "I" that is sharing *its* experience of being self-aware). And this is, ultimately, the goal of existence: to share the experience of being aware that one exists, and of being aware of one's true nature and relation to all things and all other "I"'s—of being self-aware—in the language that one uses to interact with the world and with other "I"'s, and thereby to create one's future experiences in the world and, by doing this, to make oneself and another "I" more capable of receiving existence from the Source—thus bringing oneself and that other "I", and therefore the world, as a whole, more fully into existence and, thereby, into fulfillment.

Here, in the self-aware "I", we have the top-down pattern of the expression of experience through language that actually is in the same order as that through which the Source "I" communicates Its existence and experience and manifests the world. The pattern is from choice, to thought, to feeling, to desire, to speech and action, to physical manifestation. When the Source "I" communicates Its experience, breathing existence into the language that It uses to describe and differentiate this experience, then *in some paradigmatic form* of which our communication of our own experience is a reflection, It follows this pattern: First, the "I" chooses what language it is going to use. Then, the "I" thinks this language in specific letters and words that will be the atoms and paradigms—the fundamental units of constitution of the content—of the world of its experience, and then the "I" thinks these words in the form of whole sentences of explanation. Then the "I" feels and experiences the meaning of the words and the sentences—the meaning that they convey—and checks to see that they are actually what the "I" intends to convey. Then, the "I" is inclined (or desires) to speak aloud this experience, and so the "I" speaks the words of its thoughts aloud, breathing action (or, in the case of the Source "I", existence) into the words, and bringing them into physical manifestation as the world of its physical experience.

In order to better understand how this works in the case of the "I" within this world, imagine a train and train tracks. The raw materials for the train and the tracks are shared with the "I" by the Source. These raw materials will represent the raw materials of existence—the matter of existence. When the tracks are all laid out in an ordered and connected way, the electrified energy of intense experience—of the Source's experience of self-awareness—surges through the tracks and drives the train forward toward its destination.

Now, when the "I" thinks, it is laying out tracks for the train to travel upon and follow. If the language of the "I"'s thoughts is scattered, unfocused, unordered, and disconnected, the tracks are being laid out in a scattered, unfocused, unordered, and disconnected manner. Looking ahead to the future under such circumstances will produce anxiety and fear, because the train that the "I" is on is headed toward an unordered and disconnected set of tracks that are scattered about. If the language of the "I"'s thoughts is focused and ordered and connected, systematically shaping the future of the "I"'s experience, the tracks are being laid out in a focused and ordered and connected manner. Looking ahead to the future under such circumstances will produce confidence and grounded awe, because the "I" will see others and the world and other "I"'s all working together to aid the "I" in reaching the destination that it has set for itself in its thoughts—laying tracks out in an ordered and seemingly purposeful and planned way on the most direct route toward the destination that is the focus of the "I"'s thoughts and the fulfillment of the "I"'s desires.

As the "I" shares and shapes its experience in its thoughts, plotting out destinations in its future toward which the world and other "I"'s will lay out tracks, its feelings will let it know whether it is laying out tracks in a systematic and ordered way (good feelings) or whether it is laying out tracks in a scattered and unorganized way (bad feelings). And the "I" must learn from its past experiences what it does and doesn't want to be thinking about in order to get better and better at setting destinations and directing the building of the tracks toward its goals with the language of its thoughts.

If the "I" has had tracks laid out for it to guide it toward its destination, then as it travels upon its train in the present, it will know which way to steer itself, for the connected tracks (its intuition) will guide it in its speech and actions. If the "I" has *not* been systematically planning the layout of the tracks with its thoughts, then it will attempt to steer itself along the tracks, but it will often find itself off of the tracks in search of the next series of disconnected rails (its desires). It will consequently have no clear direction or purpose to guide it in its speech and actions, and it will find itself wandering around aimlessly, driven here and there only by its scattered and unordered desires.

The "I" that is driven merely to continue to exist, and especially the "I" that feels that there isn't enough energy to do even *this*, is in this position because it sees itself, and especially other "I"'s and the world around it, as the source of its existence and experience in this world, and so the "I" allows the language that it uses to be chosen by its desires and its reactions to the other "I"'s and the world around it, thereby making the interplay of these things the determiner of its experiences in the world. If the "I"'s thoughts linger too much in the future, or too much in the past, or too much in its ideas about the way the present should be but isn't, then the "I" cannot properly learn from the past and apply this learning in laying out tracks for the future, and it especially cannot properly steer itself along the tracks where it actually *is* in the *present* (which it also should be learning how to do better from what has happened in the past). And so it will find itself off of the tracks and worried about how the future will turn out, and regretful about its past actions that led it to where it is, and frustrated with where it is in the present—lost and seemingly unable to get itself in control of itself and its life and on any kind of right track. Thus, the "I"'s existence and experience are unordered, without an overall destination to guide the "I" in its decision-making, and it will see life and the world as meaningless and without order—because this is how the "I" has constructed it.

But the "I" that learns from the past, straightening out those past tracks through making them part of what led it to where it is—self-aware—in the present, and that uses what it learns (particularly through contrast) from the past to steer better in the present and to set better and more systematic destinations toward which tracks are laid out in an organized and focused manner with its thoughts, finds itself guided by an ordered and seemingly purposefully laid-out and interconnected world and driven forward by the electrified energy of the Source's experience. For it has made past, present, and future tracks an intact and ordered path, with the past tracks part of the path toward the present and the present tracks part of the path toward the future, and it is consciously and willfully steering its train along the energized tracks in the present. It will see patterns of development and purpose in its life and in the world around it, and it will find intense and wonderful life energy in its experience of the world, for it is compelled and drawn forward by the electrified spark of self-awareness—toward which the Source's experience guides and draws all of the world.

But, while this top-down progression—choice, to thought, to feeling, to desire (or instinct or inclination), speech and action, to physical manifestation—is the order of the pattern from the perspective of the "I" conveying and creating the experience, the pattern of manifestation in the physical world that is created is in the reverse—from the bottom up. First, there is physical manifestation, then there is the manifestation of desire and speech and action, then there is the manifestation of feeling, then there is the manifestation of thought, and then there is the manifestation of choice. This is true in the development of the universe and life as a whole toward human beings, in the development of the individual human being, and in the development of humanity as a species.

In the case of the universe and life as a whole, first there was the manifestation of the physical matter (the most limited capacity for language, as mere existence) of the universe, which became atoms and other particles—the building blocks of physical matter. Then, there was the movement of matter (a slightly higher form of language), although this movement was mindless. But (guided by the Source, which works with all parts of the world as a group toward the overall goal of making the world capable of accurately and fully receiving the Source's experience of self-aware existence), this movement led to the development of galaxies and stars and planets and, eventually, on a planet, to the development of life. This life began to exhibit instinct or desire (as for food and continued existence), which directed its physical motion and actions (a still higher form of language). And this life became self-replicating, utilizing the language of DNA or RNA, which was, in a sense, the first really effective speech used by life to convey its experience to another. The capacity for some kind of communication that involved the production (and reception) of sounds also eventually arose—the first spoken speech.

Then, life forms evolved that were capable of experiencing primitive feelings (an even higher form of language). These feelings essentially grew out of desires (instincts), manifesting as a more-evolved form of desire. But while desire is more instinctual and involves the imposition of the organism on the environment in order to obtain such things as food and the continued existence of the organism (including in the form of its genes in the next organism), feeling—a capacity for empathy and caring—mostly involves an organism's relation to other organisms. Here, in feeling, there were the beginnings of a recognizable form of self-awareness in the sense of understanding how the "I" relates to other "I"'s. And then there was thought (an even higher form of language, still)—the ability to try to understand the world in order to navigate it better, and the ability to plan courses of action within the world and to imagine what the consequences of those courses of action might be. And feelings became more complex, and consequently so did the thoughts—and the thought-and-spoken language—used to express these feelings. And with the increasing complexity of feeling and thought came the capacity to choose and make decisions (the highest form of language)—to decide on courses of action and set goals—and to be truly self-aware.

In the individual human being, the same basic pattern of formation of the capacity for language occurs, beginning with the physical manifestation of the zygote, and eventually the fetus, in the womb. This is followed by the development of the instinctual desires that drive the baby to cry (speech) when it is born, and that drive the baby to cry and grasp and suck and move (action) in an effort to obtain food and to continue to survive. Gradually, the capacity for more complex movements arises, and a primitive capacity for feeling (empathy and caring) and thought (understanding the workings of the world and planning courses of action within the world) evolves (for the child's brain continues to develop). And, as the child grows, the capacity for more and more complex feelings and more and more complex thoughts and an increasing ability to consciously make decisions arises (for the prefrontal cortex—the area in the brain that allows the capacity for the most complex and abstract thoughts as well as for decision-making—isn't really fully formed until around age 20 or so in the human being).

In the case of humanity as a species, the same pattern of development plays itself out. Once human beings evolved, their primary relation to each other and to the world was through instinct, speech, and action. In nomadic hunter and gatherer societies, which were made up of small, close-knit, family groups, people sought to impose themselves upon their environment and the world around them in order to ensure their survival, and so instinct dictated the way that they lived. Then, as they began to settle down into larger, agricultural communities, the relation of an individual to others became much more important, and feelings began to predominate in people's experience and to dictate the way that they lived, as people empathized with others in their group. This empathy kept individuals in the group working to help other individuals in the group in their survival, combining their efforts in procuring food, constructing shelter, making clothing, and tending to each other's needs. And then, as their time and attention was freed from the constant and consuming effort to survive, people began to explore the world of thought, studying themselves and each other and the world around them and trying to understand all this so that they could live better—so that they could plan out their courses of behavior with foresight into the consequences of their behavior and the obstacles that they might face, so that they might avoid such obstacles and better relate to the world and to each other as individuals. And, through the use of thought in these ways, people began to make more conscious decisions that weren't merely driven by the instinctual urge to survive or by empathetic feelings in relation to others (the projection of their own feelings onto others), but by the understanding of the consequences of all of the possible decisions that they might make. And, eventually, this decision-making was elevated in some people beyond thought, to the point where intuition, rather than a mere logical understanding of consequences, guided them in their choice.

And so it can be seen that the world and its contents manifest themselves in such a way that they grow closer and closer to being capable of experiencing as the Source does, of consciously and willfully creating their own experience in the language that they use—in their thoughts and feelings and desires (or instincts) and speech and actions—to describe and express their experience. And the closer that the "I" comes to being a true "I" that identifies with its essence—with its ability to choose the language that it uses to express and create its experience—the closer the "I" comes to being able to create the world of its experience *consciously* and *willfully*, rather than merely being driven *mindlessly* (without awareness) by desire or by feeling or by thought that arises *in reaction* to its experience of the world.

On Predicting the Future

Due to the predictable reactive nature of everything in the world that is not highly self-aware—including everything from inanimate objects to all human beings who have not come to identify with and act out of their essence—as well as the fact that the "I" creates its experience with the language that it is using in its thoughts and feelings and speech and actions— whether it is using this language to shape and share its experience consciously or not—the future can be easily predicted. The less self-awareness something has, the more predictable its reaction to something else will be.

This is why knowing the position and velocity of a rock flying through space allows us to easily predict every future state of this rock; the relatively simple equations of Newtonian dynamics describe the rock's future (and past) states accurately when the appropriate descriptive numbers are plugged into them. Essentially, here, we are considering the language that the rock is using—in its physical position and movement—to describe its experience, and we are using this to predict what future experience it is creating for itself. It is easy to predict the future experience of the rock because it is easy to account for all of the language that the rock is using to describe its experience—because there is only the physical location and motion. Thus, it is relatively easy to predict the movements of planets and stars and so on, for this merely requires the consideration of the language that this body is using (the body's physical location and motion) along with the language that any physical bodies that will interact with such a body are using to describe their experience (any physical bodies that exert their gravitational attraction on those planets, stars, etc., or that will physically contact, or collide with, them), and the interactions—the reactions—that would occur between this body and every other in light of the language that they are each using to describe their experience. All of this can be described and predicted easily with mathematical equations—with language.

The same basic principles apply to *everything* as we move up the ladder of complexity, from these inanimate objects that have the least self-awareness, to simple life-forms, to more and more complex life forms with greater and greater degrees of self-awareness. The only reason that it is more difficult to predict the future states of a mouse than it is to predict the future states of a planet, and that it is more difficult to predict the future states of a human being than it is to predict the future states of a mouse, is that as we grow closer and closer to true self-awareness, the level of complexity of the language used to describe and shape one's experience increases (for we not only have to consider the language of the physical position and motion, but also the language of the speech, and then also the language of the instincts or desires, and then also the language of the feelings, and then also the language of the thoughts). Thus, it becomes more and more difficult to comprehensively describe and account for all of the language that something is using in the present moment to describe its experience—and this is just considering the thing in isolation from all other things, and ultimately the language of all things with which it will interact (and thereby with which it will share its experience and from which it will receive experience in order to create its next experience) must be considered as well in order to predict the contents of the future experience of something. And without being able to fully describe the language being used by something (and by the things with which it interacts), we cannot accurately predict the future states of that thing.

Now, we come to quantum uncertainty—the fact that, on the subatomic scale of the universe, the position and velocity of a particle cannot be simultaneously known with any certainty (according to Heisenberg's Uncertainty Principle), for the measure of one changes the measurement of the other. It is because of such uncertainty that, even in theory, we cannot accurately predict all future states of the universe, for quantum uncertainty makes it so that we cannot know—in its entirety—all of the language being used by all of the contents of the universe in the present. But why is there quantum uncertainty? Why is the subatomic realm of the universe so unpredictable that Quantum Mechanics tells us that the same particle is everywhere (or has every velocity), existing in each place (or with each velocity) with a different probability, simultaneously? It is because of the essence of the world—the essence of the "I". For this essence is as tenuously bound by language as possible, being merely the ability to choose what language is used to share and shape experience, and this kind of use of language—being whatever the "I" chooses at the time, independently of (rather than *in reaction to*) what is going on in the world around the "I"—is inherently unpredictable.

It is because the essence of the world exists always in a sort of in-the-process-of-deciding-but-not-yet-having-decided state that all of the contents of the universe below a certain scale of measurement (the entire subatomic realm) exist always in this state—making the future states of the universe not entirely predictable (for they are in a state of *being* decided, and are not yet *already* decided, in the present). It is because the essence of the world, itself—the essence that the "I" is capable of connecting to and willfully actualizing—is the potential, or ability, to choose how it will manifest itself in the next moment, that the subatomic realm of the universe is seemingly in some kind of indecisive, potential form that has not yet been actualized. For, in truth, it has *not* yet been actualized; the subatomic realm

is the fuzzy realm where decisions about how things will manifest have not yet been made, and it is only when decisions are
made that things take on a concrete and definitive existence and
nature in the universe. Until then—until observation of the
particle forces it to make some kind of definitive decision—we
can only state the likelihood—the probability—that a particle
is going to decide definitively to be in one place or another (or
to have one velocity or another) in the next moment. And,
using Schrödinger's equations, we can predict how these probabilities will evolve over time—how the likelihood that the
particle will decide one thing or another will change over time.
But only upon observation does the subatomic realm of the
universe make up its mind about how it will manifest.

The step from action to manifestation of the next experience has no wiggle room. But as we move up the ladder toward choice—from action to instinct to feeling to thought to
choice—there is an increasing amount of wiggle room. The
language of a thought doesn't *have* to lead to a feeling (or to one
particular feeling as opposed to another), for it can be changed
before it does. The language of a feeling doesn't *have* to lead
to an instinct (or to one particular instinct as opposed to another), for it can be changed via a change in the language of
thought before it does. The language of an instinct or desire
doesn't *have* to lead to an action (or to one particular action as
opposed to another), for it can be changed via a change in the
language of thought before it does. The language of a thought
can manifest any number of ways in experience, for it still has
to progress through the rest of the causal process, but the language of an action can only manifest one way in experience.

The progression of the causal process of creation of the
next experience is much like the progression up a tree—from
one thought (one trunk) ultimately to any of a number of
branches (actions) that end in leaves (physical manifestation
of experience in the world). (It is interesting that the tree as a

reflection of reality can describe so aptly the development of language in the process of the creation of experience by the "I", as it has formerly been seen to describe so aptly the development of language in the process of the creation of the world by the Source "I" and, therefore, the development of the world as a whole, and the development of the individual within that world, and so on. And it is particularly interesting that the *tree* represents the development of *language* in this reflection, in light of the fact that plants are a necessary intermediary between us and the sun as language is a necessary intermediary between us and the Source.) And the more self-awareness there is, the less fixed the whole causality of this progression toward manifestation in some definitive actual experience in the physical world is—because the more self-awareness there is, the more ability there is to catch and to alter or halt the progression of this causal flow before it completes itself.

But, ultimately, despite the kink that self-awareness throws into the works of our ability to predict the future states of things, for all practical purposes, as long as we can account for a sufficiently encompassing amount of the language that is being used by all (or even simply a large proportion of) things relevant to the prediction, we can get a pretty good idea of what is going to happen in the contents of experience of those things. Thus, we can still predict the overall motions of planets and stars and disregard the uncertainty of the subatomic particles that make up those bodies, and we can still predict the overall contents of the experience of large groups of human beings, or of humanity as a whole, and disregard the uncertainty (produced by self-awareness) of the individual (although the equations of language are much more complex, and so are much harder to determine with as complete accuracy, because of the complexity of the language involved).

Even the future states of the individual human being can be predicted, in light of one thing or another happening in the life of that individual, with some degree of accuracy that is inversely proportional to the degree of self-awareness and willful choosing of his/her language independently of what happens in the world around him/her that this individual expresses. But, on the scale of the group, the accuracy of prediction increases tremendously as compared with the scale of an individual for the most part (for everything from the bottom to the top of the evolutionary ladder—from bacteria to fish to birds to mice to dogs to monkeys to humans), similarly to the way that on the scale of a planet or star the accuracy increases tremendously as compared with the scale of a single subatomic particle. Group behavior is always rather predictable, because the uncertainty of the individual collapses into predictability in its interactions with, and reactions to, others (like the collapse of the wavefunction of a particle—the Quantum Mechanical description of the state of simultaneously being in many places or of having many velocities, each with some probability— upon observation of that particle by other particles in its interactions with, and reactions to, them).

All we need is the ability to account for a sufficiently encompassing amount of the language that is being used by the group—and in the case of humanity, we have this in the internet. With the internet, we can answer the question that we would ask on the level of the individual to monitor what we are bringing into our lives: What is humanity feeling? And then we can look to the contents of the language of the thoughts that are producing this language in our feelings by looking to the context of feeling-laden words (e.g. "afraid"—or this passive adjective's more active noun and verb form, which is therefore indicative of greater imminence or immediacy—"fear"). For example, we could look for the word "fear" amongst several million websites (to get an accurate indication of the prominence of this feeling in the group of humanity), and then we could look to see what the general context of the word is in all of these websites. Does it most often appear in the context of money or the economy? Does it most often appear in the context of the environment?

Essentially, with something like the internet, we are capable of determining in this way (to some degree of accuracy) the present "position" or state of humanity and the language that it is using to describe its experience. And if we look at the same sort of information on the internet at two or more separate times, then we can also determine the "velocity" of humanity and the language that it is using to describe its experience—what direction it is headed and how fast it is going in that direction. And so we can basically determine the information that is the equivalent of what we require of a planetary body if we wish to determine its future states, namely its position and velocity—where it is, and in what direction it is headed and how fast it is going.

Ultimately, our thoughts dictate the content of our experience, and our feelings dictate the quality of our experience. So by using the internet to monitor the language that humanity is using in its thoughts and feelings in this way,[3] we would be capable of exercising self-awareness of ourselves as a group—which would be a more-developed way of being, because we would be closer to the goal of the self-aware use of the language that we use to share and shape our experiences in

---

3   Using the internet to predict the future in a way similar to this has already been, and is being, accomplished successfully in what is known as the Web Bot Project (its predictions are known as the Web Bot Predictions), which was originally started to predict stocks and ended up predicting far more. But the information is not currently being used so actively to *change* what is going to happen, rather it is only being used to *be aware of* what is going to happen (partly because the people who developed the project don't know exactly why they are able to predict the future in this way—they don't know that humanity is *creating* the future with the language that it is using—and partly because the ideology of the people who first created the software, George Ure and Cliff High, suggests that they shouldn't try to change anything that they find).

the world. Predicting the future in this, or some similar, way (and making use of what we discover) would empower us to change the contents of the future experiences that we are in the process of creating for ourselves as a group, just as monitoring the language that we are using in our thoughts and feelings as individuals empowers us to change the contents of the future experiences that we are in the process of creating for ourselves as individuals.

We can even monitor the thoughts and feelings of humanity as a group, to a large extent, through the news media, in which what we see is a combination of the results of past thoughts and feelings and the current thoughts and feelings that are being propagated in reaction to those results. And since there are so many people, and since newspapers and television and the internet so effectively spread news about events and reactions to those events to so many people so quickly, the effects that we are having on the shaping of our future experiences in the world in our reactions to events are magnified from what they ever were in the past. Just bringing awareness to how the events and other things you see or read about make you feel, and then changing those feelings by changing your thoughts about those events and other things, could have a huge impact on the course of the events of the world in the future if millions of people were doing this. In light of humanity's ability to actualize the essence of the world, thereby taking a leadership role and acting as the brain of the world in leading the world toward self-awareness and the mindful and willful sharing and shaping of its experience—toward the fulfillment of the purpose for which the world was created—these kinds of next steps (or something like them) seem to be courses of action that we *must* take—for the sake of our own fulfillment (and therefore for our own continued existence, for the reception of existence is included in fulfillment) and for the sake of the fulfillment of the entire world.

Why the Source Created the World

Now we are capable of understanding what led the Source to bring about the existence of the world in the first place more accurately than we have been at any point prior to this. For the paradigm of experience that we put forth in the beginning can be expanded still further in terms of the associations it encompasses.

From the perspective of an "I" in this world, first there is "I", then there are others, and then there are other "I"'s. This pattern of stages of experiential development parallels the pattern of instincts that arise in concordance with these stages: Once the "I" exists, first there is the desire to preserve the existence of the "I", then there is the desire to be part of (or to belong to, or to fit into) a group of others, and then there is the desire to connect intensely with other "I"'s. Also in concordance with these stages is the following pattern: Once the "I" is physically manifested (once the "I" exists in a physical form), first there are instincts (or desires), then there are feelings, and then there is thought.

This last pattern can be seen to fit quite nicely into the paradigm that has been established. Once there is "I", there is only "I", and the "I" desires to preserve its own existence; in this stage, the "I" is driven by its instinctual desires to impose itself upon the world—perceiving the world, with all of the world's contents, as a mere extension of the "I"—and the "I" is driven by its instinctual desires to preserve its own existence in this way—through the imposition of itself upon its environment. Then, there are others, and so the "I" desires to fit in with those others that are projections of itself—to be part of a group—and as it interacts with those others, feelings arise; this is because feelings are involved in an "I"'s relation to others—with the capacity for empathy and caring that feelings, or emotions, provide—as the "I" feels what it would be like if the "I" were in an other's situation. Then, there are other "I"'s, and the "I" desires to connect intensely with an other "I"—to know what it is like to perceive the world through that other "I"'s unique subjective lens of thought and feeling and desire; thought is required at this stage because the "I" cannot merely *feel* what the other "I" feels by projecting its own lens into that other "I"'s physical circumstances—the way that the empathy of feeling, by itself, inclines the "I" to do—but rather the "I" must use thought to divide and categorize and compare and contrast in order to learn how the other "I" actually experiences the world—in order to learn in what ways that other "I"'s experience is similar to, and in what ways it is different from, the "I"'s own experience.

In order to get to really understand an other "I"—and thereby to really understand the "I", itself—an "I" must learn not only the other "I"'s *external experiences*, but also that other "I"'s *internal experience* of those external experiences—the other "I"'s *internal* perception of those experiences and how this affects (and how it affected) that other "I" and alters (and altered) that other "I"'s lens of thought and feeling and desire. And in order for an "I" to come to understand any of this, it requires thought, including imaginative thought—the ability to create the perception of circumstances that the "I" is not actually perceiving and maybe has never even actually perceived. Thus, there are two forms of thought—analytic, or divisive and categorizing, or deductive, thought, and synthetic, or unifying and imaginative, or inductive, thought. The "I" needs to use both in order to attain self-awareness, because it must be able to break down its own experiences into parts and recombine them in new and different ways in order to understand other "I"'s experiences (for other "I"'s have different proportions of the same basic desires, and so on, as the "I" has, and other "I"'s also have different external experiences from those that the "I" has, and so the "I" has to imagine these by piecing together and inferring from its own experiences). And the "I" also must be able to break down other "I"'s experiences and compare and contrast them with the parts of its own experiences in order to learn what it is to be itself, and what it is to be that other "I", and what it truly is to be an "I".

The "I" must be able to learn about and come to understand the other "I"'s experience and its own experience in such a way that it can relate aspects of one to aspects of the other, for only then can the "I" truly communicate and share its experience with the other "I" through language that that other "I" can understand and receive in its intended form and meaning. Further, without the ability to compare (and synthesize) and contrast (and analyze) different experiences, the "I" would never be able to learn from its own past experiences (which are basically the experiences of other "I"'s), let alone from completely other "I"'s. Because the "I" must be able to find similarities amongst its experiences and group them together by similarity, and also to distinguish—or differentiate—amongst the groups and within the groups of experiences. Only in this way can the "I" learn what it should do differently and what it should do similarly in the next moment in order to attain fulfillment. Only in this way can the "I" grow and progress toward self-awareness.

For, you see, thought reflects or, rather, is reflected in, materiality, for thought produces materiality. Just as thought can differentiate and divide and group by similarity, so, too, can the physical world. From unity is begot differentiated multiplicity. And then groups form, unified by their similarity—by a common goal. The world divides, and matter groups together to form atoms—driven by the common purpose of fulfilling the strong nuclear force (which holds protons and neutrons together to form nuclei) and electromagnetism (which causes the negatively charged electrons to be attracted to the positively charged protons)—and molecules—driven by the common purpose of fulfilling electromagnetism (which drives the exchange and sharing of electrons by atoms)—and stars and planets and galaxies—driven by the common purpose of fulfilling gravity (which causes all bodies to be attracted to all other bodies). The cell divides, and cells group together by their common functions to form tissues and organs and so on in a multicellular organism, which then seeks to unite with another multicellular organism in the common goal of the formation of a new organism, of a new experience of the world. First, there is division, but then there must be union. First there is analysis, but then there must be synthesis. For the ultimate goal of the world is synthesis—synthesis in itself, and synthesis with the Source, in Its experience. The world divided itself in order to learn to be self-aware, for the contrast of the other "I" is required for a true understanding of what it is to be "I", and of what it is to be an "I". But self-awareness, itself, is unifying.

Now, it should be realized from what has been discussed earlier that in this last manifestation of the paradigm—in the pattern of instinct (or desire), to feeling, to thought—there is a clear next step. After thought, there is *choice*—the ability to choose and make decisions. So, if there is a clear next step in this manifestation of the paradigm, there must be a next step in the paradigm, itself. From "I", there are others, and then there are other "I"'s. From the desire to preserve the existence of the "I", there is the desire to belong to a group of "I"'s, and then there is the desire to connect intensely with other "I"'s. After thought, there is choice. After there are other "I"'s, what is there? After there is the desire to connect intensely with other "I"'s, what follows?

The answers here are pivotal, you see, for the answers here are a step closer to how the Source began—a step closer to what the Source experienced that led It to create the world. Because development of the Source's experience is in the reverse direction from that of all "I"'s in this world. Because the development of all "I"'s in this world is toward the experience of the Source. Because the Source began where all development in this world is headed, and so to understand where all development in this world is headed is to understand, more closely, what it is to be the Source.

We are working from choice. Choice is our guide to the answer as to what the next step of the paradigm is. After there is thought, there is choice. After there are other "I"'s, there comes the ability to create others consciously and willfully, as the Source created others consciously and willfully. After there is the desire to connect intensely with other "I"'s, there is the ability to recognize all "I"'s within the "I", and so, from the "I", others can be created—*not* out of the *desire* to share the "I"'s experience, but out of the subtle but energizing guidance of intuition.

When the "I" holds onto experiences like a pond, the "I" shapes a view of itself that is fixed, and it *desires* to maintain the existence of this fixed perception, and the "I" is unable to recognize others, or those others as other "I"'s. The progression to others and to other "I"'s entails holding onto things less and less, and thereby being able to take in *new* things more and more. And so the "I" can begin to recognize others besides itself, making it capable of desiring a new thing—to fit in with those others. And so the "I" can begin to recognize others as other "I"'s, making it capable of desiring yet another new thing—to connect intensely with another "I". As the "I"'s experience develops, its view of itself evolves to manifest in new forms, and its desires consequently evolve to manifest in new forms as well. From desire, to feeling, to thought…to choice. As the "I" develops, holding onto things less and less, it can eventually begin to recognize its true nature as choice—as the ability to decide what it thinks, and what it feels, and what it desires.

But *desire* results from holding onto things. Just as when you hold onto your breath, and only then do you truly *desire* to breathe, it is, in every situation, the case that desires result *only* from holding onto experiences—*only* from being more like a pond than like a mountain stream. For the stream is always full and always filling, like our breathing allows us to be always fulfilled in terms of our requirement for taking in oxygen. Only when we do not allow our breath to pass—exhaling the carbon dioxide that is certainly not in the same form as the oxygen that we breathed in—do we experience the *desire* to breathe, for now we lack oxygen, and now we are filled with carbon dioxide instead of oxygen and so we desire oxygen even more—like a pond that is lacking in fresh water and is filled with parasite-and-bacteria-ridden murky water, thereby requiring fresh water even more in order to be filled with *fresh* water and in order to experience the rain as fresh water. When the "I" no longer holds onto things, but rather allows all things to pass, the "I" makes itself capable of receiving all of the existence that it desires for itself, and for all of the experiences that it shapes through its now-willful use of language. And so it no longer *desires* anything, for desires are the result of lack, of unfulfillment, and the "I" is no longer lacking, the "I" is no longer unfulfilled.

Instead of being guided by the exaggerated inclinations that are gnawing and nagging instinctual desires—which evolve out of materiality—in its use of language, the "I", when it identifies with and acts out of its essence, comes to be guided by the inclination that is intuition—which evolves out of the essence of the world, out of choice. Because when the "I" sees the world as the source of all that it has, it reacts to its experiences in the world, allowing its behavior to be guided by the world—via instincts, or desires—but when the "I" sees the Source as the source of all that it has, it proactively and willfully shapes its experiences in the world, allowing its behavior to be guided ultimately by the Source—via intuition—toward self-awareness and, thereby, true fulfillment. And the guidance of intuition—the guidance that stems from the essence of the world, and ultimately from the Source in that the world's direction is determined by its and the Source's common goal of the world's being capable of experiencing what the Source experiences—is that by which every "I" is guided toward the fulfillment of its purpose as part of the group that is all "I"'s, including the Source "I". As the cell is guided by the brain via the language of hormones and electrical signals toward the optimal fulfillment of its goals within the larger goals of the whole organism, the self-aware "I" is guided by the essence of the world via the language of intuition toward the optimal fulfillment of its goals within the larger goals of the whole world.

Thus, the "I" comes to encompass all "I"'s within itself—within all of its own goals. No longer is the "I" driven by desire to preserve its own existence for the sake of its own existing, or to be part of a group (that is a mere extension of itself and its own goals) for the sake of its own belonging, or to connect intensely with another "I" for the sake of its own connection. For the "I", being fulfilled, is now driven by intuition to preserve itself for the sake of being able to be there for others—in groups linked by common goals, and in intense connections of sharing and receiving experience. Essentially, once the "I" reaches fulfillment as a self-aware "I" that allows existence and experience to flow, unhindered, through itself and into all other "I"'s and the rest of the world, it begins to experience something much more closely reflecting the Source's experience. For the "I", being fulfilled in existence, is no longer driven by desire in search of existence for itself from the environment and from others and from other "I"'s.

And not only does the "I" now begin to create through the willful use of the language of thought, to produce feeling, to produce inclinations, to produce actions—the paradigm followed by the Source in creating the world—but the "I" also now begins to follow the paradigm as followed by the Source in other respects as well. For it begins to be inclined to make other "I"'s capable of receiving the experience that it experiences—the experience of being a self-aware "I". And, through its efforts to share its experience with other "I"'s, it comes to recognize other "I"'s as projections of the same essence of which *it* is a projection—it comes to recognize *them*, and *itself*, as *others* that are ultimately all projections of the *Source "I"*—and it becomes inclined to work with them, as a group, toward a common goal (which is the fulfillment of the entire world, to be achieved through the world's self-aware sharing and shaping of experience through every "I" within the world). And now that the "I" is working toward this common goal as part of the entire world—a goal that has grown out of its inclination to share its experience with other "I"'s—the "I" comes to be inclined to preserve the existence of others and of the world, in order for it to be able to reach its goal of sharing its experience with others and with the world. And so the "I" goes from recognizing others as other "I"'s, to perceiving those other "I"'s as others that stem from the same essence as *it* does—with *it* and *them* as projections of the same Source "I"—to perceiving the ultimate reality as being that there is only *one* "I"—namely, the *Source "I"*—experiencing what the Source "I" experiences. And from choice, the "I" manifests the thought of sharing its own experience, and from this thought, it experiences the loving feeling that stems from it, and from this feeling, it is inclined by its intuition—driven and energized by the purpose of it—to speak and to act in this world, to help others to experience the fulfillment that it experiences, that it knows.

So, we see that it is not the case that self-awareness gives rise to the desire to connect intensely with another, but rather the desire to connect intensely with another guides us toward the kind of experiences that give rise to self-awareness. For it is only through intense interactions with other "I"'s—and by other "I"'s, I mean any other aspects of the world, including not only other people, but even other animals, or plants, or stars, or our breath as we breathe, or our movements as we walk or run or ski or whatever—that we can truly come to understand how we are related to everything else, and what makes us *us*, and what makes *us*, as individuals, similar to and different from all other individual aspects of the world.

We can intensely interact with anything in the world—anything from the realm of thought (as abstract ideas), from the realm of feeling, from the realm of instinct (as desires), from the realm of action (as activities, like skiing or running), or from the realm of manifestation (the physical world, including other people and everything else)—for everything in the world shares the same essence and is given existence and experience by the same Source. And it is only through these kinds of interactions, in which we direct our focused attention upon a single thing, or set of things, that we can come to use language to share and shape our experience, and so it is only through these kinds of interactions that we can come to develop self-awareness.

When our desire for intense connection comes to manifest itself in our actions as mindful existence in the present moment, then we are well on our way toward the kind of self-aware existence that gives rise to an experience that most closely reflects that of the Source. For now that we have honed our ability to focus our attention willfully, the next step—after we come to experience true fulfillment in this way—is to direct our attention mindfully and proactively toward the language that we want to manifest in our experience of the world in the next moment. And the next step after this is to be inclined to share this experience of self-awareness and of fulfillment with others—thereby beginning the pattern of the Source's experience.

Thus, the desire to connect intimately and intensely with another "I" becomes the inclination to connect intimately and intensely with the Source "I" (as through mindfulness of the present moment as it is). In this way, through intimate and intense connections with other "I"'s in this world (including even the "I"'s past self, through the "I"'s memories, in its thoughts and feelings), the "I" comes to connect intimately and intensely with the Source "I". Through the experience of the other "I", the "I" comes to experience the Source "I"'s experience. And the "I" begins to create its experiences willfully as a projection of the Source "I", experiencing what the Source experiences.

In this way, when the "I" follows the paradigm of the development of experience for everything within the world to its end, the "I" comes to experience the paradigm of the development of experience for the Source in relation to the world. And the "I" comes to understand experientially that the Source did not create the world out of desire, or for Itself. Already having the fulfillment of complete existence, and so not experiencing any lack that would give rise to desire, the Source created the world out of an overflowing inclination to share Its own experience with another—to grant another the fulfillment that It experiences, that It knows.

Expanding the Paradigm
to Include the Senses

We can actually expand the paradigm of experiential development still further than we already have, and we shall do so here to include the development of the senses.

Paralleling the stage of only "I", of the desire to preserve the existence of the "I", and of instinct, speech, and action (for, in fact, not merely instinct, but also its manifestation in speech and action, is used to preserve the existence of the "I" at this stage, as instinct drives the "I" to impose itself upon its environment through its outward physical behavior), there is smell, taste, and touch (directly paralleling instinct, speech, and action, respectively). These are the most instinctual senses, and they are involved in finding optimal environmental conditions and in avoiding dangerous conditions (as of temperature), which require touch, and even smell and taste (in the case of detecting the pH of, or the chemicals present in, an environment) to sense, in finding edible food and in avoiding things that are inedible or even poisonous (which requires touch, smell, and taste as well) and so on—all to sustain the existence of the "I".

Paralleling the stage of others, of the desire to belong to a group, and of feeling, there is hearing. Hearing is the sense that is arguably most linked with feeling, or emotion, as can be seen particularly dramatically in the case of the effect of different types of music upon a listener. Also, there is a linear progression of the experience of hearing similar to the linear progression of the experience of feelings, where only one sound or group of sounds, and only one feeling or group of feelings, can be experienced at one time, and everything that is experienced at once is taken in sort of as one sound or as one feeling (and it is only able to be broken down by the analysis of thought into disparate parts separate from the initial experience). Hearing is vital in being part of a group and in group interaction, for it allows the reception of the feelings of others in the group and it thereby allows common goals to be understood so that the "I" can work toward these.

Paralleling the stage of other "I"'s, of the desire to connect intensely with other "I'"s, and of thought, there is sight. Like thought, sight is capable of taking in many disparate things at once and of recognizing them as separate and of perceiving their relation to one another. Both thought and sight can take in an entire picture whole by zooming out and putting together the parts, or break down a whole picture into pieces by zooming in on the details.

Okay, these connections are nice and all, but there is more. It has been previously mentioned that sharing and receiving are apparently fundamental interactions in the world—interactions that are a reflection of the interaction of the Source and the world and that, like with the Source and the world, have a mediating central column between them (like language). In light of this, it can be seen that we have stumbled upon sharing and receiving aspects (relative to each other, for everything in the world is receiving relative to the Source) of each stage of experiential development. The senses—touch, taste, smell, hearing, and sight—are receptive; they receive what they sense from the world. Action, speech, instinct, feeling, and thought are creative, or sharing—they bring about some effect on, or in, the world.

Touch receives language from another "I" (receives information about that other "I") through direct, unmediated, physical contact; action shares language with another "I" (impresses information upon that other "I") through direct, unmediated, physical contact. Taste receives language from another "I" (receives information about that other "I") via the mouth and tongue; speech shares language with another "I" (conveys information to that other "I") via the mouth and tongue. Smell receives language from another "I" (receives information about that other "I") via scents and odors (e.g., those of pheromones); instinct shares language with another "I" (conveys information to that other "I") via scents and odors (again, e.g., those of pheromones). Hearing receives language from another "I" (receives information about that other "I") linearly (in time) via the effect of *that other "I"* upon the environment (via the compression waves that that "I" produces in the air or water or other atmospheric molecules); feeling shares language with another "I" (conveys information to that other "I") linearly (in time) via the effect of *the "I"* upon the environment (via the impression of the feelings upon the atmosphere of the environment). Sight receives language from another "I" (receives information about that other "I") at a distance, all at once, via an intermediary (light—photons—which bounces off that other "I" and is received by the eyes of the "I"); thought shares language with another "I" (conveys information to that other "I") at a distance, all at once, via an intermediary (language—words—which is conveyed by the "I" and is received by that other "I").

Just as thought, feeling, instinct, speech, and action manifest in the development of experience in this world in the opposite order from this downward cascade of creation, sight, hearing, smell, taste, and touch manifest in the development of experience in this world in the opposite order from this progression that corresponds with the downward cascade of the creative process. This can be seen in the evolution of all of life as well as in the development of a single human being.

Before life, there was only touch, and it could hardly be considered a sense, because we usually think of senses as being at least somewhat conscious. The first single-celled organism likely relied on touch, although possibly also on some kind of chemical taste/smell, in order to receive information and food from its surroundings. Single-celled organisms, like bacteria and algae, developed a chemical sense that was the precursor to both taste and smell, and they use this sense to find food and to find optimal environmental conditions and to avoid dangerous environmental conditions that might threaten, or even end, their existence. As single cells grouped to form multicellular organisms, taste and smell soon differentiated from this primal chemical sense as new ways to experience the world. Smell, as in the ability of such things as bacteria and fish to smell chemicals in the water and the ability of such things as ants and mice to smell chemicals in the air (and taste, as in the ability of many reptiles to taste chemicals in the air with the flick of their tongues) even makes it possible to detect things at a distance via the direct contact with molecules that are carried off of those things by the atmosphere (the water or air).

The ability to sense compression waves, or vibrations, in the environment, or hearing, grew out of the sense of touch. In fish, there is a sort of combined set of these two senses (hearing and touch), and through these senses they are capable of sensing other fish and other things that are present around them, and they are capable of swimming with other fish in groups, or schools, behaving with the other fish as though they were all one fish, working toward common goals, namely the preservation of the existence of the fish and particularly of the school of fish. Such animals as dolphins and whales rely very much on hearing in their communication with other members of their species. Eventually, sight—the ability to detect a certain portion of the spectrum of electromagnetic waves in order to perceive objects at a distance more effectively—evolved, and primates, including human beings, rely highly on this sense in order to receive information that allows them to assess their surroundings, and even to seek out potential mates.

Ultimately, once a sense evolved, it became, for the organism that had it, a highly important means of taking in information, and the organism that evolved it relied on this sense more than on other senses. So, we see that bacteria rely mostly on smell/taste, many insects rely mostly on smell, many whales rely mostly on hearing, and some birds (such as hawks) and primates (including humans) rely mostly on sight. Also, in most species, the dominant senses are next to each other on the order of development of the senses. For example, many lizards rely highly on taste and smell. Mice and rats rely highly on smell and hearing. Human beings rely highly on hearing and sight (though more on sight, as can be attested to by the huge size of the portion of the brain devoted to sight). And, if we were to look at the dominant means of processing and sharing information with others (action, speech, instinct, feeling, and thought) in each of these organisms, we would see that the evolution of each of the senses as a dominant sense corresponds pretty closely with the evolution of each of the means of processing and sharing information as a dominant means (e.g., human beings, whose dominant senses are hearing and sight, with a greater emphasis on sight, and whose dominant means of processing and sharing information with others are feeling and thought, with a greater emphasis on thought).

In a single human being, development in the womb yields a form of touch first, whereby the very early developing embryo, and then fetus, is capable of detecting, and responding to, its being in physical contact with other things, including itself, and to its physical orientation in the womb. Chemical senses (like some kind of smell/taste) guide the embryo's, and then the fetus's, cells in migrating and extending and growing as they specialize, forming the different organs and so forth. And the taste buds and nasal system develop, allowing the fetus to taste and smell the amniotic fluid that surrounds it. Hearing develops next, so that the fetus is capable of detecting (and responding to) sound vibrations in its environment in the womb—the movement of blood, the mother's heartbeat and digestion, the voices and sounds outside the womb. And hearing continues its development outside the womb, as the baby increasingly associates sounds with their sources and meanings. When it comes to sight, the basic apparatus that allows for the reception of light, namely the eyes (along with general synaptic connections between the light receptors in the eyes and the visual portion of the brain), forms during development in the womb. But the neural connections that complete the development of the baby's capacity for sight and fine-tune it (so that the baby is capable of perceiving coherent images and interpreting them as being specific objects), are made during the beginning of the baby's life outside the womb, as he or she is exposed to visual stimuli.

There is something else that we can learn from the development of the senses. We have already seen that in the development or manifestation of the creative processes, we go from the bottom up—from action, to speech and instinct, to feeling, to thought, *to choice*. When we go from the bottom up in the development of the senses that correspond with these creative processes, we go from touch, to taste and smell, to hearing, to sight. But what comes after sight? What is the sense that corresponds with the creative process that is choice? The answer is intuition. The sense of choice is intuition—as the sense of thought is sight, and as the sense of feeling is hearing, and as the sense of instinct is smell, and as the sense of speech is taste, and as the sense of action is touch.

The more we actualize our essence by exercising our ability to consciously choose the language that we use to share and shape our experience, the more we gain control over the sense that is intuition—the sense that guides us toward the actualization of the contents of experience that we have chosen for ourselves. When we are self-aware, we are guided by intuition. But there is more than simply this when we are self-aware and we allow the Source to share self-aware existence through us, for just as our experience of being an "I" in relation to other "I"'s begins to express itself in the order of the expression of these stages in the Source's experience, and just as our desires turn into inclinations that express themselves in the order of their expression in the Source's experience, and just as the creative processes express themselves in us in the order of the Source's experience, the senses begin to manifest in new forms in an order that is the reverse of that of their original manifestation.

And so we gain a new kind of sight, and a new kind of hearing, and a new kind of smell, taste, and touch—all in forms that stem from choice's sense of intuition, instead of from the world of manifestation. And so, as thought, and feeling, and instinct, speech, and action become choice-driven, sight, and hearing, and smell, taste, and touch become intuition-driven. And so, as we gain conscious, willful thought, and conscious, willful feeling, and conscious, willful instinct, speech, and action—in place of reactive thought and so on—we gain intuitive sight, and intuitive hearing, and intuitive smell, taste, and touch—in place of merely mundane sight and so on.

Understanding the Complete Paradigm by which the Source Creates the World

Piecing Things Together

We have now reached a pivotal point where we are capable of piecing together different parts of the puzzle to understand the complete paradigm by which the Source created, and continues to create, the world—the paradigm of which all paradigms in this world are reflections. The paradigm that we have so far, with all the patterns or manifestations of it that we have discussed so far, is as follows:

The creative process goes from choice, to thought, to feeling, to instinct, to speech, to action, to manifestation. Since we are considering this from the perspective of the Source, it is necessary to realize now that desire, or instinct, does not exist for the Source. The Source does not experience desire because It does not experience unfulfillment (since It does not lack anything), and the Source's inclinations, or intuition, are actually equal to (the same as) its speech/actions. So, essentially, the creative process, from the perspective of the Source (but, of course, relative to this world, for this is how the Source creates the world), goes through five basic stages: from choice, to thought, to feeling, to inclination/speech/ action, to manifestation. This paradigm of five stages also manifests in the pattern: choice, to other "I"'s, to others, to only "I", to manifestation (for if we were to look at this in reverse—as it manifests in this world—the first step of the pattern, before there can be the idea that there is only "I", must be the manifestation—or the beginning of the existence—of the "I", and the last step, after there is the recognition of other "I"'s, is for the "I" to identify with, and begin to actively exercise, choice—by choosing the language with which the "I" shares and shapes its experience). This paradigm of five stages also manifests in the pattern: choice, to inclination to share experience, to inclination to work with a group toward a common goal, to inclination to preserve existence, to manifestation (remember, if we look at the pattern we begin to experience from the Source's perspective *after* we begin to identify with *choice*, our desires turn into intuitive inclinations, and then we begin to actively *manifest* the next moment of our experience). This paradigm of five stages also manifests in the pattern: intuition, to sight, to hearing, to smell/taste/touch (remember that inclination, speech, and action are all equivalent relative to the Source, and so their receptive parallels are also), to the physical world (which is the manifestation that is sensed by the senses).

Okay, now that we have reiterated what we have so far, let's start putting things together. Since we are trying to understand the paradigm by which the Source created and creates the world, we'll begin with the creative process of choice, to thought, to feeling, to inclination/speech/action, to manifestation. What can we do with this? What is incomplete about it? It is important to remember what we have discussed earlier: All things in this world manifest the paradigm of the Source and the world and their interaction (the interaction of the Source and the world). We saw this in such disparate things as the development of male and female forms of species and of sexual reproduction, the sun and us and our reception of the sun's energy via plants, the interaction of atoms to form molecules, and even in the relation between the creative processes and the senses.

Everywhere, and on every scale, there are indications in the world that the sharing and receiving (with a central column that allows this interaction to take place) that occurs between the Source and the world (via language) is part of the ultimate paradigm by which the world was and is created. After all, as we follow the paradigm of the creative process ourselves in this world in order to create the next contents of experience of the world, we must receive experience and share it via language— the language of thought, feeling, instinct, speech, and action— in order to receive *more* experience, and this certainly suggests that this kind of interaction can be found in the ultimate paradigm by which the world was and is created (since it is found here in our own part in the creation of the world).

In the situation with a holographic plate that differentiates a laser beam in order to form a holographic image, it is important now to understand how a holographic plate is formed in the first place. First, there is a laser, then there is an object that the laser is trying to capture as an image on the holographic plate, and then there is the holographic plate. The laser beam reflects off of the original object and hits the holographic plate. Only then does the holographic plate become capable of being used to differentiate a laser beam in order to create an image of the original object. This reflects the creation of each new moment of time, which is ultimately a reflection of the previous moment. But the important thing to realize here is that *first*, there is the laser that shares its light, *second*, there is the object that receives the light from the laser, and *third*, the reflection of the light off of the object, as this light has been shaped by the object, is captured on the holographic plate—which only *after this* can be used to differentiate the light of the laser to produce a new object that is an image of the original object. To apply this to the Source and the world and language, *first*, there is the Source, *second*, there is the world, and *third*, there is language (as it exists in a sort of holographic-plate analogue, where it is defined sufficiently to differentiate what the Source shares into a form that is distinctly defined as being different from the original form of what the Source is sharing).

From this, we might better understand why we cannot understand the situation of the world in between its physical existences—in between its existences with matter and space and successive time—(the situation of the world when it is like water vapor in the tree reflection), for, in fact, *there is no real or concrete language* to describe this situation, because the situation involves no concretely decided language (and it is, in this way, a bit like the subatomic realm of our universe, although it is significantly less concrete and definitive even than this strange realm). The only thing to truly separate the world from the Source at this point is the fact that the nature of the world differs from the Source so completely in being receptive and dependent upon the Source for all that it has, for the Source is sharing and creative and self-sustaining, with existence inherent in It. All the constraints and divisions of concrete language, including time and space and everything else that we know, as we know them, come after the existence of the world, in order for the Source to actually be able to share Its experience with the world in a form that the world can receive.

For when the world first comes into existence (or, in relation to the cycle of physical worlds—since the cycle doesn't actually have a beginning—when the world comes into simultaneous time and spaceless connection with the Source beyond the intermediary of language), it exists without concretely defined and differentiating language. It is merely the nature of the world as the capacity to receive—as something that is *not* the source of what it has—that makes the world separate from the Source at this point. And when the Source shares Its existence and experience with the world, the world receives what the Source shares, but then rejects it, because the world is so far from being able to understand what it is receiving, since it has no experience of its own to relate this to, and because the world doesn't understand the consequences of what it is doing; the world doesn't understand that its fulfillment—its very existence—depends upon its receiving what the Source is sharing.

But the world cannot receive what the Source is sharing in the true form in which the Source is sharing it, and the world is essentially completely overwhelmed and stressed out by all that the Source is sharing with it. It is like a bottle that threatens to burst as it is filled to overflowing with water from a hose that is attached to its opening and turned on full blast. And so the world experiences what it is receiving in the most corrupted, most negative form. But once the world has refused to receive more of what the Source is sharing with it, it begins to experience unfulfillment and, consequently, desire, as the continuation of its very existence is threatened. And so it acts upon its desire and begins once again to receive what the Source is sharing, but now it actually bursts as it is filled to overflowing. It bursts into multiple, differentiated parts because this is the only way that it can continue to receive the Source's existence and experience. This is the case because the world, being like a bottle that is threatening to burst, desires to share what it is receiving, to allow what it is receiving to flow through it and into others so that it can continue to receive more of what it is receiving—so that it can continue to be fulfilled and can continue to exist—and the only way that it can share with others what it is receiving is if there are others with which it can share. The world's differentiation provides for the existence of such others.

The world differentiates into successive time, guided by the nature of what it is receiving (which, in order to be experienced, requires the contrast of multiplicity and disparity) toward being capable of receiving more of it in an increasingly accurate manner. At the point that the world cannot receive any more, it reflects the laser beam outward and impresses its image upon the holographic plate, through which the laser beam (of what the Source is sharing) shines in order to produce the next moment. Thus begin a series of interactions that continue even now, whereby the world, in one moment of successive time, reflects and shapes what is shined upon it—what it receives—through its use of language (in all of its aspects of manifestation), and this captured reflection (the holographic plate) is used to differentiate what the Source shares in the next moment.

Now that we've established the order of sharing, receiving, and the central column, let's begin to apply this to our understanding of the paradigm. In every stage between the first and fifth (between choice and manifestation), there must be three parts to the stage—a sharing part, a receiving part, and a central column. The paradigm of the creative process cannot simply consist of choice, thought, feeling, inclination/speech/action, manifestation. Why? Well, let's look at the nature of each of these stages as they stand. The choices that we have for the divisions of the stages are as follows (this can be derived from the development of our experience from before and after when we begin to identify with choice, as well as from the central stage of being mindful and self-aware and identifying with choice, but not yet beginning to actively create, but it is displayed here in the order from the perspective of the Source): a creative and overflowing inclination to share the experience, an inclination to receive the experience and manifest it within ourselves, and an allowing the other's experience to manifest through us.

Let's skip choice in our categorization and get back to it in a moment. Thought, feeling, and inclination/speech/action are what? Are they creative and sharing? In relation to the senses, they are, for from our perspective, the experience that we receive with our senses is acted upon and shaped and shared by these creative processes. And from the perspective of the Source (and from our own perspective when we are mindfully and proactively creating our experience), they seem to be creative and sharing as well. But what about from the perspective of the world (and from our perspective when we are not self-aware)? When we are not mindfully and proactively creating, then our thought, feeling, and inclination/speech/action are either allowing the experience to manifest through us—as when we simply experience the world passively without being fully present to it with our attention—or receptive—as when we actually react to the world, in which case they are the forms of our reactively receiving from the world, the manifestation of the world within us. So, thought, feeling, and inclination/speech/action can each be any of these three parts. What about manifestation? Well, the manifestation of all aspects of the physical world in one moment is ultimately composed entirely of language, and it serves as the holographic plate that differentiates and shapes the next moment. By the time we reach manifestation in the present moment, the manifestation is not receiving anymore, because it is the result of what has been received, and it is not sharing in itself, because it is the *Source* that is sharing through it and not *it* that is sharing. So it seems to be part of the central column that allows sharing and receiving to take place—that allows the Source's experience to manifest through (and be differentiated by) it.

So what about choice? The answer to this question provides a great deal more understanding than we have hitherto had. We might be inclined to say that choice is the inclination to share. (We probably wouldn't say that choice is the inclination to receive, for choice seems to be creative.) But choice is not the origin of the inclination to share. When we come to experience the inclination to share, then we begin to *manifest* this inclination *through* the choices we make. Choice is creative in the sense that it determines the shape that existence takes, but in this way it is like the holographic plate that allows the laser light to flow through it but that ultimately differentiates and shapes the laser light into a new form as the light is *manifested through* it. Thus, we see that choice—the first stage of the creative process—is actually part of the central column, allowing what the Source shares to be manifested through it.

So when we identify and exercise choice, we are actually moving away from our desire to receive, and closer to the inclination to share, but we never *become* the inclination to share in an ultimate sense; we merely begin to allow all that we receive to flow through us, sharing all that we receive, and we never begin to share more than we receive, for this would be impossible (at least for very long)—considering that we depend upon what we receive in order to exist and so sharing more than we receive would be like a stream giving out more water than it takes in (which would result eventually in its dwindling down to nothing and ceasing to exist). The Source shares, and we receive, and we are capable of getting to the point that we share all that we receive. When we begin to actively choose, what we are actually beginning to do is actively allow the Source's experience to be manifested through our thought, feeling, inclination/speech/action—to allow all that we receive to be shaped by the guidance of intuition—by the pull toward self-awareness. Our choice is between allowing the world to choose for us, manifesting itself through us via our reactions to it, and allowing the Source to choose for us, manifesting Its existence and experience through us via our mindful and self-aware sharing and shaping of our experience.

The Language of the Source, the Language of the World

Thus, we see that we—the world—are the Source's language. The Source did not use any concrete or definitive language until the world brought about the need for this restriction and differentiation of Its flow of existence and experience—so that the world could receive these things. In light of this, *of course* no religion could have *the* language or *the* text that God uses to create the world: *We* are the language, and the *world* is the text. *We* determine the language God uses to create the world in every moment, for *we*—our thoughts, our feelings, our instincts, speech, and actions—are God's spoken language. And when we allow the world to manifest itself through our mindless patterns of reactive thought, feeling, and instinct/speech/action, the world chooses the language that is used. And when we allow the Source to manifest Its existence and experience through our self-aware and willful use of intuitive thought, feeling, and inclination/speech/action, the Source chooses the language that is used. The difference is only in how distorted a lens we are for the manifestation of the Source's existence and experience, for the less distorted a lens we are, the more accurately the Source's experience will be manifested through us.

Once the world exists, there is the desire to maintain what *is*. But as the world is guided toward self-awareness, the desire to maintain what *is* becomes the inclination to create something *new*. From the desire to receive experience, there comes the inclination to share experience. However, what happens is that once the world first begins to create something new by differentiating itself, thereby sharing its experience with the next moment of time and beginning the succession of time in a physical existence, its parts begin to see each other as the source of what they have and of their fulfillment, and so they begin to desire to receive *from each other*. Essentially, the world begins to desire to receive from *itself*—to receive what it already has. Thus, there is clinging to existence and to other parts of the world in the forms of the desire to preserve the existence of itself (of the way it is) and the desire to belong and the desire to connect to other parts of the world. This is from where the attraction element of all things in the world comes. This is where we get like attracts like and grouping by similarity and more of what we have.

When the language of the world is formed in reaction to what currently *is* instead of through the willful and self-aware creation of something new and different from what currently *is*, the image of the world that is captured by the holographic plate (through which the Source manifests the next moment) becomes very similar to, or an exaggeration of, what exists in the present moment. Thus, experiences beget thoughts about those experiences that beget feelings about those experiences that beget inclinations/speech/actions in reaction to those experiences, and the result is a new moment that looks very much like the previous moment (in the case that we were merely mindful and neutral observers of what was in that previous moment), or that is exaggeratedly warped from the previous moment (in the much-more-usual case that we were reacting with desire and stress and other distorting things—pushing and pulling at our experience of the previous moment through like and dislike, want and don't-want judgments, and thereby holding onto, and producing more of, our experience of that previous moment).

And so planets and stars attract more motion like that in which they engage—for this motion is the language that they are using to describe their experience. And human beings attract to themselves in the next moment more illness or health, more poverty or wealth, more sadness or joy, all depending upon how they are allowing themselves to experience and comment on this moment. If we react and focus on what *is*, or on trends or patterns that we perceive and believe will continue, all things in this moment will be perpetuated and exaggerated in the next moment. On the other hand, if when we are not content with what we are experiencing in the present, we willfully and proactively *choose* to use our experience in the present moment as contrast in order to learn what we actually want to experience, and we then describe in our thoughts and feelings and in our speech and actions what we *wish things to be*—as though they already *are* this way—instead of describing how things *are* or how things *were* or how things *could be* in light of how they *are*, then we will be creating a holographic plate that differentiates the Source's experience for us in the next moment into a form that we actually want to experience.

Development toward increasing self-awareness, toward an experience that increasingly resembles the Source's experience, entails receiving increasingly more from the Source—meaning we are actively creating something *new* for the *next* moment that is different from *this* moment—and decreasingly from the world—meaning we share our experiences instead of holding onto them. Remember, in order to stay in the sunshine of fulfillment, we must recognize that fulfillment does *not* come from anything in this world, and so holding onto anything in this world will not give us fulfillment. Fulfillment only comes from the Source, and so we must continually make ourselves capable of receiving more from the Source by giving up what we already have—by allowing all that we have (all of our thoughts, feelings, and inclinations, speech, and actions) to flow through us and into others and the world around us. And so we must actively create the next moment of our experience in this moment rather than holding onto our experiences in this moment.

But everything in this world is subject to falling into patterns of receiving from the world (through holding onto experiences), instead of receiving from the Source. We are inclined to passively allow our thoughts, feelings, and inclinations/speech/actions to be chosen for us by the world through our reactions to the world, instead of actively choosing these aspects of the language that we use by ourselves, by following the guidance of the Source via our intuition. *Only* the active exercise of self-aware choice—allowing the Source to create through us, using us as tools, as language, to create an accurate description or depiction of Its experience for us to experience—prevents us from falling into such reactive patterns and instead keeps us willfully choosing the language that we use and thereby willfully sharing our experiences with the next moment by shaping them anew—by shaping them into something truly different from what was before. Only when we actualize the potential of the world, and are like a mountain stream, do we overcome the reception of experience from the world—holding onto experiences, which results in the maintenance of what *is*—and, instead, begin to receive experience freely from the Source and intuitively share our experience, thereby creating something new.

[An interesting aside here is that this ability to create something completely new for the next moment of our experience actually allows us to jump out of the usual progression of moment to similar moment. Thus, through the exercise of choice, we could actually move out of the usual progressive succession of time, thereby traveling in time by sharing with a distant future moment or with a past moment (in a future universe, for the past is already over with respective to us in time) and progressing from there.[4]]

Choice Defines the World

All right, so choice is the central column. This means that, like a stream is composed of water, the world is composed of what flows from the Source—which is the Source's existence and experience of being self-aware existence. The world is the Source's language. And the ultimate essence of the world—as water may be considered the ultimate essence of a stream—*beyond* choice is the Source's existence and experience. Choice is

---

4   This will be discussed further in a later section.

the first step in the differentiation of the Source's experience. Choice is the first step in making the world separate and different from the Source, and it is, thus, the first part of the world. Choice is the essence of the world in the sense that choice is what defines the world. Choice is what determines what language is used to differentiate, to limit, to constrain the world. Choice is the cause of the existence of space and time and all that is limiting.

Everything about the shape and form of the world is determined by choice. The world, having an essence of choice, is, in essence, the capacity to limit itself. The world is capable of being unfulfilled, and of consequently experiencing desire, because its essence is choice—because it is capable of choosing to receive from itself and not from the Source—and this is why it is separate from the Source. For the Source is not limited or unfulfilled in any way, for the Source is a self-sustaining entity. The origin of all limits is choice, and this is the world's essence and not the Source's. The closest the Source got to limiting Itself was by creating something separate from Itself to receive what It was inclined to share. Ultimately, language became a limit far more for the world than for the Source, for the Source still exists beyond language, but the world is bound by it.

Choice is what defines the world, but the ultimate composition of the world is not choice or the language that is chosen; the *ultimate* essence of the world that is there to be defined and differentiated and shaped through the world's (through choice's) use of language is the Source's existence and experience. The shape of a stream is determined by the stream's flow, but the water that makes up the stream is what the stream essentially is in its composition. The world is essentially the Source's existence and experience the way that the stream is essentially water. As the stream allows itself to be shaped by the flow of water, we can allow ourselves to be shaped by the flow of the Source's existence and experience. But we are also capable of choosing to change the flow of water—either to alter its direction or to slow or halt it, becoming like a pond.

The Source created language in order to share Its experience in a form in which the world could receive it. And the world—choice—through its use of language, is the origin of space, and successive time, and all boundaries and limits, for the Source is limitless. It is through the world's use of language by which the Source continues to share Its existence and experience of the world—on the world's own terms, adapting to the world's capacity to receive Its existence and experience, within the limits set by the world in its use of language.

In the way that the soul of an individual human being is separate from the individual but manifests what it chooses in the physical form of the individual and provides the individual with life, the Source is like the soul of the world—separate from the world, but guiding the manifestation of the world and providing the world with existence. In both cases, the soul acts as the sharing element, and the physical form acts as the receiving element. In the case of the individual, the soul is choice, thought, feeling, and inclination, and it manifests itself in the body via speech and actions. Here, inclinations seem to be sort of the interface, or connection, between the soul and the body. In the case of the world, the Source is beyond choice, and it manifests itself in the world via choice—and ultimately via inclinations, and particularly intuition, by which it guides the physical actions of the various parts of the world toward self-awareness. The body guides our behavior via desire, and the soul guides our behavior via intuition. Likewise, the world guides our behavior via desire—via the physical form that is the body—and the Source guides our behavior via intuition—via the more-ethereal form that is the soul. The body manifests from the bottom up, and the soul manifests (or, rather, creates) from the top down. Likewise, the world manifests from the bottom up, and the Source manifests (or, rather, creates) from the top down.

The beginning of the separation of the world from the Source is therefore choice. And, as choice is the beginning of the world's differentiation, we are all like differentiated aspects of the world's essence of choice, capable of choosing how we use language to share and shape our individual experiences in our individual lives. Yet all of our individual shaping of experience contributes to the collective shaping of the world, and for those of us who do not actively choose, our experiences will be shaped for us by collective beliefs and trends—by the way that the majority of those around us are shaping their experiences.

Successive time is the manifestation of choice in the physical world. So, time is the essence of the world in the sense that time is how the world manifests itself. The world is simultaneous—every moment of time is completely fulfilled—in between physical existences, and the world is successive—time follows a progression from one moment to the next—during physical existences, and this is because of how the world makes it. Because when the world actualizes its essence by choosing—and thereby shaping its experience *for* the next moment and sharing its experience *with* the next moment—time becomes successive. Thus, time is the manifestation of choice. And both of these—time and choice—are aspects of the central column, allowing another's experience (the previous moment's experience or the Source's experience) to be manifested through them.

Notice also that the less the world receives from itself and the more it receives from the Source, the closer it gets to a point when it no longer receives anything from itself and it only receives from the Source. This is the point when the water evaporates from the leaves. This is the point of the singularity. This is the end of a physical existence. But in order for the world to be capable of continuing to receive from the Source, it must share what it receives, and so it shares its experience of unfulfillment—of not being self-aware—because this is what its experience is at this point, and it holds onto this experience and perpetuates this experience through the language that it begins to use to describe the experience. And the result is the beginning of a new physical stage of the world—a new world of multiplicity that begins to develop toward self-awareness and toward receiving solely from the Source and no longer from itself.

The Complete Paradigm

So, time is the manifestation of choice. But choice does not manifest time directly. It manifests each moment of time via thought, feeling, and inclination, speech, and action. And so we will now get back to these in the development of the overall paradigm by which the Source creates the world—through us, through the language of *the world's* thoughts, feelings, inclinations, speech, and actions, which the world chooses (or, rather, allows to be chosen, either by other aspects of itself, or by the Source).

Choice and manifestation are merely the central column, but thought, feeling, and inclination/speech/action each have three parts: a sharing aspect, a receiving aspect, and a central column that allows this interaction to manifest through it (and that somehow combines and reconciles the two extremes—the two opposing forces—the sharing and receiving aspects). And so, once a thought is chosen, there is the aspect of the thought that is the creative, overflowing inclination to share this thought, then there is the aspect of the thought that is the inclination to receive and manifest this thought within itself, and then there is the aspect of the thought that is the allowance of this thought to manifest through it. This is followed by an aspect of a feeling that is the creative, overflowing inclination to share this feeling, and then by an aspect of the feeling that is the inclination to receive and manifest this feeling within itself, and then by an aspect of the feeling that is the allowance of this feeling to manifest through it. This, in turn, is followed by an aspect of an inclination/speech/action that is the creative, overflowing inclination to share this inclination/speech/action, and then by an aspect of the inclination/speech/action that is the inclination to receive and manifest this inclination/speech/action within itself, and then by an aspect of the inclination/speech/action that is the allowance of this inclination/speech/action to manifest through it. And this is followed by the manifestation, in the physical world, of the language that was chosen (which is ultimately—after the initial creation of the world—the result of the intimate connection between the Source and the world, as the Source's existence and experience is shaped by the world's choice).

So, within this complete paradigm, there are five stages, with the first and the last (and, in fact, also every part in between) being the central column relative to the Source and the world, and with each of the three intermediate stages having sharing, receiving, and central-column aspects to them. However, within the paradigm itself, separate from its relation to the Source and the world, choice acts as a sharing force, and all of the intermediate stages act as a receiving force, with manifestation acting as the central column that mediates, and is the product of, the interaction between these.[5]

5   Notice that the stages of this paradigm correspond with the *sefirot* (spheres) of the tree of life in Kabbalah (Jewish mysticism), such that they can be explored further beyond this book in that form (among other forms) in *Inner Space*, by Rabbi Aryeh Kaplan, as well as in many other books. Choice corresponds with *Keter* (meaning Crown), sharing thought corresponds with *Chochmah* (meaning Wisdom), receiving thought corresponds with *Binah* (meaning Understanding), allowing thought corresponds with *Da'at* (meaning Knowledge), sharing feeling corresponds with *Chesed* (meaning Mercy or Love), receiving feeling corresponds with *Gevurah* (meaning Judgment or Restraint), allowing feeling corresponds with *Tiferet* (meaning Beauty or Harmony), sharing inclination corresponds with *Netzach* (meaning Victory or Dominance), receiving inclination corresponds with *Hod* (meaning Glory or Empathy), allowing inclination corresponds with *Yesod* (meaning Foundation), and manifestation corresponds with *Malchut* (meaning Kingdom).

Allowing the Source to Manifest Its Experience in Our Own Experience

Now we've seen that there are sharing and receiving forms of each of the intermediary parts of the creative process (namely, thought, feeling, and inclination/speech/action), but there is still definitely a relation between the creative processes and the senses, and in this relation, the creative processes are sharing, and the senses are receiving—they are the reactive reception of what is created by the creative processes. And there is still more to be learned from this relation.

In the top down manifestation of the paradigm (as occurs from the Source's perspective), first there is choice. Followed by this, there is thought, then sight, and then the object seen (the object that allows what is thought to be manifested through it and therefore seen). Followed by this, there is feeling, then hearing, and then the object (as music) heard (the object that allows what is felt to be manifested through it and therefore heard). Followed by this, there is inclination (instinct), then smell, and then the object (as pheromones) smelled (the object that allows what is inclined to be manifested through it and therefore smelled). Followed by this, there is speech, then taste, and then the object tasted (the object that allows what is said to be manifested through it and therefore tasted). Followed by this, there is action, then touch, and then the object touched (the object that allows what is acted upon—or, in the case of the Source, actualized or given existence—to be manifested through it and therefore touched). [Remember that inclination, speech, and action are all the same for the Source, and the senses with which they correspond are not our predominant ways of experiencing the world, so the correspondence of these creative processes with smell, taste, and touch might not be as close in our own experiential understanding as the correspondence of thought with sight and of feeling with hearing (remember that sight and hearing are our predominant ways of experiencing the world, and so are most familiar to us)—but they all still correspond quite closely and quite nicely for the Source, as you will see in a moment.]

Notice that this order makes no sense to our experience of things in this world. Here, we are saying that you think about what you see, then you see it, and then there is an object to be seen, that you experience feeling with regard to what you hear, then you hear it, and then there is something to be heard, and so on. But, remember, this is all from the Source's perspective. From our perspective in this world, this whole process—the manifestation of the stages of the paradigm—is from the bottom up, meaning that it is in the reverse order from what we have just stated. And so the order of things as we are familiar with it in this world is as follows: First, there is the manifestation of the world. So, there is something that exists and is capable of being touched, and so we then touch it, and then we act upon it. And there is something that exists and so is capable of being tasted, and so we then taste it, and then we speak about it. And there is something that exists and so is capable of being smelled, and so we then smell it, and then we are inclined by our instincts to do something in reaction or in response to it. And there is something that exists and so is capable of being heard, and so we hear it, and then we feel some emotion in reaction or in response to it. And there is something that exists and so is capable of being seen, and so we see it, and then we think some thought in reaction or in response to it.

Now this all makes much more sense to us. But, as we just said, for the Source, this whole progression is in the reverse from what it is for us in this world. The Source thinks, and thus there is sight, and then there is something that is capable of being seen. The Source feels, and thus there is hearing, and then there is something that is capable of being heard. The Source is inclined to do something, and thus there is smell, and then there is something that is capable of being smelled. The Source speaks, and thus there is taste, and then there is something that is capable of being tasted. The Source acts, and thus there is touch, and then there is something that is capable of being touched.

One thing that is worthy of note here is that this pattern of having a sharing element, then a receiving element, and then, only after this, something that allows this interaction to take place, which seems counterintuitive, is exactly what happens when the Source creates the world and then, only after this, creates language by which to share with the world. We can see now that this order is like having thought and sight prior to having an object that can be seen and thus thought about. It doesn't make any sense in this world, but the reverse order makes complete sense, and if we were to change the order from the Source's perspective, making it Source, then language through which to share, then world with which to share—making it thought, then object to be seen, then sight—then the reverse order (which is our experience in this world) would be clearly wrong and inaccurate for, in our experience, we would see, then have an object to be seen, and then have a thought about what we've seen. So we can understand through this that we've got our order of the paradigm correct with sharing element, followed by receiving element, followed by something that allows this interaction to take place, as strange as this order seems, here, from the top down (from the Source's perspective)—because the bottom up order is an accurate description of the order from our perspective.

Also, we can see hints of the Source's perspective in this world—of the top down order of the manifestation of the paradigm (of creation)—when we look to the subatomic realm of the universe. For, as the mathematics of Quantum Mechanics seems to suggest, our *observation* determines where a particle definitively comes to exist (or what a particle's velocity definitively comes to be). First, there is observation (sight), and then there is the object observed, as it is observed (the object that is capable of being seen *where* it is seen or *as* it is seen). Our sight determines where the object exists to be seen and *that* the object exists there to be seen. As the Source observes the world through us (for we are Its senses, essentially), It is actually, in every moment, shaping the world through our observations of the world (for what we discern through our senses is Its language—or, rather, what we discern through our senses is *part* of Its language, for *everything* that we experience is actually Its language, including what we sense, our senses, and our creative processes). And so, in reality, the object seen exists as we see it because we see it that way, and the object heard exists as we hear it because we hear it that way, and so on. *Our observations of the world are shaping the world that we observe.*

But we can take this back one step further. Because *before* all of our sensing of the world comes *thought*; from top down in the paradigm, before sight, and before all of the rest of our five physical senses, there is thought. First, there is thought, and then there is sight, and then there is the object seen. Our thoughts are determining what we see, and what we see is determining what there is to be seen. *Our thoughts are shaping our observations of the world that we observe, and are, thereby, shaping the world that we observe.* Our thoughts determine the world's form. Our thoughts determine the contents of the world's experience.

But, remember, the something that is seen is only the beginning of the manifestation of the world as we know it, for the manifestation of the physical world comes only after we pass through thought and sight and object seen, and feeling and hearing and object heard…all the way through action and touch and object touched. And so our thoughts and feelings and inclinations and speech and actions determine what we see and hear and smell and taste and touch (physically feel), and what we see and hear and smell and taste and touch (feel) determines what manifests in the world.

We are shaping the world that we experience with every aspect of our experience of it, for the Source is shaping it through us—for *we* are the Source's language, and *our experience* is the Source's experience. Our thoughts are the Source's thoughts. Our feelings are the Source's feelings. Our inclinations are the Source's inclinations. Our speech is the Source's speech. Our actions are the Source's actions. And our sight is the Source's sight. And our hearing is the Source's hearing. And our smell is the Source's smell. And our taste is the Source's taste. And our touch is the Source's touch. Our experience is the Source's experience, and when we allow the Source to work through us, we give the Source control over how *our* experience—*Its* experience—is shaped and formed, we give the Source control over the contents of our and Its experience (as *Its* experience exists within *our* experience).

But how do we do this? How do we give control to the Source, allowing the Source to guide the shaping of Its experience through us?

When we are not self-aware and mindful of our experience in the moment, our sensing is passive and reactive—we see because there is something to be seen and we see only what there *is* to be seen (although in relation to what there *was* to be seen—to what we have seen before), we hear because there is something to be heard and we hear only what there *is* to be heard (although in relation to what we have heard before), we smell because there is something to be smelled and we smell only what there *is* to be smelled (although in relation to what we have smelled before), we taste because there is something to be tasted and we taste only what there *is* to be tasted (although in relation to what we have tasted before), and we touch (feel) because there is something to be touched (felt) and we feel only what there *is* to be felt (although in relation to what we have felt before). Essentially, we take in the world passively, without awareness or consciousness, and desire arises in us as we judge all that we experience, liking this and wanting more of it, disliking that and wanting less of it. And our use of the creative processes is also passive and reactive—we allow our thoughts, feelings, inclinations (in the form of desires), speech, and actions all to arise in us and be chosen and determined by what we have seen, heard, smelled, tasted, and touched (felt).

In this way, we allow the way the world was and is—the past and present manifestation of the world—to choose for us, through us, how the world will be—how it will manifest—in the next moment. And the past is propagated in the present, and the present is propagated in the future, and we walk the same ruts of repetitive habitual patterns like planets revolving predictably around stars. And so overall predictive patterns—like those of which scientific theories are descriptions, and like those described in astrology, and like those described in the Mayan calendar, and like those that can be clearly found in the progression of history—exist to be found, in everything from our individual behavior to our behavior as a group and even to our behavior as a whole species.

But when we *are* self-aware and mindful of our experience in the moment, our sensing is active and responsive—we *watch* things as they are and we see what can be made to be, we *listen* to things as they are and we hear what we can make them, we *sniff* things as they are and smell what they are capable of becoming through our actions, we *taste* things as they are and taste their potential to be something more, we *touch* (or *feel*) things as they are and feel their potential to be something greater; we sense all things for what they are capable of becoming—through the lens of a potential that can be actualized through us. Essentially, we take in the world actively through our senses and use this as contrast in order to visualize the world and imagine it through all of our senses as though it has already fulfilled the potential that it has, as though it has already become what we want it to be—and we thereby set goals, or destinations, for the world to reach, and make it possible for the world to actualize its potential through reaching them. And our use of the creative processes is also active and responsive—we allow our thoughts, feelings, inclinations (in the form of intuition), speech, and actions all to arise in us and be chosen and determined by the Source through our intuition.

In this way, we allow the Source to choose and create the world through us, and to determine how the world will manifest in the next moment. In this way, we allow the Source to pull the world out of predictable patterns and through the process of development toward self-awareness—toward the experience of being the Source.

Instead of trying to control our own hands as we paint the picture of our lives, we allow the greatest Painter to guide our hands—so that our lives look just as we want them to. Instead of trying to steady our own hands as we sculpt the substance of our existence, we allow the greatest Sculptor to support our hands—so that our existence in this world takes the most perfect shape that it can have. Instead of trying to think through reactive and staticy thought, and to feel through reactive and overly dramatic feeling, and to be inclined by reactive and gnawing desires, in order to try to choose exactly the right words to describe our path toward fulfillment, we allow the greatest Writer and the greatest Speaker to choose our words and share them through us, through our clear and receptive minds and hearts and bodies. And we allow the Source to show us *Its* experience through our *own* experience, and our lives are as fulfilling as they can possibly be.

Ten Forces, Ten Dimensions

Reflecting upon the Tree of Life to Form the Next Moment

In the complete paradigm by which the Source creates the world, there are eleven total stages. First, there is choice, then sharing-thought, then receiving-thought, then allowing-thought, then sharing-feeling, then receiving-feeling, then allowing-feeling, then sharing-inclination/speech/action, then receiving-inclination/speech/action, then allowing-inclination/speech/action, and then manifestation. However, manifestation (which is the child that is the product of what the Source shares and what we—the world—share by dictating how we will receive what the Source shares) *is* the choice of the next moment, and so it is as though there is *either* choice *or* manifestation, but *not both* as separate things, for it is more like manifestation/choice and the process is cyclical, whereby the end is the beginning of the next cycle. Thus, in some sense, there are *ten* total, *distinct* stages to the complete paradigm.

Manifestation—the combination of the sharing and receiving elements—is choice of the next moment. Thus, this paradigm—this creative process—repeats at every moment to create the next moment and, in fact, repeats on every level of existence, including portions of lifetimes and whole lifetimes—in which the end of one lifetime determines the beginning of the next—and including the entire existence of the universe—in which the manifestation of the singularities in which the universe ends are the singularity in which the next universe begins.

However, everything in this world goes not from the top, down (from choice to manifestation), but from the bottom, up (from manifestation to choice). We are thus pulled upward toward, and by, self-awareness, as water is pulled upward in a tree by evapotranspiration. And so we see that this whole paradigm is what the tree-setup reflection conveys to us. This paradigm is the tree that contains all of spatial existence. This paradigm is the tree of life.

And as the universe progresses up the tree of life (from the bottom up in the paradigm), gravity (receiving from the world—parts of the world attracting, and being attracted to, other parts of the world)—like adhesion and cohesion—weakens in its influence upon the universe as self-awareness (a receiving from the Source and a sharing force)—like evapotranspiration—increases. This is the cause for the expansion of the universe, and this is why the universe began to expand increasingly rapidly (as it currently continues to do) not long before the emergence of the solar system and the earth: The universe reached the point where adhesion and cohesion (clinging to spatial existence and to other parts of itself) ceased to be the primary forces that kept time flowing up the tree, and evapotranspiration (the pull of self-awareness) began to take over as the primary force, pulling time up the tree, as life began to emerge in the universe—and, since then, self-awareness has built upon itself, increasing exponentially, and so the world is exponentially increasing its reception from the Source (and exponentially decreasing its reception from itself).

The world has the capacity for choice all along but, beginning from the first moment of the physical, differentiated universe, which received all that it had from the world that *was* prior to differentiation (and therefore from itself and not from the Source), the world's choice for the next moment was nothing more than the manifestation of the previous moment, with the action that this moment contained. The early physical world, thus, was inertial, clinging significantly to itself, with gravity deciding its shape and form. But as the world gradually works its way in the direction of receiving more from the Source and less from itself, it is ever-increasing its actualization of its capacity to actively choose to break out of inertial, cyclical spirals—like those of planets around stars, and of stars around the centers of galaxies.

The manifestation of predictable orbits of planets and stars under the influence of gravity is a reflection of the cyclical path through the tree of life, which merely repeats itself over and over again in the same form if no instinct, feeling, or thought intervene to make the choice for the next moment different from the manifestation of this moment. The influence of electromagnetism, as manifested in the unpredictable orbits of electrons around the nuclei of atoms, for example, as compared with the influence of gravity as manifested in the orbits of planets around a star, is what the choice for the next moment looks like in relation to the manifestation of the previous moment when instinct, feeling, and thought intervene between manifestation and action, and choice, as compared with when they don't intervene.

Here, we are reminded of the holographic nature of the universe as we see the tree of life paradigm manifested both in solar systems and in atoms. The reason that the universe is holographic in nature, such that every part contains information about the whole—such that the same paradigm is manifested on every level and in every aspect of the universe—and the reason that this pattern manifests in an increasingly large number of ways over time (as from just physical bodies to myriad forms of life), is self-awareness—is that self-awareness increases over time. For self-awareness requires self-reflection, and the repetition of the same basic paradigm—which is ultimately the paradigm of the world's relation to the Source (in central column, receiving, and sharing; in "I", others, and other "I"s; etc.)—is merely the manifestation of the world's self-reflection—its reflection on its past and how it got to where it is. The repetitive manifestation of the same paradigm is the world's attempts to understand itself and its relation to the Source, so that it can gain fulfillment.

At the point when the universe starts manifesting other self-aware "I"s, it begins to exercise choice and receive consciously from the Source, and so predictable inertial patterns (like gravitational orbits) are replaced by increasingly unpredictable changes from one moment to the next. For the world gradually reflects less on itself and more on its relation to the Source. It is this encounter with the contrasting other that vastly increases the world's self-awareness (and, thereby, its rate of expansion, as well as its manifestation of other "I"s—as it reflects upon its new experiences) and its ability to understand and receive the Source's experience accurately, in its true form.

And, so, when we observe and study the world on any and every scale—from the subatomic to the galactic realm, from insects to mice to ourselves, to the course of history over the progression of time—we see the same sorts of patterns, we see the same basic paradigm. And the only major difference in the pattern amongst these things is the addition of the complexity and unpredictability that increasingly arises with the addition to action of instinct and speech, and then feeling, and then thought, as these things arise in the world, in life—up to us.

The Physical Forces and the Physical Dimensions

Considering this nature of the world, we should expect to find aspects of things on every level of existence that correspond with the ten basic stages in yet another repetition of the overall paradigm. Okay, so there are four fundamental forces of the universe and there are four physical dimensions with which we are familiar in our daily lives in the physical world. Like the creative processes and the senses, there is a more creative, sharing form here (namely, the forces), and a more receiving form here (namely, the dimensions). So, in the forces and the dimensions, we've got the equivalent of thought and sight, and now there needs to be the equivalent of the object that is seen—that which allows the other to be manifested through it as the sharing and receiving elements interact to create something new that is this thing. This thing is matter and energy.

And so we see that matter and energy are actually the child of the interaction between the forces and the dimensions. And this certainly makes sense, particularly when we look to what Einstein's Theory of Relativity tells us, for Relativity tells us that matter and energy warp space and time with the gravity that they exert upon these, shortening space and slowing down time relative to other observers who are in some other place in relation to a large body of matter and energy. But what we see now is actually not that matter and energy are warping space and time per se, but rather (at least from a top down perspective) that the interaction of gravity (and the other forces) and space and time is producing matter and energy.

In the tree of life paradigm, we could, as we have seen, display the ten parts in terms of the creative processes alone (sharing thought and receiving thought and allowing thought, sharing feeling and receiving feeling and allowing feeling, and so on), or in terms of the creative processes and the senses (thought and sight and object seen, feeling and hearing and object heard, etc.), and we could actually display the ten parts in terms of the senses alone (watching and seeing and that which allows seeing, listening and hearing and that which allows hearing, and so on).[6] This is because there are aspects of each of the ten stages in each manifestation of the paradigm on every level of existence.

For the physical world, the creative processes manifest as forces, and the senses manifest as dimensions. So, let's find the ten parts in terms of the forces of the world, alone, and in terms of the dimensions of the world, alone. And let us keep in mind that the world's creation of itself is from the top down, even as the manifestation of this creation is from

---

6   We might actually have a more accurate display of the paradigm in terms of the senses, alone, in the directions of eye movements, which are recognized in NLP (Neurolinguistic Programming) as indicating that we are giving our attention to certain types of internal activities. For the correlation between the directions of eye movement and the types of internal activity going on perfectly corresponds with the stages of the tree of life paradigm, proving to be a manifestation of the paradigm. So, when we, in thinking, look with our eyes up to our right, we are creating an image (sharing sight, or creating sight, corresponding to sharing thought), and when we look up to our left, we are remembering an image (receiving sight, or recreating sight, corresponding to receiving thought). And when we look directly to our right side, we are creating a sound (creating hearing, corresponding to sharing feeling), and when we look directly to our left side, we are remembering a sound (recreating hearing, corresponding to receiving feeling). And when we look down to our right, we are creating a physical feeling in our bodies (creating touch, corresponding to sharing inclination), and when we look down to our left, we are remembering a physical feeling in our bodies (recreating touch, corresponding to receiving inclination). We might also notice that when we are looking straight up, we are giving our attention to allowing a sight, or seeing, by looking at something that exists in the present—unless what we are looking at is located elsewhere in our field of vision—(allowing sight, corresponding with allowing thought). And when we are looking straight forward, we are giving our attention to allowing a sound, or hearing, by listening to something that exists in the present—we usually look straight at, or toward, where the sound is coming from, like when we are looking at someone who is talking—(allowing hearing, corresponding with allowing feeling). And when we are looking straight down, we are giving our attention to allowing a physical feeling in our bodies, or feeling (touching), by feeling something that exists in the present—we look down as if to look into ourselves, to check with our bodies to see how they feel—(allowing touch, corresponding with allowing inclination).

the bottom up—just as we can see in our own experience that our shaping of the contents of our experience is from the top down, while the manifestation of the contents of our experience is from the bottom up.

Choice is not manifested as any force of this world in itself (although, as manifestation—for choice and manifestation are one, in a sense—it *does* serve as a force), but its effects are definitely made known in the thought stages—with all of the quantum uncertainty that exists there due to decisions being in the process of being made in the subatomic realm. Sharing thought, which is inductive and synthetic thought because it comes up with new insights derived from the top down—from general theory to individual instance or manifestation—and puts them together to form new thoughts that can be shared, is manifested for the world as the strong nuclear force, which is what holds together the protons and neutrons (and, more directly, holds together all the particles that compose these particles) to form the nuclei of atoms. Thus, the world, with the strong nuclear force, forms the building blocks of its physical manifestation as the world begins to put together its thoughts and to manifest the contents of its own experience, giving form to its existence (the existence that it has received from itself or, rather, from the previous universe).

Receiving thought, which is deductive and analytic thought because it builds up thoughts from the bottom up—from experience up to general theory—and divides the thoughts up into their parts in order to be able to put them together later, is manifested for the world as the weak nuclear force, which is what breaks down the atoms and their parts in radioactive decay. Thus, the world, with the weak nuclear force, does a lot of the equivalent of erasing and rewriting what it has already written, or of reorganizing its thoughts in a systematic manner, in trying to manifest its experience in language. (But it also does the equivalent of breaking down into specific words and language what has begun to be built up in a sort of language-less insight. As we will see later, the right hemisphere of the brain, as a manifestation of sharing thought, comes up with seemingly random and unorganized sparks of insight—like the atomic nuclei building blocks. And the left hemisphere of the brain, as a manifestation of receiving thought, and where the language center of the brain is most often located, breaks down such sparks of insight into systematic and linear and chronologically successive words and language—in a sort of breakdown of the particles of insight that have just been built up.)

Allowing thought, which is the combination of sharing thought and receiving thought in a new manifestation, is manifested for the world as electromagnetism, which provides for the exchange of electrons and the interactions of atoms and of ions (which are atoms that do not have the same number of protons and electrons, and that therefore have some charge other than zero)—all ultimately via the exchange of photons (from where we get the electromagnetic spectrum, which includes visible light). Thus, the atoms that were constructed of different particles by the strong nuclear force, and that were partially broken down into other particles by the weak nuclear force, are all interacting with one another based on their electronegativity (their inclination to share or receive electrons) and their charges, due to electromagnetism, in order to form such things as ions and molecules.

Here, in electromagnetic interactions, we can account for the formation of nearly everything with which we are familiar in this world (other than what is explained by gravity). And these interactions all produce light, and they thereby give rise to our very capacity to *see* everything with which we are familiar in this world. Allowing thought is, therefore, essentially the first real manifestation of choice, and it is the beginning of the definitive manifestation of all of the rest of things. Likewise, electromagnetism is the beginning of the definitive manifestation of the former probabilistic uncertainty that derives from choice.

(And again, as we will see later in correspondence with the parts of the body, the brain stem, as a manifestation of allowing thought, channels the sparks of insight and linear language to all parts of the body, where they are put together to form all other things, from the experience of feelings to instincts and speech and actions and so on—like the formation of ions and molecules that interact and combine to produce everything else with which we are familiar. Ultimately, all of this higher thought is expressed in the openly manifested picture of the entire body, which is a manifestation of the stage of manifestation, and which is, thus, an expression of a combination of everything that comes prior—the ultimate manifestation of the manifestations of all of the previous stages.)

From these three forces (the strong nuclear force, the weak nuclear force, and electromagnetism), all of the rest of the forces of the universe are manifested—those that correspond with sharing feeling, receiving feeling, allowing feeling, sharing inclination/speech/action, receiving inclination/speech/action, and allowing inclination/speech/action—except for gravity.

Manifestation is manifested for the world as gravity—that which determines the final, overall, big-picture shape of everything else when everything else is combined together and manifested through it. We see the attraction of bodies to form planets and stars as the ultimate—and the most definitive and decisive (and, therefore, the most predictable)—manifestation of the strong nuclear force's attraction of particles to form the nuclei of atoms. We see the breakdown of bodies, as stars explode and black holes evaporate, as the ultimate—and the most definitive and decisive (and, therefore, the most predictable)— manifestation of the weak nuclear force's decay of nuclei and of particles into other particles. We see the inertial paths and orbits of bodies, such as planets orbiting stars, and stars orbiting black holes, and objects flying through space out of orbit on trajectories that are straight lines unless the bodies come near enough other bodies, in which case they begin to interact with one another, forming such things as solar systems and galaxies, as the ultimate—and the most definitive and decisive (and, therefore, the most predictable)—manifestation of electromagnetism's interaction of charged particles, with electrons orbiting the nuclei of atoms and ions, and with atoms and charged particles interacting with one another in various ways when they come near enough one another, forming such things as molecules. (And so we see that choice, which *is* manifestation, in a sense, is manifested for this world as the potential for things in this world to choose to cling to one another—an attraction of the world to itself that is most defined in the manifestation of gravity.)

Now, to find all ten dimensions of the world. First of all, as we were able to see that the strong nuclear force and the weak nuclear force correspond with sharing thought and receiving thought, respectively, there must be an obvious physical dimension to correspond to each of these stages in the creative process as well, and so here we have two of the three spatial dimensions with which we are familiar in the physical world. Now, electromagnetism corresponds with allowing thought, so allowing thought corresponds with the third spatial dimension with which we are familiar in the physical world. (We'll get back to what corresponds with choice, itself.) Okay, so now we've accounted for all three spatial dimensions of the physical world with which we are familiar.

Next, we'll skip to manifestation, and then we'll come back to the other stages we're now skipping. Gravity corresponds with manifestation, and so time must correspond with manifestation, for we should be able to match the four dimensions with which we are familiar with the same stages with which the four forces (with which we are familiar) correspond. That gravity and time both correspond with the same stage (manifestation) makes sense in light of the connection, or interaction, between gravity and time, namely that gravity slows down time (somewhat like what we think affects what we see, for we are dealing here—in the relation between gravity and time—with the relation between a creative process and a sense).

And all of these connections make a lot of sense, for just as the first three forces lay the groundwork for the rest of the manifestation of the world, which is combined in the big picture with gravity, the three spatial dimensions lay the groundwork for the rest of the manifestation of the world, which is combined in the big picture with time (for each moment of time contains all of the dimensions of space).

And, to get back to choice (which is, in some way, linked with manifestation, which is manifested as time), we can see now that choice is the fuzzy next moment of time (with all of its contents of space and matter and energy only in potential form) that is in the process of being created through the capturing of the manifestation of this present moment of time (as though on the film of a holographic plate). So choice and manifestation are two aspects of time. Choice is the spaceless and immaterial moment of time when the moment merely has the potential for space, and successive time, and matter and energy—and this is why subatomic particles, which are influenced by this lack of certainty, are said to be everywhere and not definitely anywhere—and manifestation is the moment of time when the moment actually and concretely exists, with spatial definition of its contents of matter and energy, which definitely exist in definite places with definite forms and velocities and so on.

Time is merely another dimension of space that emerges from the interactions of all of the spatial dimensions above it, for time encompasses all of these dimensions; we move in another dimension besides the spatial ones in order to go from one place in space to another place in space—and this other dimension is time. Like a three-dimensional reel of movie film, which contains several essentially two-dimensional frames of film, time stretches into an extra dimension in order to serve as a compilation of all of the spatial frames. And in order to get the illusion of the flow of time, we merely need to pass the reel of film though a projector—as we need to have the Source, like the sun, shine self-aware existence upon us.

The faster we travel in space, the more slowly we move through time. This is because time is the final manifestation (and, in choice, it is the full actualization) of the spatial dimensions, and so the faster we move in space, the more we are fixating on the spatial dimensions, which slows our getting down to manifestation (or up to choice), to time—thereby slowing our actualization in time. Also, the closer we are to a lot of matter and energy—to a lot of concentrated mass—the more slowly we move through time. This is also because time is the final manifestation (and is the process of the actualization of choice), while matter and energy are manifestations of the upper stages, prior to the final manifestation (and, moving upward, prior to choice). So the more mass we are near, the more we are fixating on stages prior to manifestation (and, moving upward, prior to choice), thereby hindering our progress to manifestation (and to choice)—and thus hindering, and therefore slowing, our actualization in time.

To simplify this, we must realize that choice is essentially where the next moments of time are in the process of forming, and we must remember that all manifestation in this universe is actually from the bottom up. So, from the present, actual moment of time—in manifestation—we develop upward toward the actualization of the next potential moment of time—in choice. And if we fixate on the manifestations of the stages along the way, such as on movement or materiality, then we will slow our progression to the next moment of time (for we will slow the process of the actualization of each next potential moment of time), thereby slowing our progression through time.

In light of gravity and time being aspects of manifestation, we see that the origin of matter and energy is actually *not* the interaction of gravity and time—for gravity and time are the central-column result of all previous interactions, and they are not the interactions themselves. As the creative processes (like thought) can be broken down into their different aspects (sharing, receiving, and allowing), or collapsed into one thing in relation to the senses (for, in relation to the senses, all thought is sharing), electromagnetism and the strong and weak nuclear forces can be considered as these different forces (or fields—like the magnetic field, which is part of the electromagnetic field—as they actually turn out to be), or they can be collapsed into one force (or field) in relation to spatial dimensions. So, like thought and sight produce an object capable of being within the visual dimension and of being acted upon by the field of thought, quantum fields and space produce particles that are capable of being within the spatial dimensions and of being acted upon by the quantum fields. And so the interaction of quantum fields and space produces matter and energy—the building blocks of everything with which we are familiar.

Of course, this is from a top down perspective (a perspective that explains the seeming importance of observation in determining the existence and state of a particle). From a bottom up perspective, like we experience in our normal everyday lives in the macroatomic realm, an object exists that is capable of being seen and thought about, and then we see it, and then we think about it. And, in the case of matter and forces, matter and energy exist, and then they affect space, and then they are acted upon by quantum fields. We should note that, in a sense, quantum fields *are* the thought of the universe, and dimensions *are* the senses of the universe (with the three physical spatial dimensions being the sight of the universe).

But, now, we have a sort of problem, because we have exhausted all of the dimensions with which we are familiar in the physical world, and yet there are more stages—*six* more stages, to be precise. We have accounted for the stage of choice, the stages of thinking, and the stage of manifestation. But we have *not* accounted for the stages of feeling or the stages of inclination. We have laid the groundwork for the beginning and end of the creative process—all of the parts that provide for the physical aspects of the world with which we are familiar. But we are missing the middle stages of the process.

And yet this—the four fundamental forces and four dimensions that are accounted for by the beginning and end of the creative process—is all that Quantum Mechanics and General Relativity account for. When we look at it from a dimensional view, we see, perhaps more clearly, that something is missing (although, we didn't actually account for the specific forces that correspond with the six total stages of feeling and inclination either). And this is why Quantum Mechanics and General Relativity have been so difficult to combine mathematically in the attempts to find a unified theory of everything: They only account for the realm of choice (as it is manifested in the realm of thought and in manifestation), the realm of thought, and the realm of manifestation, and they do *not* account for the stages in between allowing-thought and manifestation.

We have already seen that matter and energy are merely the result, or manifestation, of the interaction of forces and dimensions—of the interaction of different aspects of each of the stages; we have seen that matter and energy manifest in definite locations, with definite velocities and so on, in the spatial dimensions, when we reach the product of all of the previous interactions of forces and spatial dimensions in the manifestation of (gravity and) time. So whatever we are looking for, it's part of the backdrop for the contents of experience in this world, because we are missing six forces and six dimensions.

We live in the physical world—the world that is thought and its manifestation. This world is logical within itself, for it abides by the language of thought—since it *is* the language of thought. And the only realms in which it seems not entirely logical are the realm of thought (as it is influenced by choice)—the subatomic realm—(which we have accounted for), and the realm of feeling and inclination. What we haven't accounted for is the world of feeling and inclination (or instinct, or desire). The reason life is the beginning of real lack of logic (other than what is accounted for in the subatomic, indefinitive realm), and the reason that life, as it develops, becomes seemingly less and less logical—and consequently less and less predictable—is that we have to account for feeling and inclination, which we often don't do. Without accounting for feeling and inclination, we are missing whole portions of the language being used in this moment that are going to affect how the next moment is going to manifest. If we account for thought, feeling and inclination/speech/action, then we will have all of the language being used in this moment and we will be able to predict the next moment. All of this abides by logical, rational rules because the paradigm of creation is basically logical and rational. The only thing that could make things unpredictable after we have accounted for thought, feeling, and instinct/speech/action is the active exercise of choice, for the paradigm will not be followed in predictably repetitive paths in the case in which choice is actively exercised.

By the way, it ought to be pointed out here that since gravity and time are seen to be emergent properties of all that comes before (in potentiality)—somewhat like a school of fish or a flock of birds proves to have Gestalt-like emergent properties that almost seem to be more than what composes them—a path toward an explanation of gravity and time that is compatible with an explanation of the rest of the forces and dimensions might necessarily involve avoiding a direct explanation of gravity and time. The best way to explain the properties and activities of a school of fish or a flock of birds is to describe the properties and activities—the characteristics—of the individual fish or birds that make up the emergent group. And so the best way to explain gravity—which seems to be the emergent product of the interactions of all of the other forces—and time—which seems to be the emergent product of the interactions of all of the other dimensions—is likely to explain them in terms of the interactions of all of the other forces and dimensions, respectively. This might be useful to consider in the search to combine Quantum Mechanics and General Relativity in some kind of theory of everything.

The World of the Inner Life, and of the Afterlife

So, anyway, we have to account for the world of feeling and inclination. And if everything up to now is an indication, there are actual spatial dimensions and actual forces that correspond with each of the six total stages of feeling and inclination. A little mindful introspection will reveal what these dimensions are, for we may live against the backdrop of the spatial dimensions and the forces that stem from the thinking stages, but we really live in our own worlds—in our own feelings and desires (at least until we manifest self-awareness). The extra dimensions represented by the stages of feeling and inclination are the inner dimensions—the dimensions where we dwell in self-consciousness, where we dwell in the belief that we are the only true "I".

The world of thought is the world of other "I"'s. And the arena of the three-spatial-dimensional physical world of manifestation is a world where many "I"'s physically coexist, but where most "I"'s are merely projecting themselves—through the distortions provided by different feelings and inclinations that manifest in people's thoughts as subjective perceptions that are separate from the objective reality, the reality where other "I"'s exist—unaware of all of the other lenses through which reality is being viewed. In this physical world, we are surrounded by the subatomic realm that is the manifestation of the world's willfully chosen thoughts, and yet we live in our own reactive, self-conscious, self-oriented worlds that are shaped by inclinations and feelings in an upward reactive manifestation, instead of in the self-aware world of downward, willful creation. Yet in this physical experiential realm, we always have the possibility available to us—all around us—to choose to think what we will see, and then to look and find the object that we have thereby created to find within our own experience.

But if the "I" fails to recognize, before it dies and leaves the physical world, that it is not the only true "I", it will continue to exist within its own reactive, subjective, self-conscious world of inclination and feeling. A part of it will go on to manifest upward toward choice—to choose to enter physical life again in order to receive and manifest more experience, and thereby to receive and manifest more understanding, in the effort to strive once again toward the experience of existing with self-awareness, of being able to willfully create the "I"'s own experience with self-aware understanding, and thereby to create the Source's experience within its life. But some remnant of the "I" that failed to attain self-awareness in physical life will always remain, dwelling within its own self-conscious world—in the dimensions of inclination and feeling.[7]

The afterlife—the realm of the lower parts of the soul—is the end of the realm of potentiality, of what no longer manifests in the physical world of actuality. For the contents of the dimensions of inclination and feeling do not manifest to our

---

7   This will be discussed further in later sections.

physical senses except via physicality—only through the physical realm (e.g., through our physical speech and actions when we are alive) can anything within these stages be manifested. But, just as the matter and energy within the three physical spatial dimensions manifest in the physical manifestation that is time, so too do matter and energy within the six inwardly wrapped-up spatial dimensions of inclination and feeling manifest in the physical manifestation that is time.

This world that we are missing is, therefore, the world of our inner lives and of the afterlife—where the very contents of our experience are manifestations of our feelings and our inclinations (our desires), the way the very contents of the physical world with which we are familiar in our daily lives are manifestations of our thoughts. And, ultimately, all manifestations are manifestations of our thoughts, because the thoughts that we choose to think are manifested in our feelings, which are manifested in our inclinations/speech/actions, which are manifested in the physical world. But the world of our inner lives and of the afterlife is made up of the direct manifestations of feelings and instincts—before thoughts, feelings, and instincts are combined in the ultimate manifestation of strictly defined and successive time. Yet the manifestation of thoughts before the ultimate manifestation in time is not this physical world. The ultimate manifestation in time combines the world of thought and the world of feeling and inclination/speech/action. And so the world of our inner lives and of the afterlife is very real. And there is a world of thought separate from the physical manifestation of our thoughts as well. For these things all manifest separate from the ultimate manifestation in time prior to this ultimate manifestation.

What we think exists in a world of its own. And what we feel and desire exists in a world of its own. The world of feeling and inclination (or desire), in terms of dimensional experience, is the world of the inner life, and of the afterlife.

Our life between physical lives is in the realm of feeling and inclination manifested, a bit like our physical life is in the realm of thought ultimately manifested, and these worlds are not completely separate, for they are combined in the ultimate manifestation. (We see, therefore, that we create our own heaven or hell—within the realm of feelings and desires—in this physical life as well as in the afterlife—although our experience for the afterlife is created by us in this life in the case that we do not develop to a top down, self-aware experience of reality in this life—for only part, or a copy, of our soul will go on to choice, to choose to enter physical life again.) And this is why we can access the world between lives even in physical life. For the material part of us that is produced by the interaction of the fundamental, physical forces and the physical dimensions is our physical bodies, and so there must be a material part of us that is produced by the interaction of the forces and dimensions of the world of feeling and inclination as well.

Thus, we have a very nice way to account for the soul and the body and the interaction between the soul and the body. The part of the soul that is most responsible for the connection between the higher parts of the soul and the lower parts of the soul is the allowing thought stage of the soul. Like the brainstem (to which allowing thought correlates in the relation between the brain and the body) allows interactions between the brain hemispheres (where logical thought and choice are made possible, and which correlate with sharing thought and receiving thought) and the body, the allowing thought stage of the soul is the stage that allows interactions between the world of thought and the world of feeling and inclination—the stage that, therefore, allows interactions between the choice-and-thought parts of the soul and the feeling-and-inclination parts of the soul. And the part of the soul that is most responsible for the connection between the soul and the body is the allowing instinct stage of the soul—via which our thoughts and feelings and instincts are able to be expressed through the physical speech and actions of the body.

All of the language that we use begins in our essence—in the world of choice. Then, it manifests in the world of sharing thought, then in the world of receiving thought, and then, via allowing thought, the world of receiving thought gives rise to the world of feeling and inclination, and via the world of feeling and inclination, the two worlds of thought give rise to the world of manifestation. And so there are five worlds, and there are ten dimensions (with a sort of eleventh that is an aspect of time beyond the confines of the spatial dimensions, and which has its effects most directly manifested in the world of our experience as the fuzzy quantum realm). And there are different aspects of us that exist in each of these worlds, and in each of these dimensions.

It is worthy of note that auras (which are the manifestation of things prior to their manifestation in this physical world) and ghosts and other things that seem to have no manifestation in the physical world, but that *do* exist, have been detected as having electromagnetic presence; they are detectable in this world physically as electromagnetic fields. This is interesting because electromagnetism stems from allowing thought, of which one of the physical spatial dimensions is an aspect, and which precedes the development of the feeling and inclination/speech/ action stages, thereby making electromagnetism something that influences all things after allowing thought down to manifestation, apparently (and logically) including auras and souls.

You see, the soul is merely that part of us that is prior to manifestation; it is the body in potential form before it has been fully actualized as the body. And the soul of someone who has a physical manifestation—a physical body—can be perceived through intuitive sight or intuitive touch as an aura around the body.

The fact that we can *see* the soul in some way—via intuitive sight—is fitting with the fact that the means by which electromagnetism expresses itself is via photons, which in certain wavelengths (for particles are also waves—for thoughts are influenced by choice, and so the contents of them are indecisively particles with definite states and are indecisively waves of indefinite state, and so these contents sometimes act as one and sometimes act as the other) are visible as the light of the rainbow spectrum of visible light with which we are familiar. So, electromagnetic waves allow us to see all that we see in the manifestation of the physical world with our *physical sense of sight*, and electromagnetic waves allow us to see manifestations of allowing thought and of the stages after this (in the world of feeling and inclination)—prior to their manifestation in the physical world—with our *intuitive sense of sight*. Also, the fact that we can *feel* the soul or aura in some way—via intuitive touch—is just as fitting as that we can *see* it, and for largely the same reason—for electromagnetic waves in the infrared range of the spectrum of wavelengths are felt physically as heat, and so it makes sense that they should be intuitively felt in their post-allowing-thought manifestation, prior to their physical manifestation, as some sort of warmth or heat.[8]

The world of the afterlife, being a consequence of the language of the worlds of thought, is disconnected from choice. We do not have the same kind of choice that we do in physical life when we are dead, because when we are dead we are unable to choose and create what manifests in the physical world (since the lower parts of our souls are not yet connected to the higher parts of our souls if we have not actualized those higher parts during physical life, and since the lower parts of our souls also have no grounding in physicality—in the actualization of their creations). Instead, we are compelled by our feelings and our desires, unable to work them out significantly

---

8   This will be discussed further in a later section.

further with logic through the piecing together of experiences to create new experiences (which requires sharing thought) and through the analyzing—the breaking down—of experiences in order to better understand them and learn from them (which requires receiving thought).

As we shall see later, sleep is much like the afterlife. In both, we tend toward thought and particularly choice at the end—tending toward choosing to wake up or choosing physical life. For the only way to manifest new experience and understanding of that experience is to live in the physical world. The soul is the creative element in relation to the body and the rest of the contents of the world of physical experience, which are the manifestations of the soul's creation. So without grounding in physicality, only creation in potential can occur, and no creation can be actualized. Thus, in the world of the afterlife, we cannot continue forever to grow toward self-awareness, for we cannot manifest new understanding forever without more experience in physicality. Only in the physical world can we grow closer to self-awareness, for the ability receive and manifest new experiences is required for this, so that we can grow closer to experientially understanding the Source's experience.

And this is why the physical world of matter and energy exists in the first place—so that the world can grow closer to experientially understanding the Source's experience. Originally, the world created physicality in order to express its own experience in language. But once the pull of self-awareness takes over, the goal for the existence of physicality becomes to approximate, more and more closely, the Source's experience—for the Source's experience of fulfillment is so much greater than the world's distorted experience of the Source's experience after it cut off the Source's experience in order to propagate its own experience.

When we enter physical life, we forget the goal that we came here to accomplish, and so a lot of the beginning of our physical life is consumed with trying to remember why we are here and what we are supposed to be doing here. And we see this also in goals that we set out to accomplish within each life. We plan the goal, and then we aren't quite sure what to do. But when we start to discover the path toward our goal, and we come to see our goal in the distance as it comes into view and more and more clearly takes shape, we are increasingly pulled toward our goal. And then, once we accomplish our goal, and we form a new goal, we aren't quite sure what to do again.

These are reflections of the world's situation when it enters physical existence. For it forgets what it came here to do—which was to share its experience of experiencing what the Source experiences. And as it begins to remember, it gains momentum, as the insightful remembrances come faster and faster, and it puts together why it was here, reflecting upon the basic paradigm over and over again as time speeds up and space expands to try to encompass the awe-inspiring experience—the experience of the Source's experience.

So, besides the physical world, there is the world of feeling and instinct. And there are forces and dimensions beyond the four of each with which we are familiar, and the interactions of forces and dimensions produce matter and energy, somewhat like the interactions of tectonic and erosive forces and land produce mountains and valleys. And so there is physical matter and energy in this physical universe—the matter and energy of which the body is composed—and there is also matter and energy in the world of feeling and inclination (as well as in the worlds of thought as they are separate from the world of manifestation)—the matter and energy of which the soul is composed. And all of this—all of these dimensions and forces and the matter and energy that they produce—combines to manifest in the world of manifestation—in time.

Thus, there is more matter and energy than we would account for if we just looked to the physical universe in three dimensions of space. And all matter and energy has gravity in at least some potential, not-fully-defined form, and all of it is combined to manifest in the world of manifestation—from which both time and gravity stem—in a fully-defined form. And so just as all matter and energy is manifested in some form of time (the world of the afterlife, like the physical world, is manifested in time, although in a more potential, less-strictly-defined form of time), it is all manifested with some form of gravity. Further, it is wherever we discern matter and energy manifested in these three spatial dimensions that there is matter and energy manifested in the rest of the spatial dimensions, for the matter and energy of each realm is linked—for the third spatial dimension (the one that corresponds with allowing thought) is the link between the worlds of thought and the world of feeling and inclination. And so this world of three dimensions is just the tip of the iceberg as far as material existence is concerned. And this is the cause of dark matter.

We have already seen that the dark energy that is increasing the rate of expansion of the universe is coming into this world from the world of choice, and ultimately from the Source—for it is because the universe is more actively choosing to receive from the Source and not from itself that gravity is weakening (and that gravity is, therefore, so much weaker than the other three forces, which are closer to choice) and that the universe is thus more and more rapidly expanding. And now we can explain the nature and location of dark matter—a source of gravity that causes the stars near the edges of galaxies to be moving faster in their orbits than they should be if the only source of gravity were the matter and energy that we can discern in this physical world—as well. For dark matter—this source of gravity—is merely the manifestation of the material in the world of feeling and inclination, as this material is associated with the material in this physical world (by being the material of this physical world in a sort of potential, less-fully-actualized-or-defined form). Dark matter is the sort of aura surrounding the physical matter and energy of galaxies and those galaxies' contents—it is the souls of the physical contents of this world.

Back to the Tree of Life,
Back to Experience

The Infinite Universe

If matter and energy have the effect of shortening space, then without matter and energy, space is *infinite* (completely unshortened, completely unconfined or defined by the language of matter and energy), not *absent*—which makes sense since the universe is expanding (as matter and energy evaporate out of the universe via black hole singularities as though via the pores of the leaves of a tree). So, the singularities of black holes are the singularity of the white hole that is the Big Bang of the next universe, and they are the means by which the matter and energy of this universe are shared with the next universe. However, once the black holes evaporate, *infinite* space remains—just as the tree, which represents space, remains when the water evaporates from its leaves. Time, as it exists in the physical world (successive time), evaporates out of material existence, and space remains there, infinitely expanded to encompass the Source's experience in its own understanding, and time becomes simultaneous.

But now the world's understanding of the Source's experience is no longer experiential, and it *must* be experiential—it must be based upon experience—in order to be true and accurate understanding, in order for the experience of the world to actually be the Source's experience. The Source is no longer connected with the world via language—via the matter and energy that are the Source's language, that are what define the contents of the world's experience. The Source is no longer speaking Its experience into the world. And without receiving more existence via language, the world is empty of the contents of the Source's experience. So, the world *is not receiving from the Source*. The world is empty space.

Time speeds up, becoming more fulfilled, as the physical universe progresses—as the world receives more and more from the Source (exponentially increasing the rate of the universe's expansion and diluting the matter and energy in the universe that would otherwise be slowing down time) and less and less from itself (and gravity consequentially grows weaker and weaker, thereby having less of a slowing effect on time). Momentum builds as the clear goal of self-awareness energizes the world and pulls the world toward it. And gravity has its last say as all of the matter and energy in the universe are finally consumed by black holes at the cores of galaxies—and so is the last of the universe's reception from itself. And time reaches simultaneity, and space reaches the ultimate infinity—all like a mind that races with all of its self-reflection increasingly rapidly until it has finally expanded sufficiently to encompass the grandest idea: what it is like to be the Source. And the pinnacle of it all is the greatest fulfillment, and the mind that is the entire universe is completely clear and tranquil following the greatest understanding.

But it is at that moment that the world ceases to receive from the Source, for it is at that moment that it begins to get caught up in its experience of its own fulfillment. It is in that moment that the world begins to look to *itself*—to its *own* experience—for fulfillment, and that it ceases to look to the Source for fulfillment. And so it is like the universe is now thinking and feeling and being inclined to speak and act without experiencing through its senses first. It is using its creative forces (electromagnetism, the strong and weak nuclear forces, gravity) without having these interact with its receptive aspects (its dimensions) in any way. For it is not taking in what the Source is sharing and is merely beginning to reprocess what it has already received. It has eyes, but it sees not. It has ears, but it hears not. Removed from experience, the universe's understanding loses its groundedness in the Source's experience, and it thereby loses its accuracy. The world is no longer self-aware and mindful of the Source and of what the Source is sharing with it and is, instead, self-conscious—caught up in itself, in its thoughts and feelings about its own experience, and so it is mindlessly inclined to speak and act.

And so it speaks and acts. And the world begins to manifest its own experience through its use of language. And the forces of the world begin to interact with its dimensions again. Removing itself from direct experience of the Source's experience—from reception from the Source—the world seeks to describe its own experience, like a writer who removes himself from experience in order to write the experience down and thereby create something of his own with what he has experienced, manifesting his experience in his own way. And this is the beginning—the Big Bang and beyond—of the next world.

Here, we see that we, like the world as a whole, came out of experience and thereby ended up with a flawed understanding. For the tree of life remains always; it does not collapse upon itself. And so the spatial existence that it represents exists always; it does not collapse upon itself. Like the liquid water is pulled toward the leaves of the tree, and then transpires through the stomata (pores) in the leaves of the tree, and then evaporates, thereby leaving the tree, and then condenses, and then diffuses back into the roots of the tree, the matter and energy of the universe are pulled toward the singularities of black holes, and then the matter of the black holes evaporates, thereby leaving spatial existence, and then the matter in some way condenses and diffuses back into spatial existence via the white hole (the Big Bang) at the beginning of the (next) universe.

The Progression of the Universe through the Tree

We need to remember to remain with experience if we wish to be accurate in our understanding. So, in this case, we need to remain with the reflection of the reality we wish to understand in order to understand this reality accurately. Let's look closely at the tree setup in order to see what we can glean from it so that we might better understand the world's progression.

We'll start with liquid water in the ground, entering the roots of the tree, since this is a reflection of the Big-Bang beginning of the universe with which we are somewhat familiar. The water moves up the roots of the tree, drawn upward by cohesion (the bonds of the water molecules to one another) and, to an extent, by adhesion (the bonding of the water molecules to the inside of the tree's inner tubing—xylem tissue—which transports water and nutrients up the tree), as well as by root pressure, which results from osmosis of water into the roots when the water concentration is higher outside of the roots than inside the roots (because of solutes dissolved in the water within the roots).

Okay, so the tree exists—spatial dimensions exist—and the pouring of energy out of the white hole Big Bang produces the analogue of root pressure (diffusing of water into the roots of the tree, pushing the water upward), and this propels the universe through time (as time speeds up with the spreading-out of matter in the initial explosion of the Big Bang). After the influence of root pressure, the expansion of matter, along with the progression through time, slows its pace, as the upward trek of water through the tree (through time in spatial existence) slows its pace. The water still clings to the sides of the tubing, but this doesn't produce much upward pull. This is like matter and energy clinging to existence, but this clinging doesn't propel them forward through time much. (This is like when we have nothing to drive us forward but the desire to

continue to exist; getting up in the morning and going through the day is an effort, and time seems to move slowly, because the desire to continue to exist—in this way—is not much of a driving force, because it is not much of a goal toward which we must be headed. We already exist, and so the goal of existence doesn't pull us forward much at all.) But the water clings to itself, and this is of great importance, because this is all that keeps the water going for a while—because when water molecules are pulled upward, they pull the water molecules that are behind them upward, and these water molecules pull the water molecules behind them upward, and so on.

Essentially, after the universe gets past the influence of the initial thrust of root pressure—of the Big Bang (and possibly of the inflationary period of the universe soon after)—which expands the universe and increases its pace through time, there isn't much driving force to keep the whole progression going until the upward pull caused by evaporation of water from the leaves takes effect upon the water molecules—until the pull of the beginning of the manifestation of self-awareness takes hold upon the universe (a point that is possibly marked by the arising of life). But the pull of matter toward itself is a driving force (as the universe begins to be pulled forward through time, after the initial thrust of the Big Bang, by the pull toward self-awareness—a distant goal that merely pulls the universe forward without a clear or understood purpose) as matter attracts itself under the pull of the strong nuclear force and electromagnetism and gravity—like beads of water pulled together by cohesion—forming galaxies, and stars, and planets, and black holes with singularities at their centers.

In the tree, the liquid water forms a continuous line up the tree, and this line of water is bound to itself by cohesion. When the pull of evaporation becomes great (during the day when the sun is high in the sky and the air is hot and/or dry), this pull stretches the line of water like a rubber band as the water moves rapidly upward near the top of the tree and is not as rapidly replaced at the bottom of the tree (where water is entering through the roots), and if the pull becomes too great (as in the middle of a really hot, dry day), the tree must prevent more loss of water by closing the stomata in its leaves so that it doesn't break the continuity of the line of water (because then the flow of water up the tree would cease). If the tree had no mechanism of halting the evaporation of the water from the leaves, the line would be broken and the transport of water and minerals would cease in the tree. During the night, the pull of water by the sun's energy is absent, and so more water enters the tree through the roots without so much water leaving from the leaves, making it so that the rubber-band line of water becomes no longer stretched taut. The pull of water up the tree in this case is caused by the stretched line of water, which draws more water up like a stretched rubber band unstretching. So, in the universe, there must be a continuous line of matter and energy through time. We'll get back to the implications of this later. Let's stick with the present moment as it progresses upward like a few water molecules progressing upward.

When the Source is most clearly present to the universe (like the sun during the day), the pull of self-awareness is great, and the universe expands more rapidly, and time progresses forward more rapidly as matter and energy are spread out even more, slowing time less and less. If the pull becomes too great, the singularities of black holes cease to pull as much matter into them, slowing down the loss of gravity (due to the slowing of the loss of matter, which has gravity), and so slowing down the acceleration of the expansion of the universe a bit and thereby slowing the acceleration of the forward progression through time a bit. When the Source is hidden from the universe (like the sun at night), the universe continues to expand; although, again, the acceleration of its expansion is slowed and the acceleration of the progression through time is slowed. If there were no mechanism for slowing the loss of the gravitational effect of matter and energy through the singularities of black holes, the universe would—like the tree that breaks its whole transport system of water up the tree if it loses too much water too rapidly—lose too much matter and energy too rapidly, causing the universe to expand too rapidly and time to progress too rapidly, and life within the universe would not be able to form or, in the case that it has already formed, life would not be able to continue to exist. The tree would die, and the universe would become barren without reaching its goal of self-awareness within itself.

As the water nears the leaves in the tree, the pull of evaporation becomes greater, and the water travels upward more rapidly, drawn upward by the pull. As the matter and energy nears the singularities of black holes (as when galaxies, like the Milky Way, form around black holes, and then solar systems capable of supporting life, like our own, form in those galaxies), the pull of self-awareness becomes greater and time moves more rapidly, drawn forward by this goal.

Then, the water transpires from the stomata of the leaves and is evaporated out of the tree by the sun's energy, which it finally gains directly, unmediated by the tree (through which it was pulled indirectly by the sun's energy via the attraction of water molecules to other water molecules). The matter and energy of the universe is pulled into the singularities of black holes (mainly the supermassive black holes at the centers of galaxies), and is somehow evaporated out of spatial and successively temporal existence by the Source's experience of being self-aware existence, which the universe finally gains directly, unmediated by the language of material existence (through which it was pulled indirectly by the Source's experience via the attraction of matter and energy to other matter and energy—which caused the formation of everything from atoms and molecules and galaxies and stars and planets up to simple and then complex life, with all of life's interactions). In other words, everything that has formed in the universe has done so because of the combination of the attraction of the world to itself (which causes the law of attraction) and the pull of self-awareness—the goal of experiencing what it is like to be the Source—and so all that we experience outside and inside ourselves has been produced by the attraction of aspects of the world to other like-aspects of the world (like water molecules being attracted to other water molecules), along with the pull and guidance of the Source.

Once the water has left the tree as water vapor, it is no longer in the process of receiving more of the sun's energy but (having received all of the energy that it can), rather, it is in the process of sharing that energy (as with the atmosphere and, possibly indirectly, with the next water that is transpiring from the leaves, thereby allowing that water to evaporate). Of course, basically all of the energy given up by the evaporated water (as it condenses) would be lost to the atmosphere unless the tree were in a closed system, like a dome, with the water and the ground. In either case, most of the energy for the evaporation of the water from the leaves would actually come directly from the sun, itself, and not from previously evaporated water that is condensing (due to the nature of energy conversion and loss, as entropy—the degree of disorder in a system—increases). Once the water vapor condenses back into liquid water, it reenters the ground and, eventually, the roots of the tree, thereby sharing itself with the tree again. Once the energy of the universe has left material existence, it is no longer in the process of receiving more of the Source's experience but (having received all that it can), rather, it is in the process of sharing that experience (with the next universe). The world then shares itself with the next universe via the white hole of the Big Bang.

Night Inside the Tree, Day Outside the Tree

The water only really evaporates from the leaves of the tree during the day, when the sun is in the sky, for at night there is no source of energy to evaporate the water. Then, it is mostly when it grows a bit colder (as at night, when the sun is hidden from the water vapor), that the water vapor condenses back into liquid water and forms root pressure in the beginning of its next progression up the tree. The energy of the universe evaporates as it receives the completion of the Source's experience in itself, and then it is only when the Source becomes hidden from it (due to its own movement, or change, in relation to the Source, rather than to the Source's movement or change)—when it ceases to receive the Source's existence and experience—that it condenses back into another progression through the material structure of space and successive time.

We can imagine the stages of the paradigm as concentric circles, with the physical universe beginning at the point of manifestation in the center, and expanding outward to encompass each stage, up to sharing thought (understanding) and choice—self-awareness. Once the paradigm reaches the outermost concentric circle that is choice, we might think that this whole structure of concentric circles instantaneously collapses down into a point, making choice the next manifestation. Then, the universe would expand outward from there again, with new concentric circles replacing the old ones. But this can't be so, because the tree continues to exist—the spatial (although space is infinitely expanded in the absence of matter) and temporal (although time is infinitely fast in the absence of matter) structure of material existence continues to exist—beyond the evaporation of its contents from it. What actually happens is that the universe expands outward from the point of manifestation to encompass each stage up to sharing thought and choice (self-awareness), and then it begins to contract inward, passing through each stage from choice down to the point at manifestation—where the next universe begins. In this way, the entire world is as though it is breathing in—expanding (like our lungs) with—experience, and then breathing out—contracting (like our lungs) and squeezing out—experience. However, there is more to this.

The world receives and manifests experience, working its way up from the bottom of the tree of life to the top—from manifestation to sharing thought, or understanding, and choice—during its night (relative to outside the tree) in material existence, and it shares (creates) experience, working its way down from the top of the tree of life to the bottom—from choice to manifestation—during the day outside of material existence. However, the world is also receiving and manifesting understanding of its experience from the bottom up during the night in material existence, and it is sharing (creating) understanding from the top down during the day outside of material existence—where it can face the Source and its entire past without the mediation of the lens of material existence, like water vapor facing the sun and the tree (its whole past and context for being) from the perspective outside of the tree.

There is, thus, actually something happening to the world between its exit from material existence via the singularities of black holes and its reentrance into material existence via the singularity of the white hole of the next universe, just as there is actually something happening to the water between its evaporation from the leaves and its condensation and reentrance into the tree via the tree's roots.

During material existence, the world receives and manifests experience and self-aware understanding derived from that experience (from bottom up, beginning at manifestation and manifesting each stage upward toward greater understanding and toward choice). During existence between physical universes, the world shares (creates) experience and, therefore, also self-aware understanding that can be derived from that experience (from top down, beginning at choice and understanding, and choosing each stage downward to manifestation). Essentially, within material existence, the world breathes in experience and understanding that it derives from that experience (expanding to encompass each stage from the point of manifestation outward toward sharing thought and choice). When it breathes in experience and understanding, it is manifesting (actual) self-awareness (gained from the understanding of experience) upward. Outside of material existence, the world breathes out experience and understanding that can be derived from that experience (contracting to pass back through each stage from choice and sharing thought down to the point of manifestation). When it breathes out experience and understanding, it is creating (potential) self-awareness downward.

We can think of this in terms of some of its reflective manifestations. First of all, we must realize here what we have suggested above: The world is in its "day" when it is like water vapor, for this is when the sun's energy is available to make the water into water vapor, and this is also when the water is out of the darkness of the tree and is, therefore, capable of more directly experiencing the sun, rather than merely experiencing the sun indirectly via its pull on other water molecules and such. Then, when the water vapor condenses into liquid water and enters the darkness of the tree, it is in its "night". As the world is in night during *physical* existence—at which point it is receiving more indirectly from the Source (via experience of other parts of itself)—we are in the night of our lives when we are in our physical lives, and we are in the night of the usual 24-hour day when we are awake. And as the world is in its day when it is in *nonphysical* existence—at which point it is receiving more directly from the Source—we are in the day of our lives when we are in the life between physical lives, and we are in the day of the usual 24-hour day when we are asleep.

During the night (the night—in the year—that is summer and spring, the night that is the time that we are awake, the night that is physical life, the night that is all of the physical universe), we take in (breathe in) experience through our senses from the bottom up, and we derive understanding from this experience through the exercise of our creative processes from the bottom up. During the day (the day—in the year—that is fall and winter, the day that is the time that we are asleep, the day that is existence between physical lives, the day that is the existence of the world between material universes), we create (breathe out) experience through the exercise of our senses from the top down (as through actively calling upon memories of our experience of things through our senses), and we create, with this, understanding (that can potentially be derived from this experience) through the exercise of our creative processes from top down.

Night is marked by learning from experience, and day is marked by exercising what has been learned. Night is the process of learning to be self-aware, and day is the process of creating with self-awareness. We manifest or actualize self-awareness (night), and then we create with self-awareness (day). And night followed by day is one overall day—one complete existence of whatever it is that we are breaking down into night and day. A physical universe (inside the tree, night), followed by the nonphysical stage of that universe (outside the tree, day), is one overall universe. A physical lifetime (inside the tree, night), followed by the nonphysical afterlife (outside the tree, day), is one overall lifetime. Our waking hours (inside the tree, night), followed by the period of sleep (outside the tree, day), is one overall day. The spring and summer (inside the tree, night), followed by the fall and winter (outside the tree, day), is one overall year.

This all gets quite confusing when we start to consider things like the day and the year, especially, because the time when the sun is apparent seems like it should be day, while the time when the sun is hidden seems like it should be night. After all, this is how we define day and night usually. However, we must remember that night inside the tree is marked by learning to be self-aware, and this is accomplished when we are awake, when we are alive, when the sun is out—during exposure to experience, so that we can experientially learn. This is the time when we are manifesting upward, growing closer to self-awareness. Eventually, we near the transition from night into day, at which point we begin also to *exercise* self-awareness, creating our lives and our day and so on.

But, primarily, night is a period of learning. We learn from our experiences during the physical existence of the universe, during physical life, during the day. We learn from the experience of the planting of crops during the spring and summer—we learn from the experience of the consequences of each of our actions whether certain actions are favorable or unfavorable, whether they lead us to the fulfillment of what we seek or not.

We use what we have learned to create our experiences for the next night during the day outside the tree—during the day that is the nonphysical existence of the universe, during the day that is our life between lives, during the day that is the time when we are asleep. During the fall and winter, we use what we have learned from the last spring and summer to plan and create the next season's harvest.

The day outside the tree often is less concrete-seeming, less consistently causal and systematic in its progression, than the night inside the tree. When we are asleep, our experience (in dreams and so forth) seems not to adhere to a strict temporality. A moment sleeping can seem like forever or like no time at all. Day is marked by creation, and so everything is potential, and nothing is actual yet, and so nothing has reached the concrete manifestation of time yet. This is true for the day that is the nonphysical universe as water vapor, for the nonphysical afterlife, for the period of sleep, and even to an extent for the period of fall and winter, for with the sun so often unseen, time seems not to have its usual progression and seems more difficult to measure.

To make things more confusing still (or perhaps clearer) in our reversal of our usual notion of day and night from the perspective of creation—from the perspective of the Source—it can be said and seen that the sun serves as a symbol of the Source in Its relation to us during our night inside the tree, as the sun serves this purpose for the water inside the tree, providing the energy to pull it upward in its progression up the tree toward being water vapor—toward self-awareness. And so the sun during the night that is physical life, and the night that is our waking hours, and the night that is spring and summer, is sort of like the moon (again, we're saying that our usual day is night from the perspective of the Source, and so is night in its being a reflection of the physical universe inside the tree—as opposed to being a reflection of the nonphysical universe outside the tree). For the sun is a reflection of the Source in this world for us the way the moon is a reflection of the sun's light.

Let's reverse things and put them in the context of *the physical universe's* and therefore *our* perspective (which is, therefore, an easier perspective for us to relate to and, thus, to understand)—rather than in the context of the Source's perspective, which is a mirror-image reversal of that with which we are familiar. Here, we can see that the sun during our usual day is a symbol of the Source in this world the way we experience the Source in Its true relation to us when we are self-aware, and the moon at night is a symbol of the Source as we experience It in this physical world—as a reflection of what the sun, or of what the Source, truly is. The sun is an essentially endless (from our much more finite perspective) source of all that it shares with us, and we can see it face to face during the day, but we cannot truly look directly at it without injury, and we cannot sustain ourselves on it without the intermediary of plants and trees that we must physically consume and use in order to continue to exist. Similarly, the Source is endless in Its sharing, and we can see It face to face during the true day outside the tree during the nonphysical stage of the universe, but we cannot look directly at It without injury, and we cannot sustain ourselves on what It shares during this time, and so we must enter the tree of life in a new physical existence in order to sustain ourselves upon it. Like the sun, when the Source is clearest to us, we cannot experience or receive from It directly, or else we will cease to be able to receive from It, for we will cease to exist.

The moon, on the other hand, is a reflection of the sun that we can look directly upon, and we can receive its light, and although we still cannot sustain ourselves upon it, the moon is a reminder of the sun's existence. And sometimes it is clear and illuminating (as during a full moon)—a beacon that provides for the illumination and pull of self-awareness, like the sun for the water within the tree. And sometimes it is hidden even when it is still there (as during a new moon), like the situation for the water within the tree when the sun is not in the sky to evaporate the water from the leaves and thereby to pull the water upward through the tree toward self-awareness. In such ways, the moon is like a reflection of a reflection of the Source, reminding us of our situation within the tree—of our relation to the Source when we are not fully self-aware, but are, rather, still in the process of learning to be self-aware, in the process of manifestation.

With every breath in, we create the potential to breathe out, and with every breath we breathe out, we create the potential to breathe in. And we keep breathing. As the world breathes in, it breathes in and out on every level of its experience, and so we breathe—in and out.

The water molecules in the tree move upward both through attraction to other water molecules (receiving from the world—which won't get it up the tree alone) and through attraction to the sun (receiving from the sun via its interactions with other water molecules). But then the water molecules share the energy from the sun with the next water molecules only via their interactions with other water molecules—only in the form in which the pulling energy has passed through them. When we breathe in, our lungs expand and we receive both some carbon dioxide (from ourselves and each other and other life and other processes—world receiving from itself, on which it cannot survive) and oxygen (energy from the sun via plants—other aspects of this world—world receiving through the world from the Source, on which it can survive). And, when we breathe out, we share nearly only carbon dioxide (the energy that we have received from the sun—via plants—as it has been shaped by us).

We can also see this in the beating of the heart, which is actually receiving blood as it expands (which it will then share with the next contraction) from two directions simultaneously—both deoxygenated blood from all parts of the body (other than the lungs), via the superior vena cava and the inferior vena cava into the right atrium (world receiving from itself, on which it cannot survive), and oxygenated blood from the lungs, via the pulmonary vein into the left atrium (world receiving through the world from the Source, on which it can survive). And, with the next contraction, the heart is pushing (sharing) blood out in two directions simultaneously—deoxygenated blood toward the lungs, out the right ventricle via the pulmonary artery, and oxygenated blood toward the rest of the body, out the left ventricle via the aorta. Here, we see that the heart actually serves as a central column for the exchange of blood between the body and the world, for it does not change the blood, but rather shares it as it receives it (in the form in which it receives it).

With each expansion, the world receives both from itself (liquid water from previous existence, which gives it its material contents and pushes it upward only a bit through the tree, through time) and from the Source via itself (the pull of self-awareness via other water molecules that are moving upward due to the sun's evaporation of the water from the leaves). The world creates the contents of its next experience in material existence, but the existence of those contents—and the quality of the experience of those contents—comes via the world from the Source.

Manifestations of the Paradigm, and More Aspects of the Paradigm

The Human Body and Brain

The tree of life paradigm is manifested in all things, including even the structure of our bodies. Choice is manifested above the head. Sharing thought is manifested as the right hemisphere of the brain (which is synthetic, big-picture-oriented, and creative in its thinking), receiving thought is manifested as the left hemisphere of the brain (which is analytic, detail-oriented, and systematic in its thinking—and which is where the language center of the brain is mostly located, for it is always the receiving part—like the world and not the Source—that ultimately dictates, or requires and gets caught up in, the language that is used in the interaction), and allowing thought is manifested as the brain stem (and spinal cord), which allows interaction between the brain hemispheres and the body—which allows thought to be manifested through us (notice that we experience thinking in the head). Sharing feeling is manifested as the right arm, receiving feeling is manifested as the left arm, and allowing feeling is manifested as the chest with the heart (which, we have seen, allows to flow through it exactly what it receives in the form that it receives it)—which allows feeling to be manifested through us as it circulates hormones throughout the body (notice that it is with the arms that we most express feelings for others in the group, as with hugging, and that feelings that relate to other people are often experienced in the chest). Sharing inclination is manifested as the right leg, receiving inclination is manifested as the left leg, and allowing inclination is manifested as the gut and the gonads (sex organs)—which allow instincts to flow through us (notice that we experience instincts in the gut and loins, and that we often act or move with our legs). Manifestation is manifested in offspring or in some other creation that arises through the exercise of the creative processes.

(Notice that the sharing elements of feeling and inclination are manifested as the right arm and leg, respectively. The creative, and therefore dominant-in-initiating-things, nature of the right side of the body reveals that the fact that most people are right-handed—that the right side of their bodies is dominant—is a reflection of the ultimate reality—that the right side is the creative, sharing, initiative side, while the left side receives and manifests within itself what the right side creates or initiates.)

The entire paradigm is actually repeated within the structure of the brain. In this case: Choice is manifested in the prefrontal cortex, which allows us this capacity. Sharing thought is manifested as the cerebral cortex of the right hemisphere (which makes us capable of abstract, imaginative, creative, big-picture thought about what could be), receiving thought is manifested as the cerebral cortex of the left hemisphere (which makes us capable of logical, systematic, methodical, detail-oriented thought about what actually is), and allowing thought is manifested as the corpus callosum, which relays information between the two hemispheres (thereby allowing for the interaction of imaginative or creative potential and detailed, chronological actuality). Sharing feeling is manifested as the hypothalamus, receiving feeling is manifested as the amygdala, and allowing feeling is manifested as the thalamus, which relays sensory information to the cerebral cortex (notice that these structures are all part of the limbic system, which includes the parts of the brain that are most responsible for our experience of emotion). Sharing inclination is manifested as the midbrain, receiving inclination is manifested as the pons, and allowing inclination is manifested as the medulla (notice that these structures are all part of the brain stem, which is the most instinctual, reflexive, and automatic part of the brain, the part that controls functions, like breathing and the beating of the heart, that are necessary for the maintenance and preservation of life—functions that can be brought under the control of higher parts of the brain and thereby made willful, but that are usually carried out unconsciously). And manifestation is manifested as the rest of the body (through which the brain's activities are outwardly manifested).

It is noteworthy to point out that the evolution of animals up to humans (as well as the formation of an individual human being) manifests these structures from the bottom up, such that reptiles' brains are made up mostly of the brain stem (and so reptiles are very instinctual) and, as we move up through development, emotional structures develop (allowing the capacity for complex emotions), followed by higher thought structures (allowing the capacity for complex thought).

It is also noteworthy to point out that the brain-oriented reason that we experience the manifestation of the creative processes (thought, feeling, instinct) from the bottom up and, subsequently to this, we are capable of controlling the creative processes from the top down, is that the lower, more-instinctual parts of the brain receive signals of sensory input first, and only after this do the signals reach higher, thought-involved parts of the brain, which are capable of suppressing or altering our instinctual response from the top down. For example, in a situation that evokes fear in us, the signal reaches the amygdala (which triggers the secretion of various hormones, sending signals to our body to react) before it reaches the frontal cortex. And so we are inclined to do something before our frontal cortex gets the signal and is capable of interpreting the situation and deciding not to react in that way, but rather to respond in a different way. However, through practiced response, we are capable of altering our responses to situations (so that our bodies are not told, by being flooded with hormones, to express or carry out some reaction due to signals sent by the lower portions of our brains in reaction to sensory stimuli).

The Heart of the Universe

When manifesting (from bottom up), allowing feeling—the heart—is the beginning of the manifestation of life—of living, breathing things that must work, like the heart pumps, to maintain their survival. In the physical universe, there is first manifestation in the singularity of the Big Bang, and then there is action and inclination—there is physical matter and energy that, once manifested, begins to move and to be inclined to move into groups in accordance with the forces (namely, the strong nuclear force, electromagnetism, and gravity). It is only when galaxies arise (with black holes at their centers—like leaves with stomata), and life begins to take shape on planets in those galaxies, that the universe reaches allowing feeling in its manifestation.

Life is the heart of the universe. At this point (at allowing feeling in the manifestation upward), the universe, the person, etc., has finally formed a clear goal, for now others are in the picture, and there is the desire to preserve one's existence by fitting in—there is the desire to interact with those others. And, of course, it is the interaction with the other that leads toward self-awareness, so this is when the manifestation of experience has reached a point where the ultimate goal begins to take shape. Further, like the heart, life is the first thing to arise in development from the bottom up that has a clear and individual goal or purpose toward which it must constantly work in order to achieve its fulfillment (in the case of the heart, this goal is pumping blood to maintain the survival of the organism, and in the case of life, this goal is performing the activities necessary for its survival). And so the universe, the person, etc., begins to be pulled forward by some goal—which is, here (at allowing feeling), finding one's niche and fitting in with others, working with them toward an overall goal.

The important thing to realize is that this is *not* the point where self-awareness has actually arisen. The world, the person, etc., begins—at allowing feeling, at the heart, at life—to receive from the Source via the world (via others in the world), and not just from the world, alone, but the world, the person, etc., does not realize at this point what he/she/it is doing. There is still the conception that the world and those others are the source of what the "I" is receiving. The ultimate goal of receiving only from the Source (via the world) and not from the world requires the awareness that all that the "I" *has* comes ultimately from the Source. And this turning point is choice, self-awareness. For it is with the arising of self-awareness that the universe not *only manifests* experience and understanding, but *also* begins to *create* experience and, thereby, the potential for new understanding (thus entering a sort of twilight period, in the beginning of dawn, where the night of the universe begins to resemble day a bit as the universe begins creating, although the universe is still receiving and manifesting more than it is creating, and it is, therefore, still in night—in physicality, within the tree).

Allowing feeling—life, heart—makes it possible to look back on past experiences and learn from them in order to better understand the relationship between the "I" and other "I"'s (ultimately including the Source "I"). When life begins to manifest in the world, repetition of the tree of life paradigm (by which the world relates to the Source) begins to occur at a rapidly increasing pace—in multiple individual life forms and in multiple species and types of life forms—getting closer and closer to the full paradigm as evolution progresses, as the self-reflection of the world increases in extent and rapidity with the world's having reached the feeling stages of the paradigm (beginning at allowing feeling) in its development, and with the world's consequent looking back and reflecting upon its past and itself in an effort to figure out who it is and what its relation is to the various parts of itself and to the Source. Then, with the manifestation of allowing thought (the brain, intelligent and potentially self-aware life), this reflection upon the past can begin to lead to actual figuring out, where reflection upon the past can begin to be applied intellectually to predicting the future course of things. But only upon the manifestation of choice does this figuring out lead to the kind of understanding of the true relationship between the "I" and other "I"'s—such that the "I" no longer views other "I"'s in this world as the source of its experience—that can be applied in the form of the willful creation of new experience.

Before allowing feeling manifests, there is a present-orientedness. We see this in childhood, when we cannot truly imagine anything beyond the present because we are so present-focused. We see this in the beginning of the universe, where physical bodies yielded no reflection on the past or creation of the future. Planets and stars and galaxies are just there, doing what they are doing in the present. Even at the beginning of the arising of (physical) life, the reflection on the past and the creation of the future is not self-aware, but it does begin to occur. This (the feeling stages) is ultimately the adolescence of the universe—the time when self-reflective questioning of who the "I" is and how it fits in and relates to others occurs. Only in the twilight, near the end of the physical universe and, thereby, of (physical) life, does reflection on the past and creation of the future become truly self-aware, as the self-reflective repetitive manifestation of the tree of life paradigm begins to encompass the full paradigm from manifestation to choice (in human beings).

Other Aspects of the Paradigm

And so we see, here, the suggestion of two other aspects of the various stages of the paradigm. First, there is present-orientedness, with a focus on the boundaries of the "I" (when there is only "I", and the "I" extends to encompass all that is, and there is the desire to preserve the existence of the "I", and there is instinct, speech and action that arise to accomplish this, and so on—in the present). These are the stages just above manifestation—allowing inclination, receiving inclination, and sharing inclination. Then, there is past-orientedness, with a focus on the identity of the "I" (when there are others and there is the desire to fit in with those others, working with them toward a goal, and there is feeling that arises to perceive the relation of the "I" to those others and who the "I" actually is and how the "I" is perceived by others and by the "I", and so on—in the past). These are the stages of allowing feeling, receiving feeling, and sharing feeling. Then, there is future-orientedness, with a focus on making decisions (when there are other "I"'s and there is the desire to connect intimately and intensely with those other "I"'s, and there is thought that arises to aid in this connection, and there is concern about making the decisions that will have the best consequences for the "I" and for the other "I"'s, and so on—in the future). These are the stages of allowing thought, receiving thought, and sharing thought.

We can see this manifested in our lives, in a day, in a year, and in the entire universe. In our lives, we are first— as babies and in early childhood—very present-oriented, concerned with having what we need (or think we need) to preserve ourselves, and we are very *me*-oriented (because the "I" extends to encompass everything, having no boundaries), and we are predominantly focused on what we want and what we want to do (instinct and action), particularly in relation to how this is going to help us survive (or how we believe it is going to help us survive) in some way. Then—in adolescence—we become very past-oriented, concerned with fitting in with others and with the group, and we are very others-oriented in terms of being concerned with how others perceive us, and we are concerned with who we are and how we fit in, and we are predominantly focused on how we feel (feeling), particularly in relation to others. Then, eventually—around college-age (late teens and early twenties)—we become very future-oriented, concerned with making the best decisions for ourselves and for the individuals in our lives, and we thus become more other-individuals focused, and also more abstract-focused, in the sense that we are focused on things that have not happened and that are merely ideas in our minds, and we are predominantly focused on what we think might or can or will happen (thinking), particularly in our connections with other individuals.

All of this is prior to the manifestation of choice, of self-awareness. We are starting to anticipate choice, but until we come to identify with it, all of these things are issues, because we don't have the clear-minded guidance of intuition to help us make our decisions, and we don't know who we are—we don't know that we are the ability to choose who we are—and we don't know how far our influence extends into the world—that through our willful and self-aware use of language, we can accomplish anything. Along this process, each of us is often inclined to get stuck at one stage or another in his/her manifestation of different aspects of him/herself. But we'll get back to this later.

In the course of a day, upon first waking up, various hormones in our body peak, including stress hormones and sex hormones—both associated with instinctual needs and desires. We are usually pretty present-oriented at first, and concerned with taking care of the preservation of the existence of ourselves (going to the bathroom, showering, eating, and possibly also exercising and/or meditating). We usually don't really want others to encroach upon our boundaries until we've gotten our self-preservation stuff out of the way. Then, we soon become more past-oriented, concerned with how others are perceiving us and have perceived us as we are at work or school. And then we become more future-oriented, focusing on decisions that we have to make and on what will happen the next day to ourselves and to the other individuals in our lives as a result of the decisions that we make. Then, we choose—to go to sleep.

In the course of a year, the very beginning of the year is marked by present-orientedness and self-orientedness. You are trying to preserve yourself, and it is unclear how far you extend into your world. Eventually, present-orientedness gives way to past-orientedness as you begin to reflect on how your year has gone so far, and on how you are perceived by others, and on how well you fit into the group and into the world in general. Then, past-orientedness gives way to future-orientedness as you begin to focus on your connections to other individuals in your life, and as you begin to focus on the decisions that you need to make, and as you begin to think about the possible consequences that those decisions might have, with regard to yourself and the other people close to you, in the rest of the year and in the next year.

In the course of the entire universe, the universe starts out very present- and inclination- and action-oriented in the Big

Bang and just after, and even up through the putting together of matter and energy to form galaxies and stars and planets. But then life begins to arise to look back at where it was and where it is in relation to where it was and in relation to the other life, and at who it is in relation to others, and eventually at who it is in relation to the entire universe and to the Source. Then, at this point, the universe becomes more future-oriented, pulled forward in its expansion to encompass the experience of self-awareness, and focused on what decisions to make in order to attain intimate and intense connection with others in the universe and with the Source, Itself.

Be aware that, in all of these examples, I have only really discussed the night prior to the reaching of choice—prior to the beginning of the dawning of self-awareness.

Day and Night, Night and Day

The Stages of Sleep

In order to understand the pattern of breathing out and in (of creation and manifestation) of day and night better, let us look to the stages of sleep in the sleep cycle. Here, we are dealing with day, and so we are dealing with the situation that occurs in sleep, between physical lives, between physical universes, etc.—which is a reversal of what occurs during the night—when awake, during physical life, during the physical universe, etc. However, in the stages of sleep, we will not see a pure day that consists solely of creation—a situation that is, perhaps, most closely reached in the case of the nonphysical universe in between physical universes, and that is probably only completely and truly reached in the case of the Source, Itself (for the Source only creates, or shares, and does not receive).

Sleep is very much a mixture of manifesting and creating because it is day (creating) of a day, but it is part of physical life (night), within the physical universe (night) and, being so, it is manifesting (night) overall. And this is what we will see in the pattern of a usual period of sleep, in which we are certainly doing a lot of manifesting of understanding of the day's events (in the consolidation of memory and learning), and a lot of manifesting of experience (in dreams), coming to an understanding of the dream experiences in combination with the day's events, and so on. But sleep is creative (day) relative to wake, which is, therefore, manifestive (night) relative to sleep. In REM sleep, we put together the day's events in new ways, creating new experiences, which we manifest as dreams, which we then learn from in order to create new experiences still, which we then manifest as more dreams, and so on. A similar situation exists for the afterlife. The afterlife is day (creating) of a lifetime, but it is part of the physical universe (night) and, being so, it is manifesting (night) overall. But the afterlife is creative (day) relative to physical life, which is, therefore, manifestive (night) relative to the afterlife.

You'll notice that the stages of sleep reflect the tree of life stages as well—and, in fact, the pattern of their manifestation reflects the way the paradigm is manifested throughout the course of the self-reflection of the universe, although in a mirror-image reversal such that it begins at choice, creating downward, and then manifests upward, and then creates downward, and so on (remember that sleep is a day within the night of physical life within the night of the physical universe), such that it gravitates to remaining only in higher and higher stages—closer and closer to choice and self-awareness and willful creation—with each repetition of the paradigm.

First, you choose to go to sleep. Then, you pass through stage 1 (swimming and dreamy and drifting thoughts, repeating—in patterns of neuronal firing—facts learned during the day, thereby consolidating memory of these facts in long-term memory), stage 2 (I would predict from the pattern, since studies have not yet concluded what occurs during this stage of sleep: repeating—in patterns of neuronal firing—interactions that were had during the day with other people—and with other aspects of the world—that caused strong feelings to arise in you, thereby consolidating memory of these emotional associations in long-term memory), stage 3 (repeating—in patterns of neuronal firing—physical actions or skills—things that involve the body—like playing an instrument or a sport, that were learned during the day, thereby consolidating memory of these actions in long-term memory; also, during stage 3 and stage 4 sleep, which are deep and restful sleep, repair and growth occurs—meaning maintenance of the body's existence occurs), stage 4 (very deep sleep—manifestation of sleep—during which growth and restoration and some not-very-vivid dreams may occur).

Then, you follow a pattern that is something like the following: From 4, you go up to 3 to 2 to 1 to REM (rapid eye movement, where the muscles of the body are paralyzed and the mind plays sensory experiences—dreams—piecing together things that you've learned during the day in a synthetic and imaginative fashion; this is the stage of the most vivid dreams, and sometimes the dreams are lucid—you become aware that you are dreaming while you are dreaming and you may even become capable of willfully creating what manifests in your dream—and sometimes the dreams, especially the lucid ones, are creative of potential experiences for the following waking hours—the following "night" of manifestation; also, stress dissipates during REM sleep, so that you are less stressed during the "night"—the usual day—after REM sleep) and down to 1 to 2 to 3 to 4, and up to 3 to 2 to 1 to REM, and down to 1 to 2 to 3, and up to 2 to 1 to REM, and down to 1 to 2, and up to 1 to REM, and down to 1 to 2, and up to 1 to awake.

Okay, so let's analyze what happens here. We start with a top down creating of understanding and experience. Then, we reach a turning point at manifestation in stage 4. And we go back through the stages in reverse order. Essentially, we breathe out (create) experience (and potential understanding to be gained from that experience) completely to manifestation, and then we breathe in (manifest) that experience and understanding that we have just created. So, beginning at manifestation and moving upward, we manifest—as patterns of neural firing—and learn from our *actions* of the past "night" (the usual day of our waking hours), we manifest and learn from our *feel-*

ings of the past "night", and we manifest and learn from our *thoughts* of the past "night". At this point, we reach the completion of the manifestation of experience and understanding in *choice*—in self-awareness. In sleep, choice is REM sleep. Any dreams in stages prior to this are fuzzy and dull—a bit like our experience of the physical world when we are awake and we haven't yet reached self-awareness—but in REM sleep there is the manifestation of fully self-aware experience—vivid, lucid dreams that are in the process of being created as they are occurring.

It is at this point that we begin once again to breathe out (create) new experience and understanding—now not only making use of what we have learned from the experiences of the past "night" (the past usual day of our waking hours), but also of what we have learned from the experiences of this past period of manifestation up to REM sleep. Then, we go through the stages to reach manifestation again in stage 4, where we begin to manifest experience (and self-aware understanding derived from this experience) to be manifested fully in REM sleep, where we begin to create new experience once again, making use of the self-aware understanding that we have gained from the experiences of the "night" and from the experiences of the last periods of manifestation from bottom up while we were asleep. Eventually, we breathe in upward to the point of choosing to awake, rather than to enter the REM realm of choosing the next experiences that we will create downward through stages 1, 2, and 3 for another period of manifestation upward from stage 4.

We see here that in day (represented by sleep), we begin both creating (sharing) and (receiving and) manifesting, and then we tend toward just creating (toward just choice—in this case, in REM sleep) at the end. In day, first we are like water that has just evaporated from the tree and that has thereby transformed into water vapor, but then we begin to condense back into liquid water in the process of creating the next journey up the tree. Night is largely a 180-degree rotation of this pattern of day. So, in night, we begin just receiving and manifesting, and then we end up both (receiving and) manifesting and creating (sharing). In night, first we are just moving up the tree, but then, as self-aware understanding manifests upward, we begin to be pulled upward by self-awareness toward creating the next experience that we will receive and manifest.

Day of Creation (nonphysical, sleep)

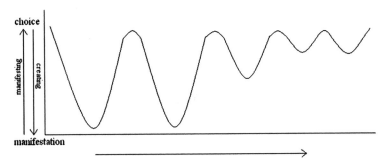

Night of Manifestation (physical, wake)

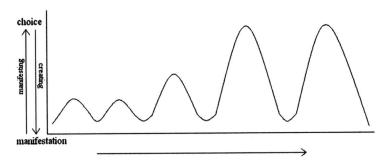

The Night of Our Lives Prior to the Dawning of Self-Awareness

During the beginning of the "night" (the night that is the usual day when we are awake, and the night that is life, and the night that is the physical universe, and so on), we are not fully awake—we are not fully self-aware. We are, instead, still passing up through the stages of sleep, stuck mostly in one stage or another, repeating thoughts or feelings or instincts and actions in our minds (especially while we are staring into space or are trying to go to sleep—during the beginning of the night that is life, prior to the dawning of self-awareness), as though in an effort to glean something—some understanding—from them. But, during the beginning of "night" (of our lives and so forth), we don't really reach any definitive conclusions regarding how to make the best decisions for the "I" and other "I"'s (which is ultimately at what much of the repetition of thoughts is aimed), or regarding who the "I" really is and how the "I" relates to others (which is ultimately at what much of the repetition of feelings is aimed), or regarding how far the "I"'s presence and influence actually extends (which is ultimately at what much of the repetition of instincts and actions is aimed).

I would predict from this that if the brainwaves of people were recorded during the usual day and the usual night, each person (at least during beginning of the night of his/her life, prior to the dawning of self-awareness) would be found to be inclined to remain in either stage 1, 2, or 3 (depending on the main stage personality type of fixation, which will be discussed in later sections) longer than in the others of these stages when going to sleep, and the types of brainwaves that mark this stage of sleep would be found to replay often in that person's brain throughout the time during which that person is awake (particularly when the person is zoned out and staring into space).

In practicality, this would suggest that of all people who are not particularly self-aware, people who are fixated on a thought stage as their main stage type would most likely have the most difficulty falling asleep, in general (since they would tend to get stuck in stage 1—which is very light sleep—with their minds very actively thinking, repeating thoughts and trying to figure out what might happen in an effort to glean some basis and guidance for how to make the best decisions—the decisions with the best consequences—for themselves and other "I"'s, and for determining what those decisions might be), people who are fixated on a feeling stage as their main stage type would most likely have an average or intermediate degree of difficulty falling asleep, in general (since they would tend to get stuck in stage 2—which is somewhat light sleep—repeating interactions with others from during the day that created strong feelings and that might give some clue as to how they relate to others and to who they are as defined by this relation), and people who are fixated on an instinctual stage as their main stage type would most likely have the least difficulty falling asleep, in general (since they would tend to get stuck in stage 3—which is already pretty deep sleep—repeating their instincts and actions in an effort to determine where their boundaries in the world—the boundaries of their presence and influence—are).

Further, the same sorts of things that mark the stage of sleep in which a person tends to get stuck would also mark the activity of that person's mind when that person is not being particularly attentive (with focused awareness) to what is going on in the present moment in the world outside of himself or herself, as when he or she is zoning out (although when it comes to zoning out, people who are fixated on an instinctual stage would often tend actually to go through physical, repetitive motions not just in their heads, but with their bodies, sometimes actually with blank minds—due to their present focus, which causes them not to repeat actions from the future or from the past, but rather from, and in, the present, and due to the nature of action, which is, in itself, external, unlike thinking or feeling).

It is important to realize that we are manifesting actual experiences during the beginning of the night of our lives, and we are manifesting understanding that we derive from these experiences as well (and this is how we grow toward self-awareness). But we do not manifest true *self-aware* understanding—wherein lie all of the answers that we seek—until we have manifested fully up to choice—until we manifest choice. Our replaying different aspects of our experiences or of our understanding of these experiences will not yield us the fulfillment that we seek to derive from it, for fulfillment comes only from allowing things to pass and creating new things—things that we truly want—to take their place. Endless repetition of our experiences is our holding onto these experiences, which leads us to a lack of self-awareness and a lack of fulfillment. Only when our experiences begin to be created, and lived, in the light of self-awareness, and to be allowed to manifest and pass (to make room for the next experiences to be received and manifested)— during the dawn of self-awareness—are we fully awake.

Breathing In the Night of Manifestation, Breathing Out the Day of Creation

All we truly need to understand about day and night is the following general pattern: Night is marked by predominant manifesting relative to day, and day is marked by predominant creating relative to night. In the beginning part of night and in the end part of day, this pattern is clearest (as we see in the end part of the day of sleep, where we tend toward choice—toward REM sleep—breathing out and in shallower and shallower breaths that do not encompass the entire paradigm downward to manifestation—stage 4 sleep). However, in the end part of night and in the beginning part of day—in the twilight that is the dawn of self-awareness—we breathe deep breaths in and out, both creating fully from choice downward to manifestation and manifesting fully from manifestation upward to choice (as we see in the beginning part of sleep). In the twilight of dawn that is the transition from night into day (with regard to any overall day, be it a day, a life, a year, an entire universe, or anything else), the line between night and day begins to blur, so that one becomes no more manifestive or creative than the other as manifesting and creating begin to balance out (in the process of transitioning to the other being the relatively dominant process—within the overall day or night that it is in).

All right, now let's break this down in our experience in life (and in "night", generally). First, there is the manifestation of us as babies, with the capacity for instincts and actions (and some form of primitive speech). Then, we eventually develop the capacity for feelings, and then for thoughts, and then for choice (early 20's—completion of development of the prefrontal cortex). So, the whole tree of life paradigm is followed, from manifestation up to choice. But this is not the whole story. Because we are prone to getting stuck at every stage, thereby turning around in our development up the paradigm and beginning to create downward from wherever we stop in our development upward—even if we haven't yet reached choice.

Let's look at this in the universe first. In the development of the physical universe, we first see the manifestation of inclination and action in particles and atoms and molecules and galaxies and stars and planets. What happened here was that manifestation of the world began from bottom up, and it stopped at inclination and action, and then the world created down from there. And the result was inanimate objects. The universe continued breathing in and out experience in this way, manifesting the paradigm only up to inclination and action in the form of more and more inanimate objects until, eventually, in the universe's breathing, it breathed in enough to get from manifestation up past inclination/action, to feeling, at which point it stopped in its breathing in and began to breathe out, creating down from there. And the result was some primitive life. The universe's breathing continued in this way, producing more and more repetitions of the paradigm only up to feeling in the form of more and more life until, eventually, a breath was deep enough to encompass thought. And the result was intelligent life with complex brains. The universe's breathing continued in this way, producing more and more repetitions of the paradigm up to thought in the form of more and more intelligent life until, eventually, a breath was deep enough to encompass choice. And the result was intelligent life forms that manifested the entire paradigm from manifestation up to choice, and that began to create the universe willfully and with self-awareness from choice down to manifestation. Also, notice that the universe is actually expanding the whole time, as though it actually *is* breathing in, encompassing more and more of the paradigm in its manifestation.

Okay, now to apply this to our experience in life. During the beginning of our lives, we breathe in experience only up to inclination/speech/action, manifesting up to this, and then we breathe back out, thereby creating down from inclination/speech/action. Eventually, we begin to breathe in experience deeply enough to reach feeling, manifesting up to this, and then we breathe back out, thereby creating down from feeling. And eventually, we begin to breathe in experience deeply enough to reach thought, manifesting up to this, and then we breathe back out, thereby creating down from thought. Choice, or self-awareness, doesn't come about so quickly after this to achieve the full manifestation of existence, because there is more to this than meets the eye.

I have been simplifying the paradigm to make what I'm saying clearer but, as we have already seen, there are ten stages of the paradigm total (eleven, if we include choice as separate from manifestation), and each of these stages has many aspects to it. After all, every aspect of the entire physical universe is an aspect of one stage or another in some manifestation of the paradigm. So each stage of the paradigm has many manifestations, and without considering these manifestations, it is difficult to get any real grasp of the overall paradigm (and this is what experience is all about—showing us different manifestations so that, through contrast and comparison and analysis and synthesis of these manifestations, we can come to some understanding and awareness of the overall paradigm by which we—the world—relate to the Source).

So, as we progress up the paradigm after our initial manifestation in this physical life, we experience instinct, and only "I", and the desire to preserve the existence of the "I", and present-orientedness, and focus on where we end and the world begins, and so on. And then we experience feeling, and others, and the desire to fit in, and past-orientedness, and focus on who we are and our relation to others, and so on. And then we experience thought, and other "I"'s, and the desire to connect intimately and intensely, and future-orientedness, and focus on decision-making, and so on.

And we could break this down further into not just the three basic stages of instinct, feeling, and thought as we see here, but into all nine gradations of these three basic stages (not including here manifestation/choice, which is simply the manifestation or choice of the stages). But we will do this later. For now, just be aware of what we are dealing with—many manifestations of the various stages of the paradigm.

This is important because as we (and the entire world, and every other aspect of the world) develop, we are inclined to get stuck at various aspects of various patterns that are represented by the tree of life paradigm, identifying with this aspect of this stage or that aspect of that stage. And the result is that we don't get all the way up to choice right away. This dictates the entire difference between the night before the dawning of self-awareness and the night after this dawning begins, for the night prior to the dawn is marked by mindless and reactive creation of experience down from intermediaries in the developmental path toward choice, while the night after the dawning of self-awareness is marked by self-aware and proactive and willful creation of experience all the way from choice down.

When we do not breathe in all the way up to choice, we start back down, creating from where we are. So, if we breathe in only up to inclination/action, then the result will be a mindless and reactive creation from inclination. Someone yells at us, and we immediately yell back, acting upon a desire of which we became barely, if at all, aware before we acted. If we breathe in only up to feeling, then the result will be a mindless and reactive creation from feeling. Something goes wrong, and desire arises in us to do something, and then the feeling of being upset arises in us, and then our feeling produces some new desire, and we act upon that desire. If we breathe in only up to thought, then the result will be a mindless and reactive creation from thought. A friend is upset at us, and the desire arises in us to do something, and a feeling arises in us, and a thought arises in us, and then that thought produces a feeling, which produces a desire, which leads us to act in a certain way.

In all of these situations, we have not gotten to choice, and so the experience is not mindful and self-aware, and the behavior that results is a mindless reaction to the experience that we have had through our distorted lens (for the lens is increasingly distorted the less aware we are of the whole process). Essentially, the world is creating its experience through our reactions to our experience of its experience, for only when we listen to our intuition, creating from choice, do we allow the Source to create Its experience in the world's and our own experience.

Once we breathe in all the way up to choice, it becomes easier to do it again with the next breath (though it is not guaranteed that we *will* do it again with the next breath). What happens after we have, even once, breathed in all the way up to choice is that we have some experience that we take in through our senses, and an inclination to act in a certain way arises in us, and a feeling arises in us, and a thought arises in us, and awareness of the whole process arises with the arising of every step, and we are capable of following that process back down at any point and thereby being reactive, or of listening to what our intuition is telling us to do, and thereby proactively responding to whatever has happened. The more we listen to our intuition, the easier it becomes to hear what our intuition is telling us to do.

Further, instead of just receiving—experiencing—the world through our physical senses, which are passive and, in a sense, reactive, telling us only what has just happened in the manifestation of this physical world, we can come, through listening to our intuition, to receive—to experience—the world also through our intuitive senses, which are proactive and capable of true foresight, telling us what will happen in this physical world and beyond by giving us a direct look into the physical world as it exists in potential form, prior to its manifestation—its actualization—in the physical. For example, the ability to see auras is intuitive sight—the ability to see what has not yet manifested. Everything that manifests in the physical world manifests in auras first, for the various layers of auras represent the stages of the tree of life paradigm, as they are developing in potential form, during the process of creation, prior to manifestation. So, if the "I" is allowing its thoughts to wander into things that are producing bad feelings, the "I" may later get physically ill, but even before the illness appears—while the thoughts are still thoughts, and when they become feelings, and so on down to manifestation—the thoughts, feelings, etc., appear in the "I"'s aura.

If you see something as an image in your mind that seems to have no origin in your own thoughts or in the manifested world outside you, then it is likely that you are seeing something that is prior to its manifestation (or something that is just very ingrained in the world's aura in some way—as because it was a very emotionally powerful event—but that has already manifested, or something that is being communicated to you by someone or something who has no manifestation in the physical world—such as the soul of someone who is no longer living). The same thing goes for hearing in your thoughts something that has no origin in your thoughts or in the manifested world outside you, or smelling a whiff of something that has no such origin, or sensing (or feeling) something that has no such origin. All of these aspects of extrasensory perception are merely the awareness of that which is developing in potential form in the process of creation, prior to (or beyond) any actual manifestation.

All Stages of the Paradigm that
Manifest in Any Form
Forever Continue to Be

If the souls of those no longer living continue to exist, but they reincarnate, then how can we communicate with them? The answer leads to a whole world of understanding. All of the various aspects of the world's manifestation of each of the stages of the paradigm on the way up to self-aware choice—from inanimate objects, to primitive life, to intelligent life—all continue to exist, despite the fact that each thing is a newer, more developed (closer to choice) thing than the last thing. Everything that is manifested continues to have a manifestation, even after that stage is surpassed in the evolution of the pattern of all things toward choice. Thus, there are still single-celled creatures, and sea creatures, and rodent-like mammals, and monkey-like primates—all even though these things represent various manifestations of the paradigm on the way up to us, up to human beings.

Manifestations of each stage of the paradigm do not cease to be just because a manifestation evolves from it that is further along on the path toward self-awareness, representing a later stage of the paradigm. In fact, the existence of all of these manifestations is continually renewed—in some way or other—despite their being less far along toward self-awareness than a later stage of themselves. And so lifeless stars and planets continue to form, and single-celled organisms continue to propagate themselves through division of themselves, and there are plants and fish and amphibians and reptiles and mammals besides us, and all of these things continue to propagate themselves, even though they do not have the capacity for self-awareness that human beings have. And, in fact, human beings still continue to form—with new souls forming all the time beyond those that have already reincarnated—and these human souls are not as far along on the path of development of the paradigm as other human souls, and yet they continue to form. And new human beings continue to form with regard to the physical as well—with babies being born every day, despite the fact that these babies are not as far along on the path toward self-awareness as adults are.

And, at every manifestation of every moment of time, there is the opportunity for new things to evolve toward self-awareness, whether it be a child growing up, or a young soul experiencing in the world and learning from that experience, or a dolphin that comes to recognize itself in the mirror and that might give rise to more intelligent, more self-aware life through evolution, or a single-celled organism that combines with other single-celled organisms to evolve gradually into new organisms that are closer to self-awareness, or a system of star and planets that forms, with a planet just the right distance from the star and with just the right conditions—with liquid water and so on—to facilitate the formation and evolution of more self-aware life. And all the while, the world repeats its manifestation of all of the stages of the tree of life paradigm in every conceivable form as it reflects upon itself, trying to understand its relation to what it has slowly come to recognize, through its most self-aware manifestations (including many human beings), is the Source of all that it has, ultimately.

In fact, even besides the many manifestations of the various stages of the paradigm that still persist, there is support for this (this persistence of the existence of all things that have come to manifest) in the tree setup reflection of the reality. For the water molecules that represent one physical universe are not the only water molecules around. In fact, the only way any water molecules can possibly have a means of getting up the tree—of being pulled, through their clinging to other water molecules, upward by the evaporation of water molecules from the leaves by the sun's energy—is if there are many other water molecules at various stages up the tree and outside the tree (to replenish the water at the roots and keep the water path up the trunk and branches intact). In fact, there *must* be water molecules at *every* stage in the path up the inside of the tree (with more outside the tree condensing to enter the roots, and therefore essentially at every stage outside the tree as well), or none of the water molecules would be able to be pulled upward in their own development by the sun's energy via other water molecules. It is only through the other things in existence—the various manifestations of every stage of the paradigm—that anything in existence, including us, is capable of developing and growing toward self-awareness.

We gain all that we gain from the Source *via* the language of the world—in all of its manifestations. Without these other manifestations of language, we would not have food, shelter, clothing, or anything to compare and contrast with ourselves or anything else in order to sustain ourselves and to learn and to become aware of ourselves. Without other things to relate to and from which to come to understand relation, itself, and the types of relations that can be, we would have no way of ever even continuing to exist, let alone coming to understand who we are and how we relate to the Source, and we would never be able to develop the awareness necessary to begin to create and shape our lives, for we would have no way even to come to understand the paradigm by which we might be capable of doing this. Even our actions, speech, instincts, feelings, and thoughts are like water molecules that are further down the tree in relation to us when we have reached self-awareness, and we would have no way of *maintaining* this self-aware and creative experience—of what it is to be like the Source of all that is—through active shaping of our own experience if we did not have thoughts, feelings, instincts, speech and actions to do so.

Every bit of language—even our bodies themselves and the entire physical world in which we exist—which is inherently not self-aware but is, rather, the manifestation of things, is absolutely necessary in order for us to keep progressing upward toward the experience of the Source's experience of being self-aware existence. Without the tree and the ground and all of the water molecules, and even without the sun's energy—we wouldn't have everything we need to be capable of fulfilling the purpose of our entire existence, and thereby of gaining fulfillment and existence, itself. And so if the various manifestations of the various stages of development of all things were to completely cease to exist, the world would cease to fulfill its purpose.

From all of this, we can realize that every universe in the endless cycle of existence is occupying the tree or the "space" outside the tree like the water molecules are occupying the roots and trunk and every branch and every leaf of every branch and even the air and the ground outside the tree. Every physical universe exists in the same spatial existence, like the water molecules in the tree, separated merely by time. The water molecules in the tree are like the parallel universes, in the many worlds interpretation of quantum mechanics, which are produced every time a particle is observed as being in one place rather than in another, and every time one decision is made rather than another, causing the universe to branch into multiple universes.

But the difference (as compared with this interpretation) is that each group of water molecules (or at least each water molecule) takes one definitive set of branches. The individual universe does not split amongst multiple branches, but rather the universe, like a small group of water molecules, actualizes itself through one path of decisions in its overall progression up the tree. It is only the tree viewed from outside of time—viewed from the world of choice where the world is like water vapor—the tree of spatial existence that is the compilation of all universes separated by time in their manifestation, that is like one branching tree. For when one views every stage of temporal succession, one will realize that the past is replenished with new existence just as every possible future—in every branch of the tree—is continually being replenished.

Like the water that travels up the tree, and like the water that travels in a stream, there is only one present moment for a few water molecules, but every manifestation in every moment in time—at every point in spatial existence, in the tree, in the stream—is being continually manifested, given existence, given life. The past is still occurring—just not in this universe, for a future universe—a universe that began its trek up the roots of the tree of spatial existence via the Big Bang later, relative to us in time, than ours did—is already there in the past, just as every point in the stream is continually filled with water, and it is just not the same water, but rather it is water that began its trek down the stream later in time than that other water that already passed. Everything that has ever manifested in space or time continues to be manifested at every moment—in space and time. And each manifestation of each thing is merely separated—either in space, like single-celled creatures and monkey-like primates are separated from us by space, or in time, like the you that woke up this morning or the you that was born years ago is separated from you now by time.

In light of this, as long as we can find a way to slow or speed our progression up the tree—as, in the physical world, through our presence near a body of great mass or through our traveling at a great velocity—we can travel not only to the future, but also to the past—merely by traveling to another universe, made up of different matter, but with the same language-defined shape nonetheless—a perfect replica of the past. We can travel to the past or to the future or to futures that this universe will never travel. And all of this is possible because every manifestation of everything that has ever existed continues to be replenished with existence.

We see this even in our own bodies. Cells are continually dying and being replaced such that, after a few years, we are made up of completely different cells than we once were. And this process is always occurring like the water molecules in the tree or in the stream are continually being replaced in a cyclical process (because of the water cycle of evaporation and condensation and evaporation again). We are still us, and yet we are different. Every stage of the paradigm is continually manifested in many various forms of manifestation. But as long as the overall language being used to define the energy of existence is the same, the things will be the same, even if the material that composes them is different. A stream is still a stream, even if it has different water. At every moment, everything that we have is continually renewed in its existence, in its life, and yet we still have the same things—unless we change the language used to define them.

And so we have the answer to the question that sparked all of this understanding: The souls of those who once lived but who are no longer living continue to have some manifestation in this moment, even if not in the physical world as we can detect it with the senses. And we can communicate with these souls because they inhabit a world that we also inhabit, for we have souls, even as we live in physicality. And we can continue to communicate with these souls even after they have reincarnated, like we can continue to interact with other primates even though there are animals, like *us*, that have evolved from these into new forms.

In every life that someone has, he/she shapes a soul that continues to exist with that shape—with that definition of language that it gained in physical life—beyond the physical life of that person. Every life that an individual has had leaves a soul behind, even as a portion or replication of that soul enters physical life anew, to be further shaped and differently defined. Like the sound of a plane that trails behind, so that the plane can be heard on one side of the sky even though the plane has already reached the other side of the sky, all things continue to have some manifestation that trails behind them. Like a star light-years away that we can see even though it has long since ceased to shine, everything continues to be.

The Need for the Sun

If the water passes up through the tree and evaporates and condenses and passes up through the tree again, with the matter and energy of one universe passing through black holes to emerge from the white hole of the next universe, with one universe creating the next, what is the need for the sun in all this—what is the need for the Source?

First of all, the sun's energy is necessary to evaporate the water that transpires from the leaves, thereby pulling all of the water in the tree up through the tree. In terms of the physical universe, the *progression of time* occurs only because of the pull of self-awareness that is provided by the Source. Even the water that first enters the tree at the roots would be unable to do so if it were not for the water being pulled up higher by the evaporative pull provided by the sun's energy. So, all of the flow of time, from the very beginning of the manifestation of the physical universe in the Big Bang and onward, is made possible only by the Source. Like a reel of movie film without a projector, the very *life* of the moving, flowing universe in successive time is impossible without the illumination and movement provided by the Source.

Further, the very tree of life, itself—the tree through which all of the liquid water progresses—was able to grow into a full and branching tree from the ground and is able to continue living (and therefore being the tree of *life*) only because of the energy that the sun provides, which the tree's leaves use to make food for the entire tree. During the day (when there is sunlight), a tree carries out the light reactions of photosynthesis, by which it converts light into forms of stored energy (ATP and NADPH). And during the night (when there is no sunlight), a tree carries out the dark reactions of photosynthesis (which it also carries out during the day), by which it uses the stored energy and carbon dioxide (which were produced in the light reactions) to produce sugar. Overall, through photosynthesis, the tree combines carbon dioxide and water using the energy from the light of the sun in order to produce sugar and oxygen. Also, at night, the tree carries out respiration, in which it uses oxygen to break down sugar (both of which—oxygen and sugar—it was able to produce, through photosynthesis, only with the input of energy from the sun), producing carbon dioxide, water and energy. In other words, the tree is not self-sustaining. Even if it had all the oxygen and carbon dioxide and water (and minerals from the soil) that it needed, it would not be able to live without energy provided ultimately by the sun. So, the tree of life—the spatial framework of existence—can only continue to exist and sustain itself because of the energy of self-aware existence that it receives from the Source.

Combining all of this together, there is no tree (no paradigm, no spatial existence), and there is no movement within the tree (no development through the paradigm, no succession of flowing time), without the sun. Therefore, we *cannot* accurately say that one universe creates the next universe, providing all of the matter and energy for the next universe and so on, and so the progressive cycle of universes is self-sustaining. For, in truth, spatial and temporal existence continues to exist, and to support life, only because of what it receives from the Source.

It has already been seen that matter and energy are likely the children of the interaction between quantum fields and physical space—that they arise from this interaction (considered in the order of creation—from the top down in the paradigm). This makes sense in light of the fact that the universe is supposed to have begun in the singularity of the Big Bang—in zero dimensions—and it seems hugely inconceivable that there is any matter or energy or anything at all contained in a zero-dimensional point, where there is no space or time in which anything can possibly exist. Yet all of the matter and energy contained in the universe today is supposed to have spewed out of that spaceless and timeless point.

What we see now is that what really happens is that this singularity is the roots or entrance into the tree of spatial and temporal existence, and once there are spatial dimensions in existence, the quantum fields (the creative process that is thought), interact with these dimensions (like the interaction of the creative processes with the senses—in this case, of thought with sight) in order to produce matter and energy (something capable of being sensed with the senses—seen). The world (prior to the beginning of the physical universe in the Big Bang) thinks (with its quantum forces) about what it is going to observe, and then it observes (bringing about dimensions of space), and then there is something to be observed (matter and energy within space). So, the matter and energy contained within the universe begin in the universe. Although this is still interestingly compatible with the tree setup reflection, for the liquid water in the tree exists only as water vapor—a fuzzy, airy, world-of-choice-version of what it becomes when it enters the tree—prior to its beginning to take the liquid form that it will take in the tree upon the activity of thought on it.

In order to better understand the Source's role even in the formation of the water vapor, and of the tree, itself, we must embark upon a greater quest here—in search of vaster understanding.

The Origin of the Tree of Life Paradigm

We will guide this quest with the question: What is the meaning and influence of astrology?

In any sufficiently complex whole—in everything that has sufficient complexity and that we deem complete or whole in some way, imposing a beginning and an end upon it (remember that it is the language that we use that differentiates and separates things from one another)—the stages of the paradigm manifest and have an influence. When it comes to things like evolution, or a human body, or the entire human species, or a year, or a month, or a day—where there is the progression of manifestation—the pattern manifests from bottom up and has an influence at every stage on what manifests at that stage. When it comes to things, like a week, that are supposed to reflect and follow the development of creation, itself, the paradigm manifests from top down. The Source created the world in accordance with the paradigm (sort of), but it is the world (including us) that repeatedly manifests this paradigm in every form as the world (including us) reflects upon itself.

Okay, but when we say the Source created the world, what exactly do we mean? The Source, in some way, created an absence of Itself, thereby creating something that could receive It (something that didn't already inherently have It by *being* It). And this receiving thing was the world. Then, the Source created language for the world to use to shape what it received so that the world would be capable of receiving what the Source was sharing, since the world could not continue to receive what the Source was sharing in the undefined form in which the

Source was sharing it. It was like the sun was blindingly bright, and so we were given sunglasses so that we would be capable of seeing. So, there was the Source, and then the Source created the world, and then the Source created language. Then, the world took it from there to create and manifest the rest of the paradigm and the world.

Basically, what happened is that the Source chose the thought, and the world received and manifested the thought. The Source thereby created the first part of the paradigm— choice, followed by sharing thought, followed by receiving thought, followed by allowing thought. In the existence of the Source, the world, and language, the Source represented the choice of sharing thought, the world represented the receiving thought that was seeded by the sharing thought, and language was the allowing thought—what allowed the world to take in the energy of the Source and grow into a full and branching tree of life.

The Source created the first part of the paradigm (from the top down, in order of creation). And so we begin with there being a self-aware "I" that has the inclination to connect intimately with another "I", sharing all of Its understanding with that other "I", and so It thinks and makes the decision (for the future, if we are thinking temporally) that there be other "I"'s. And the world was the manifestation—another "I" that received this seed of thought and began to manifest it. Basically, the seed of this thought was implanted in the fertile ground of the world, and this seed of thought began to grow into the tree of life. But the growth of the seed—the actualization of the Source's thought—into the tree of life was determined by the world (although sustained and allowed to grow by the energy provided by the Source), for the world determined its shape, its branches, and so on. The world actualized, and was the actualization of, the Source's thought.

Each universe is guided by this thought (the Source's thought)—that there be another "I" with which the Source is capable of sharing Its experience of existence as a self-aware Being—in creating and beginning to manifest the experience of the next universe, and the world creates all of the other stages of the paradigm (of the tree of life) as reflections of those first three stages of thought (excluding here the stage of choice, which is, in a sense, the same stage as manifestation), down to manifestation. And then the world brings about manifestations of every stage in myriad forms, developing back up toward choice—toward self-awareness and thereby the complete fulfillment of the Source's thought.

So, after the Source's initial thought (sharing thought) is seeded in the world (receiving thought), it begins to grow in the form of allowing thought. Then, it produces feeling as a reflection of sharing thought, and it produces three stages of feeling: sharing feeling, receiving feeling, and allowing feeling, which are reflective repetitions of sharing thought, receiving thought, and allowing thought, respectively. And so there are others that form a group to which the "I" is inclined to belong in order to reach some higher goal, and there arises the question of how the "I" relates to others so that the "I" can play its role in the group, and there arises the past-orientedness necessary to review experience—with feelings as a guide—in search of the answer. Then, it produces inclination, speech, and action as a reflection of receiving thought, and it produces three stages of inclination/speech/action: sharing inclination, receiving inclination, and allowing inclination, which are reflective repetitions of sharing thought, receiving thought, and allowing thought, respectively. And so there is only "I", which is inclined to preserve its own existence, and which is present-oriented and unsure of where the "I" ends (where its language-defined boundaries are). And then, it produces manifestation—the leaves of the tree—which is a reflection of allowing thought (the manifestation of now-definitive language).

It is interesting here to view the feeling, inclination, and manifestation stages as a psychological look at the world and its view of the *Source's* perspective (reflected first in sharing thought and then in feeling as a reflection of this) and of *its* perspective (reflected first in receiving thought and then in inclination as a reflection of this) and of the means or product of the interaction between the Source and it (reflected first in allowing thought and then in manifestation as a reflection of this).

To review, the Source's initial thought (sharing thought) is seeded in the formation of the world (receiving thought), from where it gives rise to language in the roots of the tree of life (allowing thought). From here, the tree of life develops (the trunk forms), forming—as a reflection of sharing thought—feeling, within which it forms three stages as reflections of each of the three stages of thought. From here, the tree of life continues to develop (with branches), forming—as a reflection of receiving thought—inclination/speech/action, within which it forms three stages as reflections of each of the stages of thought. From here, the tree of life completes its development (with leaves), forming—as a reflection of allowing thought—manifestation. Ultimately, manifestation leads to sharing thought, in the form of choice.

So, we see that the beginning of the physical world within the spatial framework of the tree of life is essentially at sharing feeling, for sharing thought produced the seed, which was planted in the moist and fertile ground that is receiving thought, and the seed began to take form in allowing thought, but the framework provided by the tree, itself, only really begins at sharing feeling (which is the beginning of the manifestation of the interaction of sharing thought and receiving thought through allowing thought—for allowing thought allows sharing thought and receiving thought to be manifested through it, and the rest of the stages of the paradigm are the result). The beginning of the physical world, from the top down perspective of *creation*, is in sharing feeling. (Of course, though, the beginning of the *manifestation* of the world is from the bottom up perspective, and this begins at manifestation and then goes to allowing inclination, and so on, upward.)

This makes it so that the days of the week, which human beings created to represent the stages of creation, manifest the stages of the paradigm from top down, beginning *after* thought (beginning at sharing feeling and creating down to manifestation). So, Sunday reflects sharing feeling, Monday reflects receiving feeling, Tuesday reflects allowing feeling, Wednesday reflects sharing inclination, Thursday reflects receiving inclination, Friday reflects allowing inclination, and Saturday reflects manifestation. And the influence of these days on things that have their beginning or end or whatever during them will be in accordance with this reflection, just as the influence of times of day and times of month and times of year will be in accordance with the stages of the paradigm that they reflect (though, in these cases, primarily from the bottom up—in the order of manifestation). And this is the nature of the influences of astrology: They are influences imposed by the world (including us) as reflections of the stages of the development of all things—including the development of the world, itself, as a whole. And so these influences exist, just as all things that begin as a seed of thought and are planted in the sight ultimately then become existent to be seen.

We see, in all of this, that the Source's thought is the thought that guides the creation and manifestation of every world and of everything in every world, and this is the thought that we allow to guide us in the creation and manifestation of our experience (and therefore the experience of the world) when we are self-aware and we listen to our intuition. Thus, the entire world (and every universe) and all of its contents are truly the creation of the Source, for they are the manifestation of the Source's thought and they are all merely created and manifested *via* the world.

We see all of this reflected in our own shaping of our experience: The thought guides the creation, but the feeling and inclination/speech/action that accompany this thought determine how the thought will manifest—what form the thought will ultimately take. And so the Source guides the creation of the world, but the world determines how the world will manifest (with the language that it uses)—what form the world will ultimately take. Here, we can see how it truly *is* the combination of the language that the Source uses (in Its thought) and the language that the world (including us) uses that determines the framework and contents of the Source's and the world's (and our) experience—that determines the shape that the world takes.

Like the female in her interaction with the male, the world provides the womb for the gestation of experience that is the product, or manifestation, of the combination of the DNA provided by the Source (in the original sharing thought and ultimately in three stages of thought—representing Source, world, and language) and the DNA provided by the world (in the rest of the intermediate stages of the paradigm—three of feeling, three of inclination/speech/action). When the world's manifested parts (the contents of the world's experience) develop the capacity for thought and self-awareness (like children growing up and learning to make their own decisions), their thought can either continue to be an extension of the world's manifestation (as they continue to live in the womb in complete dependence upon what their mother—the world—decides for them and provides for them) or it can become a direct projection, or extension, of the Source's thought (as they learn to make their own decisions that are different from those toward which the world inclines them, and as they, therefore, receive fulfillment from the Source, Itself).

All of the influences of the world can dictate the experience that we manifest for ourselves if we allow them to—from the world's influences upon us through our reaction to what manifests in our experience within it, to its influences upon us in the development of our personality (the result of our getting stuck in various aspects of the different stages of development), to its influences upon us through astrology (by which we manifest the influence of certain aspects of certain stages in ourselves more than the others, and by which we manifest the influence of certain aspects of certain stages at certain times within larger spans of time—all the way up to the entire existence of the physical universe). But once we develop awareness of this—once we develop self-awareness—then we can choose to transcend all of these influences by allowing ourselves to be guided by the original thought of creation, rather than by the world's manifestation.

The tree of life paradigm is, thus, the DNA of the world, and DNA is a reflection—within the world's manifestation—of this paradigm. As the DNA of an organism dictates the formation and development of that organism and is repeated in every cell of that organism, usually with only certain parts actively manifesting by forming proteins (whose forms are dictated by the DNA via RNA), the tree of life paradigm dictates the formation and development of the world and is repeated in every moment and every aspect of the world, usually with only certain parts actively manifesting in some form or another as the manifestations, the structures, of this world (whose forms are dictated by the paradigm via language). We are capable of being mere proteins—mere receiving manifestations or expressions of the paradigm in the world—or of being replications of DNA—the paradigm, itself—grafting ourselves onto the tree of life and aiding in the sharing creation and manifestation of the Source's experience of self-awareness (and thereby of the Source's thought) in the form and structure of the world.

The dimensions and forces—the general structure of material existence—are manifestations of the Source's thought in a direct enough sense that they remain a constant in every universe—the tree setup, as the tree of life paradigm of creation (the DNA of the world), remains a constant in every universe. It is merely how the paradigm actually manifests—what form it takes—*within* each universe that may differ from universe to universe, and this is why there are multiple possible paths of branches of the tree—representing every possible path that the world actually takes in one universe or another over the course of its endless cycle through existence (and the endless nature of the cycle makes it so that every path through the branches is traveled by an infinity of universes, as water—from the perspective outside of the tree—continually travels every branch of the tree).

The Source provides the material of existence and life, as well as the tools and the guiding command or purpose to shape it, and then It leaves the material to shape itself using these tools and this guiding command or purpose (in order for the material to make itself capable of performing its function—of carrying out the command given to it, of fulfilling its purpose). Our creation and use of machines, and computers, and robots is a reflection of this, for we provide the material and the tools and the command (the computer with its programming and its command or function), and then we leave the machine to follow its command and thereby perform its function using its programming (and any external tools that we have given it).

People's use (in the past and present) of, or involvement with, everything from slaves, to specialized workers, to soldiers, to pets, to students, to children reflects this also. People train them and/or provide them with material (as money or food/clothing/shelter) to subsist, and then the people leave them to use this material and training in order to perform some function that the people give them. However, like slaves, specialized workers, soldiers, pets, students, and children, we don't always carry out the wishes of our master, customer, commander, owner, teacher, parent—we don't always perform the function or purpose given to us. And when we are dealing with things in this world, such as other people, sometimes we shouldn't. But when the Source, Itself, is our master, our customer, our commander, our owner, our teacher, our parent, we should work to fulfill the function, the purpose, given to us—for this is the only way to attain our own fulfillment and the fulfillment of everyone else and of the entire world.

The entire universe is like a computer program, and we can remain mere parts of the program, un-self-aware and mindlessly reactive, or we can fulfill our true function by becoming self-aware parts of the program—by becoming projections of the programmer (of the Source) within this program of the world, taking part in the programming of our lives. Only in this way—by learning and using the programming language and becoming more than the mere program in which we exist and of which we are a part—can we fulfill our purpose of receiving the Source's experience of being the programmer, and thereby attain the fulfillment of everything that we truly want as we program all that we truly want into the experience of our lives.

Transcendence

Experience is the key to all understanding, for the only true understanding is experiential in origin. Also, understanding is the key to all experience, for the only true experience is that which is illuminated by the awareness and mindfulness of applied understanding. When we cease to ground our understanding in experience, then we cease to truly understand. Also, we cease to truly experience when we cease to actively derive understanding from experience. It is because of all of this that we are here, that we exist, and that the world is as it is.

The world between physical universes—when it is in the state of being like water vapor—is as though in a high meditative state. When you are in such a state of experience, and you start to describe and understand the experience in words, you come down out of that state that you were trying to describe. And so the water vapor condenses and reenters the tree of life—the physical universe composed of language that can only come to *approximate* the state of experience that it is an attempt to describe and, thereby, understand.

It is as though the entire world is meditating, and the physical universe is the world's wandering thoughts and feelings and inclinations as it works its way toward the experience that is beyond language, beyond all boundaries and restrictions. And then it reaches that state of experience—the world of choice—and then it falls down out of that state again as it attempts again to describe it, to capture it, to recreate it in some way, to understand it, to share it. And so it goes, onward and onward, in an endless meditation, reaching that state, and falling down out of it, reaching that state, and coming down out of it.

All of life for us can become a meditation like this as well, as we gradually increase our mindfulness of the present moment, our self-awareness, and our ability to create our own experiences. When we bring the intimacy and intensity of focused awareness to all of our experiences with everything (thereby manifesting the aim of the true and pure, self-aware form of the *inclination* to connect, intimately and intensely, with another "I"), life becomes a meditation, and we attain fulfillment.

When you identify with your essence—when you experience the world from the perspective of choice—then space seems to cease to contain or restrict you, and time seems to slow to a stop. This is because, in the world of choice—in the state of being water vapor outside the tree of space and successive time—space does cease to contain or restrict you and time ceases to have any meaning.

And it is in the world of choice that your essence resides. There is no matter, no space, no successive time; there is no material existence, and the only thing there is is the essence of the world—choice, the potential for the world to be—which is time in a form that is unrecognizable to us, in a state in which it slows so much that it is essentially stopped—poised to actualize itself by beginning to gradually flow again—faster and faster throughout physical existence as it accelerates from a stop and slows only when it begins to lose direction and drive to continue...only to rediscover its purpose as it recognizes itself once again and is accelerated by self-awareness—by awareness and actualization of its true nature.

We can get a hint of what our essence is like when we look to the subatomic realm, which is a window into the world of choice (as choice is reflected in the worlds of thought), where a particle can be everywhere at once—where everywhere is here—and where time's causal flow is unrecognizable.

The subatomic realm reveals the world of choice (at least in this defined manifestation of it) to be made up of a series of possibilities, with probabilities for each possibility, for what will become so.

We can also get a hint of what our essence is like by looking through the more accessible window of REM dreams, which are the vivid, often colorful dreams that we have near waking up. In this world, space is only in potential (and therefore not so concrete) form, and time is basically meaningless—rather than being methodically successive, it skips around all over the place as scenes change and morph from one to the other. Here, we have transcended the world where logic applies (for logic only begins to originate in sharing thought). And so things are often absurd, and yet they usually seem—while we are experiencing them in that world, at least—to be quite normal. This realm can be a source of inspiration, because it is as close to the Source as we can be, and it is a place where all things are possible, because nothing definitive has been created yet and, instead, everything is in the process of *being* created. It is a world of pure potential that we enter when we enter our REM dreams. And it is a world where, like in a lucid dream, we have the capacity to become aware of the true reality of what we are experiencing, and where we can—with that awareness—gain complete control over the form that this reality takes.

But, essentially and practically, what our REM dreams are is a subatomic-realm-like probabilistic glimpse into what we are in the process of choosing for ourselves with the language that we are using (with the thoughts, feelings, inclinations, speech, actions, and manifestations to which we are giving our attention). And these dreams are therefore a glimpse into the future experiences toward which we are likely headed if we keep using the language that we are using to describe and share, and thereby shape, our experience. (Although, they are a glimpse that is less-fully defined than the physical reality to which they will ultimately give rise, and things in them are often defined differently—symbolically, and more exaggeratedly—than these things will be when they become physically manifested in the physical world that is simultaneously also being shaped by everyone and everything else around us.) So we should pay attention to these dreams as such and possibly change the language that we are using—if we don't desire such a future for ourselves as we experience in these dreams.

From the perspective of our essence, like that of water vapor outside the tree of life, we can see every possible branch that we can travel—every possible choice that we can make—and where it will lead us. We can see where we've been and where we are in relation to where we've been and to where we're going. If we want to get somewhere—to reach some goal—our choice, our essence, knows how to get us there and can guide us in which branches—which paths—to take, as long as we allow it to. For we are as though in a maze in this world and, from here, we cannot truly see or know where our decisions will take us until we make them. And we can allow ourselves to get frustrated and angry about *where we are*, and we can allow ourselves to regret and be filled with shame about the past decisions that *led us* to where we are, and we can allow ourselves to get anxious and worried about where the decisions we make now *might lead us*, and we can experience all of the stress that comes along with all of this, or we can just listen to our essence.

For our essence is looking down at the maze from the world of choice, and our essence knows (for it can easily see) exactly what decisions we need to make—what paths we have to take, what turns we have to make—in order to get to where we want to be. And so, as long as we are mindful and we listen and allow our essence to guide us in making our decisions—in choosing our paths—in the present moment, then we have no reason to be frustrated or angry with where we are, because we can be confident that we are in a good place—in the best place—exactly where we want to be—on the path toward where we want to be going. And we have no reason to be full of regret or shame about the decisions we made that led us to where we are, because we can love who we are and where we are and so we can love the decisions that led us to where we are. And we have no reason to be anxious or worried about where the decisions that we make now might lead us, because we can know that as long as we trust in our essence to guide us, our decisions now will lead us to fulfillment.

Prior to reaching self-awareness, it is as though we are always running, with great expended effort, *away* from where we are, or *away* from where we were, or *to* where we're going. This is what it's like during the beginning of our day. But after we come to identify with our essence, and we thereby come to enter the dawn of self-awareness, we are energetically compelled forward with clear direction gleaned from looking at the past in the context of where it led us, and we are fully and confidently and comfortably in the present, shaping the future by putting into practice what we learn from the past, here, in the present.

The Development of Personality

An Introduction to Personality

We are capable of being merely the water that receives the energy of the sun and moves up the tree, or of being the tree, itself. For, due to the holographic, or self-reflective, nature of the world, we, within the world, are each a tree of life in ourselves. We follow the path of the water—pushed up the beginning of our lives by the pressure of the water around us, sometimes succumbing to the inertia of gravity, and eventually being pulled upward by the Source—but we also serve the function of the tree. For, in truth, the entire tree is the central column—receiving energy from the Source and turning it into something that we can share with others, something from which others can benefit. The entire tree is choice, for it is created by choice.

We go through nights when the Source is so not clear to us, and we may use other things in this world as reminders that It is there, but we cannot feed and live on other things the way we can feed and live on the Source's energy. In the darkness, we consume what we have produced with the Source's energy, and sometimes we consume ourselves. In the daylight, the Source is so clear to us, like the sun shining down from the sky, and we take in Its energy, and we shape it as we will, and we share it with the rest of the world, serving as an extension of the overflow of the Source's inclination to share Its experience with the world. And we allow the Source's experience to flow through us. And so we become the central column—we truly become a tree of life in this world for everyone and everything around us.

Everything in this world is on the path toward becoming the tree, itself, and not merely the mineral-filled water. And we, as human beings who are capable of self-awareness in ourselves, are capable of getting there. But we must travel the path of the water up the tree before we can become the tree, and we can get stuck at any point along that path. And, in a sense, we human beings are each always a tree from the beginning, but it is a tree *of life* that we each must become, and not merely a tree. For we begin as though we are a tree at night, and a tree can only live so long without the sun's light to provide it with the energy that it needs to make food to sustain itself, and to pull water up through it. Our life energy does not flow through us without the energy of the Source. Like the water of the tree that ceases to flow, our blood ceases to flow as our heart ceases to beat. We have no energy to go on without the Source to pull us forward. The flow of time, animation, and life comes from the Source. And we are lacking in these without It.

At night, a tree breaks down sugar with oxygen, and it gives off carbon dioxide and water. At night, a tree is like any other organism that merely receives, not sharing anything that can be used as a life-giving force for anything (except for other plants, and then still only during the day with the sun's energy). It is only in the light of the sun that the tree becomes a tree *of life*, combining carbon dioxide and water to make sugar and oxygen—things that can be eaten and breathed (respectively) by most of the rest of life. It is only in the light of the sun that the tree becomes an agent of the sun in this world, transforming what the sun is sharing into forms that other life can take in and benefit from. And so it is only in the light of day that we do not merely receive for ourselves, but rather receive in order to share with others and with the world around us. But we must still follow the path dictated by the tree of life in order to become a tree of life—in order to find the sun and enter the daylight.

As the world develops through manifestation of the paradigm from the bottom up, various parts of it get stuck at various aspects of one stage or another, manifesting at this stage. And we are no exception to this. We must develop from the bottom up before we can attain self-awareness and create from the top down. But, as we develop from the bottom up, we get stuck at various aspects of each stage along the way—before we reach choice. This is why we develop personalities—for personality is the manifestation of some stage prior to our reaching choice; personality is the result of our incomplete manifestation, or actualization, for when we manifest completely, we manifest self-aware choice.

Personality results from our holding onto certain aspects of each of the stages of development. And so these things become fixations, and since we are holding onto them, we do not allow more of what we are holding onto to flow into us, and so we are unfulfilled in this, and so we experience desire with regard to this—with regard to the aspects of the stages on which we are fixated. Meanwhile, our attention is directed to our desires (thereby bringing about more of them and magnifying them), and to our attempts to find fulfillment for our desires in this world, and so we end up ignoring the other aspects of the stages (for our attention is consumed by our desires—by the aspects of the stages on which we are fixated).

But when we cease to hold onto things, and we mindfully allow them to flow through us, then we find fulfillment in our reception of these things from the Source. And then we progress the rest of the way through the stages up to choice in our development. And, from there, we begin to progress through each of the aspects of each of the stages from the top down—from a perspective that most closely resembles the Source's experience in the creation of the world.

The Main Stage Types

There are several aspects of personality that result from our getting stuck in our development at various aspects of various stages of the tree of life, and each of these aspects of personality can be described and understood in relation to the stage (and the aspect of that stage) that is their fixation. First, we shall analyze the main aspect of personality—the fixation with one of the nine stages of development.

There are nine because choice is the goal of development and so is not an intermediate stage that can be a hindering fixation, and manifestation (which *is* choice), is the mere beginning of the existence of all things, and so as soon as there is manifestation, there is inclination/action, and so manifestation cannot be a fixation either. (Also, manifestation is the combination of the language used by us and that used by the Source, and when it comes to fixations that give rise to personality, we are concerned merely with the language that *we*, in this world, use, prior to the combination of that language with the Source's language in manifestation—which is, of course, the combination that defines the choice of the next progression through the paradigm.) With regard to the main aspect of personality, only the intermediate nine stages of development in the tree of life concern us.

Further, we must bear in mind that we are discussing the stages from the perspective of the world, and not from the perspective of the Source, and so our choice of words will reflect this. (For example, we shall call inclination "instinct" here because we are referring to a fixation, and we therefore *are* referring to an instinctual desire that comes from the world, rather than to an inclination that stems from the Source.)

We will begin from the bottom, just after manifestation, and work our way up toward choice, for this is the order of manifestation, and we shall analyze each stage, with its aspects, and we shall see that this provides us with an understanding of a series of personality types, as well as a much better understanding of the stages, themselves. As we go through the stages, keep in mind these general patterns that we will encounter: The allowing element (allowing instinct, allowing feeling, allowing thought) allows the other's experience to manifest through it, and is therefore inclined to be out of touch with the experience (the experience being either instinct, feeling, or thought). The receiving element (receiving instinct, receiving feeling, receiving thought) grasps at or desires to receive and manifest the experience within itself, and is therefore inclined to feel like there is never enough of the experience (again, the experience being instinct, feeling, or thought). The sharing element (sharing instinct, sharing feeling, sharing thought) has an overflowing desire to share the experience that it is creating, and it is therefore inclined to feel like there is always too much of the experience (again, the experience being instinct, feeling, or thought).

First, there is allowing instinct. Allowing instinct is the first stage to manifest in the physical world. It allows the instincts of others (sharing instinct and receiving instinct) to be manifested through it, rather than manifesting its own instincts, and it is consequently out of touch with its own instincts and speech and actions and body. This makes it quite passive and quiet in its interactions with others, as it allows others to dictate its actions. It is going to be the listener, as it allows others to talk. Its focus is on the "I", but it is unclear to it how far the "I" extends, and since it allows others' instincts to be manifested through it, it is inclined to see the "I" as having no real boundaries whatsoever. Whatever anyone else wants, the "I" wants, for the "I" encompasses everything, and the instincts of everything manifest through the "I". Therefore, the instincts and desires of others must be fulfilled in order for allowing instinct to be fulfilled, and so allowing instinct seeks to fulfill others' desires with the idea that this is the only way that it can be fulfilled in itself. It is concerned with preserving its existence, but because it has just manifested in the world, and therefore has no experience with the world, its attitude is generally, "Let's just do what we have to do and see what happens and make the best of it, and then we'll have a peaceful and harmonious environment in which it will be easy and comfortable to exist." Essentially, allowing instinct optimistically seeks the fulfillment of everyone, for it believes that only this kind of harmonious and peaceful situation will *allow* a situation in which it can be fulfilled itself. And since it is new to the world, and so everything is new to *it*, it just wants to relax and enjoy the experience. But it really wants to watch without engaging much itself, because it isn't familiar with its own physicality, since even *this* is new to it. With an inner blankness and pure receptivity that comes from its having just entered the world, it experiences each moment in the present moment, but in a dissociated, disconnected sort of way, for it hasn't yet grounded itself fully in this world. It dissociates from any of its own imposing instincts, and especially from anger, which is too grounding in its own desires and disruptive of the peace. Allowing instinct just wants to avoid conflict, for this is the only way to maintain its existence as far as it is concerned.

Next, there is receiving instinct. Receiving instinct is only the second stage to manifest in the physical world. Therefore, it still has much of the idealism of allowing instinct. However, by receiving instinct, there is the recognition that things are not so perfect in the world. In fact, things are quite flawed. And so receiving instinct desires to fix them, to correct them. Receiving instinct grasps at instincts, desiring to receive instincts, and so it keeps itself stirred up about things that it might have instincts about. Essentially, it seeks to *find* things to be frustrated about in the present moment—things that it feels the need to change or have be changed—and it holds onto this frustration by replaying and holding onto thoughts of anything that makes it frustrated. Receiving instinct wants to be true to its instincts, and so it feels that, in order to exist, things must be as they *should* be—things must be perfect. By maintaining this view—that, in order to preserve its existence in the world, it must make things perfect—it secures for itself a mission and a purpose—to correct the world and make things right. For it wants to want—it wants to manifest instincts within itself, and so it needs to have instincts to manifest. It wants to have things, including itself, be perfect, and it sets the bar at perfection because then things will never be as they should be, and it will always have things to have instincts about, for nothing is perfect—everything is corrupt and bad and wrong and flawed in relation to the absolute of perfection. What receiving instinct ultimately wants, therefore, is to be good and right—to be perfect itself. But, since it is focused on the "I" and is unsure of the location of the boundaries of the "I", it wants everything else to be good and right—to be perfect—also. It has its own, subjective idea of what perfection entails, however, and it will not be convinced that what *it* perceives as good and right is not *objectively* good and right. Receiving instinct seeks to find and grasp at instincts, and so it can be seemingly dominating and imposing in its instructive, or didactic, nature, as it finds things to frustrate it and seeks to correct what it perceives as flaws and wrongs in its environment and in others. But it is actually quite submissive...to its own conception of morality and rightness. True dominance and imposition appear in sharing instinct, which is next.

Sharing instinct is constantly overflowing with instincts that it seeks to impose upon itself and others and the world around it. It is still relatively new to the world, being only the third stage to manifest in the physical world, but it has been around long enough to come to the conclusion that in order to secure its existence in the world—in order to protect itself from any vulnerability or weakness that might threaten its survival—it must have complete control over itself and its environment—including all of the others and the other things around it. It is not going to let itself be walked on by others; it is not going to allow others or its environment to assert themselves upon it. And so what it wants is to be in control—in order to protect and preserve itself. And it puts more energy than is necessary into everything that it does as it overflows with its instincts, manifesting very firmly grounded and confident in its body and actions and in the physical world. Since it wants to be in control, it tends toward being the leader (it tends toward assuming this role) in situations, actively imposing its influence upon others, but also doing what it can to preserve the existence of everyone around it. Sharing instinct always wants to have its way, and it can come to think that it can do anything to get it. And since its focus is on the "I" and its issue is with boundaries, it feels like its instincts apply to its entire environment and everything and everyone within that environment. It thinks that if *it* is in control, and *it* does what it wants to do, and *it* has the final say, then everyone will be best off. And so it assertively voices its opinion and actively engages with the world to shape the world as it wills—in the present moment. And only strength and toughness is displayed; anything that might get in the way of its being in control, like showing weakness or emotion, is avoided. But this doesn't apply to anger. Sharing instinct definitely thinks that anger is okay to show, because anger gets things going, gets people moving—for anger is all about the instinctual expression of the body in getting what it wants. Sharing instinct shows toughness, and assertiveness, and forceful pursuance of its desires, and active and intense engagement with the world, and it wants the same things in return from its environment and from others. For what we give, we should get in return.

Next is allowing feeling. Allowing feeling allows others' feelings to be expressed through it, and it is therefore out of touch with its own feelings. Since it is the first of the feeling stages, it is on the borderline between past-orientation and present-orientation, and its issue is that of identity—who it is and how it fits in with others—and so it is constantly looking to its past and present interactions with others in order to find out how it should feel about things and, more specifically, how it should act. And it often looks to the past with regret or shame about how its actions might have made it not look good to others. And since it allows others' feelings to be expressed through it, and it also wants to belong, it wants to make others happy with it. It wants to meet others' expectations for who it should be, appearing the best that it possibly can in everyone else's eyes. It is therefore inclined to adapt to each person's feelings about who it should be, and this sometimes leads it to change itself depending upon who is looking at it so that it will appear in the best possible light to that particular person. Allowing feeling is the first stage where the pull of the end goal—self-awareness—begins to present itself, for it is the first stage where others start to be recognized as existing—others with which it can interact, helping it to become aware of itself, and others with which it can work toward some greater goal. Consequently, allowing feeling is extremely goal-oriented, wanting to accomplish things and to be always driven toward some goal or other. Since allowing feeling is the first of the feeling stages, it feels that it needs the basis of the instinctual stages in order to fit into the group of others. Its attitude is therefore "I need to work hard to preserve my own existence in order to be valuable to others, to the group." It thinks that if it accomplishes what other people would want it to accomplish, and it is the best at that thing of anyone, then it will be valuable in other people's eyes; this is how it seeks to find its niche—by being the best at something that others want someone to be doing and that others look well upon someone doing. Allowing feeling doesn't know how it feels about things, because it is so inclined to think that other people's feelings are *its* feelings. And it ends up covering up its own feelings, because these can get in the way of good interactions with people—in the way of being productive and accomplished and being seen well by people.

Receiving feeling, on the other hand, feels like its feelings are who it truly is, and so it grasps at and holds onto feelings, replaying thoughts and events that brought about strong emotions in it. Any strong emotion—whether good or bad—is good, because it makes receiving feeling feel like it is truly alive, for to *feel* is to be alive for it. It is past-oriented, replaying past interactions with others to recreate and explore feelings and thereby to discover, in those feelings, who it truly is. And it often looks to the past with regret and shame about how it didn't fit the identity that it has created, or found, for itself in its feelings. Receiving feeling is consequently introspective, wanting to be self-aware, but ending up self-conscious. For it always feels like it is lacking something that everyone else has—for it is so wrapped up in its own feelings that it ends up lacking, since it cannot receive new feelings when it is so busy holding onto the same feelings. It wants to fit in, but it feels like it doesn't...because it defines itself in *opposition*, or in *contrast*, to what is outside it. So, if others fit in, then *it* doesn't fit in. It wants to be true to its feelings, and it tries to such an extent to do so that it tries to be different from everyone else. Because then it can have an identity that is so unique that it will have significance for who it is and fit into the group by being something that no one else is. Like receiving instinct with its instincts, receiving feeling insists that its feelings be concerned with things being different than they are. And so receiving feeling feels it is lacking something that would make it complete—like receiving instinct feels it is lacking something that would make it perfect. Receiving feeling ends up imagining and fantasizing about its desirous feelings (its romantic longings and so forth) being fulfilled. But it is often too disorganized to accomplish the things that might ever lead it to actual fulfillment, because in order to be true to its feelings, it must do things only when it is in the mood to do them. By maintaining the identity of searching for its identity, receiving feeling assures that it will always be lacking something, and that it will therefore always have feelings to experience…feelings of lack. It is very concerned with accurately and precisely expressing its feelings, and so it is quite particular about how it manifests and expresses itself—in any and all creative avenues of expression—and it often takes things as personal attacks on its identity and therefore overdramatizes (because holding onto strong feelings makes everything quite dramatic—and makes receiving feeling quite sensitive to anything that triggers feelings in it). Yet receiving feeling can often be rather restricted in its expression of emotions, as though emotions are something to be felt and experienced fully within oneself and not to be acted out.

Sharing feeling, however, definitely feels that feelings should be acted out, for sharing feeling is overflowing with feelings that it wishes to share with everyone else. And what feeling is better to share with everyone else than love? So sharing feeling seeks to show, often with active and overt expressions of emotion, how much it cares about other people. Since it is others-oriented, with concerns about how it will fit in with others, it directs this overflowing emotion toward trying to help out everyone in every way it can. It feels like it knows what is best for everyone (because its feelings are everyone's feelings, and so if it feels that someone needs something, then that person certainly needs that thing), and it makes sure that it meets those needs to the best of its ability. Since it is past-oriented, it looks to the past, replaying interactions to see how helpful and loving and caring it has been and, perhaps more importantly, how much everyone consequently needs it. But what sharing feeling ultimately really wants is to have its overflowing, caring, loving feelings returned by others—in just as obvious displays as its own. Because the way things work is that when we give something, we get more of it in return. So while sharing feeling is always doing things for *others*, it expects everyone else to be doing things for *it*. It consequently often ends up concerned with what friendship or what a relationship really means (and how others are not fulfilling their role in these things), and it particularly expects others to be appreciating what it does for them. And it often looks to the past with regret and shame about its past actions (and especially its past failures to meet people's needs) and how these might stop people from caring about it. Like sharing instinct seeks intensity in everything and imposes intensity on everything, sharing feeling seeks closeness in everything and imposes closeness on everything. Sharing feeling is often overly intimate and physical in its trying to get people to love it and care about it and need it, because it will try to help in any way that it feels it is capable of doing so (and because it seeks the emotional return and appreciation in the intimacy). And it will impose the need for its help upon others even where it is not wanted, because it needs to be needed, needs to have an outlet for its overflowing emotion that it desires to share with others.

Allowing thought, like sharing feeling, can be very others-oriented, but in a very different way. Allowing thought allows others' thoughts to be manifested through it, and so it is out of touch with its own thought. Without being able to listen to its own thought, and not really knowing what *it* thinks—separate from what its family members or friends or religion or whatever would think—anyway, it always feels like it is resting on unstable ground. And so trust is a big issue for allowing thought, because it needs to find something to depend on, and it needs to know for sure that it can depend on it. Allowing thought is consequently very skeptical of everyone and everything to begin with. And if someone or something earns its trust, then it will defend that person or thing to the end, because it will see that person or thing as its source of thought, as its source of guidance and, consequently, as its source of security. It makes quick first-impression judgments about people (and all things), categorizing them as either *trustworthy* or *not trustworthy* and, in this way, it generally (and rather strictly) categorizes all things. Since its concern is with decision-making, it does not trust its own mind—its own thought—to make decisions, and so it looks to other people and idea systems—to others' thoughts—for guidance as to how to make the best decisions for itself and for the people close to it. And since it is future-oriented and it doesn't trust itself to make decisions, it is always anxious and worried about all of the things that could possibly go wrong if it makes one decision or another, imagining every worst possible outcome—in which it will lose its guidance, its security. Since it is the first of the thinking stages, it is on the borderline between thought and feeling, between future-orientedness and past-orientedness. And so it is often unsure of whether it should listen to its thought or its feeling, whether it should worry about the future or regret the past that is leading to that future. Its attitude is basically "I need to have security with the group or I won't have individual people to guide me in my decision-making." It tries to be loyal and dependable to the individuals—the other "I"'s—and the idea systems in which it sees itself as having security in order to maintain those people and those idea systems in its life—in order to maintain that security, that stability, that guidance.

Receiving thought doesn't consider everyone else in its decision-making like allowing thought does. Instead, it just tries to make the decisions that are best for itself, because if *it* is happy, then it will be able to be there for the other individuals—the other "I"'s—in its life…by being happy and cheery. But it really doesn't know how to make the best decisions for itself either, and all that it knows is that it needs to be constantly thinking and stimulated in its thinking or it will feel trapped. So it tries to cover every possible option in every situation—choosing every choice available. Because it seeks to receive and manifest thought within itself. And in order to find thoughts to manifest within itself, it tries to live and actively engage with every idea that it can think of, so that the resulting experiences might give rise to more ideas—more thoughts. So it sees the world as full of exciting opportunities, and it wants to experience them all—to provide fuel for more thinking, which will lead to more experiencing, which will lead to more thinking. Experience is the source of receiving thought's thinking, because from where else would one receive thought? So it wants to be thinking and doing, thinking and doing. And for receiving thought, these are practically one and the same. The moment it thinks it, it does it—spontaneously and suddenly, while whatever it is is still exciting and new and stimulating. And so receiving thought is very outgoing and extroverted, constantly engaged in some activity or another. And when it is *not* actively *doing* something, it is actively *talking* about actively *doing* something—it is talking about something exciting that it might be able to do in the future. Since all it wants is to be happy and fulfilled—so that it can be that way for other "I"'s, as well as for itself—it doesn't want to feel anything that is negative. If it feels some negative feeling, it starts to feel trapped, and it sees this as being bored, and so it jumps up to seek more mental stimulation through active engagement with experience—be it mental or physical—in the world, to try to keep itself preoccupied and happy. But because it is always thinking about the next exciting thing that it will do, it is never fully where it is in the present, doing what it's doing, and so it doesn't allow any experience to touch it fully, and it is, consequently, left unfulfilled and constantly seeking fulfillment in more and more experiences. Receiving thought tries to receive things to think about by actively physically engaging with the world, and therefore by manifesting thoughts physically; sharing thought also keeps its thoughts active, but not by immersing itself in experience the way receiving thought does.

Sharing thought is overflowing with thought already—too much thought, even, so that it can all become overwhelming. Every experience with the world provides endless fuel for thinking, because sharing thought can end up thinking about its own thoughts, and about its thoughts about its own thoughts, and so on, and so it doesn't require much experience for tons of thinking (although the thinking can end up quite removed from experience). Sharing thought is the last stage of development, and it has had enough experience already. At this point, and because it is concerned with other "I"'s and with decision making, it is ready just to learn from experience—to see what it can come to understand about it, to see if it can explain it well enough to predict what is *going* to happen. This way, it can learn all that it needs to know to weigh all the pros and cons of every option in order to make the best choices for itself and the other "I"'s around it and, this way, it can be a competent, capable, and useful source of information about the world—about what everyone else is experiencing. Sharing thought seeks objective truth, for with this it can make the objectively best decisions. But it often ends up being inclined to not act because it never feels like it knows enough in order to make a decision, and also because it thinks that since it can predict everything that would happen if it did something, there is no point in actually doing it—because knowing it is almost like living it. And so rather than engaging with things in the physical world, sharing thought engages with abstract representations of things, living very much in the world of its mind. And this can make it actually *not* so competent physically, leaving it feeling incompetent and unfulfilled. It will often observe the world with active thought (rather than with the blankness of allowing instinct, which has just entered the world and so has never experienced any of this before), as it figures out and pieces together and breaks down all of its thoughts in its head. Sharing thought can come, with the understanding that it gleans from the world, to see the world as though for the first time. Because everything looks different through the lens of sharing thought's framework of understanding. The world can be logical and systematic and brilliant as viewed through this lens (although when sharing thought feels like it doesn't understand, the world can be meaningless and terrifying as viewed through its lens). And sharing thought wants to share all of this understanding—all of this thought that it has produced. And it expects other people to be logical and to think a lot and to be sources of ideas (and to be interested in the ideas that it wants to share) as well, for this is what it gives, and it expects more of this in return.[9]

---

9   The nine main stage personality type fixations correspond with the nine Enneagram personality types, which can be explored further in books by Don Richard Riso and Russ Hudson, such as *The Wisdom of the Enneagram: The Complete Guide to Psychological and Spiritual Growth for the Nine Personality Types*, among others. The specific correlation or pairing between each of the Enneagram personality types and each of the *sefirot* of the Kabbalistic tree of life that is implied here in the explanation of each of the main personality type fixations on the stages of the tree of life paradigm is in accordance with the pairing suggested by Eyal Rav-Noy. Thus, allowing instinct corresponds with both type 9 and the *sefirah Yesod*, receiving instinct corresponds with both type 1 and the *sefirah Hod*, sharing instinct corresponds with both type 8 and the *sefirah Netzach*, allowing feeling corresponds with both type 3 and the *sefirah Tiferet*, receiving feeling corresponds with both type 4 and the *sefirah Gevurah*, sharing feeling corresponds with both type 2 and the *sefirah Chesed*, allowing thought corresponds with both type 6 and the *sefirah Da'at*, receiving thought corresponds with both type 7 and the *sefirah Binah*, and sharing thought corresponds with both type 5 and the *sefirah Chochmah*.

Personality is the Result of Varying Degrees of Fixation

It is very important to remember and understand that these are all fixations. None of these aspects of personality come from the essence of the person, but rather from the person's being stuck at one stage or another on the way up to the person's manifestation of his/her essence (which he/she has, therefore, not yet fully manifested). These aspects of personality come from the world, and not from the Source. They come from passively and reactively engaging with different aspects of the world. Essentially, these aspects of personality are all the result of getting stuck at, and manifesting, and identifying with, *one stage*, to the exclusion of a balanced and self-aware expression of all stages in their true form and order (a self-aware expression that can happen only after development all the way up to choice).

The main personality type stage of fixation remains the same throughout the life of the individual. Further, everyone who has not attained the fullest self-awareness (which basically includes everyone who is alive in this physical world) has some degree of fixation on every one of the nine stages of development, and it is merely that fixation is greatest on one stage and second greatest on another stage and so forth. Also, there are nine stages of development within each of these nine stages of development—like a tree within a tree—because every stage of the nine, considered as a personality type, has the capacity to express itself at different degrees of fixation. Basically, everyone contains every stage of the tree of life within him/her, in both the form of these personality types and the form of degrees of fixation on each of these personality type stages (as well as in other manifestations of each of the stages).

The degree of fixation in an individual can be changed by the individual's degree of exercise of self-aware choice. The higher the degree of fixation, the greater the desires that stem from the lack of the fulfillment of the stage, and the more driven by these desires behavior becomes. Because the more fixated on, and identified with, our personality type stage we are, the more we hold onto our experiences, and the more unfulfilled in our desires—the very desires that we want most to fulfill—we consequently become. Because by holding onto the things that we think we want, we do not allow ourselves to receive more of these very things, and we also increasingly corrupt the things that we have received from their original and fulfilling form (like a pond whose water becomes no longer fresh and life-sustaining for those who drink from it, because it holds onto that water). The goal is to recognize what we are doing, and to change our patterns of behavior—learning that fulfillment comes not from the things in this world that we think we want, but rather from the Source, and so it makes no sense to hold onto these things, because true fulfillment comes only from our allowing things to pass and thereby making ourselves capable of receiving more of them in their place.

In the nine levels of fixation, beginning from manifestation and going up (meaning beginning at a high degree of fixation and going up to lesser degrees), many of the general patterns associated with the stages of development apply in some way. So, in the three highest degrees of fixation—associated with the three instinct stages—there is a gradient of the view of there being only "I" (only the "I" matters and everything is ultimately for the "I") and of having a focus on preserving the existence of the "I" (which in this highly fixated state ultimately produces behaviors that are quite antithetical to this aim), of having boundary issues (in not knowing how far the "I"'s experience extends into the world), and of the "I" being out of control of what happens in the "I"'s life (because it is all determined for the "I" by what happens in the world in combination with the "I"'s set reactions to the world). In the middle three degrees of fixation—associated with the three feeling stages—there is a gradient of the view of there being others that are projections of the "I", and of the "I" needing to find some role to play (needing to find out how it relates to others) in order to have something to offer to the group (and this role is ultimately correlated with, or determined by, the personality type stage of identification) so that it will fit in with others, and of the "I" being only somewhat in control of what happens in the "I"'s life (because most of it is determined for the "I" by what happens in the world in combination with the "I"'s set reactions to the world). In the three lowest degrees of fixation—associated with the three thinking stages—there is a gradient of the view of there being other "I"'s who are separate and distinct from the "I" and who therefore must also be considered in the "I"'s decision-making and with whom the "I" is inclined to closely connect, and of the "I" being mostly in control of what happens in the "I"'s life (because very little of it is determined for the "I" by what happens in the world in combination with the "I"'s set reactions to the world).

It is interesting to note that all neuroses and psychoses and other psychological ailments and neurological disorders (e.g., obsessive compulsive disorder, obsessive compulsive personality disorder, narcissism, dyslexia, attention deficit hyperactivity disorder, autism, Williams Syndrome, etc.) represent high degrees of fixation on one stage or another (OCD and OCPD are primarily forms of fixations on receiving instinct, narcissism is a form of fixation on allowing feeling or receiving feeling, dyslexia and ADHD are forms of fixation on receiving thought, autism—along with autism-related disorders, such as Asperger's Sydrome—is a form of fixation on sharing thought, and Williams Syndrome is a form of fixation on receiving feeling).[10] Further, these associations between such disorders and fixations upon certain stages, in addition to the fact that so many of these disorders have some form of neurological aspect to them, suggest a possible association between the development of certain brain structures (their size, activity, and so forth) and the main stage personality type fixation. It may be that the part of the brain that is associated with each stage of the tree of life paradigm is, in some way, more pronounced relative to other brain structures in people who are fixated upon the same stage in terms of personality, and this may be the neurological basis of explanation for the development of personality type.

However, we must remember that the brain is not the ultimate root of things; the process of creation begins far before this physical link between the world in potential and the physical world of actualization, and so any correspondence between brain structure and personality merely suggests the form that personality takes in the beginning of its actualization in physical form—in the brain (prior to its actualization in the outward behavior of the physical body). And since the brain is not the ultimate root of things, but is, rather, merely the manifestation of the choices that we make, we have control in shaping it. This accounts for the extensive plasticity of the brain, and it also reveals that any personality-fixation-associated brain differences can be exaggerated or diminished through our own repetition of reactive patterns (of thoughts, feelings, instincts, speech and actions) or lack thereof. We can decrease the extent of the personality-fixation-related dictation of the (possibly relative) size and activity of different brain structures by changing our patterns through the active exercise of choice—by increasing self-awareness and thereby decreasing fixation.

---

10   As the nine main stage personality type fixations correspond with the nine Enneagram personality types, this association with disorders can be explored further in *Understanding the Enneagram: The Practical Guide to Personality Types*, by Don Richard Riso and Russ Hudson.

Comparing and Contrasting the Main Stage Types

Now we are in a position to compare each of the stages in order to understand the patterns that manifest amongst them as a result of the relation of one to another (with some stages being reflections of others, and so forth), and also (later) to look at the relationship between the personality type manifestations of the stages in relation to other manifestations of the stages.

In the sharing stages, we see that sharing instinct seeks to create and share intensity with the world, sharing feeling seeks to create and share closeness with people, and sharing thought seeks to create and share intimacy with ideas. In the receiving stages, we see that receiving instinct wants to receive and manifest the perfect world, receiving feeling wants to receive and manifest a complete and unique self, and receiving thought wants to receive and manifest new and exciting experiences. In the allowing stages, we see that allowing instinct wants to peacefully do whatever others want it to do, allowing feeling wants to passionately be whatever others want it to be, and allowing thought wants to loyally make the decisions that others would want it to make.

In the sharing stages, we see that sharing instinct wants to be in control of where it is; sharing feeling wants to be in control of where it was; and sharing thought wants to be in control of where it's going. In the receiving stages, we see that receiving instinct doesn't want to be where it is; receiving feeling doesn't want to be where it is and, instead, wants to be where it *was*; and receiving thought doesn't want to be where it is and, instead, wants to be where it's going. In the allowing stages, we see that allowing instinct is out of touch with, or disconnected from, where it is; allowing feeling is out of touch with, or disconnected from, where it was; and allowing thought is out of touch with, or disconnected from, where it's going.

Essentially, in the sharing stages, the instincts, feelings, and thoughts are produced by the "I" and imposed on other "I"'s and the outside world. In the receiving stages, experiences with other "I"'s and the outside world are sought and called upon to produce instincts, feelings, and thoughts in the "I". And, in the allowing stages, the instincts, feelings, and thoughts of other "I"'s and the outside world are sought so that they can be manifested through the "I".

The sharing stages want to *create new* experiences (instincts, feelings, thoughts) that originate with the "I", independent of the world, in order to impose them upon the world. Sharing instinct wants to be protected and in control of its environment, and so it seeks to create *new* instincts that originate with itself, independent of the world, in order to impose them upon the world in the form of physical efforts to be in control of its surroundings. Sharing feeling wants to be needed and wanted, and so it seeks to create *new* feelings that originate with itself, independent of the world, in order to impose them upon the world in the form of attempts to meet people's needs. Sharing thought wants to be competent and useful, and so it seeks to create *new* thoughts that originate with itself, independent of the world, in order to impose them upon the world in the form of a framework of understanding.

In all of the sharing stages, the "I" wants to have some kind of control over how it relates to the world and to other "I"'s (and it creates experiences—instincts, feelings, or thoughts—in order to try to attain this). The "I" wants to have this control in order to be helpful, and it seeks to be helpful in order to be useful in the experience that it creates and shares. Sharing instinct seeks to gain control in its relationship with its environment, and therefore to be helpful to its environment, through physical dominance; it seeks to protect itself from its environment in order to be useful to its environment—in the influence that it extends onto its environment in accordance with its own created instincts—so that it can be part of its environment through existing. Sharing feeling seeks to gain control in its relationship with others, and therefore to be helpful to others, through making itself emotionally and physically needed; it seeks to protect itself from the group in order to be useful to the group—in who it is, in accordance with its own created feelings, in its relation to others in the group—so that it can be part of the group through belonging. And sharing thought seeks to gain control in its relationships with other "I"'s, and therefore to be helpful to other "I"'s, through intellectual understanding; it seeks to protect itself from other "I"'s in order to be useful to other "I"'s—in the decisions that it makes, in accordance with its own created thoughts, with regard to other "I"'s—so that it can be part of other "I"'s experiences through connecting.

In all of the sharing stages, the "I" feels like it can't allow itself to be dependent upon the world, others, or other "I"'s, because then it would open itself up to vulnerability—to having others' experiences imposed upon *it* when it feels like it must be a source of its *own* experience (of instincts, feelings, or thoughts, depending on the stage of fixation) and a source of experience relative to *others*. Therefore, it seeks to protect itself from their experiences so that it can be in control of its relationship with them, so that *it* can be helpful and useful to *them*, rather than the other way around. For while the "I" expects and wants others to be sources of *new* experience (sources of the type of experience of which *it* is a source, be it instinct, feeling, or thought) like *it* is (and while it wants to receive such new experiences from others), it simultaneously feels like it must be a source of its *own* experience in order to hold its own and fulfill its role (largely *because* it expects others to be such sources, and so it feels like *it* has to be such a source in order to be part of the world, the group, and the experiences of other "I"'s). The "I", due to its fixation on a sharing stage, feels like it must be a source of new experience—like it must be the creative, sharing agent in its relationship with others and the world.

The sharing stages as main personality type fixations result from getting caught up in the role of one of the sharing stages within the downward creative process. Thus, the "I" here feels like it has to protect itself from incoming experience from its environment, others, and other "I"'s (from the allowing stage above it) in order to be in control of its relationship with its environment, others, and other "I"'s. (For the sharing stage is supposed to receive from the allowing stage above it and then define what it receives in order to create or produce a completely new experience—be it instinct, or feeling, or thought—for the receiving and allowing stages that follow it, and it is supposed to share this experience with the receiving stage and the allowing stage that follow it. So in order to protect itself and be in control of its relationship with the receiving stage and the allowing stage that follow it—rather than simply allowing the allowing stage prior to it to be in control of what it shares—it needs to make sure that it fulfills its role of defining, or creating something new out of, what it gets from the allowing stage prior to it—its role of creating a new experience—and of sharing this new experience.) The "I" here feels like it needs to protect itself and be in control in order to be able to be helpful and cared about, and it feels like it has to be helpful to, and cared about by, its environment, others, and other "I"'s (by defining its experience and sharing its newly defined experience with those others—with the receiving stage and allowing stage that follow it). The "I" here feels like it has to be helpful and cared about in order to be useful and capable, and it feels like it has to be useful to its environment, others, and other "I"'s (in the experience that it defines, or creates, and shares) and capable in playing its part (its part of being a source of experience) in its relationship with them.

Also, the "I" here fears being overpowered (and thus powerless), inundated (and thus helpless, unhelpful, and unloved), and overwhelmed (and thus useless and incapable) by incoming experience from its environment, others, and other "I"'s (because then it won't be able to protect itself or be in control, or be helpful and cared about, or be useful in its relationship with its environment, others, and other "I"'s). The "I" feels like it has to protect itself and be in control, and be helpful and cared about, and be useful and capable, in order to hold its own and earn its place in the world, in the group, and in the experiences of other "I"'s, by contributing something new from itself to these things.

Each of the sharing stages as fixations produces a different primary focus here, although all of these desires and fears are present to an extent in each of the sharing stages (because the sharing stages as fixations are all caused by being caught up in the role of a sharing stage in that stage's relationship with the stages around it in the creative process).

Sharing instinct primarily desires to protect itself and to be in power and in control, and it therefore primarily fears being overpowered and controlled by others' experiences and thus powerless. It fears these things because if these things become so then it won't be able to protect itself and be in control of the instincts that it creates, and so it won't have any new boundaries—any new definition—for its territory or for itself. It will therefore have to create more instincts—through more intense and forceful engagement with its surroundings—and impose these on its environment through further efforts to assert itself onto its environment in order to define new boundaries for itself and protect itself and gain control over itself and its environment.

Sharing feeling primarily desires to be helpful (so that it will be loved and cared for in return), and it therefore primarily fears being inundated by others' experiences and thus helpless and unable to help and unloved. It fears these things because if these things become so then it won't be able to be helpful in, and cared about for, the feelings that it creates, and so it won't have any new—newly defined—identity for itself. It will therefore have to create more feelings—through more outward and overt emotional displays of closeness and caring—and impose these on others through further efforts to help people in order to gain the love and caring of others.

Sharing thought primarily desires to be useful and capable, and it therefore primarily fears being overwhelmed by others' experiences and thus useless and incapable. It fears these things because if these things become so then it won't be able to be useful or capable in the thoughts that it creates, and so it won't be able to make new decisions for itself or for other "I"'s—because it won't have enough useful information to weigh all of the pros and cons of each choice. It will therefore have to create more thoughts—through more active accumulation of information and more active thinking—and impose these on other "I"'s through further efforts to figure out how to be useful and capable.

However, each of these desires requires that the previous one be fulfilled (in the order of manifestation upward) in order for *it* to be fulfilled. And so sharing instinct desires to protect itself and to be in control; sharing feeling desires to protect itself and to be in control *in order to be able* to be helpful and cared about; and sharing thought desires to protect itself and to be in control *in order to be able* to be helpful and cared about, and it desires to be helpful and cared about *in order to* be useful and capable.

Notice, here, that in all of the sharing stages, the "I"'s desire to be in control and protect itself presents a barrier to the "I"'s being part of what it wants to be part of (namely its environment, the group of others, and the experiences of other "I"'s), for the "I" seeks to protect itself from the very thing that it wants to be part of. Notice, also, that this problem arises solely due to the "I"'s fixating upon a certain stage (and consequently projecting that fixation onto the world and others), and getting caught up with merely fulfilling the role of that stage in the creative process, rather than expressing all of the stages in their true forms (and recognizing others as distinct other "I"'s).

The receiving stages want to *receive different* experiences *in reaction to* the world. Receiving instinct wants a perfect world, and so everything must be good and right, and so the "I" wants everything about the world to be different than it is (so that everything about the world can be perfect). Receiving feeling wants to be a complete and uniquely significant "I", and so everything must be unique and original, and so the "I" wants everything about itself to be different than it is (so that everything about itself can be unique). Receiving thought wants to attain joy and fulfillment, and so everything must be constantly exciting, and so the "I" wants everything about its manifested decisions—its experiences in the world—to be different than it is (so that everything about its experiences in the world can be exciting and fulfilling).

In all of the receiving stages, the "I" wants to have some kind of sense of being good in itself (and it grasps at experiences—instincts, feelings, or thoughts—in order to try to attain this). The "I" wants to be good in order to gain a sense of completion, and it seeks to have this sense of completion in order to be fulfilled in its reception of experience. Receiving instinct seeks to be good with regard to its existence in its environment, and therefore to gain a sense of completion, through the perfection of itself and its surroundings; it seeks to be good in its relationship with its environment and in its effects upon its environment—in the influence that it extends, in accordance with its reactively manifested instincts, onto its environment—in order to be fulfilled in its instincts (by being constantly filled with reactively manifested instincts), so that it can be part of the environment through existing. Receiving feeling seeks to be good with regard to its being part of the group, and therefore to gain a sense of completion, through the accurate manifestation of its feelings; it seeks to be good in its relationship with the group and in its effects upon the group—in who it is, in accordance with its reactively manifested feelings, in its relation to others in the group—in order to be fulfilled in its feelings (by being constantly filled with reactively manifested feelings), so that it can be part of the group through belonging. Receiving thought seeks to be good with regard to its intimate connections with other "I"'s, and therefore to gain a sense of completion, through the fulfillment of constant excitement; it seeks to be good in its relationships with other "I"'s and in its effects upon other "I"'s—in the decisions that it makes, in accordance with its reactively manifested thoughts, with regard to other "I"'s—in order to be fulfilled in its thoughts (by being constantly filled with reactively manifested thoughts), so that it can be part of other "I"'s experiences through connecting.

In all of the receiving stages, the "I" feels like it has to be fulfilled in itself before it can really engage with and be a part of the world around it, the group of others, and the experiences of other "I"'s—like it has to find some source of experience (of instincts, feelings, or thoughts, depending on the stage of fixation) in order to have experience to receive and manifest within itself. This is why it seeks to be good in its relationship to the world around it, others, and other "I"'s—so that it can be complete, and so that it can find fulfillment in this completion. Since the "I" expects and wants others to be reactive receivers of *different* experience (of the type of experience of which *it* is a reactive receiver, be it instinct, feeling, or thought) like *it* is, it fears not having any *source* of experience for itself. So while it feels like it must be a receiver, it comes to feel like it must also be a *source* of experience for others in order to be part of the world, the group, and the experiences of other "I"'s (since if everyone is a receiver, there will be no source for those others, and so it strongly feels like it must take on this role itself—because *someone* must do it—even though this is against its nature and is therefore difficult—and stressful—for it to do). And so it becomes a source of reactively produced, different experiences.

The receiving stages as main personality type fixations result from getting caught up in the role of one of the receiving stages within the downward creative process. Thus, the "I" here feels like it has to be perfect in its reception of experience from its environment, others, and other "I"'s (from the sharing stage prior to it) in order to be good (or right) in its relationship with its environment, others, and other "I"'s. (For the receiving stage is supposed to receive all that it receives from the sharing stage prior to it in the defined form in which it is shared, and it gets caught up in the definition, itself, and perceives this to be the source of what it receives. So it holds onto the experience in its defined form, thereby corrupting and altering it from its original form and forming a different experience from what it received. And it desires that the experience be different from the defined form shared with it, that the experience be complete and perfect, for in its defined form the experience is limited and flawed from its ultimately original form.) The "I" here feels like it needs to be perfect and good in order to be able to be complete and significant, and it feels like it has to be complete and uniquely significant in itself—performing its role as no one else would—in its relationship with its environment, others, and other "I"'s. (For when the receiving stage holds onto what it receives in its defined form and gets caught up in perceiving the definition as being the source of what it gains from it, it comes to desire an altered form—a different definition for the experience—and so it tries to produce this for itself, to reactively manifest an experience unique to itself.) The "I" here feels like it has to be complete and uniquely significant in order to be fulfilled and happy, and it feels like it has to be fulfilled and happy in the experience that it receives from the world, others, and other "I"'s (in the experience that is shared with it by the sharing stage before it).

Also, the "I" here fears being flawed and corrupt (or bad or wrong), incomplete and lacking (or insignificant), and limited and deprived (or confined and trapped or unfulfilled) in the defined experience that it receives and reactively redefines (because then it won't be perfect and good, and complete and significant, and fulfilled and happy). The "I" feels like it has to be perfect and good, and complete and uniquely significant, and fulfilled, in order to be beneficial and positive in its effects in its relationship to the world, the group, and the experiences of other "I"'s in the way that it changes its experience to be something different and distinct from what it received.

Each of the receiving stages as fixations produces a different primary focus here, although all of these desires and fears are present to an extent in each of the receiving stages (because the receiving stages as fixations are all caused by being caught up in the role of a receiving stage in that stage's relationship with the stages around it in the creative process).

Receiving instinct primarily desires to be perfect and good and right, and it therefore primarily fears being flawed and corrupt and bad and wrong—in the definition of the experience that it receives and in the way that it redefines, or fails to redefine, the experience that it receives. It fears these things because if these things become so then it won't be perfect and good and right in its receiving and reactive redefining or altering of instincts, and so it won't have any distinct boundary—any distinctly different definition—for its territory or for itself. It will therefore have to receive more instincts—by finding more things that are wrong about its surroundings to frustrate it— and repeat and hold onto these more and reactively redefine them further through further efforts to correct itself and its environment in order to make it and its environment perfect and good and right.

Receiving feeling primarily desires to be complete and uniquely significant in itself, and it therefore primarily fears being incomplete and lacking and insignificant—in the definition of the experience that it receives and in the way that it redefines, or fails to redefine, the experience that it receives. It fears these things because if these things become so then it won't be complete and uniquely significant in its receiving and reactive redefining or altering of feelings, and so it won't have any distinct—any distinctly differently defined—identity. It will therefore have to receive more feelings—by exposing itself to more things that invoke strong feelings—and repeat and hold onto these more and reactively redefine them further through further efforts to complete itself in order to make itself uniquely significant.

Receiving thought primarily desires to be fulfilled and happy, and it therefore primarily fears being limited and deprived and confined and trapped and unfulfilled—in the definition of the experience that it receives and in the way that it redefines, or fails to redefine, the experience that it receives. It fears these things because if these things become so then it won't be fulfilled and happy in its receiving and reactive redefining or altering of thoughts, and so it won't be able to make distinct—distinctly defined—decisions (meaning that, rather than choosing a single, distinct thing, it will have to choose many things at once, choosing every choice available in the hope of covering the most fulfilling one). It will therefore have to receive more thoughts—by engaging in more numerous and more exciting and stimulating activities and experiences—and repeat and hold onto these more and reactively redefine them further through further efforts to fulfill itself in order to make itself happy.

However, each of these desires requires that the previous one be fulfilled (in the order of manifestation upward) in order for *it* to be fulfilled. And so receiving instinct desires to be perfect and good; receiving feeling desires to be perfect and good *in order to be able* to be complete and uniquely significant; and receiving thought desires to be perfect and good *in order to be able* to be complete and uniquely significant, and it desires to be complete and uniquely significant *in order to* be fulfilled and happy.

Notice, here, that in all of the receiving stages, the "I"'s desire to be good and to have a sense of completion presents a barrier to the "I"'s being part of what it wants to be part of (namely its environment, the group of others, and the experiences of other "I"'s), for the "I" is too consumed with its own quest for goodness and completion—too concerned with itself and its desire for things to be different from the way they are—to be part of anything that actually *is* outside itself, and therefore to be part of what it wants to be part of. Notice, also, that this problem arises solely due to the "I"'s fixating upon a certain stage (and consequently projecting that fixation onto the world and others), and getting caught up with merely fulfilling the role of that stage in the creative process, rather than expressing all of the stages in their true forms (and recognizing others as distinct other "I"'s).

The allowing stages want to *allow whatever* the experiences of other "I"'s in the world *are* to be manifested *through them* (without those experiences really touching them). Allowing instinct wants to have peace and harmony, and so it seeks to avoid the possibility of conflict that could arise from manifesting its own instincts, and it, instead, passively allows others to manifest their instincts and actions through it. Allowing feeling wants to have value and worth, and so it seeks to avoid the possibility of not being valuable to others that could arise from manifesting its own feelings, and it, instead, passively allows others to manifest their feelings and expectations and passions through it. Allowing thought wants to have guidance and security, and so it seeks to avoid the possibility of losing the guidance and security of other "I"'s that could arise from manifesting its own thoughts in its decision-making, and it, instead, passively allows others to manifest their thoughts and ideas and beliefs through it.

In all of the allowing stages, the "I" wants to have some kind of harmony in its interactions with the world and with other "I"'s (and it dissociates from its own experiences—instincts, feelings, or thoughts—and allows others' experiences, instead of its own experiences, to be manifested through it in order to try to attain this). The "I" wants to have harmony in order to be successful in its role, and it seeks to be successful in order to have the security of having experiences to manifest through itself. Allowing instinct seeks to have harmony with regard to its existence in its environment, and therefore to be successful in its harmonization of its relationship with its environment, through passive presence and lack of assertion of its own instincts; it seeks to maintain harmony in its relationship with its environment—by not extending its own influence onto its environment, in accordance with its allowing the instincts of its environment to be manifested through it—in order to have the security of a comfortable environment, so that it can be part of the environment through existing. Allowing feeling seeks to have harmony with regard to its being part of the group, and therefore to be successful in its harmonization of its relationship with others, through its adaptation to the expectations of other "I"'s and lack of assertion of its own feelings;

it seeks to maintain harmony in its relationship with the group—by not being who it truly is in its relation to others in the group, in accordance with its allowing the feelings of others to be manifested through it—in order to have the security of its own success in the perception of others, so that it can be part of the group through belonging. Allowing thought seeks to have harmony with regard to its intimate connections with other "I"'s, and therefore to be successful in its harmonization of its relationships with other "I"'s, through making decisions in accordance with other "I"'s beliefs and through lack of assertion of its own thoughts; it seeks to maintain harmony in its relationships with other "I"'s—by not making its own decisions with regard to other "I"'s, in accordance with its allowing the thoughts of other "I"'s to be manifested through it—in order to have the security of the loyalty and dependable guidance of other "I"'s, so that it can be part of other "I"'s experiences through connecting.

In all of the allowing stages, the "I" feels like it requires the experiences (the instincts, feelings, or thoughts, depending on the stage of fixation) of the world, others, and other "I"'s in order to have any experiences to manifest through itself. This is why it seeks harmony with these things—so that it can have the security of having their experiences to manifest through itself. And this is why it seeks to dissociate from its own experience: so that it can have harmony with the environment, others, and other "I"'s, and so that it can therefore have value to them, and thus have security in, and with, them. Since the "I" expects and wants others to be allowers of experience (of the type of experience of which *it* is an allower, be it instinct, feeling, or thought) like *it* is, it fears not having any experience to allow. So while it feels like it must be an allower of others' experiences, it comes to feel like it should also be a source of experience for others, and a reactive receiver of experience as well, in order to be part of the world, the group, or the experiences of other "I"'s (since if everyone is an allower, there will be no experience for others to allow, and so it feels like it must take on these roles, itself, even though it really just wants to allow others' experiences to be manifested through it). And so it becomes, in a way, a source and a reactive receiver of allowed experiences.

The allowing stages as main personality type fixations result from getting caught up in the role of one of the allowing stages within the downward creative process. Thus, the "I" here feels like it has to have harmony (or peace) in its environment, with others, and with other "I"'s (harmony in the interactions of the sharing stage and the receiving stage prior to it). (For the allowing stage is supposed to bring the different forms of experience—the defined form of the experience shared by the sharing stage and the received and redefined form of the experience of the receiving stage—into harmonized union in some single manifestation as it manifests these experiences through itself.) The "I" here feels like it needs to have harmony in order for it to have success (in its harmonization of the different experiences) and value in its existence (and performance of its role of harmonizing the different experiences). The "I" here feels like it has to have success and value in this in order to have stability and security, and it feels like it has to have stability and security in the experience that it manifests through itself (in the experience that is shared with it by the sharing stage and the receiving stage that are prior to it) in order to fill the void left by its dissociation from its own experience.

Also, the "I" here fears having conflict (or discordance), being worthless (and a failure), and being unstable and insecure (or having no one to depend on) in the experience that it harmonizes and manifests, or fails to harmonize and manifest, through itself. The "I" feels like it has to have harmony, success and value, and stability and security, in order to maintain a place for itself in the world, the group, and the experiences of other "I"'s, so that it can continue to bring together and harmonize different experiences through the way it manifests them through itself.

Each of the allowing stages as fixations produces a different primary focus here, although all of these desires and fears are present to an extent in each of the allowing stages (because the allowing stages as fixations are all caused by being caught up in the role of an allowing stage in that stage's relationship with the stages around it in the creative process).

Allowing instinct primarily desires to have harmony and peace, and it therefore primarily fears having discordance and conflict. It fears these things because if these things become so then it won't have harmony and peace in the different instincts that it has to bring together and harmonize in order to manifest instincts through itself in the form of some kind of boundary on its territory and on itself. And so it will have no boundary, no territory, for itself. It will, therefore, have to allow instincts more, meaning that it will have to dissociate further from its body and its surroundings—from its own instincts—experiencing and expressing its own instincts less and zoning out and daydreaming more, in further efforts to gain harmony and peace.

Allowing feeling primarily desires to have success and value, and it therefore primarily fears being a failure and being worthless. It fears these things because if these things become so then it won't have success and value in the way it brings together and harmonizes different feelings in its manifestation of feelings through itself in the form of some identity. And so it will have no identity for itself. It will, therefore, have to allow feelings more, meaning that it will have to dissociate further from its own feelings, experiencing and expressing its own feelings less and working more—on stuff for a job or whatever—to try to accomplish more and be better at what it does, in further efforts to gain success and value.

Allowing thought primarily desires to have stability and security, and it therefore primarily fears being unstable and insecure and having no one to depend on. It fears these things because if these things become so then it won't have stability and security in the different thoughts that it has to bring together and harmonize in order to manifest thoughts through itself in the form of decisions. And so it will not be able to make decisions for itself or for other "I"'s (because it will be stuck in the indecision of imagining all of the insecure and unstable futures that might arise from each insecurely guided decision). It will, therefore, have to allow thoughts more, meaning that it will have to dissociate further from its own thoughts, experiencing and expressing its own thoughts less and depending on other sources of guidance more, in further efforts to gain stability and security.

However, each of these desires requires that the previous one be fulfilled (in the order of manifestation upward) in order for *it* to be fulfilled. And so allowing instinct desires to have harmony; allowing feeling desires to have harmony *in order to be able* to have success and value; and allowing thought desires to have harmony *in order to be able* to have success and value, and it desires to have success and value *in order to* have stability and security.

Notice, here, that in all of the allowing stages, the "I"'s desire to maintain harmony in order to have security presents a barrier to the "I"'s being part of what it wants to be a part of (namely its environment, the group of others, and the experiences of other "I"'s), for the "I" is not present in and as itself in order to be capable of being part of what it wants to be part of. Notice, also, that this problem arises solely due to the "I"'s fixating upon a certain stage (and consequently projecting that fixation onto the world and others), and getting caught up with merely fulfilling the role of that stage in the creative process, rather than expressing all of the stages in their true forms (and recognizing others as distinct other "I"'s).

The creative process downward traces out the flow of the Source's experience—of self-aware existence, itself—through each stage of the tree of life on its path into this world of manifestation. When we are fixated on one of these stages, we determine, in this way, what we feel like we need in order to feel like we truly exist—what we feel like we need in order to receive self-aware existence, in order to recognize the flow of existence through us—because, through this fixation, we determine a fixated role or purpose for ourselves in the formation, or creation, of this world.

The sharing stages feel like they need to be in control and helpful and useful in order to feel like they truly exist—in order to feel like they are fulfilling their role or purpose in this world, and like their existence is cared about and is needed and wanted for its effect or impact on (for what they share with) the world, others, and other "I"'s. The receiving stages feel like they need to be good and complete and fulfilled in order to feel like they truly exist—in order to feel like they are fulfilling their role or purpose in this world, and like their existence is uniquely significant to the world, others, and other "I"'s, distinct from that of everyone and everything else. The allowing stages feel like they need to have harmony and success and security in order to feel like they truly exist—in order to feel like they are fulfilling their role or purpose in this world, and like their existence is valuable and has a meaning and purpose to the world, others, and other "I"'s.

When we are self-aware, and we are not so fixated on a single stage but, instead, have developed fully upward to choice, we allow our intuition to guide us in the decisions that we make, recognizing that, in our essence, we are truly the capacity to choose how we define our experience, and acting from that essence by creating our lives downward through all of the stages from choice. And we recognize, at this point, that we don't need to *work* to *do* anything, and we don't need to *work* to *be* anything, and we don't need to *work* to *make decisions*, because merely by being a projection of willful and self-aware existence in this world, we are doing all of the things that we truly want to do, and we are being all of the things that we truly want to be, and we are making all of the decisions that we truly want to make. And we recognize that merely by *existing* as a projection of self-aware and willful existence in this world, we are cared about for the impact we have, and we are uniquely significant, and we are valuable. In truth, working against the natural flow of things, by holding onto things, will never get us what we want. When we willfully define and create our experiences in the world with awareness, and we receive these experiences with awareness, and we allow these experiences to pass with awareness, then we do not have to *work* at anything with tremendous effort, because we simply *are*, and the world flows through us, taking on the forms—in our internal and external experience—that yield us all of the things that we truly want, that yield us greater self-aware existence.

Allowing instinct feels that if it has harmony in its environment, then it will be able to preserve its existence. Receiving instinct feels that if it has a complete environment, then it will be able to preserve its existence. Sharing instinct feels that if it is in control of its environment, then it will be able to preserve its existence. Allowing feeling feels that if it has harmony in its interactions with others, then it will be able to fit in with others. Receiving feeling feels that if it is complete in its interactions with others, then it will be able to fit in with others. Sharing feeling feels that if it is in control of its interactions with others, then it will be able to fit in with others. Allowing thought feels that if it has harmony in its interactions with other "I'''s and with the world, then it will be able to make the best decisions for itself and other "I'''s. Receiving thought feels that if it is complete in its interactions with other "I'''s and with the world, then it will be able to make the best decisions for itself and other "I'''s. Sharing thought feels that if it is in control of its interactions with other "I'''s and with the world, then it will be able to make the best decisions for itself and other "I'''s.

In the allowing stages: Allowing instinct is in the transition from living in a zoned-out, timeless non-existence to living with its attention on its environment in the present, from where it gets instincts to manifest through itself in the form of its extension of its environment to itself. Allowing feeling is in the transition from living in its environment in the present to living with its attention on its relationship with others in the past, from where it gets feelings to manifest through itself in the form of its projection of others' passions upon its own self-image. Allowing thought is in the transition from living in its relationship with others in the past to living with its attention on its possible future interactions with other "I'''s, from where it gets thoughts to manifest through itself in the form of its decisions.

In the receiving stages: Receiving instinct is inclined to get stuck on the imperfection that exists in itself and in its environment in the present, and it receives instincts from this present imperfection in itself and in its environment. Receiving feeling is inclined to get stuck on the incompletion of itself in its relationship to others in the past, and it receives feelings from this past incompletion in its self-image. Receiving thought is inclined to get stuck on the possibly-more-fulfilling future interactions with other "I'''s that could result from the decisions that it makes, and it receives thoughts from the potential fulfillment of these future interactions.

In the sharing stages: Sharing instinct is inclined to take control of itself and its environment in the present, imposing its instincts upon its environment in the form of its dominating extension of itself to it. Sharing feeling is inclined to take control of its relationship with others in the past, imposing its feelings upon that relationship in the form of its helpful self-image. Sharing thought is inclined to take control of its possible future interactions with other "I"'s, imposing its thoughts upon those interactions in the form of its understanding about them and the decisions that it makes in light of this understanding.

In the sharing stages, sharing instinct seeks time with its environment to create new, action-oriented instincts, sharing feeling seeks time with other people to create new, loving and caring feelings, and sharing thought seeks time to itself to create new, innovative thoughts. In the receiving stages, receiving instinct seeks frustrating experiences to stimulate (or from which to receive) instincts, receiving feeling seeks emotionally intense experiences to stimulate (or from which to receive) feelings, and receiving thought seeks exciting experiences to stimulate (or from which to receive) thoughts. In the allowing stages, allowing instinct seeks to exist peaceably and unintrusively in its environment in order to have assertive instincts around it to manifest, allowing feeling seeks to interact harmoniously with others in order to have passionate feelings around it to manifest, and allowing thought seeks to make decisions that will maintain harmony with (and the dependability of) other "I"'s in order to have decisive thoughts around it to manifest.

Since the sharing stages seek to create, and be a source of, their own experience, they seek people who want to receive the experience that they wish to share—so that they will be useful to, and will feel in control and helpful with, (and will therefore feel like their existence is cared about for its impact on) those people. Sharing instinct seeks other people and other aspects of the world that want to receive the action-oriented instincts that it creates, so that it will be in control and have an impact on them, and will therefore be useful to, and thus able to preserve its existence with, them. Sharing feeling seeks other people and other aspects of the world that want to receive the feelings of love and caring that it creates, so that it will be helpful to them and needed by them, and therefore useful to, and thus able to fit in with, them. Sharing thought seeks other people and other aspects of the world that want to receive the innovative thoughts that it creates, so that it will be interesting to them and capable around them, and therefore useful to, and thus able to connect with, them.

Since the receiving stages seek to receive and manifest within themselves experience in reaction to their world, they seek people who are sources of the kind of experience that they are inclined to grasp at and hold onto—so that they will be fulfilled, and will feel good and complete, (and will therefore feel like their existence is uniquely significant) with those people. Receiving instinct seeks other people and other aspects of the world that are sources of strong and good instincts for it, so that it will be filled with instincts, and thus good and right, and therefore fulfilled and able to preserve its existence, with them. Receiving feeling seeks other people and other aspects of the world that are sources of intense feelings for it, so that it will be filled with feelings, and thus complete and uniquely significant, and therefore fulfilled and able to fit in, with them. Receiving thought seeks other people and other aspects of the world that are sources of exciting thoughts for it, so that it will be filled with thoughts, and thus happy and excited, and therefore fulfilled and able to connect, with them.

Since the allowing stages seek to allow the experiences of others to be manifested through them, they seek people who express the experience that they are inclined to allow to be manifested through them—so that they will be secure, and will feel that they have harmony and success, (and will therefore feel like their existence is valuable and meaningful) with those people. Allowing instinct seeks other people and other aspects of the world that express their instincts assertively, so that it will have the security of having instincts to manifest through itself, and therefore of being able to maintain a peaceful and comfortable environment in which it can preserve its existence, with them. Allowing feeling seeks other people and other aspects of the world that express their feelings passionately, so that it will have the security of having feelings to manifest through itself, and therefore of being successful and valuable in those others' perception and able to fit in, with them. Allowing thought seeks other people and other aspects of the world that express their thoughts confidently and decisively, so that it will have the security of having thoughts to manifest through itself, and therefore of having a dependable source of guidance with which it can make decisions regarding itself and other "I"'s, with them.

The Main Stage Types as they Relate to Parts of the Body

Since the tree of life paradigm manifests everywhere in an ever-increasing variety of forms, we can learn more about one thing from a seemingly completely different thing that is the reflection of the same stage of the paradigm but merely in a different context. (This is the reason that metaphors and similes and other forms of comparison used to describe or understand something better are so useful in this world—because this world is holographic, or self-reflective, in its nature, such that every part of it is a manifestation of the same paradigm as the whole and as every other part of it.) In this case, we can learn more about the main stage type fixations from the parts of the human body that correspond to the same stages of the paradigm.

Allowing instinct corresponds to the sexual organ. Like the sexual organ is inclined to merge with the other, allowing instinct is inclined to harmoniously merge with other "I"'s, and with its surroundings in the world, in its interactions with these things. Also, as the sexual organ seeks pleasure through ways that (ideally) give pleasure to the other, allowing instinct seeks the fulfillment of peace for itself through the existence of peace among others. Further, as the sexual organ single-mindedly seeks positive experiences for itself, allowing instinct is inclined to notice the positive side of things and to ignore the negative—viewing things in a positively filtered light—often with a single-minded stubbornness.

Receiving instinct corresponds to the left leg. Like the left leg tends to follow the lead of the right leg (in people who have a dominant right side of the body—who are right-handed and so on—which is most people due to the reflection of the dominant, sharing, creative, initiating nature of the sharing side of all interactions, which is the right side), receiving instinct seeks to follow the lead of the instincts it receives from the world (through its reactions to the world), manifesting these instincts in its own actions.

Sharing instinct corresponds to the right leg. Like the right leg tends to lead (when the right side of the body is dominant) or initiate walking (taking the first step forward, or up stairs), sharing instinct tends to lead in situations—particularly those requiring physical action—initiating the instincts that manifest in its environment through its and other "I"'s actions.

Allowing feeling corresponds to the heart. Like the heart has a clear function and goal that it must constantly be performing and working to achieve in order to have value to the organism, allowing feeling is constantly setting goals and working to achieve them, always trying to accomplish something, because it is inclined to feel like it must constantly be working to achieve some goal or other in order to have value to the group and to other "I"'s—it is inclined to feel that it, like the heart, has no value or purpose apart from the performance of its function.

Receiving feeling corresponds to the left arm. Like the left arm tends to be very restrictive in its actions (when the right arm is dominant), receiving feeling tends to be very restrictive in its active and outward expression of emotions. Also, as the left hand is not often used to shake hands, and so does not participate in this conventional form of outward display of emotion in relation to others, receiving feeling often does not participate—and often feels that it should be exempt from having to participate—in conventional or usual forms of expression or ways of doing things.

Sharing feeling corresponds to the right arm. Like the right arm tends to be very assertive and encompassing in its actions (when the right arm is dominant), sharing feeling tends to be very assertive in its active and outward expression of emotions. Also, notice that it is the arms that are used to hug people or to shake hands—to express feelings, like caring and love—and it is receiving feeling and sharing feeling that correspond to the arms (and it is the right hand that is usually involved in shaking hands, or even in hugging when the hug is not a full hug with both arms).

Allowing thought corresponds to the brain stem (and spinal cord). Like the brain stem (and spinal cord) receives its higher thought and decisions from the brain hemispheres and manifests these through the body's actions, allowing thought receives its higher thoughts (the contents of its thoughts)— when it comes to decision-making—from other "I"'s and manifests these through its own actions. Also, corresponding to the brain stem, which serves as the bridge between thought and the body, allowing thought's own thinking is separate or disconnected from, and is not grounded in, its body, and so allowing thought does not feel secure in trusting its own thinking to guide it in making decisions regarding its actions—which is why it, instead, seeks such guidance in other "I"'s and things outside itself.

Receiving thought corresponds to the left hemisphere of the brain. Like the left hemisphere of the brain systematizes and orders thoughts linearly, receiving thought makes lists and schedules of activities and experiences in which it might engage and gives linear order to its thoughts in the form of the order of its engagement with them in its outward experiences in the world. Also, like the left hemisphere starts with the concrete, tangible details of the physical world as it is (in its experiences with it) and then puts these together to form the whole picture, receiving thought derives its thoughts from its concrete experiences with the physical world (through its reactions to them) in pieces and then seeks to put these thoughts together afterward. Receiving thought deals in its thoughts primarily with concrete, physical objects and activities that exist or take place in the world and that receiving thought has received in its thoughts, in some form, from its active engagement with experience linearly in time.

Sharing thought corresponds to the right hemisphere of the brain. Like the right hemisphere of the brain creates new thoughts spontaneously—thoughts that are only later to be ordered—sharing thought creates new thoughts spontaneously, as (often seemingly random) sparks of insight that must later be placed systematically into sharing thought's framework of understanding. Also, like the right hemisphere of the brain starts with the whole picture and then seeks to fill in the details, dealing very much with the abstract and symbolic, sharing thought starts with a whole framework and then seeks to understand each of the parts of that framework, placing its abstract and symbolic representations of reality into that framework. Sharing thought deals in its thoughts primarily with abstract, symbolic representations of objects and activities that *could* exist or take place in the world—as viewed through sharing thought's created big-picture-framework of understanding—and that sharing thought has formed through spontaneous sparks or flashes of insight.

The Main Stage Types in Development

Remember, all stages of development are manifesting continually: Monkeys still exist even though they evolved to become human beings, who are further along on the path toward choice and self-awareness, children are still being born even though they aren't as developed on the path toward choice as older people and, likewise, new souls are still being formed even though this means that there are souls that have had more time to develop and so are further along in the development of self-aware understanding of what it is to be like the Source. And so some of us have lived more lives than others. Consequently, some of us have had more time to actualize the developmental stages and grow further toward choice, while others are still full of the potential to manifest all of the stages and haven't yet had the opportunity of many lifetimes to do this.

Ultimately, each of the stages of development encompasses something that needs to be integrated into understanding on the path toward an understanding of the relation between us (the world) and the Source, and of what it is to be the Source. And so, in order to attain this understanding, we ultimately will experience—over the course of many, many lifetimes—what it is to be fixated on various aspects of each stage on the path up toward choice (this includes our experiencing being female in some lifetimes and male in others, our experiencing being born under different astrological signs in different lifetimes, as well as our experiencing fixation upon other different aspects of each of the different stages), getting a little closer to choice each time.

Consequently, it seems quite likely that the general trend should be that we move from manifestation up toward choice, at least with regard to the main personality type stage—for the main personality type stage of fixation encompasses nearly all of the aspects of that stage, thereby truly allowing us to come to understand experientially all that we can about that stage. It is likely that, just as we can move down and up the stages of development in our degree of fixation upon our main personality type stage with the development of self-awareness or lack thereof, we can also move down and up the stages as main personality types if we fail to develop within some lifetime and possibly need to be reminded of something from a previous stage, or if we learn a great deal maybe about even more than just the stage on which we are currently fixated in this lifetime. Each new life is likely determined by the manifestation of the last life, just as each new moment is determined by the manifestation of the last moment; we can fixate to the point of stagnation or even of regression, or we can progress to the next stage. And we would almost certainly have to live many lifetimes with each single personality type fixation—probably with different gender and other things in each of these lifetimes—in order to come truly to experientially understand all that can be gleaned from this stage and its relation to all of the other stages.

[Notice that the part of you that reincarnates is not your personality, or your gender, or any other of the results of your fixation upon the different aspects of the different stages in the tree of life paradigm. The part of you that reincarnates is the part of you that is capable of fixating upon different aspects of different stages; the part of you that reincarnates is your essence—the ability to choose and, thereby, the potential to be self-aware and to share and shape the contents of your experience with self-awareness.]

But, anyway, this general trend would suggest that instinctual stage type fixations generally occur in and indicate young or beginner souls, feeling stage type fixations generally occur in and indicate intermediate level souls, and thinking stage type fixations generally occur in and indicate the souls that are oldest and furthest along in the development up the tree of life toward choice and self-aware understanding—the ultimate goal of the whole world. Another way to look at this is that instinctual stage types, like children relative to adults, have the most potential that they have yet to actualize (due, in most cases, to the lack of the opportunity of sufficient time spent within this physical world to actualize it), feeling stage types have actualized more of their potential (and they've been around longer to be able to do so), and thinking stage types, like adults relative to children (for the most part) have actualized most of their potential (and they've been around the longest to be able to do so).

This general trend would suggest that every person of every main stage type has experienced lifetimes of having each of the previous stage type fixations as his/her main stage type fixation, and (excluding instances of regression) has not experienced lifetimes of having each of the later stage type fixations (the ones closer to choice) as his/her main stage type fixation. This would explain why instinctual-stage-type people tend to be mostly present-oriented, feeling-stage-type people tend to be mostly past-oriented, and thinking-stage-type people tend to be mostly future-oriented (beyond merely attributing these orientations to aspects of the stage upon which the people are most fixated): The first haven't lived so much before and so are concerned with just experiencing what *is*, the second have lived more before and so are more inclined to reflect on what *was*, and the third have lived enough that now they are starting to become familiar with the trend of things and so start looking forward to what *is to come*. And this general trend would particularly explain the apparent general increasing familiarity with, and recognition of, (in this order of progression, from instinctual to feeling to thinking stage type fixated people) certain aspects of experience, such as all of the spectrums of the dominant positive feelings (in their entirety), which are discussed in the next sections.

Also, we must remember that at each personality type stage, there are nine possible degrees of fixation upon this stage (and upon all of the other stages, which every individual person contains), and the less fixated we are upon one stage, the more we encompass all of the other stages in our awareness and ability to create and manifest our lives. So, self-awareness can be reached by everyone, born into any main personality type stage of fixation. It is merely that there are degrees of self-aware understanding of the relation of the Source to the world, and of the Source's experience, and all understanding is rooted in experience, and so the experience of having been fixated on each and every stage, and of having overcome each of these fixations to express each stage in the form of the true role it plays in the full creative process (thereby having experientially learned, and become fluent in, the full vocabulary of the language of creation) seems to be a prerequisite to the highest possible degree of self-aware understanding of the Source's experience. And so this kind of highest possible degree of self-aware understanding of the Source's experience is accessible to all of us ultimately, but not to all of us within this particular lifetime.

But self-awareness is the goal for everyone. As long as we remain fixated upon various aspects of each stage (on anything and everything from personality features, to physical features, to weaknesses and strengths, aversions and interests, difficulties and talents, and so on), we will continue to manifest those fixations anew in every moment and in every physical life into which we reincarnate. Only through the attainment of self-awareness at some particular stage, and the overcoming of each of our fixations at that stage, can we move on, upward, in the process of development. As we overcome our obstacles—transcending our fixations—and attain self-awareness at each stage, we move further along the path toward choice, and toward the ultimate goal. And every step in the direction toward self-awareness is just as significant as every other. It is a step closer to complete fulfillment in this lifetime—achieving the goals we have set out for ourselves in this lifetime—and it is, thereby, a step closer to complete fulfillment of the ultimate goal of which all goals are a part.

Keeping this general progression from manifestation toward choice in mind, we can identify the main things that a person has to learn at each personality type stage (and therefore what he/she hasn't yet learned in previous stages) in order to become less fixated upon this stage, and thus in order to free himself/herself to progress further toward choice in this lifetime and overall.

The "I" fixated upon allowing instinct must learn to connect to its *own* instincts, manifesting *these* through itself, rather than merely submitting to other "I"'s and manifesting *other "I"'s instincts* through it detachedly. Therefore, this "I" must learn that true peace and harmony come from *it*, and therefore from actively and mindfully *creating* and *receiving within itself* and *manifesting through itself* its *own* instincts—from being fully present to, and expressive of, its *own* instincts. The "I" fixated upon receiving instinct must learn to create, actively and mindfully, its *own* instincts, rather than merely grasping at and holding onto and manifesting within itself experiences with other "I"'s and the world that *produce* instincts *in it in reaction to* these experiences. Therefore, this "I" must learn that it will only truly be good and right if it accepts what *is* in the world and lets it go, mindfully and proactively *creating* improvements in itself and in the world and fully *receiving within itself* and *manifesting through itself these*—its *own* instincts that originate with *it*. The "I" fixated upon sharing instinct must learn to *receive within itself* and *manifest through itself* instincts from other "I"s and from the world outside itself, and not just to create its *own* instincts *in disregard of* other "I"s and the world outside itself. Therefore, this "I" must learn that it will only truly be in control if it *allows* other "I"s and the world to lead and shape and control themselves *through* it, rather than *imposing* its *own* instincts on other "I"s and the world outside itself.

The "I" fixated upon allowing feeling must learn to connect to its *own* feelings, manifesting *these* through itself, rather than merely submitting to other "I"s and manifesting *other "I"s feelings* through it detachedly. Therefore, this "I" must learn that true value comes from being itself, and therefore from actively and mindfully *creating* and *receiving within itself* and *manifesting through itself* its *own* feelings—from being fully present to, and true to, and expressive of, its *own* feelings. The "I" fixated upon receiving feeling must learn to create, actively and mindfully, its *own* feelings, rather than merely grasping at and holding onto and manifesting within itself experiences with other "I"s and the world that *produce* feelings *in it in reaction to* these experiences. Therefore, this "I" must learn that it will only truly be unique if it accepts what *is* in itself and lets it go, mindfully and proactively *creating* the role it wishes to take upon itself, and fully *receiving within itself* and *manifesting through itself this*—its *own* feelings that originate with *it*. The "I" fixated upon sharing feeling must learn to *receive within itself* and *manifest through itself* feelings from other "I"s and from the world outside itself, and not just to create its *own* feelings *in disregard of* other "I"s and the world outside itself. Therefore, this "I" must learn that it will only truly be helpful if it *allows* other "I"s and the world to help and love and care for themselves *through* it, rather than *imposing* its *own* feelings on other "I"s and the world outside itself.

The "I" fixated upon allowing thought must learn to connect to its *own* thoughts, manifesting *these* through itself, rather than merely submitting to other "I"'s and manifesting *other "I"'s thoughts* through it detachedly. Therefore, this "I" must learn that true security and guidance come from *it*, and therefore from actively and mindfully *creating* and *receiving within itself* and *manifesting through itself* its *own* thoughts—from being fully present to, and trusting in, and expressive of, its *own* thoughts. The "I" fixated upon receiving thought must learn to create, actively and mindfully, its *own* thoughts, rather than merely grasping at and holding onto and manifesting within itself experiences with other "I"'s and the world that *produce* thoughts *in it in reaction to* these experiences. Therefore, this "I" must learn that it will only truly be happy and fulfilled if it accepts what *is* in its experience and lets it go, mindfully and proactively *creating* fulfilling experiences and fully *receiving within itself* and *manifesting through itself these*—its *own* thoughts that originate with *it*. The "I" fixated upon sharing thought must learn to *receive within itself* and *manifest through itself* thoughts from other "I"'s and from the world outside itself, and not just to create its *own* thoughts *in disregard of* other "I"'s and the world outside itself. Therefore, this "I" must learn that it will only truly be competent and useful if it *allows* other "I"'s and the world to understand, and be useful to, themselves *through* it, rather than *imposing* its *own* thoughts on other "I"'s and the world outside itself.

And so we learn from every stage together that we cannot allow our experiences to be created and received and manifested for us, through us; we cannot allow our experiences to be created for us in reaction to people and things outside ourselves and then grasp at and hold onto the manifestation of these experiences within us in the form in which we receive them; and we cannot create our own experiences in disregard of everyone and everything outside ourselves. The goal of self-awareness entails creating experiences (ultimately all the way from choice down through thought, feeling, and instinct) that are grounded in consideration of the perspectives of other "I"'s and the world around us, but that originate with us, and then fully receiving those experiences within ourselves (those experiences that we have created, ourselves, in mindful response to other "I"'s and the world around us) and then allowing those experiences (those experiences that have originated with us and that have been fully received in our own experience) to be manifested through us.

In this way, the goal of full self-awareness encompasses all elements—all stages—of the tree of life paradigm in their true and pure forms, uncorrupted by our fixation upon them. We create and share, receive within ourselves, and allow to be manifested through ourselves, all of our experiences—our thoughts, feelings, and instincts (and therefore also our speech and actions). And so, essentially and ultimately, by allowing the Source's experience to be manifested through ourselves, we create and manifest the Source's experience within our own experience. For when we reach choice (which *is* manifestation of the next moment), we become an allowing force—a central column—thereby revealing that we started out pretty close to the correct place in some sense after all (by beginning at allowing instinct, which is the first stage to manifest after choice becomes manifestation). We reveal that where we begin in our development reflects where we will ultimately end, in our allowing all things to flow through us, and it is merely that we must do this *mindfully* and *proactively* and with *all* experiences (including thoughts, feelings, and instincts), and *not* in a disconnected way and with just one or another aspect of our experience. We must share and receive all experiences *fully*, allowing them to touch us fully and then allowing them to pass fully.

Thus, the aim of this whole path of development, with all of its stages, is to bring us to an experiential understanding and awareness of all elements of every aspect of experience—so that we can learn, and become intimately aware of, the true function and purpose of all of them (of every stage in the tree of life paradigm) in the process of creation. For then we can use this understanding to allow the Source's experience to be created and received and manifested within our own experience mindfully and willfully and proactively. We need to attain an intimately self-aware understanding of each stage in the pattern of development so that we can come ultimately to see all aspects of the world and of every "I"'s experience within our own experience—so that we can reach the ultimate goal of seeing all aspects of the Source "I"'s experience within our own experience. In this way, we can become able to find, in our own experience, the meaning of the language that the Source is using to describe *Its* experience. In this way, we can come to experientially understand, and know, what it is to be the Source of all that is.

The Dominant Positive Feelings of the Main Stage Types

There is a dominant positive feeling associated with each of the three main parts of the paradigm—grouping the instinctual stages together as one part, the feeling stages together as another part, and the thinking stages together as the last part. Further, there is a corrupted version of each of these dominant positive feelings, and a negative version of each of them as well. And every one of these feelings is a reflection of the experience of the world (as a whole) at some stage in its development.

Beginning at the start of the physical universe, when the physical universe first begins to manifest, the world is entering the spatial framework (the tree of life), and it is empty. For, a bit like at the end of the universe, in which there are several black hole singularities but increasingly empty, cold, expanding space besides this, the universe begins in the singularity of the white hole that is the Big Bang and begins expanding into the spatial framework that exists in some sort of potential form and is merely not as actually infinite as at the end of the universe (after the universe has expanded to encompass self-awareness). Further, the very beginning of the universe is completely chaotic, full of conflict and seemingly uncontrolled disorder, as energy begins to spew out of the Big Bang singularity—a point where no laws have yet begun to manifest themselves in ordering or giving meaning to the chaos. There is almost an absence of time, and space hasn't yet begun to take any real concrete form. Here, we have the state of the world of which the negative version of the instinctual stages feeling is a reflection.

The negative version of the instinctual stages feeling is a feeling of emptiness, of utter lack of presence, of utter lack of control over the shaping of yourself and your world, of utter lack of all that is good and right and correct, of utter lack of peace and harmony. You would probably experience this feeling upon finding out that someone you knew committed suicide, or that there is right now a terrorist attack occurring in a place that is very familiar to you and many people are dying. The light of self-aware existence is completely absent, and so you feel completely nonexistent, completely empty, completely powerless, completely out of touch with the *substance* of existence, itself, because you have no control over the language necessary to shape existence. You feel like you don't have any control over your world, like you can't have any good or positive effect, or *any* effect, upon it at all (for true control comes through self-awareness, which is completely lacking at this point), and by not having any effect, it feels almost as though you are having a bad or negative or corrupt effect, increasing the conflict somehow. And so we see that the negative version of the instinctual stages feeling is the result of a high degree of fixation upon the instinctual stages (you are holding onto instincts, repeating them over and over again, and not allowing them to pass and be replaced by any new inclinations, and thus any new actions, at all), which causes them to be corrupted so extremely as to lead to the experience of their complete lack of fulfillment.

As the universe begins to take form after the Big Bang, and the chaos of the initial explosion of disorder subsides, matter begins to take definite shape, forming elegant and ordered spherical bodies that rotate on their own axes and revolve around one another in an ordered and systematic fashion—as stars, planets, galaxies, and so on, take form. Harmony and order are establishing themselves as the world begins to use the language of inclined movement of matter and energy (the manifestation of various physical forces) to shape and take control of itself and its formation. Here, we have the state of the world of which the corrupted version of the instinctual stages feeling is a reflection.

The corrupted version of the instinctual stages feeling is a feeling of chills, of waves of energy running down your body, almost through your skin, almost tingling or vibrating. You would probably experience a slightly more corrupted version of this feeling (for all of the versions of the instinctual stages feeling are part of a spectrum from negative to corrupted to positive) upon entering a dark room and suddenly hearing someone shout, "Boo!" And you would probably experience a slightly less corrupted version of this feeling if you've been kind of stressed lately and you are giving a speech before a large audience and you begin to hear the people cheering favorably in response to what you are saying. It feels almost good, but not quite completely good. It feels almost like you are having a positive and measurable effect upon your world, and yet like you aren't quite completely having a positive and measurable effect upon your world. It feels like you are almost in control, and yet like you aren't quite completely in control. It feels almost as though you are establishing goodness and correctness and order in your world and your surroundings, and yet like you aren't quite completely establishing goodness and correctness and order. It feels almost as though there is peace and harmony in your world, and yet not quite like there is complete peace and harmony. There is *some* self-aware existence, but there is a lack of *complete* self-aware existence due to your holding onto your conception that your instincts and speech and actions are the ultimate source of the energy and substance of existence that you experience, and so you cannot be fully in control of the shaping of your world, for you are not truly self-aware. And so we see that the corrupted version of the instinctual stages feeling is the result of an intermediate degree of fixation upon the instinctual stages (you are holding onto instincts, repeating them over and over, and only allowing them to pass *somewhat* and be replaced by *some* new inclinations, and thus *some* new actions), which causes them to be corrupted to the point that their complete fulfillment is incapable of being experienced, and so there is only a partial feeling of fulfillment (and, consequently, also a partial feeling of lack of fulfillment).

Just before the Big Bang, before the world enters physical existence, when the non-physical world is in the instinctual stages of creation—as it is creating the physical world from the top down—it is in the process of creating the physical world with self-awareness gained from experiential understanding. Here, we have the state of the world of which the dominant positive version of the instinctual stages feeling is a reflection—and thus we have the ultimate origin of the instinctual stages feeling in its true and pure form.

The dominant positive feeling of the instinctual stages is a feeling of complete and full presence—in your body and in the world—like your whole body is simultaneously tingling or vibrating throughout with the energy of existence, itself. You would probably experience this feeling if you have been very de-stressed for a while (either because you simply haven't had any stresses in your life or because you have been handling the stresses in your life very well) and you are actively in the process of shaping your life, following the guidance of your intuition, in the language that you are using, right now, in your thoughts and feelings and actions, and you are aware of the impact that what you are doing is having. Maybe, for example, you see the business or something else that you have been in the process of creating finally beginning to take form, really and actually, in the physical world. You are completely aware of the impact that your use of language in the present moment—your thoughts, your feelings, your inclinations and speech and actions—is having, in the context of the past that led up to this moment, and in the context of the future that this moment is in the process of creating. You feel completely in control and good and at peace—like you are having a significant and positive effect upon your world through the language that you are, at this moment, using, and like you can do anything, like you are truly powerful. You are allowing the Source's language to be manifested through you and to shape existence through you. And you are thereby allowing the Source's experience to be created and manifested through you as you allow the energy and substance of self-aware existence to flow through you—from beyond you, from the Source—while you shape it with your use of language. And so we see that the dominant positive version of the instinctual stages feeling is the result of a complete lack of fixation upon any stages at all, for it is the experience of your self-aware creating and shaping of the world.

As life begins to take shape on some planets in the universe, the starts of its propagating manifestation are repeatedly halted with changes in the environment and other events that prove that life made the wrong adaptations. The result is a number of mass extinctions, threatening to wipe out all or nearly all of the propagating life each time. Here, we have the state of the world of which the negative version of the feeling stages feeling is a reflection.

The negative version of the feeling stages feeling is a sinking feeling—a feeling, located mainly in the heart or chest area, of energy sinking. You would probably experience this feeling if you've suddenly realized that you left your keys in the car or house and the car or house doors are locked. It feels like you've made a significant mistake, and you are suddenly filled with regret as though regret has been poured into you. It feels like you are stagnating—like you are not making any progress or getting anywhere—as you linger in your past actions that got you to where you are. It feels like your past use of language—in your thoughts, in your feelings, in your inclinations, and especially in your speech and actions (for these are the most obviously impactful in your interactions with others)—has made you utterly lack personal significance and value and the love of the world and others. And so we see that the negative version of the feeling stages feeling is the result of a high degree of fixation upon the feeling stages (you are holding onto feelings, repeating them over and over again, and not allowing them to pass and be replaced by any new feelings at all), which causes them to be corrupted so extremely as to lead to the experience of their complete lack of fulfillment.

After life really begins to take hold—adapting in numerous ways to the environment—and mass extinctions happen significantly less frequently, life has proven resilient and valuable in the world. Life really begins to flourish and propagate, with little hindrance to its completely covering whole planets with its vitality. Here, we have the state of the world of which the corrupted version of the feeling stages feeling is a reflection.

The corrupted version of the feeling stages feeling is a feeling of energy flushing or flowing through the body, as though stemming from the heart or chest area, but it is as though the energy still has a bit of blockage that is restraining its flow away from the chest, and this results in a feeling of constriction or tightness in the chest and throat area—like the energy is flowing but is unable to flow completely freely, like the water in a stream that has a partial dam in it. You would probably experience this feeling if you've been stressed lately and now you are remembering when, earlier in the day, someone you care about complemented you. Or, a bit higher on the spectrum (for all of the versions of the feeling stages feeling are part of a spectrum from negative to corrupted to positive), you've been kind of stressed lately and now, suddenly, someone you care about hugs you. It feels like you are personally significant, and yet you aren't quite completely personally significant. It feels like you are valuable for who you are, and yet you aren't quite completely valuable for who you are. It feels like you are loved and cared about, and yet you aren't quite completely loved and cared about. The energy of self-aware existence is beginning to flow through you, but your holding onto things—such as your holding onto your feelings as the source of the energy and significance of existence that you experience—is preventing self-aware existence from flowing freely throughout your body. And so we see that the corrupted version of the feeling stages feeling is the result of an intermediate degree of fixation upon the feeling stages (you are holding onto feelings, repeating them over and over, and only allowing them to pass *somewhat* and be replaced by *some* new feelings), which causes them to be corrupted to the point that their complete fulfillment is incapable of being experienced, and so there is only a partial feeling of fulfillment (and, consequently, also a partial feeling of lack of fulfillment).

Before the Big Bang, when the non-physical world has reached the feeling stages of creation, it is in the process of applying experiential understanding in its self-aware creation of the physical world from the top down. Here, we have the state of the world of which the dominant positive version of the feeling stages feeling is a reflection—and thus we have the ultimate origin of the feeling stages feeling in its true and pure form.

The dominant positive feeling of the feeling stages is a feeling of energy flushing or flowing freely from the heart or chest area throughout the entire body, filling the body completely with energy as this energy simply flows through the body. You would probably experience this feeling if you have been very de-stressed for a while (either because you simply haven't had any stresses in your life or because you have been handling the stresses in your life very well) and you are, at this moment, very aware of how significant and valuable and loved you are. Maybe, for example, you just gave a homeless person a delicious meal that you prepared, and that person expressed obvious gratitude for your help. You know that the language that you have just used—in your thoughts, in your feelings, in your inclinations and speech and actions—makes you a helpful and valuable and significant part of the creation of this world, because you are allowing the love of the world to flow through you and into others. You are allowing the Source's experience to be manifested through you as you allow the energy and significance of self-aware existence to flow through you—from beyond you, from the Source—and to be shaped through you. And you are thereby sharing self-awareness with others, helping the Source to achieve Its aim of sharing Its experience with the world, and helping the world to achieve its aim of attaining the experience of what it is to be the Source. And so we see that the dominant positive version of the feeling stages feeling is the result of a complete lack of fixation upon any stages at all, for it is the experience of the process of the application of experiential understanding in the form of your aiding in the self-aware creating and shaping of the world.

As the physical universe repeats the tree of life paradigm over and over again, manifesting more and more variations of life, more and more life forms, but with none of them ever quite being able to become aware of their own existence, the physical universe expands increasingly rapidly, and time in the universe increases its pace as matter and energy disperse, increasingly diluted by relatively empty space. Here, we have the state of the world of which the negative version of the thinking stages feeling is a reflection.

The negative version of the thinking stages feeling is a feeling of the mind racing, as though the wheel of the mind is spinning wildly out of control, unable to latch onto anything or to process anything entirely. You would probably experience this feeling if you have way too many overwhelming and confining things that you have to do—way too many confining thoughts racing through your head, and it is all like roaring static. It feels like your mind can't encompass all of them, can't deal with all of them, can't process all of them, and you are flooded with anxiety. And you feel an utter lack of competence and capability and usefulness, an utter lack of stability and security and guidance, and an utter lack of fulfillment and joy. You feel completely overwhelmed and completely unstable and completely trapped. You feel like you don't understand or know anything at all, and like you aren't capable of making any decisions or of doing anything at all. Your mind is spinning so fast that it is painful, and it feels as though you are moving in slow motion relative to everything around you as the world rushes by, and you cannot possibly keep up with the pace of things—you can't do everything, and you have no idea what to do; you are completely indecisive, stuck in indecision. And so we see that the negative version of the thinking stages feeling is the result of a high degree of fixation upon the thinking stages (you are holding onto thoughts, repeating them over and over again, and not allowing them to pass and be replaced by any new thoughts at all), which causes them to be corrupted so extremely as to lead to the experience of their complete lack of fulfillment.

As the physical universe finally begins to manifest life forms that are intelligent enough to start to become aware of their own existence and their relation to each other and the world and the Source, its expansion begins to encompass self-aware-ness in its scope of experience. And so the universe expands increasingly rapidly, with time ever increasing its pace, but now this expansion is encompassing the entire paradigm of the tree of life, as the whole paradigm repeats increasingly rapidly in its entirety, bringing understanding of all of the rest of the universe, and of its true nature and purpose, into the scope of the universe's bounds. Here, we have the state of the world of which the corrupted version of the thinking stages feeling is a reflection.

The corrupted version of the thinking stages feeling is a feeling that your mind is expanding to encompass something within its understanding, but there are bounds on your mind's expansion, and so it cannot completely encompass the idea or concept within its scope of understanding. You would prob-ably experience this feeling if you have been stressed lately and now you are looking at a huge and awe-inspiring landscape or a tremendous night sky, and you can't quite take it all in. Or, a bit higher on the spectrum (for all of the versions of the think-ing stages feeling are part of a spectrum from negative to cor-rupted to positive), you have been kind of stressed lately and you are now trying to think about infinity or eternity or God or some other vast and complex idea, and you begin to understand it, but you can't quite wrap your mind around it fully. It feels like you are competent and capable and you understand, and yet you aren't quite completely competent or capable and you don't quite completely understand. It feels like you are secure and stable and have clear guidance, and yet you aren't quite completely secure or stable, and you don't quite have clear guidance. It feels like you are fulfilled and full of joy, and yet you aren't quite completely fulfilled and you aren't quite completely full of joy. It feels like your mind is racing with the repetition of ideas as it tries to encompass them in its understanding, and it is this holding onto your thoughts as the source of the energy and guiding understanding of self-aware existence that you experience that keeps your mind from expanding to encompass any part of self-aware existence fully within its scope. And so we see that the corrupted version of the thinking stages feeling is the result of an intermediate degree of fixation upon the thinking stages (you are holding onto thoughts, repeating them over and over, and only allowing them to pass *somewhat* and be replaced by *some* new thoughts), which causes them to be corrupted to the point that their complete fulfillment is incapable of being experienced, and so there is only a partial feeling of fulfillment (and, consequently, also a partial feeling of lack of fulfillment).

Before the Big Bang, when the non-physical world is beginning to create the physical world, it allows the Source's thoughts to enter its clear and completely receptive awareness and understanding as it begins to apply experiential understanding in the form of self-awareness, and thereby to define and shape the physical world from the top down. Here, we have the state of the world of which the dominant positive version of the thinking stages feeling is a reflection—and thus we have the ultimate origin of the thinking stages feeling in its true and pure form.

The dominant positive feeling of the thinking stages is a feeling of clear-minded knowing as your mind expands infinitely to encompass something (and seemingly everything) in its awareness and understanding. You would probably experience this feeling if you have been very de-stressed for a while (either because you simply haven't had any stresses in your life or because you have been handling the stresses in your life very well) and you are engaging with anything that is significantly awe-inspiring and somehow vast—be it a physical scene of seemingly endless ocean or sky or land, or a poem, or a concept (such as that of infinity, or eternity, or God, or anything somewhat—or in any way—comparably significant or encompassing). You know that the language that is forming in your thoughts is definite and dependable Truth, and you are filled with wonderful overflowing joy. You feel completely competent and capable—like you are a useful source of information. You feel completely secure and stable, for you are being guided by the Source via your intuition as this all-knowing voice of direction enters your clear and discerning mind. You feel completely fulfilled, filled with overflowing happiness and gratitude for everything as it has been and everything as it is and everything as it will be. Because you know that, as you are guided by the Source's thought that brought forth the world in the first place and that brings it forth in every moment, you will always be—and have always been and are—on the path toward fulfillment. For you are allowing the Source's language to be manifested through you, and you are thereby allowing the Source's experience to be created and manifested through you. You are allowing the energy and guiding understanding of self-aware existence to flow through you—from beyond you, from the Source. And so we see that the dominant positive version of the thinking stages feeling is the result of a complete lack of fixation upon any stages at all, for it is the experience of the completed manifestation of experiential understanding and the beginning of the application of self-awareness—of self-aware understanding—in the form of your beginning to define and shape the world.

Take note of the fact that each of the three dominant positive feelings (that of the instinctual stages, that of the feeling stages, and that of the thinking stages) is part of its own continuous spectrum consisting of the dominant positive feeling along with the corrupted version of this feeling and the negative version of this feeling. Anything less than the pure and complete fulfillment of the positive feeling is a somewhat corrupted version of the feeling, and the negative version is merely the *most corrupted* version of the positive feeling, such that the experience is that of complete *lack* of fulfillment, rather than of complete *fulfillment.* The corrupted and negative versions of each feeling result from differing degrees of fixation upon the manifestation of the stages with which the dominant positive version of that feeling correlates—be this instincts, feelings, or thoughts. Each dominant positive feeling is a reflection of the experience of certain stages (thinking, feeling, or instinctual) of the world in between physical existences during the top down process of the creation of the next physical universe, while the negative and corrupted versions of each feeling are reflections of the experience of certain stages (thinking, feeling, or instinctual) of the world within the physical universe during the bottom up process of manifestation.

The negative version of the feeling always comes first in the physical universe and results from being *out of touch* with, or detached from, the experience of those particular stages (like the allowing stages are out of touch with, or detached from, the experience) and, particularly, out of touch with the present as it *is* (for the instinctual stages feeling), the past as it *was* (for the feeling stages feeling), or the future as it *will be* (for the thought stages feeling), which causes the "I" to be out of touch with the true and pure experience of those particular stages. The corrupted version of the feeling always comes second in the physical universe and results from receiving and manifesting within yourself the experience of those particular stages (and, more specifically, the experience of the present as it is, or the past as it was, or the future as it will be, depending on the stages), but *not receiving it fully* (like the receiving stages receive and manifest experience within themselves but don't receive it fully due to their holding onto the experience in the defined form in which they receive it—as the already-received instinct, feeling, or thought). And the dominant positive feeling always comes last (after the physical universe ends) and results from truly *sharing the experience* of those particular stages (like the ideal and self-aware version of the sharing stages—and of all stages, for that matter—which are overflowing with the experience that they wish to share). This entails having *received the experience* (of the present as it is, or the past as it was, or the future as it will be) *fully* (from the Source—though for us in the world, this is via the world—and *not* from the world) and having *allowed it to flow through you* and *manifest through you* freely and unhindered, without grasping at it at all, thereby preserving the purity and true nature of its form all the way from your receiving it and manifesting it within yourself to your sharing it.

It ought to be mentioned here that the experience of each of the dominant positive feelings of the main stage types (and the corrupted and negative forms of these feelings) is likely associated with the activity of certain neurotransmitters and hormones. The dominant positive feeling of the thinking stages (and the corrupted and negative versions of this feeling) is likely associated with the activity of dopamine in certain areas of the brain. The dominant positive feeling of the feeling stages (and the corrupted and negative versions of this feeling) is likely associated with the activity of serotonin in certain areas of the brain. The dominant positive feeling of the instinctual stages (and the corrupted and negative versions of this feeling) is likely associated with the activity of norepinephrine in certain areas of the brain, and also with the activity of norepinephrine and epinephrine in the body. It is possible that the brain-and-body-based reasons for the differences among the experiences of the dominant positive feelings, the corrupted versions of these feelings, and the negative versions of these feelings, as compared with one another, are differences in experiential and perceptual context and in which areas of the brain are active (with the specified neurotransmitter, or in conjunction with the areas where this neurotransmitter is active) and how active they are.

The Inclinations

Now that we have analyzed the main stage fixation aspect of personality, we shall analyze another very important aspect of personality—the fixation upon one of the three main inclinations of preserving, belonging, and connecting (which correlate with the instinctual stages, the feeling stages, and the thinking stages, respectively, and which therefore manifest to an extent as an aspect of the main stage type fixation, but which also manifest as fixations independently of the main stage type fixation). This aspect of personality is relatively straightforward, as we have analyzed it before. But it is important to note that, like with the main stage fixation, where all of the stages are fixated upon to some degree and it is merely that *one* stage is fixated upon *primarily*, all of the inclinations are fixated upon to some degree (turning them into desires) and it is merely that one inclination is fixated upon primarily, one secondarily, and the last tertiarily.[11] Further, the more we give our attention to

11   The three inclinations of fixation correspond with the three instinctual variants of the Enneagram personality type system (such that the preserving inclination corresponds with the self-preservation instinctual variant, the belonging inclination corresponds with the social instinctual variant, and the connecting inclination corresponds with the sexual instinctual variant), which can be explored further in books by Don Richard Riso and Russ Hudson, such as *The Wisdom of the Enneagram: The Complete Guide to Psychological and Spiritual Growth for the Nine Personality Types*, among others.

one inclination (holding onto one inclination) and ignore the others, the more stress we experience, and the more stress we experience, the further down this hierarchy of our prioritization (or fixation) we are inclined to shift the main focus of our attention.

Prior to self-awareness, we experience our primary inclination of fixation as a desire (which intensifies with increasing stress to an extent) and we therefore direct all of our attention to this area. Because we direct all of our attention to this area, the inclination upon which we are fixated determines to a large extent where—in our physical environment, in groups, or with other individuals—and in what way—as part of an effort to preserve ourselves, as part of an effort to belong, or as part of an effort to connect intensely with other "I"'s—we manifest our main stage type fixation. When we are under more than a little stress, our personality compensates by shifting our attention to another area by causing the next inclination of fixation in our hierarchy to manifest as a desire (which intensifies with increasing stress to an extent). When we are under more stress still, our personality shifts our attention to yet another area by causing the last inclination of fixation in our hierarchy to manifest as a desire (which intensifies with increasing stress to an extent). And when we are under even more stress than this, all of the inclinations fail to manifest themselves within us (as we enter a sort of self-destruct mode of completely ceasing to be driven to do anything).

Also, when we are under a lot of stress for an extended period of time—when we are increasing our degree of fixation upon our main stage type, and thereby excluding the other stages from our awareness—then our fixation upon one inclination increases in degree as well, as we exclude the other inclinations (and the areas to which these inclinations lead us to attend) from our awareness.

It is fixation upon one inclination, and thereby failure to direct appropriate awareness to each of the three areas when necessary, that is causing us to experience these inclinations in their corrupted forms as desires (and that is causing the stress that accompanies our experience of these desires). Therefore, part of the goal of the attainment of self-awareness is for us to direct appropriate awareness to each of the three areas when necessary, and in a balanced fashion. And so, upon reaching self-awareness, we attend to each of these inclinations at the appropriate times and to the appropriate extent as we are guided by our intuition to do so, and we begin to experience the three inclinations in their true and pure forms as they most closely resemble and reflect their forms in the Source's experience.

These three basic desires, or instincts (to preserve, to belong, to connect) encompass all desires (all instincts)—everything that can be desired. Thus, by "desire" or "instinct", we mean one of these three or an aspect of one of these three. Intuition encompasses their pure and true forms as subtle inclinations (when we do not hold onto them and thereby corrupt them) and so it therefore encompasses all pure inclinations.

People who hold onto the desire to preserve the existence of the "I" are most inclined to project the "I"—with all of its motivations, expectations, self-judgments and criticisms, and so on (all of its fixations)—onto the environment. People who hold onto the desire to belong are most inclined to project the "I"—with all of its fixations—onto the group. People who hold onto the desire to connect are most inclined to project the "I"—with all of its fixations—onto other close individuals with whom they intimately and intensely connect.

It ought to be noted that the main stage type of fixation has the predominant influence on the formation of personality. Other influences—such as the hierarchy of fixation on the inclinations, and the effects of being born at some point in the course of the universe, at some point in the year, at some point in the month, at some point in the week, at some point in the day, and so on (and consequently under the influence of one stage or another in each of the patterns of the paradigm as these patterns manifest across these spans of time), as well as even the effects of being raised by and around people (and cultures and religions and so on) with certain fixations and ways of expressing, or manifesting, these fixations—merely serve (to different degrees) to direct the focus of the inclinations or desires of the main stage type, determining where the person will be most inclined to seek fulfillment, and therefore determining the details of how the person will actually manifest the influences of the main stage type fixation.

In the case of the inclination of fixation, where people are directing their attention is evident in the quality of the focus of their eyes.

If the "I" is fixated upon the preserving inclination, its gaze has an unfocused, sort of glazed-over quality, as though neither eye is quite focused fully in its attention on anything in the outside world, revealing that the "I"'s attention is focused inward, on things that have to do with preserving the existence of the "I" (like getting sleep, getting work done, keeping the "I" and its environment clean, etc.), because this is where the "I" perceives the fulfillment of existence to be coming from and, therefore, this is where the "I" seeks the fulfillment of existence—in its direct preservation of itself and its environment and its physical procuring of resources from that environment.

If the "I" is fixated upon the belonging inclination, its gaze has a sort of unfocused but outward-oriented quality, as though its eyes are not quite looking at a single point but are, instead, each focused on slightly different things outside the "I", as though the "I" is trying to take in many parts of the world—many people—at once, because this is where the "I" perceives the fulfillment of existence to be coming from and, therefore, this is where the "I" seeks the fulfillment of existence—in the group of other people around it of which it wants to be a part.

If the "I" is fixated upon the connecting inclination, its gaze has an extremely focused quality, as though the eyes are both fixated on a single point, almost as though to penetrate and look *into*, or even *through*, the physical object of the "I"'s attention (like a person's eyes), because this is where the "I" perceives the fulfillment of existence to be coming from and, therefore, this is where the "I" seeks the fulfillment of existence—in the single other person or object or whatever (in the other "I", itself, and not merely in the outward manifestation of the other "I"), to which the "I" seeks to connect intimately and intensely and to which the "I" wishes to give its complete attention, so that it might glean the intensity of fulfillment from that single other person or object (from that other "I").

This quality of focus of the eyes changes with shifts in fixation from one inclination to another due to short-term and long-term stress and so forth, always corresponding with, and thus accurately indicating, where a person's attention is currently primarily focused.

The Dominant Positive Feelings of the Inclinations

Like with the main stage types, there is a dominant positive feeling associated with each of the inclinations, a corrupted version of that feeling, and a negative version of that feeling. Each of these is a reflection of the world at some stage in its development—the same stages with which the main stage type feelings correlate (for the pattern of the inclinations is part of the same paradigm—with the preserving inclination associated with the instinctual stages, the belonging inclination associated with the feeling stages, and the connecting inclination associated with the thinking stages).

As the physical universe is just beginning to manifest in the Big Bang, energy that does not yet have any concrete form is spewing out of the singularity of the Big Bang into an expanding framework of space and successive time, and everything is chaotic and unorganized. Here, we have the state of the world of which the negative version of the preserving inclination feeling is a reflection.

The negative version of the preserving inclination feeling is a feeling of not having anywhere near enough of the resources necessary to continue to survive and exist. You would probably experience this feeling if you have spent an extended period of time constantly around other people, having one-on-one conversations and participating in group activities, but not getting anything done for yourself (e.g., getting work done, sleeping, etc.), or if you have not slept anywhere near enough for an extended period of time and you haven't bathed in a long time. It feels like there isn't enough time, there isn't enough space, there isn't enough money, there isn't enough food, etc. You feel disgustingly dirty, and either way too hot or way too cold, and you feel like you want to get out of your skin. You feel utterly exhausted and unaccomplished. You're either starving or you're grossly overstuffed. You are overly conscious of how extremely messy and disorganized and dirty you and everything around you seem to be. Everything about your condition and your surroundings seems terribly un-ideal for your sustenance and survival, and it all feels generally extremely uncomfortable and utterly unpleasant. And you are gnawed by the nagging desire to *have* the appropriate conditions and surroundings in order to comfortably survive, and by the frustration that arises in you because you don't have them—because you don't have *enough* of anything to have them. There is too much chaos and conflict, nothing is good or right, and you feel like you aren't in control. And so we see that the negative version of the preserving inclination feeling is the result of a high degree of fixation upon the preserving inclination (which was probably preceded and caused by complete lack of appropriate attention to the preserving inclination)—and therefore upon certain aspects of the instinctual stages—which causes it to be corrupted so extremely as to lead to the experience of its complete lack of fulfillment, and to the consequent expression of it as a nagging or gnawing desire.

Eventually after the Big Bang, matter begins to take form as atoms and molecules and stars and planets and galaxies. New elements are produced in the burning and deaths of stars, and order in the physical universe establishes itself, producing a pleasantly organized environment. Here, we have the state of the world of which the corrupted version of the preserving inclination feeling is a reflection.

The corrupted version of the preserving inclination feeling is a feeling of having pretty sufficient amounts of all of the resources necessary to continue to survive and exist. You would probably experience this feeling if you have been kind of stressed lately and you haven't generally been getting enough sleep, exercising, eating right, and so on, but now you have gotten a good night's sleep, and you have exercised, and you've bathed, and you've taken a walk outside and it's a nice day with a comfortable temperature, and you're eating a tasty and healthy meal in a well-lit room with nice coloring. It feels like there is a pocket of sufficient time, there is sufficient space, there is sufficient money, there is sufficient food, etc. You feel sufficiently clean, and your surroundings feel sufficiently clean and organized and a good temperature. You feel sufficiently well-slept and present in your surroundings, part of your environment and pretty comfortable in it. Your condition and your environment seem pretty good and all right, it is all pretty peaceful, and you feel pretty much in control. And you spend long periods of time by yourself, getting work done and getting sleep and exercising and eating and generally taking care of yourself, wanting to make sure that you take care of yourself sufficiently to ensure your comfortable survival. And so we see that the corrupted version of the preserving inclination feeling is the result of an intermediate degree of fixation upon the preserving inclination (you are holding onto the preserving inclination somewhat, giving a bit more attention to it than is necessary, and you are therefore not giving quite enough attention to the belonging inclination and the connecting inclination)—and therefore upon certain aspects of the instinctual stages—which causes it to be corrupted to the point that its complete fulfillment is incapable of being experienced (and the insufficient fulfillment of the other inclinations dampens, or hampers, the fulfillment of this one), and so there is only a partial feeling of fulfillment (and, consequently, also a partial feeling of lack of fulfillment).

Just before the Big Bang, when the non-physical world is in the preserving inclination stage of creation (the instinctual stages)—as it is creating the physical world from the top down—the world has all of the resources that it requires and more at its disposal to preserve its existence and the existence of the environment—of the physical world—that it is almost finished shaping, that the Source is creating through it. Here, we have the state of the world of which the dominant positive version of the preserving inclination feeling is a reflection—and thus we have the ultimate origin of the preserving inclination feeling in its true and pure form.

The dominant positive feeling of the preserving inclination is a feeling of having more than enough of all of the resources necessary to continue to survive and exist. You would probably experience this feeling if you have been very de-stressed for a while (either because you simply haven't had any stresses in your life or because you have been handling the stresses in your life very well) and you have been allowing your intuition to guide you in taking care of all of the things that need to get done, fulfilling all of the three main inclinations, and you have just completed a long period of working and you are walking home on a gorgeous day, where everything about your environment seems absolutely perfect—the temperature, the lighting, the coloring. You feel clean and accomplished. You feel well-slept and amazingly awake. You are extremely lucid, and the air feels almost soft, and your shoes feel like slippers, and your clothes feel like a soft robe that you put on after a wonderful shower. You feel healthy. It feels like time is moving at a comfortable pace, and space feels like a big cushion—like everything around you is amazingly comfortable, like the world is a womb. It feels like you are being provided with all of the nutrients and the requirements for your survival from the very world around you, like the energy of self-aware existence is flowing from or, rather, *through* all of your surroundings (as though from a Source beyond them) and into you, and through you and into your surroundings, like the resources available to you are endless. It feels as though everything is interconnected, like it's all part of one emanation of pure energy that encompasses beauty and comfort and vitalizing strength and immense peace. And it feels as though everything about your conditions and your surroundings is just right and perfectly comfortable and peaceful, and you are completely in control, flowing through your surroundings as though you are part of them, as though you are light, as though you are supported by them, as though they are walking through your walking, expressing themselves through your actions. And so we see that the dominant positive version of the preserving inclination feeling is the result of a complete lack of fixation upon any stages at all; it is the experience of the complete fulfillment of certain aspects of the instinctual stages, and it is the experience of your complete awareness of your ability to create and shape the world in the maintenance of its and your existence—so that it and you can continue to experience the fulfillment of self-aware existence.

As life begins to arise on some planets in the universe, environmental conditions continue to change drastically, and life is wiped out nearly completely in a series of mass extinctions, proving that the various adaptations of life forms and their attempts to find niches for themselves and to fit in have failed. Here, we have the state of the world of which the negative version of the belonging inclination feeling is a reflection.

The negative version of the belonging inclination feeling is a feeling of not fitting in anywhere at all. You would probably experience this feeling if you have not spent any time with any people, or with any more than one or two people at a time, for an extended period of time, or if you *have* spent time around a lot of people, but there were groups of people around you and none of them seemed to include you, and you were by yourself amongst them. You feel like you don't belong anywhere, like you aren't part of anything. You feel like you don't have any friends. You feel like you don't have any overall purpose, like your actions have no meaning beyond what they accomplish for you. You feel left out and lacking—like you aren't part of any kind of group, any community, any organization, any team. You really just feel like you don't fit in anywhere, like you have no group that you can call your own, and you are gnawed by the nagging desire to *have* such a group that you can call your own, and by the shame that arises in you because you don't fit in anywhere. You feel like you have no significance for who you are, no value to anyone, and like you are no help to anyone and no one cares about you. And so we see that the negative version of the belonging inclination feeling is the result of a high degree of fixation upon the belonging inclination (which was probably preceded and caused by complete lack of appropriate attention to the belonging inclination)—and therefore upon certain aspects of the feeling stages—which causes it to be corrupted so extremely as to lead to the experience of its complete lack of fulfillment, and to the consequent expression of it as a nagging or gnawing desire.

As life forms find their niches and really begin to take hold, mass extinctions become less frequent and life proves to have found its place in the universe, forming groups within itself whose members work toward the common survival of the group. Here, we have the state of the world of which the corrupted version of the belonging inclination feeling is a reflection.

The corrupted version of the belonging inclination feeling is a feeling of fitting in somewhere, of belonging to some group. You would probably experience this feeling if you have been kind of stressed lately and you are now playing some team sport, or singing, or dancing, or doing some other activity with a group of friends. You feel like you are part of something, like your actions are part of something larger than you, contributing to something and being something more than just what they are in themselves. You feel like you have some significance for who you are and what you can contribute, some value to the group, and like you are somewhat helpful to the group, and so the group cares about you at least somewhat. And you spend long periods at a time with the group, not wanting the feeling of belonging to end. And so we see that the corrupted version of the belonging inclination feeling is the result of an intermediate degree of fixation upon the belonging inclination (you are holding onto the belonging inclination somewhat, giving a bit more attention to it than is necessary, and you are therefore not giving quite enough attention to the preserving inclination and the connecting inclination)—and therefore upon certain aspects of the feeling stages—which causes it to be corrupted to the point that its complete fulfillment is incapable of being experienced (and the insufficient fulfillment of the other inclinations dampens, or hampers, the fulfillment of this one), and so there is only a partial feeling of fulfillment (and, consequently, also a partial feeling of lack of fulfillment).

Before the Big Bang, as the non-physical world is in the process of creating the physical world from the top down, when it has reached the feeling stages of creation, it is working with the Source, contributing its feelings to the Source's thought and working to shape what the Source has provided. The world is thereby working toward something larger than itself, accomplishing much more with what it is doing than merely what it is doing, alone. It is working toward a common goal with the Source—a goal that entails both the realization of the Source's thought and its own fulfillment. Here, we have the state of the world of which the dominant positive version of the belonging inclination feeling is a reflection—and thus we have the ultimate origin of the belonging inclination feeling in its true and pure form.

The dominant positive feeling of the belonging inclination is a feeling of truly being part of something larger than yourself. You would probably experience this feeling if you have been very de-stressed for a while (either because you simply haven't had any stresses in your life or because you have been handling the stresses in your life very well) and you have been allowing your intuition to guide you in taking care of all of the things that need to get done, fulfilling all of the three main inclinations, and you are working with a team or a community or some other group to accomplish some mutual goal. It feels like your actions are more than yours, like you are merely providing the voice, or the arms and legs, or whatever, for the group to work through you toward a higher purpose than that which your speech or actions have alone. You are not you; you are an appendage of the group, as though the group is a giant organism and you are a cell or an organ within it. It feels as though the energy of self-aware existence is flowing from or, rather, *through* the group (as though from a Source beyond it) and into you, and through you and into the group, and you are energized with the awareness that you truly belong. You fit in, you have your unique niche that you fill within the group, and you are valuable to the group, because you are helping the group to reach its overall goal—an overall goal that is, in some way, helping the whole world to reach its overall goal, helping the whole world to achieve fulfillment as it works toward the realization of the goal set by the Source. And so we see that the dominant positive version of the belonging inclination feeling is the result of a complete lack of fixation upon any stages at all; it is the experience of the complete fulfillment of certain aspects of the feeling stages, and it is the experience of the process of the application of your experiential understanding in the form of your allowing yourself to be a tool through which the self-aware creation and shaping of the world takes place.

The physical universe manifests the tree of life paradigm repeatedly, but incompletely, in various forms of life, and none of these life forms proves capable of experiencing the self-aware ability to shape its own existence and experience—none of these life forms proves capable of intensely connecting with the Source. And the physical universe accelerates in its expansion, with time increasing in rapidity as matter and energy spread out over increasingly empty space. Here, we have the state of the world of which the negative version of the connecting inclination feeling is a reflection.

The negative version of the connecting inclination feeling is a feeling of not having anyone with whom you can intimately and intensely connect. You would probably experience this feeling if you have not spent any time with people, or if you have spent a lot of time with many people but no time with just one or two people, for an extended period, or if you have been with one or two people, but the person's (or people's) attention didn't seem to be focused on you, and so you didn't feel any real connection or intensity in the interaction. You feel an intense feeling of lack, like you are not complete, like your experience is incomplete. You feel like you need to find your soulmate—someone with whom you can connect, someone with whom you can share your experience of the world, someone with whom you can share your life. Every experience feels like it is lacking something, because it is lacking someone with whom to share it. It is not enough just to experience things yourself, alone; you need someone to experience them with you, or someone whom you can tell about your experience of them in intimate and intense conversations—someone who would understand you, understand what you're experiencing, someone who would be there for you when you need him/her, and someone for whom you can be there. You just feel like there is no one with whom you can share your life, no one to complete you, and you are gnawed by the nagging desire to *have* such a person with whom you can share your life, and by the fear that arises in you that you might never find such a person. You feel the intense need to have someone who understands you, someone you can trust and depend on to be there for you, and you feel like only if you had such a person could you truly be happy and fulfilled. And so we see that the negative version of the connecting inclination feeling is the result of a high degree of fixation upon the connecting inclination (which was probably preceded and caused by complete lack of appropriate attention to the connecting inclination)—and therefore upon certain aspects of the thinking stages—which causes it to be corrupted so extremely as to lead to the experience of its complete lack of fulfillment, and to the consequent expression of it as a nagging or gnawing desire.

The physical universe finally begins to manifest the complete tree of life paradigm in the form of intelligent life forms who are capable of becoming aware of their own existence and of mindfully and willfully shaping the contents of their experience, thereby receiving the Source's experience in their own experience. And so the universe accelerates in its expansion of space, speeding through time, to encompass self-awareness and, thereby, an understanding of the Source's experience. Here, we have the state of the world of which the corrupted version of the connecting inclination feeling is a reflection.

The corrupted version of the connecting inclination feeling is a feeling of intimately and intensely connecting with another "I". You would probably experience this feeling if you have been kind of stressed lately and you are now having a good conversation with someone who understands a lot of what you're talking about, someone who can relate somewhat to you and to whom you can somewhat relate. It feels like you have someone with whom to share at least some of your experience, someone you can talk to about some things, someone you can depend on—at least somewhat—to be there for you, someone with whom you sort of enjoy talking. It doesn't feel quite like you found your soulmate, necessarily (although maybe), but you find some fulfillment in sharing your experience with this person. And you talk with the person for hours upon hours at a time, not wanting the conversations—and the intense connection you feel in them—to end. And so we see that the corrupted version of the connecting inclination feeling is the result of an intermediate degree of fixation upon the connecting inclination (you are holding onto the connecting inclination somewhat, giving a bit more attention to it than is necessary, and you are therefore not giving quite enough attention to the preserving inclination and the connecting inclination)—and therefore upon certain aspects of the thinking stages—which

causes it to be corrupted to the point that its complete fulfillment is incapable of being experienced (and the insufficient
fulfillment of the other inclinations dampens, or hampers,
the fulfillment of this one), and so there is only a partial feeling of fulfillment (and, consequently, also a partial feeling of
lack of fulfillment).

Before the Big Bang, when the non-physical world is beginning to create the physical world, it begins to apply experiential
understanding of what the Source experiences—the self-aware
ability to create the world—and it finds intimate and intense
connection with the Source as it so completely and thoroughly
relates to It in this way. The world begins to apply its understanding of what the Source has been sharing with it all along,
it begins to apply its understanding that it can completely trust
the Source's guidance, and it finds complete fulfillment in its
connection with the Source. Here, we have the state of the
world of which the dominant positive version of the connecting inclination feeling is a reflection—and thus we have the
ultimate origin of the connecting inclination feeling in its true
and pure form.

The dominant positive feeling of the connecting inclination is a feeling of truly intimately and intensely connecting
with another "I". You would probably experience this feeling
if you have been very de-stressed for a while (either because
you simply haven't had any stresses in your life or because you
have been handling the stresses in your life very well) and you
have been allowing your intuition to guide you in taking care of
all of the things that need to get done, fulfilling all of the three
main inclinations, and you are having a really great conversation
with someone who completely understands what you are sharing—completely understands the experience that you are conveying. It feels as though the energy of self-aware existence is
flowing from or, rather, *through* the other person (as though from
a Source beyond him/her) and into you, and through you and

into that other person, and you are energized with the intense awareness that you are truly connected with that person—in your experience, and in your core, and in the Source of both of you. It feels as though everything is brighter, clearer, crisper, as though the colors of everything are more vivid and vibrant and intense, as though the energy of self-aware existence is illuminating the world from beyond. Walls and other physical boundaries seem as though they aren't quite concrete, as though they aren't true boundaries, as though you could reach right through them, through and into the Source of illumination. It feels like you can completely trust and depend on this person with whom you are connecting, but this feeling of trust carries over to the entire world around you, because you are not seeing *the world*, you are seeing *beyond* the world, and you can feel that you can completely trust and depend upon the Source that you can discern beyond everything around you. And it feels like you can completely understand the experience that this person is conveying—like you can see in your own experience exactly what this person means to be conveying—and like the experience that you are having and sharing is being completely understood by this person in this person's own experience, but this feeling of understanding also carries over to the entire world around you, to the Source that is illuminating the entire world around you with self-aware existence. And you know that you can completely understand the experience that the Source is conveying—that you are experiencing in your own experience exactly what the Source means to be conveying—and that the experience that you are having and sharing is being completely understood by the Source. The world is glowing with the clarity of its true purpose, which you can completely understand is *this*—is to become capable of experiencing *this*. And you are completely fulfilled in your conversation with this other person, in this conversation that has turned into a conversation with the Source. And you realize that you have been conversing with the Source all along—always—and that you merely didn't understand the experience that the Source was conveying, that you couldn't relate and find in your own experience anything that would allow for such an understanding until now. And now you have found complete fulfillment in your conversation with the Source. And you come to realize that you can find complete fulfillment in your intimate and intense interaction with everything—not just with another person directly through a conversation or some other interaction, but with another person through a book you're reading or a movie you're watching, and even with an idea or your breath or something else that doesn't seem to be a self-aware "I" with which you can connect, in itself—because everything in your experience is part of the language of your conversation that you are always and continually having with the Source "I". Via everything in the world, you are capable of intimately and intensely connecting with the Source "I", and you realize that this is from where all fulfillment in this world ultimately comes. And so we see that the dominant positive version of the connecting inclination feeling is the result of a complete lack of fixation upon any stages at all; it is the experience of the complete fulfillment of certain aspects of the thinking stages, and it is the experience of the completed manifestation, and the beginning of the application, of experiential understanding in the form of your beginning to choose the words that you use to converse with the Source—and thereby to define and shape your experience in the world—with self-awareness.

We can see here that the connecting inclination is capable of leading to a kind of understanding, and an application of this understanding, of how we relate to the world and to the Source—that everything in the world is a means to communicate and connect with the Source—that brings about all aspects of the self-awareness that gives rise to our ability to share and shape our experience. Ultimately, it is from the true fulfillment of the connecting inclination that all fulfillment can be obtained—including that of the belonging inclination and the preserving inclination, which are forms of this inclination that have evolved out of it in the Source's relation to the world. And these three inclinations ultimately encompass all spheres of possible inclinations (which in their corrupted forms are desires), and so the fulfillment of every possible inclination, of every possible desire, in this world comes from our learning how we truly relate to the world and to the Source—that we communicate and connect with the Source via the world, and that the Source communicates and connects with us via the world—that the world is the language, the means of conveyance, in this interaction. As long as we recognize this, and we relate to all things in the world with this understanding that these things (including even other people), in themselves, are *not* the Source of anything that we obtain from them, but are, rather, the *means* by which we obtain from the Source all that we obtain *through* them, then we will find intimacy and intensity in our connections with the Source via the world, and we will find belonging and the feeling of being part of something larger as we work with the other parts of the world and with the Source toward the goal of the entire world, and we will find preservation of our existence with an endless supply of resources in the Source of all that exists.

Take note of the fact that each of the three dominant positive feelings (that of the preserving inclination, that of the belonging inclination, and that of the connecting inclination) is part of its own continuous spectrum consisting of the dominant positive feeling along with the corrupted version of this feeling and the negative version of this feeling. And everything written about this with regard to the instinctual stages feeling, the feeling stages feeling, and the thinking stages feeling, applies here as well. This includes, among other things, the following: The negative feeling is the result of being out of

touch with the experience of the dominant positive feeling—
the experience, in this case, of being part of the environment,
or being part of the group, or being part of the other "I"'s
experience—(like the allowing stages). The corrupted feeling
is the result of grasping and receiving and manifesting within
yourself the experience, but not letting it go (like the receiving stages). And the dominant positive feeling is the result of
creating the experience and sharing it (like the sharing stages),
but ultimately of allowing it to flow through yourself by doing
so, thus receiving the experience fully and sharing it fully in its
true and pure form.

Also, it ought to be mentioned here that the experience of
each of the dominant positive feelings of the inclinations (and
the corrupted and negative forms of these feelings) is likely
associated with the activity of certain neurotransmitters and
hormones. The dominant positive feeling of the connecting
inclination (and the corrupted and negative versions of this
feeling) is likely associated with the activity of dopamine in
certain areas of the brain. The dominant positive feeling of
the belonging inclination (and the corrupted and negative versions of this feeling) is likely associated with the activity of
serotonin in certain areas of the brain. The dominant positive
feeling of the preserving inclination (and the corrupted and
negative versions of this feeling) is likely associated with the
activity of norepinephrine in certain areas of the brain, and
also with the activity of norepinephrine and epinephrine in
the body.

Like with the dominant positive feelings of the main stage
types, it is possible that the brain-and-body-based reasons for
the differences among the experiences of the dominant positive feelings, the corrupted versions of these feelings, and the
negative versions of these feelings, as compared with one another, are differences in experiential and perceptual context
and in which areas of the brain are active (with the specified

neurotransmitter, or in conjunction with the areas where this neurotransmitter is active) and how active they are. It is also possible that the brain-and-body-based reasons for the differences in the experiences of the dominant positive feelings of the inclinations (and the corrupted and negative forms of these feelings), as compared with the experiences of those of the main stage types, are similar—based on contextual differences and activity in different brain areas.

Male and Female

The world is female in relation to the Source—making the Source male in relation to the world. In every interaction, there is both sharing and receiving, and the sharing element is male, and the receiving element is female. The male shares something that the female takes in and combines with something else, thereby forming something new (the child of the interaction) that is a combination of what the male has shared and what the female has shared. Then, this child is capable of becoming either an extension of the female element, or an extension of the male element, in an interaction with another.

So, the senses are female in relation to the creative processes, which are male in this interaction. And the dimensions are female in relation to the fields of forces, which are male in this interaction. When atoms interact with one another, the ones that receive electrons, thereby becoming negatively charged, are female in relation to the ones that share electrons, thereby becoming positively charged, and which are therefore male in the interaction.

The stereotypical differences between male and female are a reflection of the differences between the role played by the Source and that played by the world (including humanity) in the interaction between these two—a reflection of the way the

Source and the world are *in relation to each other*. We can, here, consider the role filled by the Source *in this interaction*; we can consider the way we perceive the Source in Its relation to us as we look up through all of the stages of the tree of life paradigm, and ultimately through the thought stages, and particularly through sharing thought, which is the last stage (looking upward) that has any definition that we can grasp and understand and fixate upon and manifest—because sharing thought is like the sun's light to the tree, and because choice (above it) is truly indefinite, undefined, and undefinable. This is as opposed to considering the Source as It is in Itself, which is something that we cannot do (because we cannot know the Source as It is in Itself).

Like the Source *in this interaction*, the male is more solitary and independent of the other (like the sun, which shines regardless of whether or not its light is being received), he is more logical and is better at math and other systematic things, and he is more active and imposing (producing the original thought and the goal for the both of them, and setting up the beginning of a systematic framework in which this goal can be carried out). Like the world in this interaction, the female is more social and other-oriented and group-oriented and dependent upon the other (like the world that is made up of a myriad of interdependent parts—parts that cannot continue to exist as they do without one another—and like the earth that cannot give rise to life without the sun), she is more emotional (taking in the original thought and then producing emotions from it), she is better with language and communication (being the one who really uses most of the language in the interaction), and she is more passive and receptive (receiving what the other provides and working toward the goal of the other, with the other). And, of course, like the world in the carrying out of the Source's original thought, the female has the final say as to the defining shape that the final product of any interaction takes, even as the male, like the Source, initiates and produces the general direction or aim of the interaction.

(It is interesting to see that females of most species more greatly shape the specific course of the evolution of the species—use more of the defining language of the interaction—than males. This is because while males often initiate the interaction with females, females decide which males get to pass their genes on to the next generation; females decide which language they will receive and manifest within themselves in the form of new members of the species. And so we see the plumage and mating dances of male birds, and the weaponry of male insects, and the size and strength and dominance and intelligence and so forth of the members of a species, shaped by the choice of the females who are receptive to males with certain traits and displays, willing to receive the genes of those males and to bring them into manifestation as new life with similar traits. In addition to this, it is often females who take the greatest part in the raising of the young even after birth or hatching or whatever, thereby further defining the specific course of the development of those newly manifested beings.)

Moreover, due to these roles in the relationship with the other, the male wants to be in control and helpful and useful and wanted and cared about for what he provides to the female *in his relationship with her* (like the sharing stages, and particularly sharing thought, which reflects the Source in Its interaction with the world), and the female wants to be good and uniquely significant and fulfilled in how she distinctly defines and shapes *the relationship* and *what the male provides to her*, and she also wants to be complete in her reception from the male—*in her being provided for by the male* (like the receiving stages, and particularly receiving thought, which reflects the world in its interaction with the Source). In the relationship with the other, the male wants to protect himself from being dependent upon the other because he wants to be independent and to be the source in relation to the other, and he seeks someone who wants to receive what he provides, while the female wants to be provided for, and she seeks someone who provides what she wants to receive. (Notice, by the way, that this proves true not only for human beings, but, to a very large extent, for males and females in their relation to one another regardless of species.)

These are the *stereotypes*. However, it is important to note that, as the world develops toward self-awareness, it becomes less and less a purely receiving element and becomes more and more a sharing element (ultimately up to the point that it shares all that it receives). Therefore, the differences between the world and the Source become less and less clearly defined—up to the point that the world experiences the Source's experience to as full an extent as it possibly can, transcending the separating element of language definitions. This breakdown of clarity in the differences between male and female is reflected in all elements of the world—from the breakdown of the traditional household as females take on working roles, accomplishing their own goals that are separate from their partner's goals, to increasing bisexuality and homosexuality, to the senses acting on the world to produce what is in the world instead of merely receiving what is already in the world (as we have seen, since the development of Quantum Mechanics, to be the case when it comes to the quantum realm). This breakdown of disparity in roles marks the last stages of the manifestation of the paradigm, meaning that it should reveal itself in every situation in which the final stages of the paradigm (nearing choice from bottom up) are being manifested. The end of the year (as with regard to astrological influences), the end of a lifetime (e.g., in a person's retirement years), the end of an empire, etc., would therefore be most likely to be marked by the manifestation of this kind of breakdown of distinction between roles.

[By the way, the breakdown of distinction between the Source and us in the world in the last stages of development is reflected in other relationship roles as well. What we have seen here is that the sharing form of things (the male form) is a reflection of sharing thought, and the receiving form of things (the female form) is a reflection of receiving thought. And as receiving thought (which is representative of the world in relation to the Source) comes to receive, in an increasingly accurate form, what sharing thought (which is representative of the Source in relation to the world) is sharing, the distinction between the experience of these two breaks down—and so the distinction between the male and female, or sharing and receiving, forms of all things breaks down. Sharing thought and receiving thought (as reflections of the Source and the world in their interaction with one another) give rise to allowing thought—the child produced by their interaction. Allowing thought and all of the stages below it emanate from the sharing and receiving interactions above them in hierarchical fashion as these interactions are allowed to manifest through these later stages. As we, within the world, learn to manifest the Source's experience through ourselves in an increasingly accurate form, this hierarchy becomes less distinct, for every stage comes more closely to resemble the Source of all of the stages, and every stage, thereby, comes more closely to resemble every other stage that is above it.

So, relationships within the world that are a reflection of the relationship between the Source and us within the world (between sharing thought and allowing thought, along with the stages after allowing thought) lose their hierarchical distinction near the end of the development of things similarly to the way things that are a reflection of the relationship between the Source and the world (between sharing thought and receiving thought) lose their distinction in their relation to one another near the end of the development of things.

Thus, for example, parents become less clearly simply authoritative sources of guidance and (consistent) structure in relation to their children, and children become less clearly simply receivers and allowers of such guidance and structure in relation to their parents, as the hierarchical structure of the parent-child relationship breaks down (e.g., in the adulthood of the child—when the child might even become a parent in addition to being a child—or in the last stages of a society, etc.). And teachers become no longer simply sources of information for their students but also receivers and allowers of information from their students, and students become no longer simply receivers and allowers of information from their teachers but also sources of information for their teachers. And rulers become no longer distinctly separate and different from those whom they rule (as with increasingly democratic forms of governance). And, in general, hierarchical distinctions in relationship roles (as defined by one party being a source of authority or guidance or structure and the other party allowing that authority or guidance or structure to be manifested through him/herself) break down.]

The Days of the Week

First, there was the Source. Then, there was the world. And then the Source seeded the world with Its sharing thought, and the world became representative of receiving thought. The result was allowing thought, which was the seed of the tree of life—containing the DNA that was the combination of the Source's language and the world's language. Then, the world used this paradigm of sharing thought, receiving thought, and allowing thought, to form each of the three feeling stages and each of the three instinctual stages in their relationship-image, and to form the feeling stages, the instinctual stages, and manifestation in their tripartite relationship-image as well.

Beginning with the seed of the tree of life in allowing thought, the actual beginning of the concrete growth or creation of the world began in sharing feeling. Sharing feeling (reflected in Sunday) represents the creation (or, more accurately, the *definition*, or the *defining*) of overflowing, outpouring, creative, sharing light energy that is required for the germination of the seed of the tree of life, with the resulting difference between the day, in which (the light reactions of) photosynthesis in the tree will ultimately take place, and the night, in which (the dark reactions of photosynthesis and) respiration in the tree will ultimately take place. Receiving feeling (reflected in Monday) represents the creation (or definition) of the water that is also required for the germination of the seed of the tree of life, and this water receives the energy from the light, manifesting it within itself and causing the water to have a division in itself, so that the water exists in two forms—as liquid water, and as water vapor. Allowing feeling (reflected in Tuesday) represents the creation (or definition) of the dry land in which the seed must be planted, and now, with light and water merging in land with the seed that came before, the seed germinates to produce the tree of life, growing out of and away from the land, and providing a means of interaction between the light and the water, such that the liquid water in the ground becomes water vapor through its reception of light energy via the tree of life.

Now that the basic elements for the tree of life have been created (or defined), they are each created (defined) in a more actualized or concretized form (for the stages of the tree of life progress from potentiality to actuality), such that sharing instinct is a more actualized form of sharing feeling (as sharing feeling is a more actualized form of sharing thought), receiving instinct is a more actualized form of receiving feeling (as receiving feeling is a more actualized form of receiving thought), and allowing instinct is a more actualized form of allowing feeling (as allowing feeling is a more actualized form of allowing thought).

Sharing instinct (reflected in Wednesday) represents the creation (or definition) of the more strictly language-defined and actualized overflowing, outpouring light—in the form of its (causal, or effectual) relationship to the tree of life—as the sun and moon and stars. Receiving instinct (reflected in Thursday) represents the creation (or definition) of the more strictly language-defined and actualized receiving water (in its two forms—liquid water and water vapor—which exist as separate realms that interact with one another, with one realm being inside the ground and the tree in a more physical, tangible state, and the other realm being outside the ground and the tree, up in the air in a more ethereal state). This water represents the constituents and substance of the two realms—the more physical and actual realm, and the more nonphysical and potential or imagined realm that precedes and leads to the physical realm of actual and concrete reality that is a reflection of it, thereby being no longer distinctly separate from it (for things from each realm pass into the other, like water vapor becoming liquid water and vice versa). The constituents and substance (created in receiving instinct) of these two realms receive and manifest within themselves the influence of the sun and the moon and the stars (sharing instinct). Allowing instinct (reflected in Friday) represents the creation (or definition) of the more strictly language-defined and actualized tree of life—in the form of mammals and, more specifically, human beings, which are capable of manifesting the tree of life fully and of creating, with self-awareness, from the top down, thereby serving as the means through which the sun and the moon and the stars—the lights from above—and the constituents and substance of the two realms of water (the realm of actuality within the tree and the realm of potentiality outside the tree) interact. Humans are, like the tree, the bridge between Earth and sky, but they are the tree in a more strictly defined and actualized form, for they can actively exercise self-aware creation via themselves—via the tree of life that is manifested as each of them, as their bodies, as their choice and thoughts and feelings and instincts/actions and body, and so on. Then, the ultimate manifestation (reflected in Saturday) represents the completed result of humanity's self-aware creation of the world, after humanity has brought all of the stages into harmony through its allowance of their manifestation through itself.[12]

So, sharing thought is the Source's form of sharing that is received by, and manifested within, the world (receiving thought), and sharing feeling is the light energy that is received by, and manifested within, the water (receiving feeling), and sharing instinct is the sun and moon and stars that are received by, and manifested within, the substance and constituents of the liquid water state of the world—within the tree—and the water vapor state of the world—outside the tree—(receiving instinct). And allowing thought is the ungerminated seed of the tree of life that allows the Source and the world to interact and be manifested through itself, allowing feeling is the grown-up tree of life that allows the light energy and the water to interact and be manifested through itself, and allowing instinct is the tree of life as manifested through higher animals and human beings that allow the sun and moon and stars and the substance and constituents of the physical (or real or actual) and nonphysical (or imaginary or potential) realms to interact and be manifested through themselves, with manifestation be-

---

12   Notice the resemblance of this metaphorical understanding of what was created or defined on each weekday to the Genesis account of what was created on each weekday.

ing the final result of that manifestation through higher animals, and particularly through humans.

As is hinted at in the reception of the influence of the sun and the moon and the stars by the substance of the physical and nonphysical realms via humans, astrology comes into play. It is not the physical bodies in space that are affecting us directly, however (although the sun and the moon certainly have an influence upon nearly all of life on Earth, including us, with their gravity and light and so forth); these bodies are merely manifestations of the same paradigm that is manifesting as, and through, us. For they and we both exist in manifestation—the result of the interactions of all of the stages of the tree of life paradigm. We are influenced by the stages of the paradigm, such that our use of language, and therefore our manifestation, is completely dictated by them in predictable ways, unless we are self-aware and we act out of choice, creating (defining) the contents of the world *through the paradigm* rather than allowing the world to create (or define) its contents *through us via the paradigm* (via our reactive manifestation of the stages of the paradigm).

Here, we can see one of the types of "astrological" influences that manifests through us—and through everything else that manifests in the physical world, via the world of feeling and instinct—in the days of the week. For the stages that correspond with the days of the week have an observable influence upon us—in the form of the parts of the tree of life setup that were defined in those stages during the process of the creation (or definition) of the world.

We have seen that an entire "day" begins at the beginning of the physical stage and ends at the end of the following nonphysical stage. For the universe begins as a physical manifestation, and then it works its way up to being like water vapor (learning to be self-aware), and it ends when the next universe begins—when the water vapor condenses back into liquid water and begins up the tree again (when it has fully created the next physical universe). And a life begins as a physical life, and then it works its way up to self-awareness, and then the afterlife of being like water vapor begins, and a single lifetime, as a whole, ends upon the beginning of the manifestation of the next physical life. Essentially, a day begins at manifestation, manifests (inside the tree) all the way up to choice, and then creates (outside the tree) all the way down to manifestation, at which point the next day begins. Day (an overall day) is thus composed of the night that is manifestation, followed by the day that is creation.

However, the order of day and night in the overall day depends upon the perspective. As we have just seen here with a universe or a life, night comes first (before day) in the order of manifestation (from the universe's and our perspective). This is because night is marked by the process of manifestation—of learning what it is to be self-aware and of learning the language of creation—which must come into actuality before any creating can be accomplished. But day comes first (before night) in the order of creation (from the Source's perspective), because day is marked by the process of creation, which must come before anything manifests.

The weekdays represent the order of creation, meaning that we should have day (creation) come first, followed by night (manifestation). In the terms of our usual understanding of the terms (since we are dealing here with day as referring to the creation outside the tree and with night as referring to the manifestation inside the tree, and therefore not with these terms as they are commonly used), this means that our (usual) night comes first, followed by our (usual) day. And so a day, for the purposes of the influence of the different stages of creation, is to be considered to begin upon the beginning of (the usual) night (sunset), and to end upon the beginning of the next (usual) night (the next sunset).

The creations of each of the days of the week (what is defined on each of these days) influence all that begins to manifest upon these days—all that begins to manifest within the influence of these days. Thus, if a person is born or an event occurs, the influence of the day (the day of birth or of occurrence) will be apparent in that event or in that person. Exploring the influence of the day of the week on people and on all other things that begin to manifest within a particular weekday's scope can yield us a greater awareness of such things as the perspective of a particular person or the place or purpose of a particular event in relation to the larger scheme of history.

[It ought to be noted that the weekday influence holds regardless of calendar changes in history, for the definitions of days of the week, and their resulting stage-related effects, have been created by the world's (and particularly humanity's) use of language. *We* define which day is which day, and so when a large enough portion of our language (the language that concerns and describes what day someone born in some particular place at some particular time was born or what day some event occurred) determines that the calendar is to be (or is not to be) changed (as in the case of the switch from the Julian to the Gregorian calendar), the influence of the newly-defined (or already-defined) weekday upon all things that manifest in that area and realm of influence reflects this.

Also, it must be recognized that the date of birth, alone, does not actually yield the weekday of birth as we seek to find it (the weekday defined as being from one sunset to the next sunset), for it does not tell us whether the person was born before or after sunset, and so we need the time of birth to be sure of the weekday of birth as we seek to find it—for the purposes of finding the influence of the creations of that day on that person, event, etc. However, the duration of time from midnight (the beginning of a certain date, or usual day) to sunset is much greater than the duration of time from sunset to midnight in most places (the weekday of birth is defined here by the sunset-to-sunset timeframe at the location of birth), and so if a particular date of birth is, say, a Sunday, there is a much greater chance that the person was born *before* sunset, and therefore on Sunday as we are defining it, than that the person was born *after* sunset (and therefore on Monday as we are defining it). So the weekday of birth as we seek to find it likely corresponds with the date-of-birth calendar day, although it may not (the weekday of birth may be the next day).

Due to the discernable influence of the weekday of birth as defined by sunset to sunset in the location of birth, this information (that concerning the influence of each day) can be used to determine accurately whether a person was born before or after sunset in the location of birth in cases in which the time of birth has been forgotten.]

As was explained above, in the personality section on the inclinations, everything other than the main stage type fixation—including the inclinations, as well as astrological influences and so on—serves to direct or define where one seeks fulfillment of the desires that result from the main stage type fixation. So, in the case of the weekday's influence (which we shall consider here as it regards people, even though it regards everything that begins to manifest within its influence), people born on each day tend to seek fulfillment of their main-stage-type-fixation-related desires in the creations of that weekday.

People born on Sunday tend to seek fulfillment in light-associated things, simple things—like riding a bicycle rather than driving, or finding simple solutions and avoiding complexity when possible—(for this day holds the potential for all of the following days, but is not the actualization of any of those days), the creation or definition or formation of completely new things (for this day is the beginning of the actual creation of a whole universe), and the like.

People born on Monday tend to seek fulfillment in watery areas (like pools and ponds and lakes and oceans and rivers and even showers) and water-related things (like waves), and in paradoxical, infinity-related things (like the singularity meeting-point of the liquid-water stage of the world and the water-vapor stage of the world, which cannot be understood or comprehended fully within the constrictions of the laws and language of the world, resulting in mathematical infinities and undefineds and so on), and the like.

People born on Tuesday tend to seek fulfillment amongst trees and foresty areas, and in rising above the land from which they came, rising up from where their roots are—such as their origins in some religion, culture, family, the human body, physicality, human psychological inclinations, etc.—(as the tree grows up and away from the land in which it was planted), and the like.

People born on Wednesday tend to seek fulfillment in the open sky and its contents (in the sun and the moon and the stars), and in the manifestations of their influence (of their light, gravity, and so on), and in the distinction between these—the ultimate cause (as the celestial bodies) and the more immediate cause that is the effect of that ultimate cause (as the light, etc. of those bodies—the language that they use in their interactions with us—the ways by which, or in which, they affect us)—in cosmological, overall-picture, ultimate-influence-of-things perspectives (as the sun and the moon and the stars share themselves with the substance and constituents of the entirety of the physical and nonphysical realms, manifesting their influence in everything within the physical world), and the like.

People born on Thursday tend to seek fulfillment within their own (either made-up or actual) stories and worlds (as there is the realm of the physical and the realm of the non-physical, and the contents of these realms intermingle and transition from one to the other), and in the substance and constituents of the physical and nonphysical realms (in what makes them up, in what populates them, in what exists in or happens in them, in how things can go from being part of one realm to being part of another, and so on), and particularly in the fusion or intermingling or almost-seamless inter-action of the ethereal or potential or theoretical or divine or imagined with the more tangible or actual or practical or mundane or real (like where water vapor becomes liquid water and vice versa), and the like.

People born on Friday tend to seek fulfillment in other people and in people-related or people-constructed things (for human beings were defined on this day), and the like.

People born on Saturday tend to seek fulfillment in all of the manifestations of the world in those manifestations' complete and finished (and particularly harmoniously or peacefully completed) forms, in the completion or perfection of anything (like the completion of a day's work, when they can relax) or of everything, or in the consideration of things as an integrated whole (as the world is brought through humans to a complete, perfect, peacefully integrated whole on this day), and the like.

It must be recognized that the influence of the weekday (of birth) is due to a fixation. Consequently, there can be a greater or lesser influence of that weekday upon a person due to greater or lesser fixation. Everyone has some fixation on every one of the days (like everyone has some fixation on every one of the stages in the form of main stage types, inclinations, and so forth) that he/she must overcome in the process of developing toward self-awareness, but the weekday of birth is the primary day of fixation. And when the fixation is of a sufficiently large degree, the result is that the person finds only *unfulfillment* of his/her main-stage-type-fixation-related desires in the creations of his/her weekday of birth, rather than fulfillment, although since the person still has a fixation upon that day, he/she is still inclined to seek out that day's creations (what is defined on that day) despite this.

Essentially, all of our fixations shape the lens through which we view the world—shape what aspects of the world we are most inclined to notice and receive, and shape how we view everything.

People born on Sunday tend to be particularly concerned with light (e.g. Ernst Mach, who is known for his study of sound, but who studied light much more; or Albert Michelson, who measured the speed of light several times and carried out the Michelson-Morley experiment—which involved sending two beams of light out from the earth, one in the direction the earth was moving, and one in the opposite direction, in order to measure the speed of light by measuring the ether that was believed to permeate space, much like water—and Edward Morley, with whom Michelson carried out the experiment, was born on a Monday, and so probably viewed this as a measure of the propagation of waves of light in a sea of ether), or with simplicity (e.g. Enrico Fermi, who always sought simple methods of approximation and conveyance of information when complex mathematics and theories could be avoided, such as when he estimated the strength of the blast of the first atomic explosion in the Manhattan Project by dropping some pieces of paper where he was in order to allow them to drift in the air when the blast wave came by; or Paul Ehrenfest, who sought clarity in simplicity, writing papers that each concerned only very few basic points and using simple examples and models to the exclusion of complex mathematics in his publications, his conversations, and his teaching; or Bernhard Riemann, who simplified physics by proposing a theory of higher dimensions; or John Archibald Wheeler, who sought to reduce all physical phenomena to the geometry of spacetime, and who coined such simplifying terms as "black hole" and "wormhole", and who also proposed, with his idea of the wavefunction of the universe, that we bring the universe—both past and present—into being, essentially from nothing, through our observation and explanation of it), or with the creation or definition or formation of completely new worlds or other completely new things—either in their writing (e.g. Arthur C. Clarke, author of *2001: A Space Odyssey*; or J. R. R. Tolkien, author of *The Hobbit* and *The Lord of the Rings*; or George Lucas, creator of *Star Wars*), or in the real world (e.g. Abraham Lincoln, who, in his words and actions, was pivotal in the formation of a United States without slavery; or Charles Darwin, who developed the theory of the evolution of entirely new species; or Jean Piaget, who described the developmental process for new human beings—the development of children from birth into beings with the capacity for logical and abstract thought).

People born on Monday tend to see water-related things, like waves and flowing and bodies of receptive—or collective—water, in everything (e.g. Alessandro Volta and Georg Ohm, both of whom studied the flow of electricity; or James Clerk Maxwell, who saw the commonality of the wavelike nature of electric fields and magnetic fields and light and so saw that he could combine all of them in the single theory of electromagnetism; or Hendrik Lorentz, who proposed that light comes from the wavelike motions of charged particles in atoms, and who sought to describe the propagation of electromagnetic waves in different reference frames that are in motion relative to one another, and who also worked on such explicitly water-involved projects as the prediction of the effects of flood control in Dutch dikes; or Carl Jung, who proposed that there are universal psychological archetypes that reside in the ocean-like collective unconscious), or to concern themselves with infinity or with paradoxical things—and often to write with the abstruseness suggested by such content—(e.g. Georg Wilhelm Friedrich Hegel, who developed a concept of mind or spirit that arises out of the integration of a series of contradictions and oppositions—much like the horizon arises in the mind out of the union of the liquid water of the sea and the water vapor of the sky—and whose writing is notoriously difficult to read and understand; or Georg Cantor, who proved the existence of an infinity of infinities; or Paul Davies, who has concerned himself with the paradoxes of time's arrow and of time travel, as well as with curved space and even black holes—those objects wherein our understanding of the universe breaks down in paradoxical infinities), or simply to seek out and particularly focus on water (e.g. Daniel Bernoulli, who studied hydrodynamics, writing the book *Hydrodynamica*, which gave the field its name, and who formed Bernoulli's principle—regarding the inverse relationship between the velocity and pressure of a fluid—and who worked on several projects concerning such things as tides, ocean currents, and ships; or Horace R. Byers, who studied cloud physics and the lifecycle of thunderstorms; or Rachel Carson, who loved to read about the ocean, and who wrote plenty about life in the ocean, herself, including in the books *The Sea Around Us*, *The Edge of the Sea*, and *Under the Sea Wind*, and who also wrote about environmental pollution by pesticides in the book *Silent Spring*; or Hermann Hesse, who chose to live on Lake Constance, and then right by Lake Lugano, and who wrote extensively about the flowing water of a river in his book *Siddhartha*, making the river a pivotal influence in the main character's spiritual development toward the peace and contentment of enlightenment).

People born on Tuesday tend to view the world through the struggle to rise up and away from where their roots are (e.g. Martin Luther King, Jr., whose words and actions were pivotal in the American civil rights movement, in which African Americans struggled to rise up and away from their roots in slavery, subjugation, and segregation; or Sigmund Freud, who based the development of his theories of human psychology—as that of the id, ego and superego—on the idea of our struggling to overcome repressed desires; or Lev Vygotsky, who studied child development and saw it as being shaped, through internalization, by the culture from which a person comes—by the social interactions with parents and other important people in a person's life in which the person has his/her roots of language and knowledge; or Franz Kafka, who wrote of characters who were constantly struggling, and whose writing has been interpreted as being about his own struggles with his family or with his Jewish roots or with other aspects of his life; or C. S. Lewis, who constantly struggled with his Christian roots and with Christian belief in general in all of his writing, becoming an atheist and then returning as a defender of the faith; or Richard Leakey, who has struggled throughout his life to try to get away from the archaelogical world of his parents in which he was brought up; or Thomas Kuhn, who struggled with the accepted rule-following view of the nature of science in which he was educated, and who wrote in *The Structure of Scientific Revolutions* of how science develops basically as a series of struggles to grow away from accepted paradigms; or Friedrich Nietzsche, who came up with the idea of the *ubermensch*, the over-man who rose above the constraints of man; or Karl Marx and Friedrich Engels, who both developed ideas about the working class rising up out of its condition of poverty; or Deepak Chopra, who grew away from Western medicine—and its idea of health as merely being without illness—to advocate alternative medicine, mainly self-awareness and meditation, in order to heal—or rise above and away from—illness and toward wellness, toward perfect health), and to spend a lot of time around trees or foresty areas (e.g. Jane Goodall, who studied chimpanzees in the forest; or John James Audubon, who studied birds—primarily surrounded by plant life).

People born on Wednesday tend to view the world through the model of the celestial bodies (e.g. Ernest Rutherford and Niels Bohr, both of whom saw in the atom an image of the planets orbiting the sun and described the atom from this perspective; or Edward Teller, who worked on the Manhattan Project to develop the atomic bomb, but who wanted to be working on a fusion weapon—using the power that fuels the stars—rather than on a fission weapon), or to look to those bodies themselves and their effects (e.g. Isaac Newton, who developed the theory of gravity to explain the orbits and interactions of the celestial bodies and their effects upon us, and who looked to the light of those bodies in his study of optics and the rainbow spectrum of light; or Giovanni Domenico Cassini, who was drawn to the sky and studied both astrology and astronomy, discovering, among other things, the Great Red Spot on Jupiter, which was discovered near the same time by Robert Hooke, who was also born on a Wednesday, and who also explored the planets, as well as their gravitational relations, and the moon and stars, through telescopes; or Edwin Hubble, who looked through a telescope and discovered galaxies beyond the Milky Way, and also discovered the redshift of the light from stars, which would later be used to determine that the universe is expanding; or Al Gore, who has become very involved with trying to stop global warming—the effect of the sun on the earth in combination with the carbon dioxide that we are emitting), or to look to the ultimate source or influencer of experience as being something distinctly separate from the form in which, or the means by which, we experience it, like the distinction between the sun, along with other celestial objects, and the light that we receive from them, or between the celestial bodies and their effects upon the world (e.g. John Locke, who held that there are primary qualities of objects that exist inherently in objects and that there are also secondary qualities of objects that are dependent upon our experience of those objects; or Immanuel Kant, who developed a theory of things in themselves—things that cannot be directly experienced but that in some way give rise to what we experience; or Gottlob Frege, who distinguished between the sense—the means by which one refers to something—and the reference—the thing to which one refers), or simply to surround themselves or concern themselves with the stars and the sky (e.g. William Herschel, who made hundreds of telescopes and discovered the planet Uranus—on a Tuesday, and necessarily after sunset, making it a Wednesday as we are defining the days—and two of its moons, as well as two moons of Saturn, and who, while studying the light from the sun, discovered infrared radiation; or Subrahmanyan Chandrasekhar, who studied the structure and development of stars; or Vincent Van Gogh, who is famous particularly for his painting *Starry Night*).

People born on Thursday tend to concern themselves with the substance and constituents of the physical and nonphysical (or more ethereal) realms and how things in one realm become things in the other realm (e.g. Michael Faraday, who studied electromagnetism and electrochemistry and how these can become other more practical and tangible things, such as through the use of the electric motor, the basis of which he formed; or Thomas Edison or Nikola Tesla, both of whom were thoroughly involved in inventing more tangible things with the use of the more ethereal electricity; or George Berkeley, who decided that the contents of the world must be observed in order to exist in the world—in order to be brought from a sort of potential or theoretical existence into an actual existence; or Werner Heisenberg, who revealed the inherent unknowability of the state of the universe's contents with his Uncertainty Principle and showed mathematically that, in the subatomic realm, particles go from being in a state of being everywhere with every velocity—all with various probabilities—to being in just one place or to having just one velocity upon observation of them; or David Bohm, who studied the flow of electrons in plasmas and quantum theory and came up with his own quantum theory about the origin of the contents of the physical universe from the implicate, or potential, realm; or Stephen Hawking, who studies black holes and who did so even when he wasn't sure if they were merely theoretical objects without any reality in this physical world or not, and who proposed the existence of Hawking radiation, by which black holes evaporate and appear to emit subatomic particles—which are actually particles that came into existence near the black hole's event horizon as members of pairs of virtual particles, and that then became real particles in order to preserve the total energy when their virtual partners fell into the black hole), or they tend to concern themselves with real or imaginary stories or worlds that somehow intermingle fiction and reality, imagination and truth, with things from one realm entering into the other (e.g. Alex Haley, who wrote *Roots* about his African ancestry but who interwove fictional stories into his depiction of his own past; or John Steinbeck, who wrote *The Grapes of Wrath* about a family in the Dust Bowl during the Great Depression and *East of Eden* about Steinbeck's maternal grandfather's family interwoven with the biblical Adam and his family; or George Orwell, who wrote *Animal Farm* about the Soviet Union in the form of an allegorical story of animals and *1984* about a totalitarian future society—both of which brought reality into a fictional world, dealing with an intermingling of the two; or Walt Disney, who created the cartoon character Mickey Mouse—along with Ub Iwerks, who was born on a Sunday, and who worked with Disney in the creation of new companies and characters—and other cartoon characters that are a melding of human beings and animals in appearance and relationships and so forth, and who formed Disneyland and Disney World, both of which are places where fictional characters and imagined worlds intermingle with, and enter into, reality; or Stan Lee, who created several Marvel Comic book characters and often included himself and other real people in the comic book world where he and they interacted with the fictional characters whom he created).

People born on Friday tend to be spokespeople (or people who communicate a lot with the public and other people in the field and generally with other people) for whatever field they enter, and so their names tend to be very recognizable (e.g. the physicist Max Planck, whose work helped found quantum theory; or the physicist J. Robert Oppenheimer, who was the scientific director of the Manhattan Project; or the chemist Stanley Miller, who sought to understand the origin of life on the early Earth; or the *New York Times* science writer Dennis Overbye), they tend to bring people and human-made objects to whatever they study or do, imagining people or human-like creatures in realms where they may or may not exist (e.g. Albert Einstein, who imagined people and buses and elevators in space traveling at the speed of light; or the physicist Michio Kaku, who imagines people colonizing space and living in space and on other planets and in other universes; or the astronomer Carl Sagan, who believed that it was highly likely that intelligent, human-like extraterrestrial beings exist elsewhere in the universe), they tend to be drawn to people and human-made objects (e.g. the historian Stephen Ambrose, who studied people and human history, particularly WWII; or Bill Gates, who is the founder and chairman of Microsoft and therefore works with human-produced technology; or Gene Roddenberry, who created *Star Trek*, which, of course, involves the imagining of people or human-like creatures all throughout the universe; or

James Watson, who discovered the structure of DNA—along with Francis Crick, who was born on a Thursday, and who was seeking in the endeavor to find how non-living molecules become living molecules, and who later sought to discover how proteins come from the coding of DNA, and how the non-conscious brain becomes a conscious mind—and who worked on the Human Genome Project, as well as on genetics projects that had the aim of furthering our understanding of cancers and other diseases that affect humans; or Francis Collins, who succeeded Watson as Director of the Human Genome Project, and who has searched for a genetic basis for various diseases that affect humans), and if they write, their writing is very people and character and often technology focused (e.g. Jules Verne, who imagined people traveling into the earth and under the sea and into the air and space, writing of technologies that we didn't then have; or H. G. Wells, who imagined people traveling in time and going to the moon and finding and fighting with extraterrestrial life; or Frank Herbert, who explored the interactions of human societal forces in his *Dune* novels; or Michael Crichton, whose writing is filled with dialogue and whose books concern technology, imagining, for example, people in a world filled with biotechnologically-developed dinosaurs, as in *Jurassic Park*).

People born on Saturday tend to be concerned with the perfection or completion, and often harmonious integration, of things (e.g. Brian Greene, who studies string theory and sees in it the potential for a complete and elegant theory of everything; or Kurt Gödel, who formulated the incompleteness theorem in mathematics; or William Thomson, 1st Baron Kelvin, who sought in the interrelation of various forms of energy a complete and unified theory of physics, and who completed the temperature scale of measurement by making it absolute, so that it begins at absolute zero—zero Kelvin, where there is no energy—and progresses upward by equal increments of energy per temperature number, and who also worked on perfecting such devices as the compass and the telegraph; or Richard Feynman, who worked in several different areas of quantum physics and who, among various other things, developed a sum-over-paths formulation of quantum mechanics that is essentially a complete description of all possible paths of a particle going from one point to another point; or Roger Penrose, who has worked on general relativity as well as quantum mechanics, thereby involving himself in areas all across physics, and who wrote *The Road to Reality: A Complete Guide to the Laws of Physics*, and has suggested requirements for a complete theory of physics that might be able to explain human consciousness; or Adolf Hitler, who had his extremely fixated and therefore not-at-all-harmonious idea of the "Final Solution" that entailed, in his view, the completion and "perfection" of things—as with his conception of the Arian race and so forth), or with a complete and completed peace (e.g. the 14th Dalai Lama, who has been active in working peacefully toward an autonomous Tibet—the completion of Tibet—and who has also been active in establishing a dialogue between different religions and between religion and science, and generally in promoting peace; or Mihaly Csikszentmihalyi, who has studied the experience of "flow"—of being "in the zone", with complete concentration on the activity in which one is engaged—which he believes is part of a happy and contented and peaceful experience of life), or with considering things as an integrated whole (e.g. Baruch Spinoza, who considered nature to be equivalent to God, and the mind to be equivalent to the body, and essentially all of reality to be of the same substance, and to be a coherent and systematic perfection that only seems imperfect due to our lack of perception of the whole; or Fritz Perls, who developed Gestalt therapy, which emphasizes complete awareness of what one is feeling and doing, as well as the consideration of the whole person, including the person's relation to him/herself and to all other things), and they often tend to be popularizers of their field due to their willingness to relate things to almost any other things, the wide purview of their attention and involvement across a field or fields, and the completeness of their explanations (e.g. Kip Thorne, who studies space, time and gravity—in topics from all across the field of general relativity—and who popularized such ideas as that wormholes might be used for time travel; or Henri Poincaré, who contributed to several different and varied fields of mathematics, sought in many ways to complete and perfect some of Hendrik Lorentz's work, and popularized several aspects of mathematics and physics), or they simply tend to view everything in the world without bias toward one thing or another, showing much variety of involvement (e.g. Leonardo da Vinci, who was involved with a huge variety of things—from painting, to inventing, to studying the body, to sculpting, to building, to writing, to writing music, to studying math, etc.).[13]

Be aware that the categorical breakdown of the different aspects of the influence of each day (with people being cited as examples of these different aspects), here, is merely for demonstration purposes—to bring us to a greater understanding of the influences of each day. For, in reality, every person manifests several or all of the aspects of the influence of the weekday of birth to some degree or other (as is suggested in some of the examples above).

---

13   Dates of birth—which were used to find the calendar weekday of birth using timeanddate.com/calendar—and other information about people in this section were, or can be, obtained mostly from Wikipedia.org. By the way, the examples used here only include people who seem, based on the influence of the days, to have been born *before* sunset (in which case the weekday of birth as we are defining it—from sunset to sunset in the location of birth—corresponds with the calendar weekday of birth); people who seem, based on the influence of the days, to have been born *after* sunset (in which case the weekday of birth as we are defining it is the day *after* the calendar weekday of birth) were not used as examples here.

Also, note that the majority of people used as examples here had, or (in the case of those who are still alive) have, sharing thought as their main stage type fixation. So, with the desire to understand, and to create new thoughts, that arose from their fixation on sharing thought, they became scientists, philosophers, and so forth, and they directed their desire to understand—and their thoughts—toward things that are related to their weekday of birth, seeking fulfillment in the understanding of such things.

It is not so much what people pay attention to in the world or what they do, but rather how they view it all (they are inclined to see the creations of their weekday of birth, and aspects of the nature of these creations, in everything, so that they see everything as resembling these things) and where they are inclined (where their attention is drawn first—and so what they notice first—when they step outside, where they choose to live, where they choose to spend their time, what pictures they choose to hang up and surround themselves with, what they take pictures of and write about and think about and so on) that is influenced, or defined, by the weekday of birth. And this influence can be only very slight if the person has not fixated to a very large degree upon the creations of his/her weekday of birth, or if the person has largely overcome these fixations in the development of self-awareness.

Astrological Influences on Personality

In the course of a year, the tree of life paradigm is manifested from the bottom up. If we wish to learn where this manifestation begins with regard to its influence upon what manifests during some particular time (such as with regard to people who are born during some particular time in the year), then we can look again to the idea of day and night. Unlike with the day of the week, the year has no strong association with creation, and so we are coming at the year from the perspective of manifestation (and the year is the process of manifestation from bottom up in the paradigm, instead of from top down as the weekdays are). Therefore, the overall day that is the year begins in night (manifestation), which is followed by day (creation). Spring and summer parallel the "night" that is our waking hours, and the "night" that is physical life, and the "night" that is the physical universe—inside the tree—and so spring and summer represent the night of the year. Fall and winter parallel the "day" that is the time during which we are asleep, and the "day" that is the nonphysical life between lives, and the "day" that is the nonphysical universe between physical universes—outside the tree—and so fall and winter represent the day of the year. Therefore, the year (from the perspective of manifestation, which is night followed by day), begins in spring and summer, and then continues with fall and winter.

Spring begins around March 21, on the spring equinox (when the earth is oriented in relation to the sun so that its axis does not tilt either toward or away from the sun), and so this marks the beginning (and the end) of the day that is the year—the beginning of the manifestation of the year, from the bottom up. From here, we ought to expect the several patterns of the paradigm to play out in everything that manifests during the different stages. The stages represent the development of experience—from self-orientedness, to other-orientedness, to other "I"-orientedness; from inclination to preserve the self, to inclination to belong to the group and fit in, to inclination to connect intensely and intimately with other "I"'s; from instinct-oriented, to feeling-oriented, to thought-oriented; from present-oriented, to past-oriented, to future-oriented; from issues with boundaries of the "I", to issues with identity of the "I" and the "I"'s relation to others, to issues with making decisions that are the best for the "I" and for other "I"'s.

All of these different aspects of the stages ought to apply to anything that manifests during the manifestation of a particular stage of the year. And so anyone born during any particular stage will manifest the fixation of having manifested at that stage in all of these ways and in other ways that have been previously mentioned and discussed.

Since the development of a single year follows the same paradigm as the development of a single lifetime (just the physical lifetime—the manifestation stage—for we are just considering the *manifestation* of a year), one useful way to determine how the fixation upon a particular date of birth will influence personality is to determine the approximate time of a single lifetime of a person that parallels a particular time in the course of the year (considering how far along it is from the beginning and how close it is to the end). We can also consider the distinctions between males and females at different stages of life, for there are certainly distinctions (in relation to how they express themselves during adolescence, during child-bearing age, and so on). Remember, the distinctions between male and female come from reflections of the Source and the world, respectively, in their relation to one another. And remember that the distinctions break down as the paradigm progresses—as whatever is developing grows to create and share more actively in addition to receiving and manifesting within itself, thereby growing to resemble, more closely, the Source. This breakdown in gender distinctions is reflected to an extent in the development of an individual and in the development of a year as well. So you might look to the section above on stereotypes for specific differences.

But the important thing to consider is how someone of a particular gender would stereotypically express him/herself at a particular stage of life, and then consider that a person born during the time of year that corresponds with this stage is fixated on this stage of development, so that all of his/her life is a reflection of this stage in the development of life to an extent—as though the person is forever a single age in a lot of ways (always old, or always young, or always middle-aged, for instance, but more specifically tailored to particular ages). This is similar to the way that the inclinations are manifested at different points in the early development of a single person's life, but throughout all of life—barring the development of a high degree of self-awareness—a person will fixate upon one inclination primarily. Every aspect of the paradigm is manifested over the course of a person's life, for a person's life follows the paradigm in its development from bottom up, but every person fixates on different aspects of the different stages, manifesting all of the aspects of each of the stages with a bias toward certain aspects of certain stages—the aspects upon which the person is most fixated.

This pattern of manifestation—from bottom up in the paradigm—is the form in which the paradigm manifests in most things in this world, dictating the development over the course of a day, of a year, of a single lifetime, of spans of history, and of the entire universe. Within this development, there is sometimes a divide between night and day, such that manifestation occurs throughout the overall day—or, rather, the overall night, as the case is with pretty much all things within the physical universe, within this period of overall manifestation—(the overall day, or rather the overall night, being all of the year or all of a lifetime, including both physical and nonphysical stages, etc.), but the night also reflects the entire paradigm manifesting from bottom up, while the day reflects the entire paradigm creating from top down—all within an overall manifestation from bottom up (within the overall day, or rather the overall night, that is the year, or that is a single lifetime, or whatever). But here we have a simple way of discerning the general patterns in things: Just consider the paradigm manifesting from bottom up, beginning at manifestation and heading upward toward choice. Choice is never a fixation in the process of manifestation upward. And so we consider everything up to, but prior to, choice.

However, with regard to astrological influences, there are more things to consider that can help us to describe all that manifests within any particular point of time in the year. There are aspects of creation within the year, as well as aspects of manifestation, besides the overall general pattern of development from bottom up through each of the individual ten stages (excluding choice as a stage of manifestation that can be fixated upon).

First of all, let us consider why there are inherently aspects of creation manifested in creation-order throughout the manifestation of the universe.

Even though, from the universe's perspective, we are in the process of manifestation (in the overall night of the physical universe, within the darkness of the inside of the tree), from the Source's perspective, the process of creation is ongoing (in the endless day of the sun's perspective, within its own light—outside the tree). It is easy to see that if light ceased to be shined through a holographic plate, the hologram would cease to exist. So it is with the physical universe—if the Source ever ceased to share self-aware existence with it, if the Source ever ceased to create it in any moment, the universe would cease to exist. If the sun ceased to shine upon the tree, the water within the tree would cease to progress upward through time and physical existence. The physical universe—and even the entire world within which it exists—depends upon all that the Source provides it to continue to exist.

(Notice, therefore, that just because it is night from *our* perspective doesn't mean it is night from *every* perspective. We can see, on the earth, that one person can be experiencing nighttime while another person somewhere else can simultaneously be experiencing daytime. And, likewise, we can see, in the tree setup, that there is liquid water within the tree in night even as there is simultaneously also water vapor outside the tree in day. Manifestation may be predominant for us—from our perspective within this physical universe—but creation is ongoing—and is predominant from the perspective of the Source, as well as from the perspective of the world outside the tree—nonetheless.)

So, every once in a while, within the universe, we will simply see reflections of the relationship between the Source and the world in a creative pattern and order.

We see this in the quantum realm, where we think and then look and then find that the particle ends up where we look for it. We see this in the manifestation of male and female elements of all things, where something shares, and something receives, and this produces (or creates) something new—the child of this interaction that allows the interaction to be manifested (like an understanding derived from a conversation that allows the communication to have been effective, such that the intended meaning was conveyed, or like the exchange of electrons between two atoms that produces a new molecule or that produces ions—the production of which allowed the exchange of electrons to occur and be effective or, more precisely, which allowed this exchange to be manifested). And we see this pattern of sharing, followed by receiving, followed by allowing, repeated within the development of the year as well. Before we explain how, we need just a bit more information.

There are definitively four seasons on Earth (even though this is not really practically so in some places on Earth), defined by two separate equinoxes and two separate solstices. We begin spring—and the whole year—with the spring equinox, around March 21st. We begin the next season, summer, with the summer solstice, around June 22nd. We begin the next season, fall, with the fall equinox, around September 23rd. And we begin the next and final season, winter, with the winter solstice, around December 22nd.

It is important to note here that we are biasing our assessment of which equinox is which season and which solstice is which season toward the seasons they begin in the *northern* hemisphere. The equinoxes are defined by *neither* the north nor the south pole of the earth's axis pointing toward or away from the sun, and the solstices are defined by one of the poles pointing toward or away from the sun. In the northern hemisphere, the summer solstice is defined by the *north pole* pointing *toward* the sun (producing the longest day of the year with regard to duration of daylight), and the winter solstice is defined by the *north pole* pointing *away* from the sun (producing the shortest day of the year with regard to duration of daylight). Then, the spring equinox is the equinox that directly follows the winter solstice (the equinox during which the length of days—with regard to duration of daylight—in the northern hemisphere is in the process of increasing), and the fall equinox is the equinox that directly follows the summer solstice (the equinox during which the length of days—with regard to duration of daylight—in the northern hemisphere is in the process of decreasing).

It is justifiable that we define the beginning of the year in the spring of the northern hemisphere in accordance with this bias, because about 90 percent of the human population lives in the northern hemisphere, and since it is our use of language that shapes the universe, causing things to manifest in the forms that we ascribe to them—causing the paradigm to manifest in anything and in any span of time that the universe deems, or that *we* deem, complete—the manifestation of the paradigm over the course of the year is certainly to be defined by the overwhelming majority of the language used by the overall human population. This is just as events and other things manifest in accordance with majority force of beliefs and other language, with where the majority of the language of the aspects of the universe—the majority of the aspects that are using any language to describe some particular thing whatsoever—is directing its attention and definition, considering in the balance how active and self-aware and energetic the attention and language of each aspect is and so on. If the majority of the language being used in the universe (concerning which equinox and which solstice is to be defined as the beginning of which season) is actually to *determine* what the resulting manifestation is, then we can safely consider the seasons from the perspective of the northern hemisphere in determining what shall be accurately deemed the beginning of the year.

Okay, so there are four seasons on Earth, and they each have pretty definite beginnings, and they each encompass a similar duration of time. So, to consider the creative element of the progression of the year, it would make a lot of sense to have a sharing component, a receiving component, and a resulting allowing component (which combines elements of the previous sharing and receiving components, and really of all of the previous components to an extent—an accumulation that we see in the allowing components of the paradigm in the order of creation from top down), in this order, dividing up each of the four seasons into three parts of approximately equal duration.

It is not really important which particular sharing, receiving, and allowing components in the tree of life paradigm are placed in each season, because we are not considering the sharing, receiving, and allowing of things that are defined by those stages, as we shall soon see. But if we *were* to consider particular stages, we would consider the creation-order of the stages that are particularly relevant—in their being sufficiently defined to consider as something that could manifest—to the creation of the physical universe (the feeling and instinctual stages, as we saw in the days of the week). This is where the seed of the tree of life has already been produced (by sharing thought and receiving thought, in allowing thought), and we are considering the elements provided for its growth, as well as its growth, itself.

Of course, this only gives us six stages, and there are four seasons to have three stages each, producing a total of twelve stages. Here, we must consider both the night and the day of the year. And we must consider that we are, here, describing a creation-order element of the defining of a year, and so we begin, as per creation-order (for the sake of this particular aspect of the defining of the year), with the day that is creation, and we follow this with the night that is manifestation (for, in the order of creation, things must be created before they can manifest). The feeling and allowing stages are repeated twice—once for the creation of the day, and once for the creation of the night—giving us a total of twelve stages, with three for each season.

The spring is composed of the three feeling stages, and the summer is composed of the three instinctual stages, and then the fall is composed of the three feeling stages, and the winter is composed of the three instinctual stages. There is a difference amongst the stages, even as they are repeated, because the first set of stages represents the creation of the day of the year, and the second set of stages represents the creation of the night of the year. And this is the creation of a single entire year, so there is a continued progression, with the latter stages being more manifesting and receptive (receiving from the former stages) and less creative and sharing (for the former stages share with them), making the second set of stages female (receptive) in relation to the first set of stages, which are therefore male (sharing) in relation to the second set of stages.

(It is interesting to consider what is suggested here—that spring and summer create and share what is then received by fall and winter, and that fall and winter are thus dependent upon spring and summer. These things are very true with regard to what manifests during these periods of time—with regard to the existence of life during these periods of time—for in order to continue to exist through fall and winter, we and other life are dependent upon the things that grow, or are created, by the sunlight, and/or are dependent upon the sunlight itself, that is available in spring and summer.)

But what are we to consider as being the objects of sharing and receiving and allowing? What is being shared and received and allowed?

It is significant to consider something here. If we had only one such thing to be shared and received and allowed, there would be repetition of the same stages in each season, with only the continued progression to distinguish them. If we had only two such things, there would still be repetition of the same stages in each season—each set of three stages occurring twice. If we had three such things, or more than four such things, we would not come out even over the course of four seasons. There cannot really be more than four, and it doesn't allow for much distinction to have fewer than four, and so we ought to have four such things—four different things that can be shared, received, and allowed.

But what are the four things? We have a creative component (a creation-order element) in the ordering of stages here—in the creative order of sharing, followed by receiving, followed by allowing—so we ought to combine this with a manifesting component (a manifestation-order element). After all, the year is manifesting overall, since it occurs within the overall night (the overall process of manifestation) that is the physical universe.

We can look to the tree of life paradigm for what we seek.

Choice is not a part of manifestation that can be a fixation, for it is the end of the whole process, and so fixation upon it doesn't make any sense—since fixations hinder our progress to the end goal, which *is* choice. We have seen with the days of the week, however, that manifestation can be considered as a fixation in that case.

Remember, now, how the whole paradigm formed in the first place. The Source shared a thought with the world, and the world received that thought in whatever form it interpreted the thought to mean, and the result of this communication was allowing thought. Then, from there, the world essentially produced the rest of the paradigm by repeating each of these stages in new, more defined forms, such that the feeling stages are a reflection of sharing thought, the instinctual stages are a reflection of receiving thought, and manifestation is a reflection of allowing thought (and the three stages of feeling and the three stages of instinct are each reflections of the three stages of thought). And these repetitions produced the contents of the physical universe, which is why we consider these in creation with regard to the progression of the week and of the year, excluding the thought stages (which are the same for every universe, determined, as they are, by the Source and the world to begin the creation of the tree of life in which the universe progresses in its existence). So, if we consider these stages in the order of manifestation, we have manifestation, then the instinctual stages, then the feeling stages, and then the thought stages. And here we have four things to be shared and received and allowed.

But we still need to specify what aspects of each of these stages are being shared, received, and allowed.

Manifestation is illuminating of immediate experience, for this is where our physical senses receive all of the information that they receive. This is where the energy of existence exists, and it is where actual manifestation is initiated. It can be consuming as well (think of time as like the eating of each moment, or gravity in the sense of black holes that swallow all that comes close enough to them), and it is dominated by desire, for it receives from all of the stages above it, being in this sense the most feminine of all of the stages, and if it holds onto what it receives, then this is where desires would be produced. So, in manifestation we have an illuminating, but also consuming, energy that is driven by desire in the immediacy of the moment. This sounds quite a lot like fire, and so we shall consider manifestation in this sense as fire for the sake of simplicity of reference and clear conveyance of intended meaning. (In relation to manifestation, it is like fire, but it should be considered that we might alternatively associate it, in the tree setup, with the sunlight, which is illuminating and creative and actively imparting of enlivening energy in relation to the tree. However, in its form of fire in manifestation, it is full of desire and is potentially receptive and even consuming, as opposed to in its form of sunlight. And aspects of both fire and sunlight can be considered and, in fact, reconciled in the consideration of the fire that is the sun, which does, in fact, consume—although in a creative way in the form of the fusion of hydrogen atoms to form helium atoms—and which, in so consuming, produces and radiates the energy used by the tree in the tree's growth and by the water in the tree in the form of the pull of evapotranspiration.)

The instinctual stages are very resources and environment and territoriality oriented, unsure of where they end and their environment begins, and concerned with having the material resources that are necessary for their own survival. In the tree setup, this sounds a lot like the earth—the ground, the land, the soil—the very environment and nutrient resources that are necessary for the survival of the seed of the tree, and ultimately for the stability and survival of the tree, and so we shall consider the instinctual stages in this sense as earth and refer to them as such.

The feeling stages are concerned with their interactions with others, and they are inclined to project themselves onto others—onto groups of others, regardless of the size of the group—seeing others as projections or extensions of them, with those others having no clear distinction from them other than their difference in spatial location and the resulting difference in perspective. It is as though there is a single, objective, ideal perspective (that of the "I") that is merely made subjective and different by difference in spatial location and outer conditions and the consequent difference in experiences (and therefore in all past experiences). What is true for the "I" is true for all, for all others are merely extensions or projections of the "I". It is not much of a stretch to say that this sounds like air—extending or projecting itself to fill any space, regardless of size, and flowing into and out of all living creatures as though there is no real distinction amongst anything linked by it other than the separation in space and the resulting difference in perspective. And, in the tree setup, it certainly does sound like the air outside the tree that has a single, objective, ideal perspective of all of the possible branches that the water inside the tree may take, and that allows for the communication between the water of one universe and that of the next (as the water becomes water vapor, thereby becoming part of the air, and then the water condenses out of the air to reenter the tree). And so we shall consider the feeling stages in this sense as air and refer to them as such.

The thought stages are concerned with treating other "I"'s as other "I"'s—recognizing them as distinct from one another in who they are beyond a mere difference in spatial location. Empathy may begin to arise in the feeling stages, but the feeling-stages version of empathy is like *literally* putting yourself in the other person's shoes—putting yourself in his/her external situation—and seeing how *you* would feel in that external situation, rather than considering the differences in that person's internal perspective—considering how that person is different from you in the way he/she is inclined to feel and react and so on—and trying to understand how that person would actually be experiencing the situation differently from the way you would. This individual-specific true kind of empathy only arises in the thought stages, providing at least a greater *potential* for sensitivity to an individual's feelings (whether or not this potential is actualized). Also, the thought stages are concerned with what will be, always having an eye toward the future, imagining what *might* happen or what *could* happen. And because thought is required for any real creation of new ideas and experiences—and ultimately new understanding that allows for the true departure from patterns of past ideas and experiences—the thought stages are the first stages where real growth—growth into a future that is distinctly different from the past—is able to occur. And there is the overflowing desire to share the experience of growth when it occurs—to aid other individuals in their own growth. Sexual reproduction is associated with the thought stages as well—as real distinction between individuals provides for the ability to unite with another and produce something new and different from both components that went into the production of that thing. Also, this kind of overflowing sharing of one's individual experience of growth, in combination with true empathy that considers separate individuals as separate and distinct individuals, provides for the potential for real love—love that is not merely love of some projection of oneself, but love of another "I", another individual who is separate and distinct from oneself. In the tree setup, this overflowing element of love and imagination and growth and individual feeling and experience sounds a bit like water, which provides for the growth of the seed into a tree. Also, the actualization of the potential of the tree—what only exists in imaginary, potential form—depends upon the abundance and availability of water to the seed and the tree. And water can take on different unique and truly individual forms—in solid, liquid, or gaseous stages, each of which can take a myriad of forms—adapting to the distinct environment, the distinct other. So we shall consider the thought stages in this sense as water and refer to them as such.

Remember that metaphors are not mere contrived things but are, rather (if the comparisons are accurate), reflections of reality. So as we consider manifestation as fire (as the fire of the sun that produces sunlight), the instinctual stages as earth, the feeling stages as air, and the thought stages as water, we will likely find that these reflections of reality (which quite nicely provide all of the elements in the tree setup other than the tree, itself, which they all interact with one another in different ways to produce and aid in the growth of) can be extended beyond what we have discussed here. But, for here, this is sufficient.

Now, we must figure out how to put this all together into the stages of the year. We have the creative components of sharing, receiving, and allowing for each season (in this order—the order of creation), and we have the manifesting components of fire, earth, air, and water (in this order—the order of manifestation), upon which the creative components can act. If we repeat the set of three creative components four times in a row, and we repeat the set of four manifesting components three times in a row, then we shall have twelve distinct stages—all of the permutations of these three creative components with these four manifesting components. And since we are dividing each of the four seasons (which begin on specific dates) into three approximately equal parts (represented by the three creative components), we can provide the dates—the specific beginning and ending points in the year—for each of the stages here as well.

Sharing fire, beginning on March 21st and ending on April 20th, creates its own illumination and initiative desire in disregard of others and the world outside itself and imposes these things upon others and the world outside itself, seeking to be in control and to be helpful and useful through this overflowing creation.

Receiving earth, beginning on April 21st and ending on May 21st, grasps at and holds onto the resources and stability produced within it in reaction to others and the world outside itself, seeking for itself to be good and complete and fulfilled through this grasping manifestation within itself.

Allowing air, beginning on May 22nd and ending on June 21st, allows others' and the world's projected perspectives and ideals to be communicated and manifested through it, seeking harmony and success and security through this submissive allowance.

Sharing water, beginning on June 22nd and ending on July 22nd, creates its own love and insightful sensitivity and growth in disregard of others and the world outside itself and imposes these things upon others and the world outside itself, seeking to be in control and to be helpful and useful through this overflowing creation.

Receiving fire, beginning on July 23rd and ending on August 22nd, grasps at and holds onto the illumination and initiative desire produced within it in reaction to others and the world outside itself, seeking for itself to be good and complete and fulfilled through this grasping manifestation within itself.

Allowing earth, beginning on August 23rd and ending on September 22nd, allows others' and the world's resources and stability to be manifested through it, seeking harmony and success and security through this submissive allowance.

Sharing air, beginning on September 23rd and ending on October 23rd, creates and projects its own perspective and ideals in communication with others and the world in disregard of others and the world outside itself, seeking to be in control and to be helpful and useful through this overflowing creation.

Receiving water, beginning on October 24th and ending on November 21st, grasps at and holds onto the love and insightful sensitivity and growth produced within it in reaction to others and the world outside itself, seeking for itself to be good and complete and fulfilled through this grasping manifestation within itself.

Allowing fire, beginning on November 22nd and ending on December 21st, allows others' and the world's illumination and initiative desire to be manifested through it, seeking harmony and success and security through this submissive allowance.

Sharing earth, beginning on December 22nd and ending on January 20th, creates its own resources and stability in disregard of others and the world outside itself and imposes these things upon others and the world outside itself, seeking to be in control and to be helpful and useful through this overflowing creation.

Receiving air, beginning on January 21st and ending on February 19th, grasps at and holds onto the projected perspectives and ideals communicated to it and produced within it in reaction to others and the world outside itself, seeking for itself to be good and complete and fulfilled through this grasping manifestation within itself.

Allowing water, beginning on February 20th and ending on March 20th, allows others' and the world's love and insightful sensitivity and growth to be manifested through it, seeking harmony and success and security through this submissive allowance.

All of this can obviously be expanded upon, as was done with the personality types, and the experience of things manifested within the influence of each of these stages in the year (such as people born during each of these stages) can certainly yield much more information about these stages. Also, remember that we can consider the differences in gender in our application of this information to understanding specific individual people—with males being more logical and solitary and independent and self-oriented (due to being like the sun around which the world revolves, with the obligation of having to work to provide that goes along with this) and so on, and with females being more emotional and sociable and dependent upon the other and others-oriented (due to being like the earth in its revolution around the sun that provides it with life-giving and life-sustaining energy) and so on. And we can consider the placement of each stage in the overall development of the year from bottom up in the paradigm.

Here, the first three stages (spring) correspond with manifestation and the development of a person from birth and self-centered and preservation-of-self-oriented youth (sharing fire), through adolescence and learning to be a man or a woman (receiving earth), and into a young, but manifested, adult who is beginning to really interact with others in the world around him/her (allowing air)—like the budding and growth of plants to maturity and flowering during the spring.

The next three stages (summer) correspond with the three instinctual stages from bottom up and the development of a person from young adulthood and marrying and child-bearing age (sharing water—corresponding with allowing instinct), through full recognition of manhood or womanhood and child-rearing and supporting (receiving fire—corresponding with receiving instinct), and into middle age and mid-life crises and hard work to shape his/her life (allowing earth—corresponding with sharing instinct)—like the flowering and pollinating and seed-dispersal of plants during the summer.

The next three stages (fall) correspond with the three feeling stages from bottom up and the development of a person from just past middle age when a person becomes very accomplishment and achievement and success focused and raises children (sharing air—corresponding with allowing feeling), through the self-reflective and introspective later years and menopause and the consequent tuning into oneself and one's body and so on (receiving water—corresponding with receiving feeling), to the age of esteemed status and desire and expectation for such status among social groups (allowing fire—corresponding with sharing feeling)—like the plants after seed dispersal, and the shedding of flowers, and the changing of the colors of the leaves of trees and the shedding of those leaves.

The last three stages (winter) correspond with the thinking stages and the development of a person from retirement and conservative and conserving reduction of spending and relaxed but serious and cautious focus on pursuits for him/herself (sharing earth—corresponding with allowing thought), a period of returned youthfulness and appreciation of enjoyable things in life and concern with the end and connecting with what comes after (receiving air—corresponding with receiving thought), to living in thoughts and dreams and imaginings before death (allowing water—corresponding with sharing thought)—like the hibernation of plants and trees and animals, and the blanketing of the earth in white and playful fluff that can be enjoyed or taken in seriousness, and like the bareness of plants and trees as animals sleep and dream.[14]

In our assessment of the effects of astrological influences, we must remember that, as noted above, the main stage type fixation has the predominant influence upon the formation of our personality. Things like the inclination of fixation, the weekday of fixation, and the point in the year of fixation all serve merely to modify the expression of the main stage type fixation—lessening and exaggerating different features of our

---

14   Correspondence of astrological signs with ages (and stages) in the life of an individual in this way, as well as the differentiation of expression of the astrological signs in people by gender, can be found in *Sextrology: The Astrology of Sex and the Sexes*, by Starsky and Cox.

main stage type fixation, and determining where we are inclined to seek fulfillment of the desires that arise due to our main stage type fixation.

Also, we must remember that all of these effects are the result of *fixations*—of the manifestation of one stage more than the others, and of getting stuck at that stage and holding onto that stage, which results in the formation of desires (because we are not allowing that stage to pass), and which prevents us from growing upward fully toward choice and complete self-awareness. We are not our personality. We are nothing that results from fixations. We are the ability to experience and learn and grow and understand and create. We are "I"'s with the potential to be self-aware. And all of the aspects of personality—all of our fixations—are hindrances to the actualization of this potential. It is important that we remember this so that we are not held down and prevented from further growth toward greater self-awareness by mistaken beliefs about who we truly are—by mistakenly identifying with our fixations. For when we identify with our fixations, we give up the self-aware ability to choose and we allow our identified-with fixations to choose for us in our reactions to the world as our identifications attempt to preserve our belief that they are who we truly are, and as they thereby attempt to uphold and propagate themselves—their own existence (for all things that exist seek to preserve their own existence)—through our (their) choices.

Giving and Getting

Due to the nature of the tree of life paradigm by which all things in this world abide, we tend to receive more of whatever we give, for when we give, we make room for the reception of more of whatever we have given. In a twisted corruption of this, we often tend to *want* to receive—from others and the world around us—more of whatever *we* desire to give (whatever *we* are inclined to be giving). We tend to *expect* to get what we give, and we also tend to give what we get. Thus, we project our personalities onto others and the world around us (in the first and second of the three stages, when the "I" fails to recognize the existence of distinct other "I"'s), expecting that they have the same desires, the same motivations, the same thoughts and feelings, as *we* do—or as we *would* if we were in that same situation in the outside world.

And so our expectations of others and of the world around us tend to be the same as our expectations of ourselves, and our judgments of others and of the world around us tend to be the same as our judgments of ourselves (the same as our judgments of ourselves would be if we did what those others did if we were in those others' external situation). And when we are yelled at, we tend to yell, and when we are abused, we tend to abuse others. And so negativity spreads as patterns of behavior are propagated from individual to individual.

Notice, though, that this is a corrupted reflection of the true relation between us and other "I"'s or, more specifically, between us and the Source "I". For the true relation between us and the Source "I" entails our receiving more of what we share—like water in a stream or in a tree, which is shared, and so more is received. This relation—this interaction—does not entail expectation. It is merely that when we allow things to pass, more of those same things, or similar things, will come to replace them in our experience.

The language that we use (in our thoughts, feelings, inclinations) to describe our experience inevitably becomes accurate in describing our *future* experience—regardless of whether or not this language accurately describes our past or present experience. But other people have their own control over things in this way as well. We can alter our interactions with them via the language we use to describe our interactions with them, but what is true of the interaction between us and the Source is not always true in the extreme of our interactions with other beings who are capable of describing their own experiences in this world.

When it comes to our interactions with other people in this world, we must remember that they have the same essence of choice that we do. And it is not merely that they have an essence that is *like* ours, but rather that they actually have the *exact same* essence as we do. In order to understand our interactions with other people in the world, we might best imagine ourselves and them as leaves on a tree. As long as we are just paying attention to our physical manifestations as bodies in this world, we will see ourselves as separate from everyone else, for you are a leaf here, and I am a leaf over there on the end of a different set of branches, and someone else is a leaf way over there on the end of an entirely different set of branches. But what we must recognize is that we are not merely our physical selves; we are not merely the leaves. For the leaves grew out of the branches, which grew out of other branches, which grew out of other branches, which ultimately grew out of the exact same trunk—our essence of choice, in which there is no distinction between you and everyone else. Our physical selves are merely the last differentiation of a series of differentiations of the essence that we hold in common.

So, whenever we choose—whether consciously or not—the language that we use, we are actually choosing from the trunk of the tree. We are doing something that inherently affects not only us, but everyone and everything else, for it is as though we are directing the course of the water up the trunk of the tree, into certain branches and not others. Ultimately, we can aid in the growth of other leaves, and we can hinder the growth of other leaves, all with the part of ourselves that is the trunk of the tree.

To understand this even better, we must recognize that hypnotic states of consciousness are indistinguishable from normal everyday states of consciousness. In actuality, we are all constantly in a sort of state of mass hypnosis. Everyone and everything else in this world, having the same essence as *we* do, are ever-influencing our thoughts and feelings and instincts and speech and actions and the outward physical manifestation of our lives, all through the language that they choose to give rise to with their—our—essence. And, likewise, all of *our* choices of our *own* use of language are influencing *everyone and everything else in this world*. From the same trunk, we and they branch off into distinctly differentiated—distinctly fixated—selves that culminate in our physical manifestations. And so, essentially, we are all subtly influencing one another, as though we are all hypnotizing one another, with the language that we choose to use to shape and share our experiences in this world.

It is not that we can get other people to do just anything. Just as with usual hypnosis, we cannot get anyone to do anything that he/she wouldn't be willing to do. If someone is strongly against killing people, you aren't going to be able to get that person to kill someone just by using language to that effect in your own thoughts and feelings and actions. And no matter how much you try with your use of language to get someone to show interest in you, if that person is strongly-enough *not* interested in you then that person's use of language is going to outweigh your subtly influencing choice of language.

Basically, there is all of this language being used to shape the world and each of our own thoughts and feelings and instincts and speech and actions, and it is all like the radio waves that are all around us all the time. It is to which station we turn our own radios that determines what we allow to influence us, and if we are not clear in the focus of our attention, then we will receive the static of many stations at once without our being aware of exactly what we are creating in our lives.

This is what it means to allow the world to choose our language for us. When we are not willfully choosing to focus our attention on specific language to describe and thereby shape our experiences in this world, we are allowing our use of language in describing these—our language of our thoughts, feelings, instincts, speech and actions—to be determined by the language that everyone else is using to describe these. We allow others to define in our lives whatever we are not willfully defining ourselves. In this way, we allow the world to choose for us, through us.

But when we willfully choose our use of language with awareness, then we are allowing the Source to choose for us, through us. Merely being aware of the thoughts and feelings and instincts that enter our experience, *as they enter our experience*, gives us the opportunity and the ability to choose something different from what the world is influencing us to do.

Remember, we want to be listening to our intuition, which stems directly from choice, rather than to the staticy group-use of language that exists in the stages after choice. The world will determine our lives for us if we don't willfully determine our lives for ourselves. We have to make our own willfully-chosen language the predominant language that we use. And then no matter what happens in the world around us, *we* will be the ones shaping our lives—as *we* want them to be—rather than having our families, our friends, our cultures, our religions, and the rest of the world around us shape our lives for us.

Through our use of language, we can subtly influence all of our interactions with the world, and we can also allow ourselves to be used by the Source—through the essence of the world—to guide each of the various differentiated parts of the world, including us, toward their and our own fulfillment. In this way, we become an aid in the actualization of the true essence of ourselves and of everyone around us, guiding ourselves and them toward the goals that we truly wish to reach, and ultimately toward the ultimate goal of allowing the Source to create Its experience in the world's experience—in our experience and the experience of everyone around us.

We should never merely give what we get, for what we give will determine what we get, and so approaching any interaction in this way will only result in our *not* obtaining our own fulfillment—or, thereby, the fulfillment of the entire world—for it will merely result in our getting more of what we have been getting.

The truth about the world's interaction with the Source— the true nature of our relation and interaction with the Source—is everywhere in our experience to be found—in our thoughts, in our feelings, in our inclinations, in all of our external experience. But the less far we are along the path of the development of experience—the path up the tree of life paradigm of the development of this world—the more corrupted the reflection of this truth becomes. It becomes a bit like looking in a funhouse mirror and expecting to see things as they really are. When we progress along the path of development, we gain an increasingly clear and accurate view of the truth of things.

We gain a clear and accurate view, in our own experience, of the Source's experience, for this is what we receive when we allow the Source to share it through us—when we share this, we receive more of it. We may face obstacles in our experience along the way, but if we allow ourselves to be guided by our intuition in allowing our use of language to become the Source's use of language through us, then these obstacles will become part of the experience from which we gain a more accurate understanding of our relation to the Source and of the experience that we are receiving from the Source.

Nothing in this world is the source of what we receive from it—not our thoughts, not our feelings, not our inclinations or speech or actions, and not the other things and the other "I"'s of this world. We do not receive any fulfillment from these things. But everything that we receive from the Source comes *via* our experiences in this world—*via* all of these things. Our fulfillment comes via all of these things.

When we allow our use of language to become the Source's use of language, everything in our experience becomes part of the experience that the Source is sharing with us. And so all of the things of this world—in our internal and external experience—become intertwined and interconnected in this way. We should never ignore any of it, for experience is the key to our understanding, and our understanding is the key to our ability to experience what the Source is sharing with us.

And so we must bring the awareness of understanding to all of our experience in this world, and we must use our experience to learn and grow from it, so that we will have greater understanding to bring to the next experience in the form of greater awareness. In this way, our self-awareness builds upon itself and we progress toward experiencing as the Source experiences. In this way, we progress along the path toward fulfillment—for us and for all of the world.

The Source, the World, the Tree of Life, an Infinite Number of Universes, and Our Place and Purpose in it All

How Many Worlds, How Many Universes?

The Source seems to have brought forth the world because of the overflowing inclination to share Its experience of being It—self-aware of Its own existence and capable of creating the world with a self-aware thought, and so on—this inclination being in some sort of form of which our experience of this inclination is a projection or reflection of an image. And so It had the thought that there be another "I" with which It might share this experience. And the result was the world.

The most probable reason that the world differentiated seems to be that it sought to capture its experience in words in some way—causing it to come out of its meditative state and experience. The world began to think its own thoughts about the experience and it thereby ceased to experience the experience, itself. And these thoughts gave rise to feelings, which gave rise to inclinations, which gave rise to actions, which gave rise to a newly manifested physical world. Thus, the differentiated physical world that is composed of language began to manifest—from the bottom up, in order to actualize everything up to the thoughts and the choice that brought forth the world in the first place.

However, everything after this is a bit fuzzy (or, rather, even fuzzier) in terms of what we might know with any certainty. The question might arise as to whether the world differentiated into one or multiple physical worlds. It seems already, as we have seen with the water molecules that pass repeatedly through the tree, that there are multiple worlds, all existing separate in time, such that each world enters the tree, giving rise to the next world, which in some sense is already in the tree—as the water molecules fill the tree.

The water molecules certainly seem to fill the tree, with its every possible branch and so on, from the perspective of outside the tree—outside of actualized, and therefore meaningful, time (be it slow or fast). And so, due to the nature of the pure potential and meaningless time of choice—of the water vapor outside the tree—it may simply be as we have said—that there is, in a sense, one world repeatedly passing through the tree of spatial and temporal existence. And yet it seems as though this cannot be so from the perspective inside the tree, for there are certainly several water molecules that *must* exist in order for any of them to be pulled up the tree—for the tree must be filled in order for each water molecule to be able to have the pull of the sun exerted upon it via the water molecules above it (in order for it to receive the sun's energy in this way), and in order for each water molecule to be able to exert the pull of the sun upon the water molecules below it (in order for it to share the sun's energy that it receives). It may simply be that the world fills the entire tree in some way, but this is not so if the world is merely like a single (or a couple, or even a few) water molecule(s).

And so it seems that there must be several worlds separated by time—that the original world or worlds created by the Source differentiated into multiple worlds, like multiple water molecules. Perhaps the Source's thought that formed the world and that guides the world's formation is that there be several other "I"'s and not just another "I", although this seems less likely if one considers that the inclination to share one's experience as it is manifested within this world is manifested as the inclination to share with another "I"—in a small-group, intimate setting of only two or three people.

We might question whether the fact that males tend to be rather sexually promiscuous—such that they seek to engage in intimate and intense interactions with multiple females—is a reflection of the Source's seeking to engage in intimate and intense interactions with multiple worlds (seeking to give rise to multiple other "I"'s with which It might share Its experience). And perhaps polygamy—when one man has multiple wives— is a reflection of the same thing. But it is possible that these are reflections of the Source's interaction with what seems to be multiple worlds within the tree, or even of the Source's interaction with the multiple parts of the world within the world (as with multiple human beings and so on), and not actually with multiple worlds.

However, it seems that we should also consider that the Source is infinite and so perhaps the tendency toward an infinite number of worlds is inevitable. For why share such an experience as that of self-awareness with only *one* other when one can share it with *many* others? Regardless of whether the Source's thought was that there be *one* other "I" or *multiple* other "I"'s, *multiple* other "I"'s have resulted—at least *within* the world. And it seems inevitable that they must, for the contrast of the other within the world is required for any self-awareness (and even the mere recognition of the Source's *existence*, let alone the recognition of Its purpose in creating the world and the way by which It interacts with the world) to arise, and the contrast of other self-aware "I"'s (or nearly self-aware "I"'s) that have also arisen within the world seems to be the best means of bringing about self-awareness in anything. For with the contrast of multiple other such "I"'s, self-awareness can truly build upon itself.

It may even be that there are several worlds separated by space that exist simultaneously in time, rather than merely several worlds separated by time. This idea could be suggested by the fact that water molecules travel up many tubes within the tree, up the same branches, and up different branches, so perhaps there are actually several water molecules existing within each branch and every branch at what is the same point in time but merely a different point in space. Or maybe, again, this can all be explained by the timeless perspective outside of the tree and there is actually only one world differentiated. And maybe it is one world differentiated but it is differentiated into several different physical universes.

If we are truly to look to experience for the answer, we can still find ourselves lacking, for here we need to know to what experience to look. If we look to the arising of the first single-celled organism, for example, we would first of all need to know if one organism arose from which all others arose (in the case that only one organism arose that gained the capacity to replicate and share itself with another via RNA or DNA or something), or if many single-celled organisms arose independently of one another (which, of course, must be the case in the situation that life arose independently in multiple places in the universe).

It would seem from this situation that the Source gave rise to one or many worlds, and then those worlds—like the single-celled organisms—divided and multiplied, forming several single-celled organisms, some of which eventually evolved into simple multicellular organisms (mere collections of universes) and some then even into complex multicellular organisms (with individual universes differentiating within themselves and developing to form matter and energy, and perhaps galaxies in some, and perhaps life in some). Thus, the development of universes from the original world (or worlds) might be something of which the evolution of life within the universe is a reflection.

It might be that a world or worlds divided into multiple worlds, some of which formed universes. Or it might be that a world within itself gave rise to dimensions and universes like the universe within itself gave rise to galaxies and stars and planets and single-celled organisms.

It could, therefore, be that there are multiple universes that arise within the world like multiple organisms arise within the universe—some single-celled and some more evolved and developed, all propagating into more and more organisms through their division and/or union (being of what asexual reproduction of single-celled organisms and sexual reproduction of complex multicellular organisms would be reflections, respectively).

Yet, again, we might look to a different aspect of experience and say that the universe is like a single child, formed from the combination of the Source's language and the world's language. And so the universe was manifested and began to differentiate into the analogue of a single multicellular organism, like a single human being, with its parts being as we see them.

Ultimately, the goal of all of this, if the Source's thought gave rise to it in the manner suggested, would be to form other "I"'s that are capable of receiving the experience of self-awareness. The goal would therefore be the development of a world or worlds that are capable of manifesting all the way up the paradigm and eventually creating themselves (or a new world) with self-awareness. And yet we see that everything within our universe creates its own experience whether it is self-aware or not, merely through its use of language, which it cannot avoid. Once there is matter and energy, the movement of bodies, itself, gives rise to more experiences—of like-movement.

Maybe we should be looking to the very beginning of the physical universe for a reflection of the world's beginning. Perhaps there was a single manifestation of a world that ultimately gave rise spontaneously to particle-like universes that eventually coalesced and combined and collided, like particles forming nuclei and forming molecules and forming stars and planets and galaxies. Perhaps this single world's thoughts are actually the nuclear and electromagnetic forces that form this universe in which we live, and perhaps this single world's senses are the dimensions that contain this universe in which we live, thereby making all that occurs within this universe the experience of the world. And perhaps its thoughts began to form and concretize, and to give rise to feelings and to give rise to instincts and actions, and then they manifested in the singularity of the Big Bang, and they gave rise to instincts and movement in energy and matter, and they gave rise to life and eventually to intelligent life with the capacity for self-awareness. This would all suggest a single tree of life, with physical laws that hold throughout it, unless even the forces and dimensions are a reflection of some higher world's thoughts and senses.

Regardless of how many worlds there are, or whether the universes to which they (it) give(s) rise are separated merely by time or also by space, there is only one tree of life. Ultimately, overall, there is only one tree of life—the paradigm that is manifested (or, rather, created) once to be manifested again innumerable times within itself.

The original tree of life seems to be the result of the Source's original thought that is received by the world and is manifested as allowing thought, and then as the feeling stages, and then as the inclination and action stages, and then as manifestation; the original tree of life seems to be the result of there being Source, then world, and then language, and then all of that to which language gives rise. [Notice that allowing thought is language here, and that it gives rise to, and influences, everything after it, like electromagnetism influences everything in the world after it (everything besides the nuclear forces), and like the brain stem influences everything in the body after it, and like other manifestations of the allowing-thought stage influence all of the manifestations of the stages after them.] Therefore, it seems likely that the original tree of life was formed by the interaction of the Source and *one* world. And so there is one world, and there is one overarching tree of life, and everything else exists as a part of that world—either within the tree that is composed of the world's and the Source's language (as liquid water), or merely within the world but not within the tree (as water vapor).

And there are certainly an infinite number of universes separated by time, for the tree is always filled with water that passes from its roots up through it and evaporates from its leaves. And there may also be an infinite number of universes separated by space.

The World as an Organism

The world, thus, is like an organism, and its cells are like universes. For the world is like the female in its interaction with the Source, and the seed of the Source's thought was sown within the world's womb, and this seed gave rise to the rest of the tree of life and thereby, ultimately, to all of life. Whatever exists is like the tree within the tree-setup, with water (in liquid and vapor forms) and ground and so on—with the Source being like the sun and the Source's self-aware existence being like the sun's energy. Whatever exists is like the zygote and then embryo and then fetus within the womb, with an umbilical cord through which it gains all that it needs to continue to develop via its mother, which is the world, but ultimately from the Source, which provides all that is necessary for the world to remain in existence (like the male providing for the female).

The world could not receive what the Source was sharing forever without being able to share it with another. And so it gave rise to its child, the tree of life, so that it could share all that it received from the Source and thereby receive more. And this child, in order to continue to receive what it was receiving from the Source via the world, gave rise to an infinite number of universes as cells within itself, which, in turn, gave rise to numerous parts of themselves—as parts of the cells which are manifested in the universes ultimately as galaxies and stars and planets and life, which, in turn, gave rise to numerous others as well—each and every one of them containing the same DNA that was formed ultimately from the combination of that of the Source (the language of the Source, in Its chosen shared thought) and that of the world (the language of the world, in the form of the thought as the world receives it). This DNA is the tree of life paradigm, which guides the development of the child within the womb of the world as well as every one of the child's cells (with their allowing-thought combination of the prior stages, and their feeling and instinct and manifestation repetitions of the thought in all of its forms)—every one of the universes.

And as the child's cells are differentiated, so are the universes differentiated. And as cells are differentiated differently from one another, to produce different protein contents of themselves and to fulfill different functions for the organism, so are the universes differentiated differently from one another, to produce different allowed thoughts (which act like messenger-RNA, carrying a copy of the DNA template of choice, sharing thought, and receiving thought out of the nucleus of the world and into each of the universes) and thus also different feelings and instincts (which act like the proteins formed from the mRNA copy of the DNA choice and thought stages) and different manifestations (which are here like the outward manifestation of the cells, in the appearance and function each cell has as a result of the particular proteins—the particular feelings and instincts—that it forms). And as cells arise from the cells before them to replace these cells, performing the same functions as these previous cells, so there are infinite universes that are exactly the same as one another. But as all of the cells have a common purpose—to develop in accordance with the same DNA, merely manifesting different parts of it in different ways, and thereby to maintain the existence of the child—all of the infinite number of universes, some of which are apparently separated in space (like the cells of the child) just as some of them are separated in time (like the cells that give rise to other cells and then no longer exist in themselves), have a common purpose—to develop in accordance with the tree of life paradigm, merely manifesting different parts of it in different ways, and thereby to maintain the existence of the multiverse (the child) and ultimately of the world.

Our universe is thus one of an infinite number of universes, a single cell in the child that is the multiverse, which exists, in its entirety, within the world, which is dependent, in its entirety, upon what it receives from the Source to exist and for everything that it has. Each universe manifests itself in some form—likely in a singularity (which would be allowing thought in terms of the carrying of DNA, in the form of the allowing-thought mRNA, into each universe)—and then progresses from there, manifesting the paradigm in its own way.

Several universes (an infinite number, in fact) get stuck in one stage or another of their development, as we see in the evolution of species within our universe, so that they do not develop fully. Perhaps their gravity (stemming from manifestation as a reflection of this stage) is too strong, and their nuclear and electromagnetic forces (stemming from the thought stages— the higher stages near choice—as reflections of these stages) are too weak in their development, and so these universes do not expand in their space (also corresponding with the thought stages as reflections of these stages) with self-awareness, and their time (corresponding with manifestation as a reflection of this stage) passes unduly slowly, with the entirety of their contents unable to come together and form atoms and molecules and so on, resulting in gravity-dominated, or receiving-from-themselves-dominated, universes where matter falls into itself and eventually the entire universes collapse into themselves (rather than expanding increasingly rapidly outward infinitely, as ours seems to be doing, as they receive increasingly from the Source and decreasingly from themselves). Yet, such universes will still end in singularities (of black holes into which they collapse in their entirety), and they will still give rise to new universes via their singularities.

And like cells give rise to cells that manifest their DNA in similar forms (with heart cells giving rise to heart cells, and lung cells giving rise to lung cells, and brain cells giving rise to brain cells, and so on)—even though all of the cells have the same overall DNA guiding their development—universes give rise to universes that manifest the tree of life paradigm in similar forms (with universes that manifest only up to instinct and action giving rise to universes that manifest only up to instinct and action, and with universes that manifest stars and planets and life giving rise to universes that manifest stars and planets and life, and with universes that manifest human beings giving rise to universes that manifest human beings)—even though all of the universes have the same overall tree of life paradigm guiding their development.

And so, in the tree of life, like in a tree that might show the evolution of life, each branch has a common origin that is its past, and any development that extends with that past as a basis will be on some branch extending from that point. All of the universes begin at the roots of the tree of life (allowing thought), having a common trunk of their singularity (allowing thought) origin—like all of the cells of a developing child in the womb begin at the zygote that is the combination of sperm cell and egg cell, having a single common cell (the zygote—allowing thought) as their ultimate origin. But from there, universes proliferate outward, manifesting the paradigm in different ways, with universes giving rise to universes that manifest in similar, although sometimes very slightly different, ways. And so every possibility that can be manifested is manifested—in some universe or other. So, there are an infinite number of universes in which you are reading this right now, but there are an infinite number of universes in which you are doing something else, and there are an infinite number of universes in which you don't even exist, and there are an infinite number of universes in which humanity, itself, doesn't exist.

Every universe describes its experience of the Source's experience differently, thereby sharing and receiving and allowing to manifest—and thus *experiencing*—the Source's experience differently. And the less self-awareness it has developed, the less true to the Source's experience its experience is. So there are an infinite number of universes that develop, proliferating somewhat like cancer in the multiverse-child of the world (and of which cancer is likely a reflection), creating new universes like themselves in place of themselves when they cease to be, themselves, and failing to fulfill their purpose and function in existence, which is to receive the Source's experience and pass that experience—in its true and uncorrupted form—onward, so that the world can continue to be able to receive from the Source. It is as though the world eats, and the cells in its stomach and intestines fail to digest the food, and the other cells fail to integrate the food into themselves, and so the world cannot continue to receive more food, and it cannot continue to exist because the cells within it cannot receive the energy they need to exist since they are not performing their proper functions and fulfilling their purpose.

Parts of a Cell of the Child
of the World and the Source

So, the Source gives rise to the world, and the Source and the world, together (in a conscious and willful decision), give rise to the multiverse-child—an infinite number of proliferating universes in a sort of branching tree of propagation (the tree of life)—and they do this in what is the paradigmatic original form of which sexual reproduction is a reflection (part of the thought stages, where there are other "I"'s, for there are the Source—the male component—and the world—the female component—making two "I"'s in existence). Then, the multiverse-child zygote, which begins in the combination of the sharing thought or sperm or seed of the Source and the receiving thought or egg or fertile soil of the world, and which is the core of the paradigm of the tree of life, gives rise to new universes (as it tries to understand its relation to them and ultimately, eventually, via them, its relation to the Source), and it does this in what is the paradigmatic original form of which asexual reproduction (and mitosis within developing multicellular organisms) is a reflection (part of the feeling stages, where there are others that are projections of the "I"). And these universes cluster together and develop together in groups (from the perspective of choice—of the eleventh dimension, of mere potential, unactualized time, and therefore timelessness—for, in actuality, it seems that these universes are all the same universe, for one gave rise to another, which gave rise to another, and so on, ad infinitem, in an endless cycle of existence, and they simply all continue to exist in timelessness, as though they were multiple) based on their similarity to one another as they begin to manifest differently from one another (like cells clustering and developing together into tissues and organs, and like wolves clustering in packs, and birds clustering in flocks, and so on). And within each physical universe, all matter and energy that arises seeks merely to maintain its own existence, as it is cut off from all other universes and so on in its perception, and the universe within itself essentially sees itself as the only "I" in existence (the instinctual stages, where there is only "I", experiencing what the "I" experiences, and the "I" seeks to preserve its own existence).

So, we see that the paradigm was created, in its original form, from the top down, and then, within each universe, the paradigm manifests from the bottom up, as the universe follows the paradigm as its guide in all of its manifestation (following the path of a tree)—like a cell reading and using DNA to produce its protein contents and structure—and as the multiverse of all universes follows the paradigm as its guide in all of its overall manifestation (following the path of the ultimate tree) in its proliferation of universes, through which it evolves closer and closer to self-awareness.

However, there will always (from the perspective of the timelessness of the eleventh dimension that is choice) be universes using language to share and shape their experience in ways that do not give rise to self-awareness. Like a menagerie of species—like what we see has evolved and continues to proliferate in its manifestation on our planet in our universe—the multiverse of universes will always have more universes that have not developed self-awareness than those that have.

But the essence of the world that guides all of the development of the multiverse, like it guides all of the development within each universe, is the potential to be self-aware and to choose how it creates and manifests its experience. And this essence—the eleventh dimension that contains all universes (which contain no more than ten dimensions in themselves—and possibly fewer if they don't fully manifest the paradigm—with one of these dimensions necessarily being time and the rest being spatial)—is beyond time, being merely the potential for time, which it must actualize in order to have development of the paradigm progress and occur—in order to have receiving and sharing take place within the confines of language that shapes it into the multiverse-child's various differentiated cells.

And so we see that all of the infinite universes—the cells in the multiverse-child—are separated neither by time nor by space (and, in actuality, they exist in the *same* time and space— like all water molecules passing through the same spots in the spatial and temporal framework that is represented by the same tree), for they are separated only by the eleventh dimension— by *choice*—which is the mere potential for time and space and all other things to be. (Of course, this makes the very nature of the separation rather incomprehensible to us as we attempt to bring the familiarity of the language of thought and of manifestation to bear on understanding this. For even the very nature of understanding, itself—an aspect of the higher thought stages—is part of the beginning of the actualization of choice in language and is not choice in the original form in which it separates the universes.)

The tree of life is a pattern of development. The child within the world's womb is forever in the process of developing (although within the timelessness of choice, making it fixed in its state—with every one of its cells at every point in time that it exists being forever in existence—in the form of a fractal-like tree of differently actualized or manifested versions of the same paradigm). And (within timelessness, and therefore as though it has already forever been, rather than as though it is actively in the process of becoming) every one of its cells develops and eventually divides to form new cells (as universes may thus divide up their contents to form new universes—possibly via black-hole singularities, so that other universes receive these universes' contents via their own white-hole singularity beginnings) and ceases to exist in itself (from the perspective of time being actualized) as it shares all that it has received with other cells, thus fulfilling its purpose. And every one of the parts of its cells (every one of the parts of each universe) develops and eventually ceases to be (again, from the perspective of actualizing time) as it shares all that it has received with other parts of the cell.

This is what we are like—parts of a cell of the child of the world and the Source. And we thereby have a purpose—to share all that we receive, to allow the DNA of the cell to guide us in how we share and shape our experience (and, thereby, the experience of the cell—the universe) via language. For the parts of the cell can only perform their proper functions if they allow themselves to be guided in their functioning by the DNA of the cell.

All that we receive is via the universe, via the tree-of-life-child, via the world, ultimately from the Source. And we exist because the world cannot continue to receive from the Source without sharing what it receives. And when we allow the tree of life paradigm, in its entirety, to guide our manifestation—when we allow the Source's original shared thought to guide us in the creation of the contents of our experience—and we thereby come to see the Source's experience within our own experience, it is almost as though the divide of language between us and the Source (or, rather, between our experience and the Source's experience) breaks down, so that the cells and the womb and so on become transparent, and we can see (or sense, or experience) the Source as It manifests Itself to us in the form of Its experience—we can see (or sense, or experience) the sun as it manifests itself to us in the forms of light and heat, even from our perspective as a part of a cell of the child in the world's womb. In this way, we come to be no longer confined by the opacity of the world's manifestations, in which we live in self-consciousness, and we come, instead, to be able to see through the world's manifestations as though they were transparent, so that we can see the light of the Source's experience through it all, so that we can become self-aware—completely and clearly aware of ourselves, of our relation to all of the world's other manifestations, and of our relation and the relation of it all to the Source.

The essence of the "I" within the world is a differentiated form (a more-confined-by-language form) of the world's essence, which is the potential to be self-aware and to create with self-awareness. When the "I" proactively and willfully actualizes that essence, it becomes a projection of the Source in the world. The specificity of that actualization—all of the details of the contents of the "I"'s experience within the universe—however, is determined by the choices of the "I" within this world. And so our purpose is to share what we receive, so that we can become capable, as parts of the world, ultimately, of receiving what the Source is sharing in its true form—the experience of being self-aware and of being inclined to share this experience through the self-aware shaping of one's own experience—and of thereby being fulfilled.

The Embryonic Tree of Life

In essence, the entire tree of life paradigm—in all of its stages—is created by the Source, existing in a very undefined potential form within the very choice that the Source made to create the world; all of the stages of the tree of life paradigm are contained within the world of choice. And the entire tree of life paradigm is shared with the world by the Source—all contained in a very undefined potential form—within the thought that the Source shared with the world—within sharing thought; all of the stages of the tree of life paradigm are contained within the world of sharing thought. Also, the entire tree of life paradigm—all of the stages—is contained within the thought as it is received by the world, but still in an undefined potential form; all of the stages of the tree of life are contained within the world of receiving thought.

Then, we see that each of the thought stages is reflected in each of the next groups of stages—with sharing thought reflected in the feeling stages, receiving thought reflected in the instinctual stages, and allowing thought reflected in manifestation. Relative to this tripartite completion of a reflection, allowing thought is the reflection of choice, as choice precedes all of the three thought stages.

Allowing thought contains choice, sharing thought, and receiving thought in potential form—this is the nature of these upper worlds within the world of feeling and instinct. And as the universe becomes self-aware, these upper worlds become gradually actualized in the world of our experience—as the physical spatial dimensions expand, becoming actualized and manifested in the expansion of the universe. This actualization and manifestation and reception of the upper worlds within our world of experience is evident in the developments in the modern understanding of our world—from the Theory of Relativity, in which we have seen the relative nature of time and space, the dependence of the experience of these upon the state of the observer, to Quantum Mechanics, in which we have seen the importance of the observer and of the act of observation in determining the state of the particles of matter, of the contents within this universe.

We determine our experience of the framework and of the contents within this universe but, more than this, *we determine the framework and the contents of the universe.* The language we use in our thoughts and feelings and speech and actions determines it all, shaping what we observe and measure with our senses, for this language is the language that defines the shape that the universe takes as it is renewed in its existence from moment to moment. The evolution of the universe and of life has led along this path of the increasing capacity to shape and define our world, and to use tools to do so. The greater our self-awareness becomes, the greater becomes our willful control and capacity to use the ultimate tools to shape and define the universe, guided with awareness by the very thought that brought the entire world into being—the overflowing inclination of the Source to share Its experience, so that another could experience what It experiences.

And so allowing thought is part of the world of feeling and instinct. And this is the nature of all of our thought within this world—the thought that shapes all that comes after in the downward process of creation. Our thought is merely allowing thought—our thought is created by the Source and received by the world and is then manifested through us—either as a reaction to the world (and therefore in a form that is corrupted from the original purity of the form in which it was shared) or as a willful, self-aware response to the world. The thought that manifests within this world of feeling and instinct that we inhabit is nothing but allowing thought; it is neither sharing thought nor receiving thought in their true actuality as worlds in themselves.

And all of the stages of the tree of life paradigm are contained within manifestation as well—all in a sort of potentially actualized form, as all of the elements of all of the stages are combined together in actualization, in a process of manifestation upward that begins here. This makes for five separate worlds—the world of choice, the world of sharing thought, the world of receiving thought, the world of feeling and instinct, and the world of manifestation—with each one containing all of the stages of the tree of life paradigm in some form, and all of which together make up the one *overall* world (the one overall and complete tree of life paradigm).

The tree of life—the universe (or, rather, all of the universes in the multiverse)—consists of the last seven stages of the paradigm, including the three feeling stages, the three instinctual stages, and manifestation—the stages represented by the days of the week—as well as allowing thought, in the form of the "choice" that began all of this process of creation (as the world chose to allow the Source to create the universe—or, rather, the entire multiverse of universes—through itself). The internal structure of the tree of life—as determined by the three physical spatial dimensions and the three physical forces that interact to produce the matter and energy contents of the universe in the undefined form that matter and energy take in the subatomic realm—is determined by the thought stages, the first three stages of the paradigm and the DNA of the multiverse (with all of its universes). All universes exist in the same physical space, with the same physical forces—determined as these are by the interaction of the Source and the world—and this interaction produces physical matter and energy—the raw substance of the physical universe. And it is merely the shape of the internal contents of each universe—the inner dimensions and forces of feeling and instinct—that differs (since these dimensions and forces are produced anew in the creation of each universe), producing a different overall manifestation of matter and energy within time as these are defined differently.

We normally live with our attention in the world of feeling and instinct, but we are capable of recognizing that we live in all of the worlds in some sense, and all we need to do is actualize the parts of us—the parts of our souls, the potential forms of us—that exist in the thought and choice worlds above us. We exist within the thought realms, and they are all around us, manifesting as the framework of the physical world in which we live. They are the glue (the nuclear forces and electromagnetism) that holds us together, and they are the space in which we exist. But we tend to live in our feelings and instincts, producing all of the contents of our world from these inner dimensions, without self-awareness, living always in the physical product of our self-conscious reactions to the world of our own production that we allowed to be manifested through us—through our allowing thought. The contents of this world are defined and shaped by our feelings and our instincts. It is only the bare framework and the raw, undefined contents, themselves, that are defined in their existence by the worlds of thought.

When we are self-aware, we allow our feelings and instincts/speech/actions to be produced and guided by that original sharing thought of the Source to the best of our ability to understand and receive it and to allow it to be manifested through us (although, in some sense, we *always* do this "to the best of our ability," even when we are *not* self-aware)—which can become pretty accurate indeed as we become like a stream that keeps the fresh rainwater freshly flowing through itself. This is where choice lies in all of this—in our capacity to choose to allow ourselves to be guided by that sharing thought in our creation of the contents of the physical world. And, in this way, we produce the material resources and contents in our experience in this world that we truly desire to receive, bringing fulfillment to ourselves through the exercise of the capacity to choose and create—and through the *experience* of that capacity and of the actualization of that capacity—that the Source contained within that original shared thought, that the Source intended to share with us all along.

The Purpose of the Universe

The physical universe (inside the tree) consists of the manifestation of experience and understanding, while the non-physical universe (outside the tree) consists of the creation of experience and understanding.

We therefore see that, essentially, physical life (and, in fact, all life in this physical universe) is about learning through experience. It is about learning to understand experientially what it is to be self-aware, what it is to be like the Source. Physical life is for the purpose of making us capable of being able to experience what the Source experiences by taking us through the process of how we can get to that point.

You could not simply tell a caveman about the internet and expect him to be able to understand what you are talking about. You would have to familiarize him first with the language that you are using to describe the internet, bringing him to an understanding of the meaning of the words—an understanding of each part of the process of getting from where *he* is in *his* understanding to where *you* are in *your* understanding. Likewise, the Source could not simply tell us about Its experience of being self-aware existence that is capable of bringing other things into existence without first familiarizing us with the language that It is using to describe that experience—the language that It is using to bring other things into existence.

The entire physical universe is the nighttime with regard to self-awareness because we need to use this time to learn to understand what it is to be self-aware before we can actually *be* self-aware—in the daytime outside of all physical existence.

We cannot be aware during the day—even when everything is made apparent before us in the light of the sun—without sleeping at night. In order for our senses to be capable of taking in what the Source is sharing with us, we need to be self-aware—we need to be mindful and present where we are. And the physical universe exists so that we can learn this—so that we can learn the language of self-aware creation. We must become familiar with all of the words, understanding the purpose and meaning of each one, so that we can begin to create with self-awareness as the Source creates with self-awareness.

The night that is the physical stage of the universe (the stage of manifestation) is when we have senses to take in the experience that the Source is sharing with us. We *cannot* receive from the Source during the day, when we are already like water vapor outside the tree. (Although we must remember that all of the physical universe is night, and so we are always receiving from the Source within this overall night even if we are in some day—and therefore creating rather than receiving—with respect to life or a year or a day or something.) We breathe in (manifest) both experience and understanding during the night, and we breathe out (create) both experience and understanding during the day. (Although, again, during any day of anything within the overall night that is the physical universe, we are breathing in—manifesting—overall, even if we breathe out—create—to some degree or other as well.)

In every moment or any span of time, we receive experience that has manifested in the present moment, then we reflect upon the experience of the past moment, and then we think about the experience and learn from it, looking to the next moment of experience with this new understanding that we have gained from the previous experience. Thus, during the process of manifestation from bottom up, we manifest both experience and understanding derived from that experience. And we can only do this within the physical world and, most significantly, within physical life—in the night where manifestation occurs.

All experience in this world is for the purpose of making us capable of understanding the experience that the Source truly wishes to share with us, so that we can receive this experience. This entire physical existence is largely a monologue until we really begin to take an active role in speaking and using language ourselves, and eventually the back and forth yields us the understanding that we require to be able to behold and receive the experience of the Source in its true form. We use language in the present, we look back at the result, and then we try to understand how to use language better—how to use language to shape the world with greater self-awareness—and then we use language again, repeating the process, growing closer and closer to self-awareness.

Essentially, we speak to the Source, we look back at the Source's response, and then we try to understand how to use language better in our conversation with the Source—how to communicate better what we are truly wishing to communicate about what we wish to receive from the Source—and then we speak to the Source again, repeating the process, growing better and better at effectively communicating with the Source so that we receive what we wish from It—so that It can share the experience of fulfillment with us. This is what it is to manifest experientially-based understanding from the bottom up. This is what it is to fulfill the purpose of life and of all of existence. It is to learn the language that the Source is using to create the world, so that we can learn to allow It to create the world through *us* as Its language.

And this language that we must learn is, therefore, the means by which we can effectively communicate with the Source. And this language consists of the stages of the tree of life paradigm—with all of their various aspects and nuances, and their true purpose in the overall process of creation. The purpose of the existence of the entire physical universe is to make it so that something can arise within it that can learn how it relates to the Source, and how it can effectively communicate with the Source, so that the Source can share Its experience with it. When we learn to understand the language of creation, the Source guides us, via our intuition, in using that language to create, through us, what we truly wish to manifest and receive. The universe is, thus, like a schoolhouse where we must experientially learn the language by which the Source creates us so that we can experientially understand the Source's words in their true meaning—in the meaning that the Source wishes to convey—where we must learn *to be capable* of experiencing what it is to be like the Source, so that we can head out into the day and behold the Source in Its true form with respect to Its relation to us—so that we can behold the Source's experience in its true form.

After we have experientially become intimately understanding and aware of all of the stages of the tree of life—of all of the language by which the Source creates the world—it seems likely that we cease to be reborn into physical lives. We transcend the world of feeling and instinct, beginning to take an active role in allowing the Source to create the framework of the world—and to guide the defining and development of the contents of the world—through us. For we have ascended the tree of life from purely receiving and holding onto what we receive (like a pond), learning through many physical lives to let go of and share what we receive, shaping it as we do so, so that the world becomes manifested *through* us, rather than *in* us.

We have learned how to be a mountain stream, becoming a link between the Source and this world, becoming a messenger of the Source in this world. We have learned to identify with this nature—the capacity to be self-aware and to choose. We have learned how to allow the fresh rainwater from the heavens to be received by us and to flow through us, and to be shared by us—all in its pure and uncorrupted form. We have learned to be a fount of the Source's experience in this universe, a link between the sky and the earth, between the Source and this universe.

And so this is the role—the purpose—that we continue to fulfill, dwelling in the world of choice and becoming part of the ultimate seed of the tree of life, itself, where it first begins to form, guiding its growth toward the development of self-awareness. When the universe ends and a new universe begins, however, we will once again enter the cycle of incarnation in physical life, reliving many of our physical lives as much of time repeats itself, and working our way back up the stages of the tree of life, toward transcendence of physical life, toward being a messenger of the Source and a guide in the development of the universe.

Sharing, Receiving, and Allowing

Another Pattern of the Paradigm

At this point, we are in a position in which we can put forth another aspect of the tree of life paradigm and analyze its implications for the nature of the world in which we live in order to bring ourselves to a more specified understanding of the way this world has been defined. We saw in the different versions of the dominant positive feelings that there was a version that corresponded with an allowing stage, a version that corresponded with a receiving stage, and a version that corresponded with a sharing stage—thereby giving us a full spectrum of the experience from the most corrupted and negative form all the way to the purest, most positive form. And we saw this tripartite pattern displayed repetitively over the course of the year in terms of astrological influences, just as this tripartite pattern is displayed repetitively in the tree of life paradigm, itself. But we have not yet fully considered or elaborated upon the possibility that this tripartite pattern of allowing, receiving, and sharing might actually be another pattern that is part of the manifestation of the tree of life in terms of these aspects corresponding to the instinctual stages, the feeling stages, and the thought stages, respectively.

After manifestation, we allow the instinctual desire of the world to preserve its existence to be manifested through us, but we are out of touch with existence, and with how existence is to be preserved, and with the nature of the extension of our boundaries in the world (with the fact that we can only truly exist by being present with, and fully aware of, existence as it is, so that we can create it and receive it fully, and by actively and willfully creating our experience within the world from a self-aware perspective). Then, we receive and manifest within ourselves the feeling-related desire of the different parts of the world to belong to the world, to fit into the group, but we manifest this belonging, as well as our view of ourselves, of who we are, in *reaction* to the group—defining ourselves in contrast to the others in the group in order to fit into the group (identifying with things other than our essence in order to have a niche for ourselves within the group). Then, we create and share the thought-related desire to connect with other "I"'s in our experience, but we create this connection, as well as our decisions, in disregard of other "I"'s (connecting with activities and ideas in disregard of other people and other aspects of the world as they are).

No experience can be fully actualized in its pure form unless it is fully allowed to pass and is fully shared, for any blockage resulting from grasping at or holding onto it will corrupt it from its pure form. And grasping only ceases upon the attainment of self-awareness (and, even then, only while self-awareness is maintained). We must willfully create and mindfully receive all experience fully and allow it to be manifested through us in its pure and uncorrupted form, for this is what it is to be self-aware, and this is how fulfillment is to be obtained.

We can notice here that these stages of sharing, receiving, and allowing are the fundamental stages of the world—this is what all of the repetition in the world is getting at. All of the self-reflection we discern in manifestation began truly within creation itself—when the world reflected upon the Source's shared thought that produced the receiving thought in the form of itself and that combined with its own understanding of the thought to produce something new in allowing thought—in the creation of the three stages of feeling, and the three stages of instinct, and manifestation. Creating and sharing, receiving and manifesting within oneself, and allowing to be manifested through oneself—this is the fundamental relation between the Source and the world. In fact, allowing thought, itself, is merely a reflection of choice, for before all else, the Source created choice—something that would allow Its sharing thought to be manifested through it, so that that thought could be received and manifested as the world. Everything in all of creation is a series of repetitions, and this is reflected in manifestation—in the self-reflective nature of this world of manifestation.

The World of Manifestation

And now we can more fully realize and understand: We live, physically, in the world of manifestation.

In the section on astrological influences, we saw that the first season (spring) is composed of this tripartite pattern of sharing, receiving, and allowing, and yet the entire season is contained within manifestation. And these stages correspond with our birth and youth, our adolescence, and our young adulthood. They account for our entire life up until our early twenties, when we reach maturity, when our frontal (and pre-frontal) cortices are fully developed and we have thus developed the capacity to make decisions—to choose. Our lives up until maturity are contained entirely within manifestation, and yet they reflect the entire tree of life in a sort of potential form—all contained within three stages that have not truly separated out into their full actualization as nine stages, with three of instinct, three of feeling, and three of thought. So many of the patterns that we have seen in development have been easily contained within a three-stage form, as though they have not yet come into full actualization as the entirety of the tree of life. These patterns are all contained in a three-stage potential form within manifestation. And it is after we have passed through these patterns in this form, fixating upon each stage along the way, that we continue our lives stuck in fixation upon one aspect or another of each stage of each pattern—stuck in fixations that we have been developing all along—the goal of that lifetime being to overcome these fixations.

Yet it is fixation that makes the world of manifestation. Everything that is physical is contained within the world of manifestation, for everything that is physical exists as a manifestation of one stage or another (or of a combination of stages, as the case basically always is in this self-reflective world) of the paradigm. Things develop up to a point and then get stuck there, settling out into actualization in the world of manifestation at that stage and failing to develop all the way upward to choice.

This, where we live, is the world of fixations, of manifestation—the result of receiving and holding onto aspects of stages prior to the development of choice. We live in the physical world of manifestation. And there are three basic parts contained within this world—an allowing part, a receiving part, and a sharing part—reflections of the allowing part, the receiving part, and the sharing part of the thought stages, the feeling stages, and the instinctual stages, or simply reflections of the instinctual stages as the allowing stage, the feeling stages as the receiving stage, and the thought stages as the sharing stage, all sort of collapsed down into three parts that contain all of these things in incompletely actualized form. This is why the world is as we perceive it, with three dimensions of space and one of time, with three quantum fields and gravity—for we live physically in the world of manifestation (of time, of gravity) and within this world is contained three parts (three spatial dimensions, three quantum fields), and within these three parts are contained all instinct and action, all feeling, all thought (all in a condensed, potential sort of form, the way our development up to young adulthood is like an embryonic version of the full tree of life paradigm of development).

And this world of manifestation—this physical world of fixations (where we must learn to overcome fixations in order to transcend this world, thereby fulfilling our purpose in existing within this world and achieving the ultimate goal)—is constantly being created, being shared with, for *it*, in *itself*, is only truly allowing all things (all fixations, all things that are held onto) to manifest through itself. And this is where everything beyond the physical comes into the picture; this is where souls come into the picture. While our bodies, with their physical senses, reside in the world of manifestation, our souls reside in the world of feeling and instinct, which contains all of the stages of instinct, all of the stages of feeling, and the stage of allowing thought. But these aspects of our souls are not our souls in their entirety; they are only the lower parts of our souls, and they are disconnected from the higher parts of our souls that reside in the upper worlds (those of receiving thought, sharing thought, and choice), which exist purely in a created potential and unactualized form until we actualize them and thereby connect to them. And we can only connect to them and actualize them through the actualization of self-awareness, and therefore through experiential understanding—which can only be obtained in a physical world of manifestation, in which we can become intimately familiar with, and understanding of, each of the stages of the tree of life paradigm and their role in our relation to the Source of all that we receive and have.

All of creation is initiated by the Source, via the world of choice, in the world of sharing thought, and then is furthered in the world of receiving thought, via which the world receives and manifests within itself the thought shared by the Source (the shared thought via which the Source shares Its experience—and which can only be received in its true form by another self-aware "I", making the development of such an

"I" by the world of receiving thought necessary in order for the world to truly receive this thought in its true and pure and fulfilling form). From here, therefore, the world of receiving thought gives rise to the world of feeling and instinct via allowing thought (to which it has given rise in combination with the world of sharing thought in order to give rise through it, eventually, to a self-aware "I" that is capable of receiving and understanding the Source's shared thought).

(I get the image here of someone having said something to someone else in a language that this receiving person cannot understand, and so the receiving person finds someone who can translate the language of the sharing person into another language that is still not understood by the receiving person, and so that other person finds another person who can translate into another language, and that other person finds another person who can translate into another language, and so on, until the sharing person's language is finally translated into a language that the receiving person can understand.)

And from here, the world of feeling and instinct gives rise to the world of manifestation. And in each world, there is repetition of what came before and led to its existence. This is like the way in which the DNA of a person that is the result of what was given by the person's father in combination with how it was received by the person's mother—what egg containing what DNA received it within the person's mother—repeats over and over again in the formation of the person who is the result of that original interaction. Except in the case of the Source and the world, the Source shared everything in potential form in some way—by first forming an allowing stage of choice, and then, via this, forming a sharing stage, and thereby forming a receiving stage in the form of the world.

So, in summary, the process of creation goes from the Source, via the world of choice, to the world of sharing thought, to the world of receiving thought, to the world of feeling and instinct (via allowing thought, which is part of this world), to the world of manifestation.

Then, from the world of manifestation, manifestation begins to take place in the reverse order. However, all of the process of manifestation upward through the worlds is reflected in the upward manifestation—the actualization of the higher stages—within manifestation itself, with upward-developing souls connected to and affecting bodies that form in the world of manifestation. And so within the tripartite reflection of allowing, receiving, and sharing stages that exists within manifestation, inclination and action are manifested first (in the form of the movements of physical bodies) and then feeling manifests (in the form of life) and then thought manifests (in the form of complex and intelligent life), and then the capacity for choice manifests (in human beings, with developed prefrontal cortices). And the brain develops with life, manifesting up the paradigm and becoming a manifestation of allowing thought within this world in terms of its capacity to be a link between the soul of potentiality and the body of actuality—in terms of its capacity to allow the instincts, speech, and actions, feelings, thoughts, and choice of the soul to be manifested through it (in downward creation beginning at the highest stage that has been actualized and thereby connected to) in the speech and actions of the physical body.

And as all of this development within the tripartite world of manifestation in time occurs, there is a bottom-up manifestation going on of which what manifests in physicality is merely a reflection. For the instinct and action expressed by the physical bodies of the physical world are a reflection of the manifestation and actualization of the stages of instinct and action in the world of feeling and instinct (which is creating this manifestation in the world from itself downward). And the feeling expressed by life in the physical world is a reflection of the manifestation and actualization of the stages of feeling in the world of feeling and instinct (which is creating this manifestation in the world from itself downward). And the thought expressed by life in the physical world is a reflection of the manifestation and actualization of the stage of allowing thought in the world of feeling and instinct (which is creating this manifestation in the world from itself downward).

When we fully transcend fixation upon the world—when we come to identify no longer with fixations, and we come to truly recognize all of the physically manifested fixations of the world as not being the source of what we receive from them, but rather as being what allows all that we receive from them to be shared with us by the Source—when we begin to apply self-awareness to our experience of the world and to our creation of our experience of the world, allowing the Source to create and manifest Its experience through us, then we thereby actualize and connect to the higher parts of our souls that reside in the upper worlds of receiving thought, and sharing thought, and choice. This is the purpose of the physical world of manifestation and of our physical lives within it: to develop and progress up the paradigm through experiential understanding in order to connect to and actualize the higher parts of our souls.

And as every stage of development is actualized in an upward progression, there is a reflection of this progression in the world of manifestation (even decisions and thoughts and feelings and instincts are manifested physically—as the firing of neurons and the release of neurotransmitters in the brain and the release of hormones in the body—as speech and actions are then manifested physically more outwardly in the body), for the creation of each new moment of physical experience within time begins at the highest actualized stage of development and progresses all the way downward to manifestation in time.

Fixating

When we are fixated upon any stage prior to choice, we are reactive creations of the world of feeling and instinct—which corresponds with the stages of allowing the instinctual desire of the world to preserve its existence through us, and of receiving and manifesting within ourselves our identities in relation to the world in reaction to the world (in order to belong and fit in with the group). This is the point in the progression up the tree of life where we are still like water molecules depending upon our clinging to existence (adhesion) and our clinging to each other (cohesion) to keep us progressing upward.

But this will only take us so far. For true existence comes from the Source, and our holding onto existence and depending on the finite manifestations in this world to give us more of it (more existence) will keep us never fully existing. And true belonging to the other parts of the world comes from the commonality in our essence, which we aren't actualizing and connecting to when we are identifying with our reactively manifested identities. We must learn to create and share our experience, but we can even go wrong in this, for we can even come to identify with and fixate upon ourselves as being the source of what we have.

In fact, in our essence—in the highest level of our soul that is still us and not the Source, and that we are capable of actualizing and connecting to—we are choice, which is merely the ability to allow the Source's experience to be manifested through us. In this way, we do not fixate upon any stage. Prior to our actualization of the higher parts of our souls, when we have only actualized upward to allowing thought, we allow the world's misunderstanding of the Source's shared thought to be manifested through us. And so we are left unfulfilled, with our world being created through us in reaction to itself, for we do not experience the Source's experience in its pure, true, and uncorrupted form. But when we actualize the higher parts of our souls, we come to receive from the Source directly, in the purest and truest of forms possible, as we extend ourselves upward in our actualization and manifestation all the way to choice itself—the very first stage that can be called the Source's creation and not the Source, the stage that precedes even the Source's shared thought and the world of receiving thought. We come to be part of what allows the Source's experience to be shared with the world, becoming a true link between the Source and all else that exists.

And we can accomplish all this only from the world of manifestation—only in physical life—for only here can experiential understanding be manifested upward, and so only here can self-awareness be attained—through our connection to the higher parts of our souls in the upper worlds. Prior to actualization of the higher parts of our souls, the afterlife is composed of the experience of our souls in the reactively manifested world of feeling and instinct, and this is followed by our touching down again in the physical world of manifestation as we create our next physical lives downward from where we are in the world of feeling and instinct (as we fixate and hold onto certain allowed thoughts, certain feelings, and certain instincts). But after the actualization of the higher parts of our souls, we need not touch down in the physical world of manifestation again—for we have learned what we needed to learn and achieved the purpose of physical existence within the physical universe—at least until the universe is created anew and we must reconnect with the higher parts of our souls once again, learning through experiential understanding to allow the Source to create through us, and thereby earning such a place so close to the Source once again. For the nature of all that is not the Source is such that it must continually relearn what it must know, for it forgets and comes to hold onto things again that are not the Source but are, instead, what it receives from the Source.

When this physical universe that is contained within the world of manifestation first begins to manifest, it is a world that is just beginning to be the actualization of potentiality. And so it begins in a point that cannot actually exist, and then it expands outward from there within the world of manifestation, from which time and gravity stem, to contain a tripartite reflection of the allowing, receiving, and sharing relationship that ultimately brought it into existence—a reflection from which three spatial dimensions and three quantum fields stem. And the quantum fields and the spatial dimensions interact to produce matter and energy upon which the quantum fields act within space to form nuclei and atoms and molecules, as the relationship that formed the world of manifestation ultimately is reflected in the contents of this world. And clinging to existence and to other parts of the world is thereby manifested within the physical universe in this way immediately upon the universe's coming into existence, for the world of manifestation is a product of all that came before it in creation. And as soon as there is matter, gravity also acts upon it, forming larger and larger bodies in stars and planets and galaxies, thereby giving shape to the universe and slowing down time in different parts of it, allowing for the eventual arising of life and self-aware-ness, for this is the ultimate purpose of the existence of the physical world, and this is what guides its manifestation.

This clinging to existence and grouping together to bet-ter do so—these desires that stem from the world of feeling and instinct—is manifested immediately, and this is where the world gets stuck; this is what the parts of the universe must learn to overcome, learning to connect intimately and thereby to become aware of one another as other "I"'s. But this is the world of fixation. And even when we connect with one another, we are inclined to see each other as the source of what we get from each other. And so sex is consuming of the other and is merely for the gratification of the self, and conversations with the other are conversations with ourselves, and interactions with the other are in every way mere interactions with projections of ourselves, aimed at fulfilling our own self-oriented desires that have arisen due to our fixations and consequential unfulfillment. Connections with others that are extensions of ourselves must eventually become connections with other "I"'s. But the world we live in is largely the result of the failure of this to be the case.

In this world of manifestation, where we have not developed the higher parts of our souls and so where we do not create out of self-awareness, we manifest as fixations, and everything that we create is the reactive manifestation of fixations—including our personalities, which we falsely view as being ourselves. And the world has become a series of groups, each one a projection of certain personality fixations to some extent or other. Of course, it is inevitable that some degree of fixation manifest, for we cease to exist in this physical world when we have no fixation whatsoever, since existence in this world, itself, is the result of falling out of upward progression due to some fixation that holds us down and causes us to manifest at some stage—or, rather, at different aspects of different stages (the aspects upon which we are fixated)—and thereby to come into some physical form that is the manifestation of that stage (or those aspects of those stages).

But the result, in this world, is nations and religions and cultures and philosophies, science and academia and business and politics, and every other kind of group (including even the field of self-help) that is cohered under a fixation upon certain aspects of certain stages, with every group essentially having a series of personality fixations in itself that are the result of the projection of the personality fixations of the individuals that compose and contribute to the formation and perpetuation of the group. The United States is largely a fixation upon allowing feeling and a dominant fixation upon the inclination to belong and a secondary fixation upon the inclination to preserve and a tertiary (and therefore largely ignored) fixation upon the inclination to connect. Science is a fixation upon sharing thought. Academia is a fixation upon allowing thought. Business is a combination of a fixation upon allowing feeling and a fixation upon allowing thought. (American) politics is largely a fixation upon a combination of allowing feeling, allowing thought, and receiving instinct. Self-help is largely a fixation upon allowing feeling. And so on.

(We are capable of fixating upon the higher stages of sharing thought and receiving thought because what we are doing here is fixating upon the higher stages as they exist in a potential, not-fully-actualized form. In fact, none of the stages are truly fully actualized until we reach choice and then begin to create downward, thereby manifesting each of the stages in their top-down, true form.)

Further, these groups define and manifest themselves, via the individuals who compose and contribute to them, in *reaction* to one another; they each define themselves in their relation to other (particularly similar) groups (groups of the same or of a similar category, as other religions, or other nations, etc.). In order to assure the perpetuation of the existence of the group, each group defines itself in such a way that it will continue to fill a niche that is different from that filled by other groups, for then it will continue to have a niche within which it can exist.

Everything that we see here is aspects of the world of feeling and instinct being manifested within this world. This is happening as different parts of the world allow the existence of the world to be manifested through them as the only true "I"'s with the only fixations that can possibly exist as far as they are concerned or aware of. And this is happening as different parts of the world group together and project their own fixations onto others and onto the group, seeking to preserve and perpetuate the existence of their own fixations, for they perceive these things as being who they are and as therefore being what must be preserved in order for them to (continue to) exist.

The Teachers through which We are Guided

And so, now, we come to a truth that is made clearer here and that must be truly understood and remembered and applied if self-awareness is ever to be attained: Nothing in the world is the source of what we gain from it. The higher the degree of fixation, the more corrupted from the purity of its true form something is, and so what we ought to seek is things with lower degrees of fixation. When we see groups or even individuals or anything else of any sort in this world as the source of what we obtain from them, we are fixating upon things that are fixations in themselves. True understanding comes only from the Source, via our intuition, and we must learn to allow our intuition to guide us in all that we say and do in this world—and even in all that we think and thereby allow ourselves to feel and to be inclined to say and do in this world. When we allow others or groups or anything else in this world to decide for us what we shall think or feel or be inclined to say or do or what we shall actually say or do, then we are allowing fixations in this world to manifest themselves through us. Our goal should be to find that inner voice of intuition and to listen to this, alone, for this is the Source speaking to us, and only the Source is a certain guide toward all fulfillment and toward the attainment of our true purpose in existence.

This is not to say that we should not listen to others in this world. For just as the Source provides us with physical sustenance for the maintenance of our existence via food, which we must continue to eat in order to gain such sustenance, and just as the Source provides us with shelter and clothing for the protection of our existence via other things in this physical world, which we must take in and receive in order to gain such protection, the Source provides us with everything else via this world as well, which we must receive in order to gain the fulfillment that the Source intends for us to gain from it.

This is what it means for us to need to help ourselves in order for the Source to be able to help us, for the Source provides us with everything that we require for us to receive fulfillment and work our way upward toward self-awareness, but It does this via *us*—via our own willful creation of our experience in this world, via our choices and thoughts and feelings and instincts and speech and actions. If we do not learn to listen to our intuition and actually use the tools that we have in accordance with the guidance provided via our intuition, then the Source will not provide us with what we want, and we will not achieve our purpose in existing. But usually what we need to learn is not to be gained directly via intuition, for our ability to listen to this voice is not immediately so great that it could possibly be the most direct and complete means of our learning extensive things. Our intuition will, instead, guide us to "teachers" in this world, whether these are things that happen to us or obstacles that we face and must overcome, or they are conversations with someone, or they are a group of people who help us along our path. And we must remain mindful and aware enough to remember that we must allow ourselves to be guided by the Source, and not by this world.

So it would be wrong ever to come to the conclusion that *everything* that someone says is correct, or that some person or group is the *source* of all that we require, for coming to these kinds of conclusions entails coming to see something in this world as the source of what we gain from it. And, in fact, we should *not* listen blindly to anyone or to the teachings or influence of any group—for such blind listening and following inherently entails the absence of awareness. We must learn to make our own decisions and judgments about what we should think and feel and say and do—and especially about what we should believe—applying awareness and discernment in every case. We cannot allow other aspects of this world, including even our own fixations (our reactively manifested physical experiences or instincts or feelings or thoughts), to make these decisions and judgments for us, and so we must learn to identify with our true essence of choice and to listen to the voice that comes to us via that essence, directly from the Source—the voice that is our intuition.

This world is filled with guides, but we need to recognize that the only true and sure guide is the Source, and that this world is merely the means—the tools—by which the Source guides us. And even *this*—that the world is the means by which the Source guides us—is the case only when we are listening to our intuition about what we should be allowing to manifest through us. For all of our experience in this physical universe is manifested through us, and it does not do us well to follow the results of our own fixations, for these will only guide us toward further fixation, as our fixations seek to maintain and propagate their own existence through us.

If we actively learn from experience how we must go about our lives and how we must interact with other "I"'s, allowing experience to lead us to understanding, and then we actively apply that understanding in the form of awareness and the active and willful, self-aware creation of our lives, then we will assure that we remain on the right track—on the path toward greater actualization of ourselves. And as long as we are on this path, "teachers" will continue to reveal themselves in our experience, to aid us along this path.

Combining Ideas in Understanding the Nature of the World

Overcoming Fixation and Ascending to Choice

We can now synthesize many of the ideas that we have discussed about how we are to define and understand the world. When we say that there is one world, we mean to include in this reference all that the Source created besides Itself, and therefore we mean to include all five worlds, each of which contains the tree of life paradigm in some form or other, and all of which make up some part of a single, overall tree of life paradigm.

If we consider our tree setup idea, then when we say there is one world, we mean to include in this reference the entire tree setup—with tree, sunlight, earth, air, and water (in liquid and gaseous forms). We do not mean to include the sun in this reference of one world because, here, the sun would be the Source as viewed from the perspective of the world (in Its relation to the world). The world of manifestation includes in its contents all of the liquid water inside the tree, and it thereby contains all physical universes, in every path that any particular universe may take up the branches. The structure of the tree, itself, is the world of feeling and instinct (including allowing thought).

In the tree, we can cling to (or fixate upon) existence and to other fixations of existence, including one another, and thereby allow our thoughts (and all that our thoughts create) to be formed in *reaction* to the world around us—thereby allowing the world to determine our path for us. Or we can allow self-awareness (in the form of evaporative pull) to pull us upward *via* the other fixations of existence around us, as we create our own path (in consideration of the other fixations of existence around us, and particularly of the other "I"'s around us)—allowing the Source to guide us via Its shared experience (represented by the sunlight).

When we learn to allow the force of the sunlight, which is outside of the tree, to pull us upward, rather than merely allowing ourselves to be reactively affected (and allowing our thoughts and feelings and instincts and actions to be determined) by the tree and its contents, then we thereby actualize the parts of our souls that are within the worlds of receiving thought and sharing thought and, eventually, the part of our souls that is within the world of choice. These three higher worlds exist outside the tree in the tree setup (although they are part of the overall tree of life paradigm, which, here, refers to the entire world that is the whole tree setup).

Before we allow ourselves to be pulled upward solely by the sunlight, not clinging to anything that is a fixation upon existence within the tree, we continue to exist within the tree—as part of the tree (within the world of feeling and instinct) and, when we exist in a physical body, as part of the water within the tubes of the tree (within the world of manifestation), in which form we are capable of progressing up the tree toward the leaves, as well. But as we shift our attention to the Source beyond all fixations—to the sunlight and, ultimately, the sun that provides for all that we experience—we actualize the higher parts of our souls that exist outside the tree, and we become like water vapor. At this point, we are connected to the part of us that exists in the world of choice, the part of us that is able to convey the energy of the sunlight to the water that has yet to evaporate from the tree; we are connected to the part of us that is, thus, able to aid in the pulling of the water (the physical contents of the world of manifestation) up the tree toward self-awareness, and that is thereby able to aid in the growth of the tree (the contents of the world of feeling and instinct), itself.

When we reach this point in the world of choice, we exist in a sort of timelessness and spacelessness, with no personality of our own (for time and space and all other things are only in potential form in the world of choice, and personality is a fixation that, like all other fixations, does not exist in the world of choice). Essentially, we, as ourselves, cease to exist at this point, for we exist in such a potential, undefined form that we cannot be defined as being *us* as opposed to some other fully self-aware part of the universe—and so we cease to exist to be reincarnated as anything that we could truly call ourselves. We are *not* the *world of choice*, however; we are merely part of the *contents* of the world of choice—we are merely water vapor and not the sunlight. And water vapor cannot remain water vapor; it must eventually condense back into liquid water.

So we have freed ourselves from fixation entirely, ceasing to exist as anything that could be defined as us (for all that makes us capable of being distinguished from other things is a bunch of fixations). Within choice, water vapor is water vapor, indistinguishable from itself. This choice part of our souls is what is most uniquely us and, at the same time, it is the essence that we all have in common. This is as close as we can get to the Source while still in this world—while still being part of the creation and not the Source, Itself. And we are still infinitely far from the Source, as the water vapor is still seemingly just as far from the sun as it was when it was liquid water within the tree, even as we are so much closer to It. We are still merely *allowing* the world to be created through us—allowing the Source's experience to be shared through us—and are not actually *creating* the way the Source is *creating* through us. And yet this is as far as we can get (which is actually quite far, indeed, from our own perspective, even if it seems not all that far in relation to the infinite Source). We simply cannot *be* the

Source; we cannot be anything more than a messenger of the Source—part of the Source's language of communication with which It shares Its experience with the world.

We are still in the world, but we are as close as we can get to the Source while still being in the world. But even as we cease to exist, the water vapor that is our essence cannot remain forever as water vapor, for once it shares the energy that it has received from the sunlight—the energy of self-awareness that has made it water vapor—it condenses again. From the perspective of timeless choice, it is as though we have been up there, face to face with the sun, for an instant. But from the perspective of time within the physical world, it is as though our water vapor substance has transcended the physical world for all eternity. For the physical universe from which we left will end before we pass from the timelessness of choice back into the time of the physical world, and so when we reenter the physical world, it will be a different physical universe from the one we left—one that may or may not differ from the one we left in the paths it takes. Once the water vapor that is our essence condenses again, it inherently must enter the tree in the form of a new and different universe from the one that it left, for it has already left the tree, and the rest of the universe from which it ascended is still progressing through time in the physical world and the world of feeling and instinct (where time is not the same as in the physical world, but where it is still much more defined and actualized than it is in the world of choice, where it has no definition or actuality at all).

[By the way, the less-defined nature of time in the world of feeling and instinct—where a part of the tree is always part of the tree, where it is, remaining there indefinitely in relation to the water that passes by—is what actually allows for us to communicate with those who are no longer living, even if they have since reincarnated. This is because everything that has ever come to be a part of the tree forever remains a part of the tree—fixated there—and so we can actually access anything and anyone that has ever existed in the world of feeling and instinct—or that ever will exist in some branch or other of this tree—at any point in time. Notice that we can get lost in re-active thoughts—which are ultimately allowed thoughts—and reactive feelings and completely lose track of the actual amount of time that has passed, as though we have not existed with our attention in the usual defined progression of time. All things that exist in the world of feeling and instinct—including our souls during physical life (which we experience whenever we are lost in thoughts and feelings and instinctual desires) and after physical life—are stuck in a sort of less-defined, less-strict pro-gression of time than that which exists in the physical universe within the world of manifestation, itself, from which the most-strictly-defined time emanates.]

This complete transcendence of the tree (and consequent entrance into a different universe from the one that we left) makes transcendence to choice different from anything prior. For before we actualize the higher parts of our souls, we remain within the tree (the world of feeling and instinct), following the course of the universe from which we left (due to our fixa-tion on the things in that particular physical universe), and are reborn into that same universe (due to our fixations that cause us to manifest physically again and again until we cease to fixate in ways that keep us tied to the physical world, until we cease to view certain defined things within that world as the sources of the fulfillment that we gain from them) as we progress together with it as part of it. (It may be noted here that ghosts are merely the souls of people who no longer have a physical body in the physical world but who are so fixated upon things in the physical world, for some reason or another, that they cannot even leave the physical world to dwell in the world of feeling and instinct separate from the physical world.)

When we transcend to choice, *we* are freed from fixation and the cycle of rebirth into physical life, but our essence— which is, in essence, not really *us* in any sense (again, as we are defined by our fixations—by the language we use)—will fixate once again upon some aspect of what it receives from the Source, forming a thought and holding onto this thought, thereby transforming it into a feeling, which becomes an instinct, which becomes an action, which becomes a defined physical manifestation—a physical incarnation. Any sustained (and repeated) thought will inherently manifest itself in the physical world of manifestation, for any sustained thought is grasping and defining in itself. This is because any sustained thought involves holding onto what has been received from the Source, and it thereby becomes a fixation, however slight, which will grow like a snowball rolling down a snow-covered slope, or like a condensed water droplet in the air (which, itself, condensed upon some dust particle or something else other than other water) upon which other water condenses and accumulates. And the ultimate result is manifestation in physicality—as the snowball reaches the bottom of the slope, as the water droplet becomes a rain drop that falls to the ground, to reenter the roots of the tree once again.

Existing in the world of choice is like existing in a high state of meditation, and then there is the thought of "Wow, this feels amazing!" or "I wish I could describe this experience so that I could share it with someone," or "Others should be able to experience this." And as soon as you shift your attention and awareness to this thought that has been formed, and away from the experience of awareness, itself, you are no longer in that state, having returned to your own definition of the Source's experience and ultimately to physicality, to the world of fixation. For you have fixated upon the experience, holding onto it in its form as a defined thought, and thereby forming a blockage in the flow of energy through you—a blockage that prevents the Source's experience from flowing through you in its pure form, a blockage that falls down the tree of life and into the world of physical manifestation, becoming further defined through the repetition of sharing, receiving and allowing all along the way.

Basically, the physical world of manifestation is a condensed, or repetitively defined and thereby fixated, version of self-aware existence, a fixated choice—as liquid water is condensed water vapor. But when it is fixated, it is inherently no longer fully self-aware—having existence, but not being aware of this, or of how far it extends into its surroundings, or of who or what it is and how it relates to others, or of how it can make the best decisions for itself and other "I"'s.

And when we increase our degree of fixation upon any one thing, this increase in fixation generalizes to all aspects of our lives as our self-awareness decreases, leading us to unfulfillment in all aspects of our lives. Likewise, when we decrease our degree of fixation upon one aspect of our lives, this decrease in fixation generalizes as our self-awareness increases, leading us to fulfillment in all aspects of our lives.

Fixating vs. Merely Defining

It is fixation—holding onto what is received from the Source—that brings all things in the physical universe into existence in the physical universe, and it is fixation that keeps us here in unfulfillment. In order to achieve fulfillment, we must learn to allow all that we receive to be shared and to pass through us, rather than holding onto what we receive. Everything in this physical world is a fixation, because matter and energy are fixations—they persist in existence because the quantum forces (the thought of the world) repeat them over and over again, holding onto them, and thereby holding them in existence.

The natural course of everything that ultimately is to enter this world is to come from the Source originally—in a completely undefined form as utterly raw self-aware existence of some sort—and then to pass through choice, where its general possible direction is determined, and then to pass through sharing thought and receiving thought, where it begins to be built up in its core constituents, being defined somewhat more clearly in its general direction, and then to pass through allowing thought (where true repetition—of allowing, sharing, and receiving stages—and, thereby, true fixation, begins to occur), and then to pass through the feeling stages, where it is defined further in its quality, and then to pass through the instinctual stages, where it is defined the rest of the way, so that when it comes into manifestation, it does so with a completely defined form. Then, once it is fully manifested (once it has manifested upward as far as is necessary for it to have fully manifested and actualized the full potential of definition with which it was created), it passes out of physical existence.

The only way anything—be it a thought, a feeling, an inclination, a physical object, or whatever—will persist in its physical existence beyond its fully manifesting all of its potential of definition, is if something holds onto it—is if something fixates upon it in its defined form, in its definition, giving it sustained attention. But getting to manifestation in this physical world entails fixation in itself, for it entails a shifting of attention away from the Source's experience in its pure undefined form and toward some definition of that experience, and it thereby entails holding onto something and seeking fulfillment in something that is not the Source's experience or the true Source of fulfillment.

It is important to distinguish here between actualizing, which entails defining, and fixating, which entails holding onto what has been defined. Things are not truly being fixated upon or held onto merely by being defined. We could remain self-aware and define the general nature of the world from self-awareness without having fixations drag us down from choice and thought and back into unfulfillment. It is only when we are in the world of choice that defining takes us out of our current state of fulfillment (and, even then, we can remain up in the sharing and receiving thought worlds of definition without any fixation occurring). As long as we have physical forms in this world, defining is our path toward actualization, for it allows us to receive things in physical form—things that our physical forms can experience and from which they, we, can thereby attain fulfillment.

In both the case of us in the world of choice and the case of us in the world of manifestation, we must allow what we receive to pass through us. It is merely that when we exist in the world of choice, what is flowing through us remains always undefined experience, and when we define it, we are inherently no longer in choice, passing into the thought worlds temporarily (and downward further if our attention does not remain on the experience, itself, but rather shifts to our definition—our understanding—of the experience). And so defining is, in a way, tantamount to fixating for us when we are in the world of choice, but defining what is to manifest is the only way to actualize ourselves, and thereby to work our way up to the world of choice, as long as we exist in the physical world of manifestation—where fulfillment is provided to us via other physical manifestations.

The only way for us, in this physical world of manifestation, to attain fulfillment is through defining—through describing and thereby shaping our experience and, in this way, actualizing our potential. And this is because we are not fully actualized in the manifestation of the potential with which we have been defined, and thereby created, until we achieve full self-awareness and fully shape our experience with self-awareness. The natural course of things is to remain in existence until they achieve their complete actualization—until they achieve the purpose for which they were created—always developing and manifesting upward and thereby actualizing themselves. As long as we are constantly in the process of actualizing upward toward greater self-awareness, we will be constantly fulfilled (as fulfilled as we can be at each point in our development), all the way through our entire existence.

However, until self-awareness is achieved, the inclination is for things to cling to existence and to other things in existence. When this inclination is acted upon, unfulfillment occurs, because the natural flow of things is interrupted—because such clinging, or holding onto, or grasping, or fixating, slows or even halts the process of actualization upward. We are like flowers that were meant to bloom, and it is when we prevent ourselves from doing so that we end up feeling unfulfilled, for we end up unfulfilled in our potential. Our goal is to be always moving on the path of development upward, always defining and actualizing, for this is the path toward the fulfillment of our potential and thereby toward the experience of fulfillment.

There are basically two aspects to exercising self-awareness in this world of manifestation—*defining*, and thereby shaping, our experience, and *letting pass* what has been received and manifested, so that it can achieve the full actualization of its intended definition and then can pass out of existence, allowing for something else to take its place. (This can actually be broken down into three aspects—creating and sharing, receiving and manifesting within ourselves, and allowing to be manifested through ourselves, or defining and shaping and sharing, experiencing within us, and allowing to pass through us.) While we are in the world of choice without any physical form in the world of manifestation, doing the first is tantamount to *not* doing the second, which is tantamount to fixating, and so in the world of choice, self-awareness merely entails allowing things to be manifested through us—allowing what we receive to pass completely. However, we can remain in the world of choice and the thought worlds without fixating and entering into the world of feeling and instinct and the world of manifestation, for we can do exactly what we must do in order to remain self-aware—we can allow the Source's experience to pass through us (the choice part of our soul) and to be defined and shared (the sharing thought part of our soul) and to be received (the receiving thought part of our soul).

(Notice that, at every point prior to choice, the ideal is: *first* creating and sharing an experience, *then* receiving this experience in our own experience, and *then* allowing this experience to manifest through us—flowing to others and the world around us and into the past. But when we reach the world of choice and the worlds of thought and we are outside of the physical world of the progression of time, the ideal is changed, for we actually come to allow the Source's experience to flow through us, and then we create and share it, and then we receive it. Instead of initiating our reception of the experience by defining the experience, and only afterward allowing it to pass through us—an approach that is necessary as long as we require that things come to us in a defined form, as in physical form, in order for us to be capable of receiving them in our experience and gaining fulfillment from them, and therefore in order for us to be capable of allowing them to manifest through us, which will ultimately always result in a *defined* and *fixated* new manifestation—we actually come to begin by allowing the experience to flow through us and into the world in an *undefined* form, only defining it and receiving it afterward, and never fixating upon the definition we give to it and with which we receive it.)

And the truth is that this is where we would remain after we have developed the higher parts of our soul—in the worlds of choice, sharing thought, and receiving thought—and so we can define and receive, and thereby guide the world in its formation—in its manifestation of the Source's experience. In fact, fixation entails repetition—which is how we hold onto things. And repetition does not truly occur at all in the worlds of choice, sharing thought, and receiving thought (except to the extent that the Source's experience is being repeated in increasing definition, which possibly makes the world of choice, alone, the most ideal dwelling place in the overall world). Repetition, and therefore fixation, only really begins to occur in any significant sense at allowing thought, for allowing thought is a repetition (or a reflection) of choice as an allowing stage, and then the feeling stages and the instinctual stages and the stage of manifestation are all repetitions (or reflections) of the thought stages.

So fixation only really begins in any significant and notable sense after the worlds of choice, sharing thought, and receiving thought. And this is why our goal of complete self-awareness entails developing or actualizing the parts of our souls that exist in these first three worlds and then dwelling only in those worlds—because when we exist only in those worlds, we do not truly fixate at all, and so we are able to be as completely self-aware as is possible for us in this overall world of dependent existence, allowing the Source's experience to flow through us in as true a form as possible, and to be shared by us in as true a form as possible, and to be received by us in as true a form as possible.

For, in truth, the Source's experience is undefined and is that of a Source of all that is, and so this experience cannot truly be maintained in its true form once it enters the overall world, even in the worlds of choice, sharing thought, and receiving thought, where it is at its purest with respect to this overall world. Because we will always be *us* experiencing what the Source experiences, and we can never be the *Source* experiencing what the Source experiences; we will never truly be the

Source of what we are experiencing in the way that the Source is the Source of what *It* experiences.

[Notice, by the way, that this end goal of existing just in the worlds of choice and thought is reflected in the end of the sleep cycle, where we end up passing from REM (choice) to stage I (thought) and back to REM (choice), settling around these stages until we awake. And we awake into a new period of wake or, in the case of the ultimate end goal (the goal of dwelling just in the realms of choice and thought—a goal that we can only reach, like with the end of sleep that comes after wake, after we pass through all of the stages from the bottom up and then repeatedly pass through all of the stages up and down in a self-reflective way, eventually settling out in just choice and thought), in a new physical life in a new universe, where we begin once again from the bottom, in the world of manifestation, actualizing upward, but beginning by lingering around manifestation and the instinctual stages.]

While we are in the physical world of manifestation, defining beyond the worlds of choice, sharing thought and receiving thought—all the way through allowing thought and the feeling and instinctual stages and to manifestation—allows us to receive, where we are (in the physical world), the Source's experience in as direct a form as we can while we are here. It allows us to receive the Source's experience in forms that provide us fulfillment by making us increasingly capable of receiving the Source's experience in purer and truer forms, in forms that allow us to continue to exist and to increasingly actualize and connect to the higher parts of our souls. And so while we are in this physical world of manifestation, it is only when we repeat and hold onto things that already exist and/or that will not bring us fulfillment through their actualized existence—when we view things other than the Source as sources of fulfillment in themselves—that we are fixating beyond what we need to in order to obtain fulfillment in the form of actual things in this physical and actual world, and that we are thereby preventing ourselves from becoming ever-more capable of receiving and manifesting the Source's experience within our own experience.

Everything in this physical world comes from the Source, is defined in its potential increasingly until it comes into a definite actuality, and actualizes until it has achieved its complete actualization—fulfilling its definition—or until it is too completely interrupted in its actualization to be able to achieve it. And then it passes out of existence. Thus, for example, there are plants that die after they have flowered, and there are insects and other creatures that die after they've produced the next generation of the species—laying eggs or whatever. They fulfill the full definition—the purpose—of their being, and then they cease to be. It is only when something prevents things from taking their natural course of actualization that fixation is occurring beyond what is necessary with respect to us in this physical world of manifestation—of actualization.

For us in this physical world, the inertia of fixation prevents our progression upward in development, up the tree. In order to overcome this inertia, we must be constantly in the process of actualizing our potential to be self-aware—defining our experience and allowing it to pass (shaping and sharing our experience). In this way, we do not fixate beyond what is necessary to receive the Source's experience in this physical world, and in this way, we fulfill our purpose in existence—the purpose for which we have been defined and thereby brought into existence: to become capable of receiving (and ultimately to receive) the Source's experience of self-aware existence, in as pure and true a form as possible, from the Source.

The Air of Choice

In the tree setup, the tree can grow and change, the liquid water within it is constantly moving and developing and choosing its paths, but the world of choice outside the tree—the air surrounding the tree into which the water from the tree can evaporate—remains the same.

There are an infinite number of physical universes existing within the world of manifestation, and this infinite number of physical universes (which together form a multiverse of physical universes) has a corresponding infinite number of extensions into the world of feeling and instinct (the lower levels of souls—which have definition and are distinctly identifiable due to fixation—of that which exists in the physical universes). But beyond the tree—beyond the world of feeling and instinct—things become so difficult to define as separate and different, due to the lack of specifically defining language, that nothing is really different.

The world of sharing thought and the world of receiving thought that combine to produce the tree in the tree setup and that are reflected in every part of it, including in the physical world of manifestation (as two of the three spatial dimensions and as the nuclear forces that allow for the formation and breakdown of atoms), are essentially the same for every universe—differing only in how they combine in allowing thought, which is reflected in every part of the tree, including in the physical world of manifestation, as well (as the third spatial dimension and as the force of electromagnetism, which determines how atoms and other particles combine to produce ions and molecules and all of the rest of the specific contents of the physical world). And so it seems that the formation and breakdown of atoms as the basic building blocks of the physical world, due to the interaction of nuclear forces and space (the basic thoughts and senses of the world), is the same for all of the infinite universes in the multiverse—and it is merely how these basic building blocks combine into seeable (or sensible) objects that interact with one another in specific ways where different universes begin to differ.

And, beyond it all, the world of choice remains utterly un-changed, being the pure potential for all things to be.

In the tree setup, we can say that the air represents the world of choice, the sunlight represents the sharing thought that passes through choice, and the earth in which the tree grows represents receiving thought, where the sunlight begins to break down. When we are like water vapor, existing as part of the air (as part of the world of choice), and we begin to condense back into liquid water and move into the tree (the world of feeling and instinct), we first pass through the sunlight of sharing thought (with a thought of sharing that begins to give rise to the world), and then we condense into the earth—into the soil of receiving thought—where we feed the growth of the world of feeling and instinct that is the tree, and become a new physical universe in a new incarnation within the world of manifestation (within the tube system of the tree which, here, is the world of manifestation, with the liquid water being this world's contents that the world allows to manifest through it).

In this way, we become, as water vapor existing in the world of choice, a means by which the sunlight can interact with the earth—we, as water vapor (choice) that condenses into liquid water, *allow* the sunlight (sharing thought) to interact with the earth (receiving thought) in a way that might aid the seed of the tree (allowing thought) in its growth into a tree, and that might aid in the growth of the tree, itself. The earth (receiving thought), itself, cannot aid the growth of the tree unless there exists water to transport the nutrients of the soil into the roots of the tree. And so the water that evaporates with the energy of the sunlight (sharing thought), and thereby passes into the air (the world of choice), becomes the means by which the sunlight (the world of sharing thought) can interact with the earth (the world of receiving thought) to feed the growth of the tree in its continued existence.

And so while the sunlight (the world of sharing thought) is different sunlight at every moment, even as it serves the same purpose, and as the earth (the world of receiving thought) is different earth as its nutrients are used and replaced, again even as it serves the same purpose, the air (the world of choice) into which the water from the tree evaporates remains, relative to the rest of the tree setup, basically the same. The sunlight (the world of sharing thought) shines and doesn't shine and shines again and is always different sunlight shining, the earth's (the world of receiving thought) nutrients are used and replaced, the tree (the world of feeling and instinct) grows and changes, the tube system of the tree (the world of manifestation) grows and changes with the tree, the liquid water (the contents of the worlds after choice and sharing thought, for the water is vapor in choice and sharing thought, and liquid water is the altered form in which the ground that is receiving thought receives it—due to its holding onto what it receives in the defined form in which it receives it—and passes it on to the rest of the worlds after it) inside the ground and the tree is constantly cycling through and is always different water from one moment to the next. But the air (the world of choice) outside the tree is, relative to all of the rest, basically the same—a constant from one universe to the next, being that within which all of the rest of the tree setup (the rest of the world of all that is the Source's creation) exists.

So nothing truly separates one universe (in its entirety of actual and potential forms) from the next other than the dimension of choice—within which is contained the pure potential to be anything and to be defined in any way—within which all universes—the entire multiverse of an infinite number of universes—exist. All universes exist in their definition of fixations that make them themselves, separated only by that which contains no definitions, no fixations, no actualized anything within it in itself, and this is the dimension that is choice.

[We may note here that the things that change the most relative to the rest are the tree and its contents—the world of feeling and instinct and the world of manifestation—unless we consider the fact that the sunlight truly is always different from moment to moment—that the self-aware existence shared by the Source is always of the same quality but is always truly renewed in every moment. Although, the sunlight *is* always of the same nature even though it is different sunlight, and the tree really does have discernable changes. Also, the ground—receiving thought—provides a firm and largely unchanging foundation in which the tree can grow. So we can point out that all these things remain in *common* for all universes—the air, the sunlight, the ground, the tree, and the water—the overall world, the overall tree of life paradigm.

But what we seek to point out and emphasize here is that the air—choice—is what *separates* (or *allows to be separate*) each of the branches, each of the possible paths of the universe and, thus, each of the different universes. And the air (including its water vapor contents)—choice—allows the sunlight—sharing thought—and the earth—receiving thought—to interact to feed the tree with the liquid water contents that are necessary for the tree's growth. This interaction occurs continually, although it is truly the contents of everything—the water that cycles through the air and the sun's energy and the ground and the tree—that are, in any particular part of this cycle, changing from moment to moment, even as they remain the same overall if the system (excluding the sun) is closed. And the water then merely allows the sun's energy—self-aware existence—to be received by the system—the overall world—continually (for the water is also losing, or giving up, that energy continually). In any closed system, entropy (the degree of disorder) increases perpetually, so for this system of tree and cycling water to remain in its structured and ordered and continuing form—in order for the existence of the tree and the entire tree setup as it is (the overall world) to be preserved and for the tree thus to remain *alive*—there needs to be an outside source of energy, which is, in this case, the sun (the Source).]

As we get caught up in the liquid water—the experience of choice in the redefined form given to it by receiving thought's holding onto it—we get caught up in fixation. And this liquid water includes all of the contents of what we choose—from allowing thought onward, and so it includes all of our thought, our feeling, our instincts (or desires), our speech, our actions, our bodies, and the entire contents of the physical universe around us. So we can see here that none of these things are the sources of what we receive from them, and none of these things are even the experience in the pure form in which it is being shared with us. These things are all defined forms of that experience—they are all liquid water relative to the water vapor, which is the closest to the Source's experience in its purest form that we can get in the overall world (while we are not the Source, Itself). And so we must not get caught up in the definitions—the liquid nature of it—but, instead, must recognize that what we are receiving is the experience, itself—the water. This is what is being shared with us—life-giving water—and the defined form in which we receive it (its liquid form) is merely what allows us to receive it while we exist in the world of feeling and instinct and the world of manifestation—where we are defined, ourselves. But our essence is undefined—our essence is water vapor that is part of the air that is choice. And we must recognize this, and we must allow our essence to be fed by the water that is shared with us, consciously receiving the present and not merely the box in which the present is given to us.

When we get caught up in the contents of the world of feeling and instinct—in thoughts and feelings and instincts (or desires)—then we are as though we are part of the liquid water in the tree that is clinging to the inside of the tree instead of being like part of the liquid water in the tree that is surrounded by other liquid water and is not clinging to the tree. And so instead of allowing ourselves to be effortlessly carried forward by the flowing wave of time, we are fighting against this flow. And this causes the tension, or stress, of trying to make things different than they are or were or will be, and this also alters our perception of time.

If we are clinging to our instincts or desires for things to be different from the way they actually are in the present, it makes us feel like we are out of synch with the flow of time as it is, like we are playing a tape with terrible picture and sound quality (which results in frustration and anger and ultimately in a very corrupted or even negative version of the dominant positive feeling of the instinctual stages). If we are clinging to our feelings regarding the past, it makes us feel like we are stagnating within the flow of time, repeatedly rewinding and replaying events as time plays onward without our getting anything done within it (which results in regret and shame and ultimately in a very corrupted or even negative version of the dominant positive feeling of the feeling stages). If we are clinging to our thoughts regarding the future, it makes us feel like time is flowing uncomfortably rapidly by us, or fast-forwarding by without us (which results in anxiety and fear and ultimately in a very corrupted or even negative version of the dominant positive feeling of the thought stages). For even as our bodies are flowing forward with time, we are essentially separating from our bodies, which exist in the present moment at every moment, and we are fighting against the flow as our bodies and everything else pass by without our full presence in them—without the full awareness of our attention on each of those moments as they actually are.

At the worst (at the point where we experience the negative versions of feelings, rather than merely corrupted versions), we are so fixated upon our thoughts or feelings or instincts, replaying them over and over, that we cling to the inside of the tree without budging at all as the water flows by us—without taking in what the water (the experience of the Source that is shared with us) provides us at all. And we merely allow all of the physical experience in the physical world around us to manifest through us, without our being in touch with any of it as it is at all—like we are automatic machines (for our physical bodies are all that is truly there in the present), giving a set output of a thoroughly practiced and mindlessly habitual pattern for every set input, without any awareness or willfulness at all.

We must learn to let go of the things—the thoughts, the feelings, the instincts, the external physical experiences—that we pass by; we must not cling to them, and we must, instead, allow ourselves—our awareness and ability to choose—to be drawn forward by the flowing water all around us (including our physical bodies and our outward, physical experience in the world with everyone and everything around us). We must allow ourselves to be drawn upward by all of these things, gaining through them this upward pulling force as we and they are pulled upward through the tree by the pull of evaporation, by the pull of self-awareness—awareness of them, and of ourselves, and of our relation to them and ultimately to the Source that is ultimately providing this pull of awareness through them. We must allow ourselves to be drawn upward by all of these things toward complete actualization as water vapor, in which form we become part of the air that is the world of choice, within which this tree in which we exist grows.

As the tree grows and branches, all that separates one branch from the next is the air—is choice. Through the air, all of the branches of the tree strive upward toward the sunlight. Through choice, all of the universes strive upward toward the Source's experience. Every one of the infinite number of universes in the multiverse exists in the same time and space and so on, and the only thing that separates one from another is *choice*—the different ways each chooses to actualize its potential, the different places a particle is observed in each one when it is observed, the different choices we make in each one.[15]

---

15   This is, by the way, the many worlds interpretation of quantum mechanics (an interpretation developed by Hugh Everett III), which says that every time a choice is made or a particle is observed, the universe splits— like a branching tree—to account for every one of the possible outcomes, such that each possible outcome is realized in a separate universe.

The Possibility of Time Travel

Travel in Time

Considering that choice is what distinguishes one universe from another, making it separate and distinct from every other universe, it becomes clear that any time travel that might be engaged in would inherently result in travel to a different universe from one's own—a different universe from the universe of origination. For example, let's say that I travel back in time and kill my grandfather before he met my grandmother (the infamous grandfather paradox, for then how could I have been born to go back in time and kill my grandfather?). I could very well do this, but in the universe from which I came, I did not exist in that part of what is now my past. I wasn't there to kill my grandfather. In fact, I wasn't there, period. I was born in such and such a year, and I, as I am now, only exist *now* in this universe. Therefore, if I were to travel back in time, I would inherently be choosing a path for the universe that I enter that is different from the path that was chosen by my own universe of origination.

If we imagine the course of universes like a branching tree, my traveling to the past would mark a point of branching at the time that I enter, with the time I enter being the first point of a different branch from the one traveled by my own universe of origination. This would be the case regardless of my type of travel (be it the travel of my physical body, or merely the travel of a part of my consciousness or soul in some form of remote viewing, or possibly regression to the past in one's current physical life or to past lives, or progression to the future in one's current physical life or to future lives, or something else). Because the fact is that if choice is what separates universes, distinguishing one from another, then every moment is an opportunity to travel one branch out of several possible branches, and the choice of the universe, with all of its contents (all of its contents' choices), determines its path of travel. So everything that we think or feel or say or do at every moment determines the path of this particular universe.

It is important to realize that time is not yet fully defined until manifestation in the physical world, but it still has some potential form in the stages prior to this. Further, the physical universe exists in potential form in the world of feeling and instinct. So, even though some form of spiritual travel—travel of awareness or consciousness or soul separate from the body—would likely have less of a pronounced or defined effect upon the universe we enter, we would still be creating a different branch for that universe (as well as for this one) by our mere presence there in any form (and our consequent absence from here, and our potential learning from our experience of there—in the case of spiritual travel where our physical body remains here—which might lead us to make different choices here after this experience).

Since traveling to another point in time (either past or future) is inherently the actualization of choice, and thereby the choosing of the path of travel for the universe (both the universe of origination and the universe that we enter), there are various forms of travel within the same universe (within the universe of origination) that are impossible for us to engage in.

Travel to the past in any form—physical or spiritual—will create an alternate path for a universe that is therefore separated from that of origination by choice and that is therefore inherently a separate universe.

Travel physically to the future might allow for travel within the same universe, for such travel is allowed by Einstein's Theory of Relativity such that existence near a body of great mass or travel at some velocity relative to another observer will result, practically, in travel to the future of that other observer, since time is slowed relative to that other observer. So, if I, for example, were to travel on some form of spaceship out into space at near the speed of light and then return to Earth, I could travel (and age) a week and find that a century has passed on Earth and everyone I knew is dead. Essentially, due to the warping of time here—or, rather, the alteration of the rate of passage of time relative to other observers—I never have to leave the sequential and successive moment-to-moment progression of the universe into the future in order to travel physically into the future. And so it seems that I would remain in the same universe throughout my travel.

Travel spiritually into the future—like travel to the past—on the other hand, will not only create a situation like that of physical travel to the future, in which my very presence in the future will be a choice of a path for that future, regardless of what I communicate to anyone there or how I otherwise affect anything there. Because although this is the future, and so my effect on it should not causally affect the path of my own universe of origination toward that future (the way my effect on the past causally affects the path of that universe toward the present in the universe from which I came), we must remember that my experience of the future will inherently, in some way, affect the course of my universe toward that exact future. My thoughts and feelings and inclinations regarding that future are inherently choices for the universe in which I exist (for thoughts and feelings and inclinations are all consequences, or forms of actualization, of choice, which precedes them). Therefore, I cannot travel to the future spiritually without affecting the course of my own universe. And so my own universe will not travel the path toward that same future to which I travel (ed). Thus, my travel spiritually to a future point in time is inherently travel to a different universe—one separated by choice from that from which I am traveling. Such travel is, therefore, travel to the future that would occur if I had not traveled to it and experienced it and thereby altered the course of the actualization of my own universe through my thoughts and feelings and inclinations and speech and actions that were part of, or that resulted from, my experience of that future (of course, this alteration could be very small, and large events—or even various small events—that I experience in my spiritual travel to the future could still take place in my own universe's future).

So, to summarize: Physical travel to the future can occur within the same, single universe. But physical travel to the past, and spiritual travel to the past or to the future, will inherently determine a different path for a consequentially separate universe—a universe that is separated from the universe of origination by the altered actualization of choice.

We can travel up and down the branches of the tree of the actualization of choice. But when we travel back, we cannot travel forward along the same branch in that past as our universe of origination traveled (and so physical travel to the past will result in our being unable ever to return to the exact same universe from which we left, although we might return to a universe that very closely resembles the universe of origination if we have not greatly affected the past beyond our mere presence in it, and if we *have* more greatly affected the past, we could, before traveling forward again, travel back further into the past—to some time that is prior to the previous past that we entered—so that our presence, now in the more distant past, is the only distinction between the universe of origination and the final universe to which we travel "back"). And when we travel forward spiritually, we cause the branch that our universe travels to be a different branch from that through which we travel forward spiritually. And in order to travel to some future that could have resulted from an altered past, but that is not a possible path for the universe now in the present, we would have to engage in physical time travel (for spiritual time travel always must involve travel forward or backward from *now*—to a future that is only different in that we are now traveling a different path due to our knowledge of the original future, or to a past that is only different in that we are, in some form, in it), and we would have to go first to the past and make some alteration, and then go forward (either physically or spiritually) from there to the future.

Basically, we can only travel along the branches of the tree of actualizing time, and whether we go backward or forward, we cannot simply jump from one branch to another, but rather must travel along the branches back to a junction with other branches and go forward from there in this case. We can only travel, physically or spiritually, to a past that is like ours except for our presence in it, and we can only travel spiritually to a future that would have been ours if we had not had knowledge of it, and we can only travel physically to a future that *is* ours, because we never leave the universe in order to travel to it. The only way to do anything other than these is to travel multiple times, beginning with physically traveling backward, so that we have a different starting point from which to travel forward to an alternate past or future (relative to the original point of departure).

Due to these limitations on travel within the same universe—due to the fact that every universe is separated from every other universe by choice (and choice, alone)—time travel paradoxes of all sorts are inherently avoided.

Even if we were to come up with some elaborate scenario, such as in which someone travels forward spiritually in time one day, and then gets in a car accident the next day, and then travels forward spiritually (or physically) in time the next day to the exact same future point as last time and communicates to his slightly younger self there in the future that he should not get in the car, we would not be able to come up with a situation in which the past of the universe of origination would be altered. For example, in this particular scenario, the person would not be able to alter his own past and make it so that he never got in the car accident (and therefore, paradoxically, make it so that he also had no reason to go tell his past self that he shouldn't get in the car, no reason to try to prevent the car accident from happening).

The reason that the person would not be able to alter his own past is as follows: The first time he traveled forward spiritually in time, he traveled to a universe that was inherently *not* that from which he originated because it was a universe that traveled the path that his universe *would have* traveled if he had not altered its direction through his experience of the future. The second time he traveled forward in time, he traveled to a universe that was inherently neither that from which he originated (for the same reason as was just stated, although if he traveled forward physically, it *would* be the same universe from which he originated and therefore *not* the universe to which he traveled last, and so he wouldn't be able to tell his past self from his universe of origination anything at all) nor that to which he traveled last, for the future to which he travels the second time is the one to which his universe would travel due to his having traveled to the future the first time and thereby affected the chosen course of his universe (and so he would still be able to encounter himself in the future, but it would be himself on a path—in a universe—that is no longer that of his universe of origination due to his current traveling to the future, which is altering his universe's path from that universe's path).

Because choice is what separates every universe in the multiverse from every other universe in the multiverse, we cannot, in any way, alter the past of our current universe—the past branches that our current universe has traveled, the past choices that have been made that have led it to here, now, as it is.

This does not mean that there cannot be people from the future in our past, however. It merely means that if they were in our past, they were *always* in our past—they were always part of the actualization of choice that led to our universe taking the path that it has since that time that they were here, as a result of their existing (and having whatever effects that they had) at that point in our past. And it also means that such people could not be from our universe originally (from our universe's future), for when they traveled to the past and ended up in our universe, they inherently created a different choice for the path of the universe of their destination (our universe) as compared with their universe of origination, and so our universe could not be their universe; they could be from what is the future relative to where we are now (further up the branching tree of time, or rather of actualizing choice, than we are now), but it would have to be a future in a different universe.

But even as it is choice that limits our ability to travel in time and still remain in the same universe, it is choice that makes it possible for us to travel in time at all, and therefore to travel to different universes in the multiverse (which, again, are separated by choice, which is why choice makes it possible for us to travel from one to another, thereby allowing us a form of travel in time). In the case of spiritual time travel, it is choice as manifested in our decisions (our decisions that are informed with the knowledge of how to go about traveling in such a way) that allows us the capacity for this form of travel. And in the case of physical time travel, it is choice as manifested in such things as the singularities of black holes—the pores of the leaves of the tree, where water becomes water vapor that can then condense and reenter the tree to become part of the contents of a different universe—that allows us the capacity for this form of travel.

Choice is where all definition breaks down, or rather where all definition has not yet been formed, and all things exist there only in a purely potential form—the potential for anything to be or to occur. Singularities, as physical manifestations of choice, are where all of the definitions and laws of the physical world cease to be, where space and time, themselves, are ripped apart. When we transcend the definitions of the physical world, we are capable of breaking out of the usual progression of things, for time, itself, breaks down. All we need to do is learn how to make use of singularities in such a way that we benefit from the breakdown of the definition of time without having the definition of us break down as well (for then we would die and be ripped apart and fail to travel in time as ourselves in any meaningful way).

Nonetheless, the possibility of traveling in time (outside of the usual progression of time)—physically or spiritually—is within our capacity to choose once we figure out how to do it. For, ultimately, anything and everything is within our capacity to choose (once we learn how to willfully use the language of creation to bring it to bear on shaping one thing or another in some certain way), since choice is the source of all definition in the entire world of existence.

Travel in Choice

All forms of travel in time are also sort of travel in space in that we travel to a different universe. But we must remember that, in fact, we are traveling *neither in time nor in space* (no matter how much we might want to call it "time travel" due to its resemblance to this). We are traveling in choice, and in choice, alone, and we can here gain a greater understanding of how different universes—parallel universes—in the multiverse relate to one another (and of how they can interact with one another via their contents, such as us).

Only choice separates what is the present moment in one universe from what is the present moment in another universe. And it is merely that we *seem* to be traveling in time when we travel in choice; it is merely that the present in another universe seems to be a different point in time as compared with the present in our own universe when we travel to that other present moment—that other moment that is in the process of occurring, that other moment that is illuminated with self-aware existence (which is why it was earlier suspected and considered that the universes were separated by time, with one universe coming after another in time).

How we actualize choice determines how quickly we progress upward through development, how soon and how quickly and how consistently we allow ourselves to be pulled upward by self-awareness. It is due to this that the separation of universes by choice can seem like a separation in time, because the specific exercise and actualization of choice by each universe determines where it is in its overall progression through the cycle up the tree through time, into the air as water vapor, and back to the ground and up the tree, through time, again. Even in the case of the usual progression of time from moment to moment, we are, in essence, traveling through nothing other than choice, for the usual progression of time is actually the progressive actualization of choice.

The other water molecules that pass through the tree seem either to be lower or higher in the tree—less far or further along in the process of development upward—than the water molecules that are our own universe. And when we travel up or down the branches, we encounter different water molecules (different universes) from our own—different substance (different self-aware existence) that has the same definition of point in time and contents and so forth as some point in our future or past. Therefore, it would seem when we travel up or down the branches that we are traveling in time within our own universe, when the truth is that we are traveling to a different universe (illuminated by different photons of sunlight, different self-aware existence) that merely has the exact same language defining it as the future or past in our own universe; it is like another watch of exactly the same brand and model and so forth as our own, but it is still *another* watch, *another* universe, made up of different material that was merely shaped identically to our own—identical in every way *except*, of course, for our presence within it and the effects that we have upon it in the choices that we make while we are there (such as for the scratch across the band that we accidently make on the other watch, or the initials that we carve into the back of it).

We might better understand the proliferation of universes in choice by looking to a reflection of this in the developing embryo in the womb. As a reflection of the creative process from the thought stages downward, sexual reproduction is the uniting of the language descriptions of two individuals that results in the formation of a single cell that divides over and over again to give rise to many cells. [Notice, by the way, that in evolution, development occurred in the reverse direction (upward instead of downward), with the mitotic division of cells to produce other cells with the same DNA, in the form of asexual reproduction (an aspect of the feeling stages), coming prior to sexual reproduction (an aspect of the thought stages).]

Here, we see what is perhaps the most accurate reflection (in many ways) of the proliferation of universes, which begins in a single point in the singularity of the Big Bang (a single zygote, a single trunk of the tree). From here, the universe (the cell, the trunk) divides with the actualization of choice at every moment (with the collapse of wavefunctions upon the observation of particles and the world in general, with the making of decisions), dividing more and more frequently into an increasing number of universes (of cells, of branches) as self-awareness increases and the actualization of choice becomes greater (and as time in the universes consequently increases in rapidity as the universes are ever-diluting their matter and energy contents in ever-expanding space, as the universes are expanding to encompass and actualize the full potential of their DNA, and of the Source's experience).

So, it would seem from the reflection in the development of the embryo from a single-celled zygote (as well as from the single trunk of the tree) that there is only one singularity origin of the entire multiverse (one Big Bang that is continually occurring as it is renewed with water molecules, with self-aware existence), and from this single point (like from a single seed), each of the universes arise through ever-increasing division (like the division of cells or the branching of the tree) upon the actualization of choice at every moment, whereby many different choices are made, with a different universe to account for each one—a different universe to account for each direction that the universe might take at each moment. And through this actualization, as the universes divide or branch, they increasingly differentiate and specialize in various ways (like cells in an embryo becoming heart cells or liver cells or lung cells or skin cells, etc.).

But every defined moment in every universe is being continuously illuminated by self-aware existence, continuously fed with the substance of water molecules passing through them (in actuality, with no time, there is no need for "continuous" illumination, for illumination of the present *ever* is illumination of the present *forever* in the absence of time). And since all points in time that have ever existed or will ever exist are always the *present* for some universe, travel through choice to a different point in time—in what seems like travel in time—is possible.

Gravity and Related Things

As we have seen, the world of manifestation, in which every physical universe exists, is divided up by its manifestation of three basic components—sharing, receiving, and allowing. And these three basic components contain all of the other stages (besides manifestation) in a sort of not-fully-actualized form. As the universe manifests upward toward the actualization of self-awareness—with the arising of life, and then of intelligent life—it increasingly actualizes each of the other stages within itself, and so, essentially, every one of the dimensions is expanding as it unfolds in its actualization (besides choice, into which all of the other dimensions are expanding). This is significant because it means that it is likely that the expansion of the universe is occurring in more dimensions than the three that we perceive, and if this is true, then this world of manifestation—and time and gravity, which are manifestations of it—is expanding in nine dimensions of space altogether (if we don't include time—manifestation—which is doing the expanding, and choice, into which all of this expansion is occurring), since manifestation is the manifestation of all of the previous stages. And so the more the universe expands, the more gravity spreads out—exponentially in nine different actualizing and expanding dimensions—and the weaker gravity seems, as its force is diluted in expanding space.

Here, in this case, we have a physical mechanism to explain the relative weakness of gravity as compared with the three subatomic forces, for gravity's influence, stemming from manifestation, itself, is actually diminished as the universe actualizes upward and manifests more sharing in comparison to its receiving and allowing (for gravity is a solely attractive, allowing force), and gravity's influence also moves freely everywhere throughout all of the dimensions that actualize within manifestation, and so it is diluted greatly with their expansion. This is as opposed to the subatomic forces, which are manifestations of the thought stages (and which are consequently relatively balanced in their sharing, receiving, and allowing—which is the goal of actualization) and so are being increasingly actualized in the world of manifestation as they stem from the very stages from which the three main expanding dimensions stem, and which extend their influence only on small scales (and so are not threatened with being diluted in all of the expanding dimensions as gravity is).

We also have a physical mechanism here to explain the nature of the dark energy that is increasing the rate of expansion of the universe, because the universe would be expanding increasingly rapidly, as we perceive it to be, due to the diluted nature of the very attractive force that keeps all of its contents clinging to one another (the attractive force that would, therefore, be a possible mechanism for the slowing of the universe's expansion if it were not being increasingly diluted). And so, as the universe actualizes upward toward self-awareness, expanding to encompass more and more of the actualization of choice, its self-awareness builds upon itself, and its expansion increases at an exponential rate.

We might make note here that time differs from the three spatial dimensions similarly to the way gravity differs from the three subatomic forces (as manifestation, from which time and gravity stem, differs from the three thought stages, from which the three spatial dimensions and the three subatomic forces stem). In both cases, due to the stage of which they are a manifestation, the former is significantly more defined and limited than the latter. Gravity is significantly weaker in its influence than the other forces, and it is also solely allowing (as its activity draws matter and energy together from being spread out over vast distances, thereby making possible—or *allowing*—the activity of the other forces, which project their influence only across very tiny distances), as compared with the other forces, which are also sharing and receiving. And time allows movement solely in one direction (forward—up the tree, upward in development along the path of increasing actualization) and doesn't allow much freedom of movement in general (since we are always stuck in the ever-moving present, and it is not so easy to change our rate of movement through time significantly—and, again, we can only change our rate of movement *forward*, and cannot go successively backward), and time is thus solely allowing (for movement in time passively *allows* movement in space—in the other dimensions, which are spatial). This is as compared with the three spatial dimensions, which allow free movement in two directions—both sharing and receiving—per dimension.

(Note, by the way, that allowing-stage manifestations encompass aspects of both sharing and receiving stages, but in a less-true form. Thus, gravity has aspects of the creative and receptive stages that come before its manifestation, as it forms new planets and stars and even black holes and singularities—in a creative fashion—but it does so by drawing all matter and energy toward all other matter and energy—in a receptive fashion. And time has aspects of the creative and receptive stages that come before its manifestation, as it contains two directions, with the past receiving present moments and the future creating and sharing present moments. But in both the case of gravity and that of time, there is less freedom of choice, of decision, of movement than in the case of the subatomic forces and that of the spatial dimensions, respectively, because gravity and time are more defined, and they are manifestations of an allowing stage—namely, of manifestation.)

With what we have learned, we have another mechanism that can be contributing to the acceleration of the expansion of the universe (and therefore another aspect of dark energy) as well: Loss of gravity (along with matter and energy) via black holes. As the pores of the leaves of the tree in the tree setup, the singularities of black holes actually reveal gravity's (and manifestation's) relation to choice. Gravity in the universe allows different parts of existence to cling to other parts of existence, and in this way it allows the formation of the gravity wells that are singularities—infinitely massive concentrations of matter and energy contained within infinitely small points. However, as matter is pulled toward black holes, it is like the water molecules that are being pulled upward by evaporative pull. As water molecules leave the tree, they pull other water molecules upward. And so as matter and energy are pulled toward black holes, they are not actually clinging to other things in existence but are, rather, being pulled *via* other things in existence *toward* self-awareness. Just as we can learn to recognize the things in the world as *not* being the sources of what we receive from them, but rather as being that through which we receive from the Source, Itself, beyond the world, the universe as a whole manifests this realization also as its contents are pulled toward singularities, where space and time, themselves, tear and break down and physical existence ceases to be.

It is interesting to note that supermassive black holes exist at the cores of galaxies wherein conditions are suitable to life, including our own Milky Way Galaxy. And so when black holes arose (and when they arise), they became a mechanism for the pull of self-awareness. They became a mechanism for the parts of the group of matter and energy within galaxies to connect intimately and intensely in ways that yield a true understanding of the relationship between different parts of the world—an understanding that the other parts of the world are a means of receiving from the Source, Itself, beyond the world (where this world's laws as they are break down) and are not the sources of what anything in this world gains from them in themselves. And as matter and energy, along with their gravity, leave the physical existence of the universe via black holes, and as black holes, themselves, evaporate (in the very distant future), the universe expands increasingly rapidly with self-awareness as its contents, themselves, are pulled *toward the Source through each other*, instead of merely *toward each other*.

Remember that singularities—as those of black holes and as that of the Big Bang white hole—are zero-dimensional in the sense that they are the absence of time and space. And so nothing can truly exist within them (for there is no space or time within them within which to exist). Therefore, logically, nothing can truly come from them or go into them. And yet all of the matter and energy that exist in the universe came into the universe via the Big Bang singularity, and all of the matter and energy that exist in the universe will eventually fall into black hole singularities. We have already seen that the forces and dimensions of the universe interact to produce matter and energy, and so matter and energy as we know them don't actually come from the Big Bang singularity (a manifestation of choice), but rather they emerge in some kind of defined form just after that singularity, in the interaction of the thought and senses of the universe. And here we can see that matter and energy don't actually fall into the singularities of black holes either, but rather matter and energy cease to exist just before reaching those points that are manifestations of choice.

For, at singularities, as at choice, all definition ceases to exist (although to a lesser extent than at the primordial choice itself—the choice of the overall tree of life paradigm—for every manifestation of choice is only undefined relative to all that is defined after it—in the case of singularities, relative to all of the physical universe—but, being *manifestations* of choice, and particularly *physical manifestations* of choice in the *physical* world, singularities have some kind of definition, particularly relative to that which comes before them in the tree of life paradigm). All of the definitions of the physical world cease to exist at singularities, and so as matter and energy fall toward singularities, they come to a point where they pass out of existence like fleeting thoughts in the mind of the universe upon the universe's reaching the high-meditative state of choice. All that defines them as physical matter and energy melts away, including the definitions of their spacial and temporal extension, leaving nothing but undefined self-aware existence, like water vapor intermingling with the air of choice. In the clear mind of the universe at choice, the thoughts that have become fixated to produce the definition of the structure and contents of the physical world cease to be fixated. And so they pass, like vapor, from physical existence.

More Precisely Defining Terms

The Roles of the Sharing, Receiving, and Allowing Stages

It may be realized that we have, hitherto, been a bit loose with our language in describing the nature of the sharing, receiving, and allowing stages. By this, I mean that our definitions now can actually be a bit clearer and more precise, even though our descriptions up to this point have been entirely sufficient in understanding everything up to this point, and can even be used from here on with accuracy.

(This, of course, is the nature of the progression of all things anyway, for the precision of the language involved ever-increases as we progress through the creative process, and everything that is manifesting is being simultaneously created as well—remember the holographic plate idea, where the manifestation in the world of manifestation is used as the holographic plate through which the Source may shine Its self-aware existence in the creation of the world in the next moment; this book is being created just as it is manifesting, and its formation is taking on greater specificity in the definitions and separation of its concepts just as all things do. As we progress through the creative process downward to manifestation, our definitions become more limiting, more precise in their separation of one thing from another, and as we progress through the process of manifestation upward—of actualization—the manifestations increase in number and variety as the world takes on increasing specificity, with every specifically defined thing reflecting the same general paradigm.)

In truth, there is no actual *creation*, in the strictest sense of the word, going on in any of the stages of the tree of life paradigm—in the entire *overall world* that contains each of the five worlds (and therefore all of the physical universes in the multiverse of the world of manifestation) within it. Everything that seems like *creation* within the overall world—within the entire paradigm of the world—is, in actuality, merely *allowing*. The only true *creation* occurs *prior* to choice. The Source carries out the only true creation in Its creation of the overall paradigm, the overall world, in the first place. The Source creates *choice*, itself—and therefore the potential for everything that is chosen, everything that comes after. This is the only real "creation" in the strictest sense of the word. It seems impossible even for us to *imagine* the creation of choice, for how can one *create choice* without *choosing* to do so? This is real creation.

The sharing stages are reflections of this initial and true creation. They are creative in the sense that they begin to define how things will be. For example, in the downward process of creation, sharing thought comes first in the thought stages, and it serves to define what thought shall be in the next stages. There is no such thing as thought (in the creative process from top down) prior to the defining of thought in sharing thought. (And so the Source's experience and the reason that the Source created the world becomes defined as a thought—becomes defined as something that we, within the world, can begin to understand—only in sharing thought. Prior to this in the downward creative process, the Source's experience has no definition or limitation that would allow us, within the world, to experience and understand it at all.) Likewise, sharing feeling is the first of the feeling stages, and it serves to define what feeling shall be, and sharing instinct is the first of the instinctual stages, and it serves to define what instinct shall be. So there *is* some kind of creation going on in the sharing stages, but it is not quite like the creation of the creative process, itself, which is a kind of creation that is only within the Source's capability—beyond the confines of the creative process, within which only the stages of the creative process can be utilized in any "creation".

In order to best understand the roles of the sharing stages, the receiving stages, and the allowing stages, we might look to the reflection of these stages in the male, the female, and the child produced from the interaction of the male and the female. The Source intimately connects with the world, and the thought stages reflect this, and the result is allowing thought—the seed of the tree of life paradigm, which develops into the world of feeling and instinct and then the world of manifestation, which are the worlds in which we reside solely in any actuality until we actualize the higher parts of our souls (at which point we cease to be reborn in this universe). Likewise, the male intimately connects with the female (in the thought stages, in the intimate connection between different "I"'s that provides for the possibility of sexual reproduction, which is associated with these stages), and the result is a zygote, which develops into a new person who experiences in a different way (through a different lens of thought and feeling and instinct, sensing the world from a different spatial location at every point in its life) than the parents who gave rise to it. And, likewise, people can connect (in the thought stages, in the kind of intimate and intense connection that is associated with these stages) and give rise to a new way of experiencing the world that didn't exist prior to their interaction.

[Notice that the manifestation upward to the development of sexual reproduction progressed through the stages of the paradigm (manifesting the various stages upward repeatedly, with the stages being more fully and more accurately represented each time). First, there was a single-celled organism that was only "I" preserving itself. Then, a single-celled organism gave rise, through asexual reproduction, to others that were projections of itself. Then, single-celled organisms somehow exchanged DNA, as through conjugation, thereby altering the "I"'s involved in the interaction and thus forming new "I"'s. Eventually, there was a multicellular organism that was only "I" preserving itself. Then, multicellular organisms grouped together by similarity, as by species and often by relatedness, in extended family groups such that others truly were, in a sense, projections of the "I". And then multicellular organisms intimately connected with one another through sexual reproduction in order to give rise to a new "I".

Notice also that, just as this development upward through the paradigm to sexual reproduction occurred, even the ways of intimately connecting with another "I" developed and manifested upward through the paradigm over time as the conception of another "I" developed and manifested upward through the paradigm over time (as did, by the way, the ways of preserving and the ways of belonging—every stage can be broken down into stages of development within itself, just as we see that instinct, feeling, and thought can each be broken down into allowing, receiving, and sharing, and as we see that the paradigm is manifested on every scale, even within manifestations of each stage).

The first kind of such connection that manifested is in the act of sexual reproduction, which corresponds here with the instinctual stages, since it is a very instinctual form of connection that has to do with the physical preservation of the "I"'s existence and the fulfillment the desires of the "I" as though the "I" is all that exists. The next kind of such connection that developed in manifestation, and which corresponds with the feeling stages in development, is connecting with another "I", who is a projection of the "I", through simple empathy— through feeling—putting the "I" in the other's external, physical situation and feeling what the "I" would feel if the "I" were in that external, physical situation—so that the "I" might connect with that other in a way that would aid in the "I"'s belonging to the group and in the perpetuation of the existence of the group, which is ultimately just a projection of the "I". In this case, the connection with the other is really still about the "I" and not about the other, for it is about the fulfillment of "I"'s desire to belong and the fulfillment of the "I"'s feelings—the "I"'s reflection upon who it is in relation to others in order to figure out who it is and how it fits in with others—in a similar way to sexual reproduction's truly being about the fulfillment of the "I"'s desire to preserve itself and the fulfillment of the "I"'s instinctual desires. The next kind of such connection that developed in manifestation, and which corresponds with the thought stages in development, is connecting with another "I" who is truly an other "I"—with a different internal and external experience and even a different *way* of experiencing. You might think that this is the highest form of intimate connection with another "I", but it is not. Because, in this case, the connection with the other is still about the "I" and not about the other, for it is about the fulfillment of the "I"'s desire to connect and the fulfillment of the "I"'s thoughts—the "I"'s figuring out the world around it in order to understand the other "I"'s in the world so that it might learn how to go about making decisions and so that it might learn what it should be deciding.

In order to reach the highest form of intimate connection with another "I", we have to reach choice in our development and manifestation—we have to reach self-awareness. The kind of connection that arises with self-awareness is a connection that is no longer about the fulfillment of the "I"'s desires in any way, for the "I" does not hold onto things and so does not experience desires but, instead, only experiences subtle inclinations that stem from intuition and, ultimately, from the Source.

And so this kind of connection is the truest connection, for when the "I" is not seeking fulfillment of desires and holding onto aspects of the connection in search of fulfillment, then the truest and greatest fulfillment can actually come from the connection.

It is at this point that the intimate and intense connection with the other "I" becomes an intimate and intense connection with the Source, for the "I" does not seek fulfillment *from* the other "I", and so the "I" is able to receive fulfillment *through* the other "I"—*from* the Source, from which all fulfillment truly and ultimately comes. When the "I" is self-aware, it is capable of connecting with any aspect of the world in the present moment, essentially through the practice of mindfulness, and that other aspect of the world becomes a means through which the "I" obtains greater self-aware existence from the Source. And it is in this way that the "I" comes to allow the Source to shape the world through it, as it allows the Source to direct its use of language via its intuition, thereby shaping the very self-aware existence that it gains through its interactions with all aspects of the world. Thus, the "I" comes to be a means of conveyance of self-aware existence into the world, itself, in all of its connections, as it becomes a projection of the Source in this world, and as the experience that it shapes for itself and the world around it comes to resemble, most closely, the Source's experience, itself—as far as it *can* within the constraints of language within the world, which allow the Source's experience to take many forms that approximate it, but no forms that are exactly it.]

It is connections in which experience is shared, received, and allowed that provide us the information that we seek about the true nature of the sharing, receiving, and allowing stages. The male does not truly create anything in the strictest sense, but there is creation in the sense of the definition of something that wasn't there before—sperm cells, each containing certain DNA. (Notice that, like in the case of the sun with its light energy and in the case of the Source with Its experience, the male shares in a sort of radiation outward of a lot more than is ever actually going to manifest in the allowing stage ultimately—and, in fact, it is possible that none of what he shares will manifest ultimately, and yet he shares nonetheless.) And the female receives what was shared with her and combines some of this (usually only a single sperm cell in the case of human beings) with an egg (or eggs), which contains certain DNA within it as well. Then, the result is the allowing stage: the zygote that allows the interaction—the connection between male and female, between what was shared and what was received—to be manifested through it. And this zygote, as the manifestation of allowing thought, develops further in the process of creation (through the feeling and instinct stages) before it manifests in the world of manifestation—being born into the world, when the process of actualization upward truly begins to occur.

Okay, so what can we learn from this? The sharing stages define something new and share—something that is to be manifested in another after it has been received. The receiving stages receive what has been shared (and, therefore, they receive *reactively*, for they receive when there is something that is shared, and so they receive in reaction to the sharing that has occurred, and they actually grasp at what is shared, holding onto it within themselves) and combine this with some modifying definition of their own, bringing a greater completion to what has been shared. And the allowing stages are the result—and it is in the allowing stages that complete and true manifestation ultimately occurs, like the zygote is the first potential manifestation of the new person as a complete, although still potential, new person.

[Also, if we look at the male as sharing thought, the female as receiving thought, the zygote as allowing thought, and the baby that is born as manifestation, then we can get a better, more precise idea about the relationship amongst all of the stages of the paradigm. For example, we can see in this reflection of the stages and their relationship why sharing thought and receiving thought are each separate worlds in themselves—for these worlds are like the male and the female, who are two separate people. And we can also see why the world of feeling and instinct contains everything from allowing thought downward through the feeling stages and the instinct stages—for this world is like the egg (in the case of such things as reptiles and amphibians and birds) or the womb (in the case of most mammals) in which the baby is formed, from conception (when it is merely a single cell, or a zygote, resulting from the merging of sperm and egg) onward through its development and the definition of each of its parts via the multiple division of the zygotic cell and the growth and specialization and division of each of the resulting cells. And we can see why manifestation is a separate world as well—for this world is like the physical, outside world into which the baby is born when it hatches from its egg or leaves the womb. And we can even see how connected the world of feeling and instinct and the world of manifestation are, just as we can see why these worlds are separate from the worlds above—for the world of feeling and instinct contains the baby as it begins to develop, and the world of manifestation contains the baby as that development manifests itself in the physical world outside the womb. These worlds contain the same person—the same multicellular organism composed of cells, the same multiverse composed of an infinity of universes—and it is merely that one world (the world of feeling and instinct) is the place where development in potential occurs, and the other world (the world of manifestation) is the place, discernable by the physical senses, where the actualization of that development occurs.

From this reflection, we can discern how much we are truly confined in our experience within the stages from allowing thought downward. And to transcend allowing thought is to transcend the multiverse of universes (like leaving the tree through its leaves) and to become the egg (receiving thought) and the sperm (sharing thought), themselves—the contributions of the mother and father that combine to produce the multiverse (in its development and in its actualization) in which we currently reside. But remember what we saw with the tree setup, where sharing thought is the sunlight and receiving thought is the earth. We do not become these things; we merely aid in the sharing of the sunlight with the earth—by being water that receives the sunlight to become water vapor and then shares that energy with the next water in the leaves of the tree, so that we can become liquid water again, which can moisten the soil and thereby allow the soil to give rise to the tree and the tree's contents. So we do not truly become the sperm or the egg. For we are essentially manifestations—we are allowing—and so we reside in the world of choice (an allowing stage) and allow this interaction between male and female to take place—so that sperm and egg can be combined.

Choice is that which allows the decision for the father and mother to produce the tree-of-life-child that is to gestate within the womb (the world of feeling and instinct) and that is ultimately to be born into the world of manifestation. And so when we ascend to the world of choice and reside there, we become part of the decision to conceive the entire multiverse, with all of the infinity of universes and all of their contents, but upon aiding in that decision, we also become those contents, themselves. We become like the particles that compose the molecules that are the water vapor that is capable of becoming the next liquid water contents of the tree-of-life-multiverse. We become part of the contents of the universes in that multiverse, projecting our essence of choice into them to be developed in potential and then actualized once again. In this way, we can become fully actualized once again, coming once again to reside in the world of choice, where we can aid in the continuing creation of the entire multiverse of potential and actual physical existence through our choice for all of this to continue to exist. In this way, we—as part of the essence of the overall world—can become capable of continuing to receive the Source's experience (of being self-aware existence that, by being self-aware, is inclined to share its experience through the creation of other self-aware existence), in its pure form, within our own experience.]

This close analysis of the sharing, receiving, and allowing stages is important because it tells us what truly occurs in each stage. When we look to how the stages manifest as personality type fixations, for example, we can now see how this plays out a bit, although we will see a slight modification from what we have here because there is actually manifestation occurring at each stage—as the personality type fixation—when usually true manifestation really only occurs in the allowing stages in some sense. (In the union of male and female, there are actual things being shared and received, but this is because the entire interaction is occurring within the world of manifestation, and so every stage has an actual manifestation.) Let's see what we mean:

In the personality type fixations, the sharing stages define new experiences for themselves and share these with others, to be manifested in those others (like the male shares sperm that is to be combined with an egg outside itself, in the female, and thereby allowed to manifest within the female as a zygote). For example, sharing thought defines, or creates (in the less-strict sense that applies to all creation within the paradigm, within the overall world), new thoughts and shares these with others and with the world (or imposes these on others and on the world), to be manifested in the world (as an imposed framework of understanding, for example). However, because this is all taking place in the world of manifestation, the sharing stages actually also receive and allow their experience to be manifested through themselves to some extent—although the greater the degree of fixation, the greater the bias toward just sharing becomes (with regard to a particular manifestation, such as, in this case, the manifestation of personality).

The receiving stages reactively receive experiences from others and from the world outside themselves so that these experiences can be manifested within themselves (like the female receives sperm and manifests the zygote of the new, distinct person within herself). For example, receiving thought reactively receives thoughts from its interactions with others and with the world and grasps at and holds onto these thoughts so that these thoughts can be manifested within itself. However, because this is all taking place in the world of manifestation, the receiving stages actually do everything from sharing to receiving to allowing their experience to be manifested through themselves to some extent—although the greater the degree of fixation, the greater the bias toward just receiving becomes (with regard to a particular manifestation, such as, in this case, the manifestation of personality).

The allowing stages allow the experiences of others and of the world outside themselves to be manifested through themselves (like the zygote that is the offspring of the male and female allows what the male has shared, in the form that the female has received it and combined it with her own experience, her own DNA, to be manifested through itself, and the zygote has no DNA of its own except that which came from the male and the female). For example, allowing thought allows the thoughts of others to be manifested through itself, in its own decisions that are made with the thoughts of others. However, because this is all taking place in the world of manifestation, the allowing stages actually do everything from sharing to receiving to allowing their experience to be manifested through themselves to some extent—although the greater the degree of fixation, the greater the bias toward just allowing (which requires dissociation from their own experience) becomes (with regard to a particular manifestation, such as, in this case, the manifestation of personality).

Gleaning a Precise Understanding of the Roles of the Stages and Our Relation to Them

What we have learned here is all very subtle, but it is important to realize some things here. The sharing stages define something new that they share—to be received by, and manifested in, another (as it is further defined by the understanding of that other, by the way it is received by that other). The receiving stages reactively receive what has been shared, as they understand it (and they understand it as having come *from* the other from which they got it, even though it actually came *through* that other and has merely been more greatly and specifically defined by that other), and they allow what they have received, in the form that they have received it and held onto it, to be manifested within themselves. And the allowing stages begin to grow in the receiving stages—like a seed beginning to grow within the earth—but they eventually grow out of the receiving stages—like a tree growing out of the earth—and they are the manifestation of what has been shared in the form that it has been reactively received and held onto.

It is holding onto things that results in fixation, so the first real fixation occurs in allowing thought—which is the *result* of the holding onto what has been received that is carried out by receiving thought. This is why when we exist in the upper worlds—in the worlds of choice, sharing thought, and receiving thought—we can do so without fixating. Prior to this, the overall world merely receives the Source's experience in the most undefined form and allows it to flow through itself in this form (in choice), and then it begins to define it into a new form—that form being thought—(in sharing thought), and then it reactively receives what has been shared (in receiving thought). At this point, the overall world's holding onto what has been received in this form as it was defined by sharing thought—as though sharing thought was the *source*, in itself, of what has been received—results in the formation of allowing thought—the first real manifestation, and the first real fixation. And this—the very beginning of the world of feeling and instinct from the top down—is as far as we can develop upward as long as we exist in the world of manifestation (although we can, within the world of manifestation, reach a point where development progresses into, or continues in, the afterlife, resulting in our transcendence to, and dwelling in, the higher worlds, in a manner similar to the way we can reach a point in our waking hours where development progresses into, or continues in, sleep, resulting in our eventually settling into just stage I and REM sleep near the end of our sleeping hours).

As long as we live in the world of manifestation, we can only receive *via* manifestations—we can only receive the Source's experience as it has been allowed to manifest in some kind of defined form. Remember, the world of manifestation is an allowing stage in the paradigm. And so everything that manifests in this world is merely the result of having allowed something else to manifest through this physical world—that something else being the Source's experience as it has been extensively defined and shaped by all of the previous stages in the paradigm. And we, as predominantly receiving agents that are inclined to hold onto what we receive in defined form, must learn that this results in fixation, and that what we must do is recognize that the defined things in this world from which we receive anything are not the *source* of what we receive from them, and so we must be like the stage of choice in simply allowing everything to flow through us in its pure form.

However, since we exist in this world, and since we therefore can only receive via *defined* manifestations, we cannot be *just* like choice (which, although it is an allowing stage, is a manifestation of the Source's experience in an *undefined* form). We must allow the Source's experience as we receive it in defined form to be manifested through us, and we must further define and shape it into what will allow us fulfillment, so that what we allow to manifest through ourselves is fulfilling to us—so that we can gain further self-aware existence from the Source through what we allow to manifest through ourselves, in our internal and external experience. Further, we must share what we have manifested, like moving from choice to sharing thought, so that it can be received by another. For only if we share what we have allowed to manifest through ourselves (and we simultaneously define and create the next thing to be received by us and allowed to manifest through us), will we be capable of continuing to receive fulfillment through what we manifest. *Not* sharing what we receive and allow to be manifested through ourselves is fixation beyond what is necessary to manifest, and so it actually results in the diminishing of our fulfillment, since we cannot receive (and allow to manifest) more things that will yield us fulfillment if we are too busy holding onto things that once yielded us fulfillment but no longer do.

So, to review what we have learned here: True creation is only accomplished by the Source. Manifestation only truly occurs in the allowing stages except as all stages can be fixated upon and caused to manifest in this world of manifestation. And we can only receive from the Source in this world *via* manifestations—via allowing thought and all that comes after it (which is all repetitive holding onto and fixating upon what came before). By the way, this is part of why we can talk of thoughts, feelings, and instincts and perceive each of these things as being singular things—for they only truly manifest in the allowing stages, and so the way we experience them can be (to some extent) attributed simply to the allowing forms of each one (to the way that the sharing and receiving stages have been combined and allowed to manifest in the allowing stage of each one).

The Meaning of Upward Manifestation

Another thing that requires more precise defining is what we mean by the idea that all things manifest upward. Everything is created, or develops in potential form, downward—from choice, to sharing thought, to receiving thought, to allowing thought, to sharing feeling, to receiving feeling, to allowing feeling, to sharing instinct, to receiving instinct, to allowing instinct, to manifestation. When we say that everything then manifests, or actualizes, upward—in the reverse direction of creation—what we really mean is that awareness of what was created expands from the bottom up—that what is more strictly and closely defined in later stages of creation comes into the light of awareness before what is more subtly and openly defined in earlier stages of creation. So, the most definitely and strictly defined manifestation comes into the light of awareness first, and then the slightly less definitely defined allowing instinct comes into the light of awareness, and so on.

Generally, we are aware of the existence, or manifestation, of the world, first. Then we become aware of movement and inclination (including in its corrupted form as desire) within the world and others and other "I"'s and within ourselves. Then we become aware of feeling within others and within other "I"'s and within ourselves. Then we become aware of thought within other "I"'s and within ourselves. And then we become aware of our capacity to choose all of these things—and we become aware *that* we are choosing all of these things, always.

When we see in the brain that the neurons in lower, more instinctual parts of the brain fire first, and the neurons in higher thought parts of the brain only fire later—and, in actuality, last—we are merely seeing the order of our becoming aware of what is going on. In fact, we are always choosing our actions and what we manifest in our experience (along with everything else that comes before these)—even when we only become aware that we are simply acting, or that we are inclined to act; it is merely that, in the case that we only become aware of our action as it is occurring, we have not extended our awareness to contain what came before our action (and so our action, in this case, is reactive, rather than conscious and willful). Remember, the brain merely represents an allowing stage relative to everything else, because the highest we get in the world of feeling and instinct, in which we reside, is allowing thought and, in the case of the brain, more precisely because this is a physical manifestation in the physical world that is merely allowing what develops in the world of feeling and instinct and above to be manifested through it in our physical bodies (making the brain the link between our bodies in potential form—or our souls—in the world of feeling and instinct and the upper worlds, and our bodies in actual form in the world of manifestation, and making the brain the point of the beginning of the manifestation, or actualization, in the body and in the world, of what is above, in the soul, in potential form).

Everything is created downward, but the world of manifestation actualizes its awareness of each of these stages in the reverse order from the order in which they are being created—climbing the ladder, which is descending from above, from the bottom up. We are always creating by choosing what we think, which causes what we feel, which causes what we are inclined to say and do, which guides us in what we actually say and do, which causes what manifests in the physical world. And we are, in this way, a link between the higher worlds and this one—but so is everything else in this world, for everything is creating in this order. The only difference between us and other things in this world is that we are capable of being aware of the true order of creation all the way from the top down and of making use of this—taking control of our lives and our experience by willfully and consciously choosing the language that we use to define our world.

But we choose always. The entire world does. And it is merely that awareness of what has been created and defined builds gradually—from the most definitive and obvious outward manifestation upward to the pretty concrete inclination that likely would have led to that manifestation, but that could have led to another one, to the somewhat less concrete feeling that could have led to that manifestation but probably could have led to other manifestations as well, to the sort of concretized but still abstract thought that really could have led to quite a lot of different manifestations depending on how it was further defined, to the completely undefined choice that could have led to any manifestation at all. Like the entire universe was created, and is continually being created, in its full potential before it even came, and comes, into being, we are full human beings, created in our full potential before we were born, and our lives are merely the development of awareness of that full potential—the potential for the capacity to choose, with self-awareness, how we define our lives and our world.

Actualizing Our Essence

When we learn to actualize our essence, we learn that this is how all of time progresses—through the actualization of the world's essence. For when distinct choices are made, paths are chosen and other paths are eliminated from our awareness as we choose to bring all of our awareness fully to one, single, distinct path at a time—one choice amongst all of the possibilities. The wavefunction of possibilities collapses and one choice is made, completing the strictly precise and limiting definition of the Source's experience as it is to appear to us in the moment that becomes the present—in all of its various forms that we give to it. And with this focused attention—this laser beam of awareness—we actually are choosing how we are defining our experience. Our choice lies in the ability to cultivate that focus, to narrow the light of our awareness to a single, focused beam, and to direct that beam in order to illuminate, with it, the language that we wish to use to define our experience for the next moment. It is in this way that we choose the definitions that shall be captured upon the holographic plate through which the Source shall shine Its experience to produce the next moment. For this is how every holographic plate is formed and used to produce a hologram.

First, you shine a laser beam through a beam splitter (choice) to form two beams (sharing thought and receiving thought) from that single beam, and then one of these beams (receiving thought) is shined through a lens (the rest of the stages of the tree of life) so that it is caused to diffuse (into the world of feeling and instinct) and shine upon some object or objects (in the world of manifestation). This scattered beam reflects off of this object and onto a holographic plate, where it combines with the other part of the original split beam that has also been shined through a diffusing lens (allowing thought). [For sharing thought does not merely share with receiving thought; sharing thought also shares with allowing thought (like every sharing stage shares with the receiving stage and, in a way, directly with the allowing stage just after it as well, although sort of via the receiving stage), for allowing thought is the result of the interaction of both sharing thought and receiving thought. As we see in the tree setup, the sunlight—sharing thought—is providing the original energy that brings the water into vapor that can condense out of being vapor—out of choice—to descend back into the ground—into receiving thought—and up the tree. Here, we see that sharing thought shares with receiving thought in this way. But the sunlight is also providing the energy that draws the water up the tree—the energy that guides the world in its development. Here, we see that sharing thought seems almost to bypass receiving thought to share with allowing thought and the stages beyond. It does this in order to convey the Source's experience to allowing thought and the rest of the world of feeling and instinct in a truer form—in the form of self-aware choice, of water vapor—prior to its being received by receiving thought and held onto in its defined form (with the definition or limit given to it by sharing thought) and thereby corrupted and altered from its intended content. We might better understand this by looking to the interaction of the male and the female to produce a child. The male shares his DNA with the female, but as he does this, he is also, in a way, directly sharing his DNA with the child that is produced in the female when this DNA is combined with the female's DNA, and the child, thereby, actually receives the male's unaltered DNA as part of its own DNA—its own DNA becoming a true combination of the male's DNA and the female's DNA.] The result is a holographic plate (the world of feeling and instinct—the tree in the tree setup, and the combined DNA of male and female in the zygote) that captures the interference pattern, or the interaction, of our manifestation in this world—the language that we use to define and share our experience—and the Source's experience that is projected down into this world—the language that the Source uses to define and share Its experience. Then, a light is shined through the completed holographic plate (the Source shines self-aware existence through the holographic plate that has been completed prior to manifestation), and a holographic image (the next moment of experience in the world of manifestation) is formed—a projected reflection of the interaction of the Source's experience and our experience of it.

We must remember that even the first object upon which one laser beam shines is merely a hologram in this case of reality. So, essentially, the Source's experience (the original laser beam) is shined through choice (the beam splitter) and is thereby divided into sharing thought and receiving thought (two beams). From there, receiving thought (one of the beams) shines through the world of feeling and instinct (which serves as both the diffusing lens and the holographic plate), which defines and divides the Source's experience to produce the world of manifestation (the hologram). And the present moment in the world of manifestation (the hologram) becomes the object of which the next holographic plate (the next moment in the world of feeling and instinct) becomes a picture, making each moment of time a projected reflection of the previous one. And as we choose to direct the awareness of our thoughts and feelings and instincts and actions toward one thing or another, we thereby shape the holographic plate that is to be used for the next moment, through which the Source's experience is to shine to produce the defined contents of our experience. The universe is, thus, an interference pattern that is formed by waves that are produced by, and emanate from, a single, ultimate Source, when these waves of self-aware existence pass through the holographic plate of our thoughts, and feelings, and instincts, speech and actions.

We might think of the world of feeling and instinct (the tree in the tree setup; the zygote, with its complete DNA, which becomes an embryo and then a fetus) alternatively as a prism that divides the white light of sharing thought ultimately into the many different colors of this world's thoughts and feelings and instincts and all of the other aspects and manifestations of the paradigm, which shine as a multiple-colored, and thereby multiply-defined, rainbow into the world of manifestation.

Perhaps most beautiful of all, the formation and utilization of a holographic plate (with choice as beam splitter, thought worlds as split laser beam, world of feeling and instinct as holographic plate, and world of manifestation as object and hologram) and the use of a prism in refracting and dispersing, and thereby dividing and thus defining, white light (with thought worlds as white light, world of feeling and instinct as prism, and world of manifestation as rainbow), are not mere metaphors, for they are both manifestations, and thus reflections, of the reality—of the way by which the stages of the paradigm relate to one another as the Source relates, via them, with this world in which we reside. And, with the language we use to define and shape and share our lives and this world, we shape the way the holographic plate diffracts, and determine the way the prism refracts, the Source's experience, thereby giving form to the pure illumination that is the Source's experience as it manifests in this universe in each next moment. And when we take in the world through our senses, we are perceiving nothing but the Source's experience, merely in the divided and diffracted and refracted and dispersed form it takes within this world. We live in a world illuminated by self-aware existence, and the language of each stage of the paradigm serves to give it some more-specifically-defined and multiplicitous form, dividing up and shaping the original unified purity—a purity that is greater even than that of the laser light or the white light of sharing thought, for here, the laser, the light source, is the Source, Itself.

Knowing and Understanding

One *cannot* know everything—in all of its specifics and details—but, due to the holographic, or self-reflective, nature of the world, one *can* understand everything—in its general nature and relationship to everything else. All one needs to do is attain an understanding of the basic paradigm—with each of its stages—in one of its innumerable manifested forms (preferably a form in which the entire paradigm, including its upper stages near choice, is manifested), and then a mere bit of information about some other of its manifested forms (which includes any and every aspect of reality) will yield one all that is required to understand this other realm—for this other realm is just another reflection of the same basic paradigm, with the same basic stages and relationships among these stages, and so all one needs to do is find the analogues between the aspects of this new manifestation and those of the manifestation with which one is familiar.

Thus, through understanding anything—from the development of the universe, to the development of a year, to the development of a day, to the evolution of life, to a single sufficiently complex organism's body, to the personalities of human beings, to the inner workings of oneself—to a sufficient degree so that one becomes aware of the nature and relationship of its parts, one can understand everything to quite a large extent. Of course, even our efforts to understand are thoughts, and these thoughts are creative, giving rise to new manifestations of the paradigm in themselves, so that our efforts to understand produce the very complexity of the world—a complexity that arises from increasing varieties of manifestations of the same paradigm, and from increasing manifestations within manifestations within manifestations, and manifestations containing manifestations containing manifestations, of the same paradigm—that we describe and then consequently observe as existing. Wherever we look, we will find more manifestations of the paradigm, and the sheer number and variety of manifestations—all of the details that arise and that might be known—can be overwhelming, but it must be remembered that the paradigm of it all is the same. We can take comfort in this, and we can find understanding in this.

Once we become sufficiently experientially familiar with some manifestation of the tree of life paradigm, we have an experience to which to relate all manifestations of the paradigm, and so then, when things are true, they resonate with us as being true. Because then we have something within our own experience to which to attach the words and descriptions and other definitions of objects and ideas, and so we have a way to judge the truth or accuracy of something with which we are presented—for we can see whether this fits with our previous experience, which was of some other manifestation of the same basic paradigm. We can, in this way, have an understanding of all things.

Ultimately, everything within this overall world is a manifestation of the same basic paradigm in some way, to some degree or other of fixation and, thus, to some degree or other of warping and corruption in the way that it reflects the true forms of the stages and their relations to one another. And so everything in this world is true to some extent by this definition—true in that it expresses the basic paradigm of all reality, of the relationship between the Source and the world—for nothing can exist within this world that does not express this paradigm.

However, the more we hold onto things—the more fixated we are on a single aspect of a single stage in the paradigm, on the way the Source's experience is defined in that stage—the more corrupted from the true nature of the entire paradigm-relation (between the Source and the world) our manifestations become—the more corrupted our experience (in our thought, feeling, instinct and speech and action, and external experience in our body and in the physical world) becomes. The result is that the more fixated we are on any particular definition of any particular stage in any one of that stage's manifestations (including, especially, in the manifestation of our main stage type, although any fixation will extend to this and to everything else in its corrupting effects), the more corrupted from the Source's experience in its true form our own experience becomes. And so the further from the truth our thought-patterns—our beliefs about the world—become.

But when we are not very fixated and we are more self-aware, we can begin to listen and hear as our intuition guides us toward truth—toward an accurate understanding and expression of the tree-of-life-paradigm-relation between us and the Source, via each other and everything else in this world. And our reflection upon the world—our comparing present experiences with past ones, and comparing each of these with ones that might come about—guides us toward the kind of understanding that leads to self-awareness, which leads ultimately to more understanding, which leads to more self-awareness, and so on.

Knowing everything entails knowing all of the ever-increasing number of manifestations in all of their ever-widening diversity of defined forms, and this is beyond our ability. But *understanding* everything merely entails understanding the basic paradigm of the nature and relationship of things that is repeated everywhere—of which everything is a manifestation. And this we can do. And, in fact, it is only by doing this that we can truly attain self-awareness and thereby fulfill our purpose in life and in existence—because only once we learn the language of creation can we learn to receive, in a true and accurate form, the experience that the Source is actually intending to be sharing with us.

In order to learn anything, we must begin somewhere and be present there. Then, after we've progressed somewhat, we must look back to where we came from in order to view it in the new context of where it got us (where we are). Then we must look and progress forward. And then we must begin again—looking at where we are, looking at how we got here, looking at where we're going. In every moment, and in every portion of our lives, and in our entire lives, and in whole sections of history, and in the entire universe, this path must be repeated, must be manifested again, in order for progression to occur—this path that is represented by the tree of life paradigm, from present to past to future. This is how all learning takes place; this is the nature of self-reflection. All learning and, ultimately, all true understanding, comes not just from the final manifestation of a process, but from the entire process of manifestation—from all of the manifestations that led to that final manifestation. And this is why the universe is as it is, and this is why our lives are as they are, and this is why this book is as it is—starting somewhere and progressing from there, looking back at where we were in the context of where we are, and then looking and progressing forward with this new understanding in order to develop further, manifesting the same paradigm over and over again, in numerous forms (with each one slightly different from the last), approaching an increasingly accurate understanding of its true nature with each new manifestation.

Without seeing the process of development—without going through it—one cannot truly understand or be intimately aware of anything. All reception in this world occurs through a process of manifestation that begins at (physical) experience, goes through reflection upon that experience and then figuring out from that reflection, and then, ultimately, comes to an understanding of that experience—and an understanding that can be applied to more general experience in the form of awareness. The term "experiential understanding" can therefore be used to refer to the whole process of manifestation—from experience to understanding—and self-awareness is merely *applied* experiential understanding. And this is why the world is as it is and why this book is as it is—manifesting gradually, in the form of a process, to reach and attain the true understanding that leads to awareness.

And so here we have another pattern contained in the paradigm—other aspects of the stages (aspects that have been touched upon in earlier sections). In manifesting from bottom up, we go from physically experiencing (corresponding with the instinctual stages), to self-reflecting (corresponding with the feeling stages), to figuring out and then understanding (corresponding with the thought stages), and then ultimately to the application of understanding in the form of self-aware choice (corresponding with choice) and creation from the top down.

We can see this pattern quite clearly played out in any overall day or, rather, night, within the physical universe—in any complete manifestation from bottom up. If we consider a usual day of sleep and wake in the order of manifestation (the order in which the night of manifestation inside the tree comes first and is followed by the day of creation outside the tree), we have wake, followed by sleep, or daylight in which we physically experience (as we hover around manifestation and the instinct stages at the beginning of wake), followed by nighttime, where we begin to reflect upon all of the stages in our recent experience of the past period of wake, transitioning into sleep with repetitive reflection upon all of the stages and eventually tending toward figuring out and real understanding as we progress to the end of sleep (where we tend toward stage 1 sleep—thought—and REM sleep—self-aware choice), and then we exercise choice in creating the next day from top down and waking up and beginning the pattern of manifestation from bottom up once again. If we consider a lifetime in the order of manifestation, we have the night of physical life, where we physically experience (hovering around manifestation and the instinct stages) and begin to self-reflect, repeating the entire paradigm over and over, followed by the day that is the afterlife, where we continue the self-reflective repetition of the entire paradigm until we eventually begin to figure out and understand (tending toward just the thought stages and self-aware choice), at which point we apply that understanding in the form of the self-aware exercise of choice in creating a new physical life from top down to manifestation, where we then manifest from bottom up once again.

This pattern is evident, also, in the development of the experience of an individual human being. We each begin life, in our young childhood, by merely experiencing what is going on in the present—for everything is new, and so we do not yet have any understanding of it or ourselves or our relation to it. And as we experience the present, we seek to find the boundaries of ourselves; we seek to find how far we—our influence—extends into the world around us. Then, in adolescence, we begin to reflect upon our past experience, repeating over and over again what has happened in our interactions— between us and everyone and everything else in the world—in an effort to figure out who we are and how we relate to others. And then, in young adulthood, we begin to figure out things about ourselves and others and life from our reflection upon our experience. We begin to figure out how different "I"'s differ and how they are similar and how we relate to particular other "I"'s, including our past and future selves and other people and other aspects of the world. And we thus begin to figure out how our choices—concerning how we use the language of our thought, feeling, instinct, speech, and action—manifest differently with regard to different situations and different people and so on. We therefore begin to figure out—based on our reflection upon our past experience—how to make decisions that will have consequences that are in line with our goals, consequences that we want to bring about. And we come to some understanding of ourselves and of others and of our relation to everything in the world around us that can be brought to our future experience in the form of greater awareness.

The purpose of all that exists within the world is to manifest and receive experiential understanding in order to share it (for this is the bottom-up order of the manifestation of the stages)—in order to apply it in the form of self-awareness, thereby creating the potential for further reception of experiential understanding from the Source.

[Notice that we, as manifesting beings who are part of this manifesting world, but who also have the capacity to create with self-awareness, are at a crossroads. As manifestations of the world, we require that things manifest before we can receive them and then share them, like all other beings in this physical world. But as projections of the Source, we also have the capacity to create willfully and with self-awareness, creating things first, then receiving them in our experience, and then manifesting them through ourselves (at which point we can physically receive, and then share, them). And so, from our origins in the upwardly manifesting world, we are capable of reaching a point where we can bring awareness and conscious choice to the downward creative process that defines the world that manifests.]

If we linger upon any of the stages of development in the tree of life paradigm, fixating upon them and failing to progress forward at all to the next stage, then we will not achieve the ultimate aim, which is to actualize self-awareness. We can see clear examples of this in the pattern of development from experiencing to self-reflecting to figuring out and understanding. If we just experience, but do not move on to reflect upon this experience, then we will learn nothing to bring to our next experience. If we get to self-reflection but then remain there, we will stagnate, for we will linger on the past without ever experiencing anything anew or learning from our reflection, and our past experience will become warped in our reflection. If we get to figuring out but then fixate there, our figuring out will become detached from the actuality of experience, for it will cease to be based on the experience of, and reflection upon, our true relation to everything in the world around us. In all of these cases, we will fail to achieve any real understanding (of our true nature and of our relation to everything, including the Source of everything) that can be brought to our next experience in the form of greater self-awareness; we will fail to achieve the development and continuation of self-awareness—the true goal and purpose of our existence. And so we must progress through all of the stages, upward toward self-aware choice.

As we become intimately familiar with, and understanding of, each of the stages of the tree of life paradigm in this experientially repetitive and self-reflective way, we can come to connect intensely with anyone or anything, relating on everything, for we can come to find the analogue and the equivalent (and can differentiate between these if need be—as due to differences in fixation and so on) of the experience of that other "I" within our own experience. In this way, we can come to be capable of intimately and intensely connecting with the

Source, for we will have the experiential understanding of our relationship to the Source that is required to be brought to our experience in the form of self-awareness (an application that, in itself, requires to be practiced and learned) in order to allow the Source to create Its experience through us, in our own experience—in order to fulfill the purpose for which the Source created the world.

Communication

Successful Communication

We can learn quite a lot about how we communicate with the Source "I" from how we communicate with other "I"'s, and we can, likewise, learn quite a lot about how we communicate with other "I"'s from how we communicate with the Source "I". Communication cannot occur without a common ground of experience that can be communicated. So, in the example that we have previously seen, you cannot simply communicate information about the internet to a caveman successfully, such that you share the information and he receives the information in the form that you shared it. But there is another barrier to this communication as well: a lack of common language.

We shall, therefore, refer to "successful communication" or, more simply, "communication" to mean that: a) something is shared, and b) what is shared is received in the form in which it was shared. And now we can state that two things are required for communication to occur: a) a common ground of experience, and b) a common language (or means of referring to that experience).

If you wish to successfully communicate something to someone, you need to speak in a language that this person understands, and you need to refer, with this language, to an experience that you and that other person have in common. So, if you want to communicate something to someone, you can use some form of spoken language, such as English or Spanish or Russian, or some form of physical-action type of language, such as pointing or gesturing or mimicking or smiling or frowning. But, in order for communication to be successful, whatever language you use needs to be one that is understood by the other person. So you cannot use English to communicate something to someone who does not understand English, for whatever you share in this case will not be received in the form in which it is shared—your intended meaning (the experience you are trying to convey) will not be received, because the person will not understand the references of your words and combinations of words. So that is for the language. Now, for the meaning, or experience, to which you refer.

If you wish to convey your experience of a snowstorm to someone who has never experienced snow, you cannot simply say you were caught in a snowstorm and expect anything like what you have shared to have been received. You need to refer to things a person actually *has* experienced (and so you need to consider your audience and adapt your communication to this audience in terms of the experiences to which you refer as well as in terms of the language that you use to refer to these experiences and the way that you use this language to refer to these experiences), and the person will hopefully (using thought) be able to take different aspects of different experiences of his own and piece them together to form something somewhat like what you are referring to. So, you might want to refer to a rainstorm in which he was caught in his car last year and his experiences at the beach on a windy day and say that it was a bit like when he was caught in the rainstorm in that you were also caught in your car and were unable to get anywhere and the sky was dark with clouds and it was terrifying because you thought that you wouldn't survive, except that, instead of being in a sort of river of water, it was a little like driving along a beach on a windy day, except much more windy, and the sand was completely white and freezing cold. Anyway, you get the idea.

And you can realize here that it would be a lot easier to communicate your experience of being caught in a snowstorm if the other person had actually experienced snow, and even easier if the other person had actually been caught in a snowstorm before, and even easier if the other person had been caught in this same snowstorm, and even easier still if the other person had been in the car with you when you were trapped in the snowstorm. And, even then, that other person is not *you*, with your exact spatial location, and therefore your exact *external* experience, and with your *internal* experience.

The more closely in common your experience and another's experience is, the easier it is to communicate this experience. And so the easiest person to communicate something to would be yourself, except that then there would be no actual communication—no sharing and receiving—going on, unless, perhaps, you are communicating something to your future self—writing a letter to him or her, maybe—in which case your present self would be sharing an experience that your future self would be capable of receiving due to the common language and common experience (so long as he or she remembers the language and the experience).

However, the truest and most fulfilling communication does not occur between two people with the exact same experience (although no two people have *exactly* the same experience). If you want to tell someone about your experience in a snowstorm, it will likely be more enjoyable to tell someone who wasn't in the same car with you, unless you are actually talking about your very specific experience, where your experience differed from that of that other person. The fulfillment in communication comes from conveying to another person an experience that you have, or have had, that the other person does *not* have, or has *not* had. To be more precise, there isn't really communication occurring if the other person already has the exact same thing that you are giving, because then there isn't anything truly being received, since it has already been received. You can tell someone about an experience a second time, but if you refer to it in exactly the same way with exactly the same words and with no new information or context, you are bordering on no communication actually occurring.

Although it is rare (if it ever can happen at all within this world) that the number of same things can be in place for it to be the case that no communication occurs due to the exact same thing being communicated, for there will always at least be the different context of a different time in which the communication is occurring, if nothing else, and the different context will change what is being communicated, allowing for communication actually to occur. So, if someone says, "I'm hungry," for example, we might say that this means something different from when the same person said, "I'm hungry," yesterday—because the intended meaning is time-specific in the sense that the person could have been hungry then and now, but *now* he is likely intending to convey that he wants food *now*, while *then* he was likely intending to convey that he wanted food *then*.

The Pattern of the Development of Attraction

It is interesting to note something here regarding the kind of communication that occurs, or rather that becomes necessary, at the thought stages of development.

In the instinctual stages, existing and acting things cling to existence and to like-action (as with the inertial motions dictated by gravity in the orbits of bodies, and with the persistence of living creatures in finding food and such). In the feeling stages, things cling to like-things (as with the gravitational attraction of bodies to one another, and with the grouping of living creatures into packs and herds and flocks and so forth). But in the thought stages, things are actually attracted to *unlike*-things (as with the electromagnetic attraction between things that have a negative charge and things that have a positive charge, and with the attraction between male and female). Thus, when it comes to thought-stage-related intimate interactions, we are often drawn toward people with whom, and things with which, we would likely *not* group together (due to our difference from them in structure, form, personality, interests, and so forth).

When it comes to intimate relationships, we are usually most inclined—at first—to be attracted to people who are very different from us in various ways. We might be attracted to other members of the same species, but often to other members who are as different as can be within this species—who are the opposite of us in many respects. Ultimately, this provides benefits evolutionarily in that we are more likely to produce offspring with varied genes, making those offspring better able to adapt and survive in a changing environment, and this also provides benefits in accordance with the overall purpose of existence in general, for it is through our interactions with a truly *other*, *distinctly different* "I" that we might best come to understand ourselves and our relationship to others and ultimately to the Source.

However, when we give into this inclination to connect with an other "I" that is very different from us in its fixations, we are faced with a situation resembling that of the Source and the world at first, when the world is so different from the Source in only receiving and not sharing (while the Source is only sharing and not receiving) that it cannot receive the experience that the Source is sharing in its true form (even as it *wants* or *desires* it the *most* at this point, due to its complete *emptiness* or *lack* of it, similar to the case of our fixated attraction toward other members of our species who are extremely different from us even as they are, in some significant ways, like us—in the capacity for compatibility such that union with them will potentially result in the creation of new experiences and even new *ways* of experiencing).

(Notice that here in this beginning form of our attraction to other "I"'s, we are attracted to the *experience* of existence—when it comes to the Source—for we do not have existence inherently, and we seek it, but it doesn't really matter to us from where it comes, for it is the *experience* and *not* the *Source* of it that we want and seek. And it is, likewise, the *experience*—the thoughts, feelings, and instincts—involved in our attraction to another person who is very unlike us—who has what we lack—that we want and toward which we are drawn, rather than the *person*, himself or herself.)

And so learning to communicate well in such a relationship is highly important, because otherwise there will be a pronounced absence of understanding of the (very different) other "I" in the relationship. Understanding of the other "I" is more likely to arise and remain a continuously present facilitator of interactions when we intimately connect with an other "I" that is *like* us in various ways (in some basic interests and ideals, in certain aspects of personality—e.g., degree of willingness to look beyond the surface of things and abstract from past and present experience vs. desire to stick with the experience of the senses and that experience as it is retained in memory, primary inclination of fixation, degree of extraversion vs. introversion, etc.—and so forth).

The goal of existence is to become more like the Source in our experience, and so learning to intimately connect with an other "I" that is more like we are (in certain ways—someone with whom we can experience the kind of intimate and intense union that *not just potentially* but *actually* results in the *willful* creation of new experiences and even new *ways* of experiencing) is actually the next step of development. (Notice that here in this more-developed form of our attraction to other "I"'s, we are attracted to the *Source*, Itself, and not just to the *experience* of existence, and we are, likewise, attracted to the other *person*, himself or herself, rather than merely to the *experience* that we get from him or her. We come to recognize the other "I" not just as an other "I" that is different from us in its experience and that therefore might fulfill our own desires by providing us with what we lack and in some way completing us, but as an other "I" that is truly separate and distinct from us in its fixations and that has its own desires that we should work to fulfill in conjunction with our striving toward our own fulfillment.)

For, moving upward, we pass through allowing thought, from which the electromagnetic, *opposites-attracting* phenomenon stems. But then, after we pass through receiving thought (from which the weak-nuclear-force *breakdown* of atomic nuclei and of other particles, and ultimately of our attraction to other "I"s that are completely unlike us, stems), we reach sharing thought (from which the strong-nuclear-force *attraction* of *like*-charged protons in atomic nuclei stems), where we are most like the Source in creating the world, and where we come to be attracted toward other "I"s to which we can relate in various ways (revealing again the breakdown of distinctions between male and female elements—sharing and receiving elements—in the relationship between these, as we near the end of development, due to the attraction of "I"s to more-similar other "I"s), as we have come to be attracted and drawn toward the Source, to which we can, at this point, relate in various ways.

(Notice, by the way, that we have, here, revealed the reason that our three-stage breakdown of patterns often seems somehow to have a sort of fourth stage. The third stage—in the order of manifestation—always corresponds to the thought stages. But, more specifically, it truly only corresponds with allowing thought—the only one of the thought stages that is part of the world of feeling and instinct. And so in a careful breakdown, we will find ourselves with three truly fixated stages, with the third stage sort of extending into a related, although self-aware and therefore *unfixated*, version of it—a sort of fourth stage that seems to grow out of, or to be a part of, the third stage.

Thus, for example, we see that in the pattern of allowing, receiving, and then sharing, the third stage—sharing—can certainly be a fixation, as in various aspects of personality, although it is also the path toward a self-aware, unfixated state of being, whereby we can make ourselves capable of receiving the Source's experience in its true form. And we can see that in the pattern of preserving, belonging, and connecting, the third stage—connecting—can certainly be a fixation, as in the inclinations of fixation, although it is also the path toward true, self-aware connection with the Source through all things in this world. And we can see that in the pattern of "I", others, other "I"'s, the third stage—recognition of other "I"'s—can be a fixation, as when we become caught up in making decisions that are the best for ourselves and other "I"'s or when we seek overly to analyze those other "I"'s, all in search of our own fulfillment, but it is only through the recognition of the existence of other "I"'s that we can ultimately come truly to recognize the existence of the Source "I". And we can see that in the pattern of instinct, feeling, thought, the third stage—thought—can be a fixation, as in the main stage personality identification with it, but it is only through thought that we can come to understand our true relation to other "I"'s and, thereby, our true relation to the Source "I".)

We might better understand this development—from attraction between like-things in the instinctual and feeling stages, to attraction between unlike-things in allowing thought, and ultimately to attraction between like-things in sharing thought—by considering another manifestation of it. First, we define and attract to ourselves—with our thoughts, feelings, instincts and speech and actions—things that are (in a stagnant and unchanging way) like what we have already defined and attracted to ourselves, because we are stuck in inertial, habitual, reactive patterns, recreating and magnifying our current experience. Then, we define and attract to ourselves things that are *un*like what we have already defined and attracted to ourselves (as we increase awareness and break out of inertial, habitual, reactive patterns). And then, after we change all of our negative patterns into positive ones, we reach a point of the breakdown of attracting unlike things, because we come to define and attract to ourselves things that are (in certain ways—in a sort of continuously developing way) like what we have already defined and attracted to ourselves (as we continue to further ourselves consistently along the path toward ever-greater self-awareness and willful shaping of our lives and, thereby, toward ever-greater fulfillment).

Comparing and Contrasting Communication between "I"'s within this World and that between Us and the Source

In the case of communication between two "I"'s within this world, the experience to which the "I" refers and the language that the "I" uses to refer to it are basically always separate things that can *easily* be separated or paired up, due to the fact that no "I"'s experience is exactly the same as any other "I"'s experience. If we use a description in language to refer to an experience, for example, we are not giving someone the experience, but are merely referring to something that is within our own experience in order for this person to relate this to his own experience in order to gain some understanding of what our experience is like. However, in the case of communication between the Source "I" and this world (including us), the experience to which we refer (and that to which the Source refers) and the language that we use (and that It uses) to refer to that experience are *inseparable.* The language *is* the experience, in a way, *at least as far as the perspective of the fact that they always coincide with one another is concerned.* The thoughts and feelings and instincts and external experience in the physical world are all part of the language that the Source is using, via the world, to convey Its experience to us, but they are also all part of the experience, itself, for us, and they are all part of the language that we use to convey to the Source what we want more of in our experience, even as they are also our experience, itself.

The situation with communication between the Source and us is a bit like telling someone what it is like to be hugged by hugging the person. And, of course there will be tremendous variation in this experience, so that your specific experience of being hugged by one or another person will not be the same as the experience that this person has when you hug him or her. In the case of the Source communicating Its experience to this world, the experience is also specific to every individual "I" within this world, for the experience is defined differently, with different language, in every case.

If you wanted to communicate to someone who has always been blind what it is like to be able to see, the most effective way to do this (if it were possible) would be to give him the ability to see. Essentially, this is what the Source does with the world. It is inclined to share Its experience with another, for this is part of what Its experience *is,* and even after It creates the world, the world does not have self-awareness (like not having sight), and so, in order to share Its experience of being self-aware existence that is capable of sharing its experience with another—and, thereby, of creating the world—through the use of language, It gives the world the ability to be self-aware (the ability to see), so that the world can experience for itself what this is like. And when we, as "I"'s within the world, come to experience this to the fullest extent that we can possibly receive it ultimately (reaching the world of choice), the Source has effectively communicated Its experience to another "I" that is not Itself to the greatest extent that It possibly can without that other "I" *being* Itself.

So the experience (of an "I" within the world) is different from the Source's experience even at the completion of the communication of Its experience, a bit like giving a blind man the ability to see in order to show him what it is like to be able to see does not give that blind man the experience of what it is like for *you* to see, but merely gives him the ability to see and the experience of what it is like for *him* to see.

And then, when we reach this fullest extent of experience in the world of choice, we cease to receive what the Source is conveying, for communication has already been successful, and the experience is flowing through us, but there is no language to define it for us, and we cease to receive the experience as it is. And then we get caught up in some language definition of the experience in receiving thought (as this definition is formed in sharing thought), and we have to learn the language all over again, and gain experience through this language (that of choice, thought, feeling, instinct, and physical manifestation) all over again.

It should be recognized that the language that the Source uses to communicate with the world is not actually the experience that the Source is conveying (even though the language and the experience, in this case, are inseparable in that we cannot receive the experience without the language). This conflation is what leads receiving thought astray in the first place, for it comes to believe that the definition of what it receives is the intended meaning (or is what it is actually receiving), itself. And this conflation is what we engage in when we believe that we get fulfillment from our thoughts or our feelings or our instincts or the physical things that we have, in themselves.

The truth is that these are merely the packaging, in a way. We cannot receive the Source's experience without them—we cannot receive the Source's experience in any way except *via* them (and, in this way, the language that the Source is using via the world *is* the experience for us, for we know the experience in no other way)—but they, themselves, are *not* the Source's experience. They are merely defined forms of the Source's experience—the means of conveyance of the Source's experience that allow us to receive it.

This situation is akin to saying that sunshine is being shared with us by the sun, and that this—the sunshine in the forms in which we experience it—is the sun's experience that it is conveying. When we receive the sunshine from the sun, our experience of the sunshine—what we gain from it—is different from the sunshine, itself. The language here might be a stream of photons that are also acting as electromagnetic waves, but this is not our experience of it. Our experience of it—what we gain from it—may be warmth and light and whatever else, but this is not quite how it is being conveyed to us, for this is merely our *experience* of what is being conveyed to us. Only in our experience of it is the sunshine warm (as perceived via our skin) and light (as perceived via our eyes). The sunshine is, in itself, not inherently warm or light. And yet we might refer to the sunshine, loosely, as being both the means of conveying the experience and the experience that is conveyed, for we know the experience in no other way.

Also, realize that we are never actually communicating with the Source, per se, for our language merely modifies the way that we receive the Source's experience, somewhat like we are never actually communicating with the sun, for we merely alter how we receive what it is sharing and we do not affect the sun, itself. We can shape the light of existence into any form, but we are not affecting the Source of existence when we do this. The Source merely shares; It does not receive. When we share, we share merely with other parts of the world, and not with the Source. The Source is unaffected by us, but we are affected by It via what It shares, and we can alter how we are affected by It like we can alter how we are affected by the sun—by moving in relation to It (as the earth moves in relation to the sun and thereby gives us day and night and the seasons), by defining what we receive from It differently, mediating this differently (as we can mediate sunlight through a colored window, or through plants that we use for food or shelter or clothing, or whatever).

In the case of communication between the Source and the world, the Source has to teach the world the language by which It is communicating Its experience so that the intended meaning of what It is sharing will be received by the world. If a person does not already know the language that you are using, then in order to actually communicate something to him, you first need to teach him the language, otherwise what you intend to be sharing will not be received. So, basically, the Source really has to begin with us from the very beginning, as though we were just born.

Except when we teach a child something, and we use language and experience, we don't have to do everything ourselves, because the world provides the child with experience, to which we can attach words and so on, and as the experience builds and becomes more complex, we add more words—more language—to refer to it. But the Source has to create everything from scratch—via the world that It creates—by speaking Its experience to the world, sharing with us both the language and the experience together, even as these are separate in the sense that the language is merely the means of conveyance of the experience of being self-aware existence. And so the Source shares Its experience with us, teaching us the language by which It is sharing Its experience *via* our experience along the way. As we receive the experience that the Source is communicating, we learn the language by which It is communicating this experience, and as we learn the language, we more fully and more accurately receive the experience.

The aim and means in teaching a child and the aim and means in the Source's teaching us are reversed. When we raise a child, we have the goal of teaching the child language and, through the child's experience, this is accomplished. But as the Source raises us, It has the goal of sharing Its experience with us and, through language, this is accomplished.

When we teach a child language, the hard part is getting the child to associate the words with what they are referring to, because the language seems obviously separate and different from what it describes. The word "bread" doesn't have any obvious relation to bread, for example; it is not made of flour and yeast and water, and you can't eat it or gain physical sustenance from eating it, and so on, so why are we saying it has a relation to bread?

When it comes to the Source teaching us the language of creation, we encounter the reverse problem, for the hard part is getting us to understand that the language and the experience being shared are *separate* things. Try telling someone that bread is merely the form through which the sustenance you seem to receive from it is being given to you, and that the bread, itself, is not giving you sustenance. Or try getting someone to understand that his or her happiness does not come from the new car, or the girlfriend or boyfriend, or even the rush of dopamine in the pleasure center of the brain that might accompany experiences with such things. All of these things are merely part of the language, part of the means of conveyance—you gain the experience of happiness *through* these things, for these things allow happiness to be manifested through them and in you, but they are *not* the *sources* of the happiness. If you didn't have these things, you might not be happy, but this is not because these things are the sources of the happiness that you gain from them; they are merely the means by which you are allowed to receive happiness—part of the experience that the Source is sharing with you via them.

The reason it is so difficult for us to understand that the language used to define and convey the Source's experience is not what we are receiving through that language—that what we are receiving is not actually thoughts and feelings and instincts and physical objects, but rather self-aware existence, itself—is that we cannot gain the experience except through these language-defined forms. Like water molecules in a tree cannot experience the pull of the sun's energy except *via* other water molecules, we cannot be pulled upward toward self-awareness and fulfillment except *via* the things in this world. And since we never truly experience the fulfillment that we gain from these things and the things, themselves, separately, we come to believe that they are one and the same—that the defined things are the sources of the fulfillment, that the definition is the experience.

But when we believe this, we prevent ourselves from exercising our essence—which is the capacity to willfully choose these things—because we allow these things to choose themselves for us, through us, through our reactions to them (as we try to gain more of what we think we get from them by getting more of *them*—by getting more of these language-defined forms). And we end up straying from the present as it is because we seek to gain fulfillment from language-defined things that may not be in the present—language-defined things that may not exist now or that we may not have now—and this results in a lack of self-awareness and, consequently, a lack of fulfillment.

In order for any communication to occur between two "I"'s, there needs to be a common ground of experience and a common language used to refer to that experience. And so in order for the Source to communicate Its experience to us—in order for us to receive it in the form in which It is sharing it—

It needs to give us the experience, itself, and It does this via the language that is the stages of the tree of life paradigm. And in order for us to actually receive what the Source is sharing with us in its original and intended form, we need to learn the language that the Source is using—the language of the tree of life paradigm of creation—and we need to recognize that this is the language, itself, and is *not* the experience that is being conveyed through it. As we learn to understand and speak this language ourselves, we learn to receive through it the experience that the Source is intending to share, and thereby to communicate, with us.

The Path of Life that We Travel

Tracing the Path in the Specificity of Experience

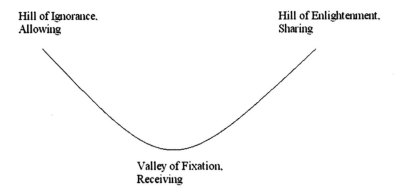

Hill of Ignorance.
Allowing

Hill of Enlightenment.
Sharing

Valley of Fixation,
Receiving

In this world where everything that exists is a manifestation of the tree of life paradigm and, more specifically, in this world of manifestation where three stages—allowing, receiving, and sharing—are manifested, over and over again, in this order (manifesting upward), we progress through the repetition of these stages, over and over again. We can look to the dominant positive feelings, with their corrupted and negative versions, and to the main personality type fixations, and to the tree setup, and to several other reflections of the stages, for guidance in understanding how we relate to the experience that we are receiving (ultimately from the Source, but via the world) at each of these stages.

We begin in this world in manifestation—in life—atop a hill of ignorance, allowing all that we receive (in its defined form) to be manifested through us. We can think about this in terms of the physical senses for the sake of having some particular manifestation to consider. We begin by taking everything in as we perceive it, without any understanding of our place in it or of how we relate to it. It is all raw experience, as the world's desire to preserve its existence is manifested through us, and the only significantly prominent inclination that keeps us going is the inclination to continue to exist. This is when we are like liquid water clinging to the inside of the roots, moving upward because of our clinging. Atop the hill of ignorance, we are engulfed in darkness, unable to perceive anything. And so we blindly grope for the things we need to survive, and we have nothing to be truly angry or shameful or fearful about, because we don't understand anything about the world yet; we're just experiencing it for the first time, and so we're just going to see what happens.

But what we are truly doing is simply *allowing* things to happen. We don't have any conception of the possibility of our control over what we experience. We feel like we don't truly have any control over what we experience, and so we simply allow things to happen, as they are dictated by the world—by the environment and the people—around us. At every allowing stage other than choice, we are not allowing the Source's pure and undefined experience to flow through us; we are merely allowing the world's definitions—the world's understanding, as it began to be reactively formed in the stage of receiving thought—to flow through us. And as we can learn from the negative versions of the dominant positive experiences, or from the allowing stages as main personality type fixations, we do not truly *experience* what we allow to be manifested through us. The world sort of just happens, and we aren't truly aware of it. We are on autopilot, allowing our lives to be manifested through us without our even being conscious of what we are doing—without our living in the present moment as it is, but rather in a sort of zoned-out trance, in our thoughts and feelings and inclinations regarding the present.

And, as we do this, we descend this hill of allowing and begin to transition into the valley below—into receiving—because the more we simply go through the motions, the more deeply we create patterns, or wear ruts, for ourselves, and the result is that the habitual patterns end up truly mindless and reactive. And so we begin to receive reactively from the world, more and more. Allowing the world to manifest itself through us, and perceiving what we get from it as truly originating with *it*, will ultimately always lead us into the valley—a valley of stress, and upset, and confusion, and even depression, a valley of reactive manifestation of our lives.

Now, we have some conception that we might have some control over our lives, but only if we exert a tremendous amount of energy to do so. We really have to work at life, because living, itself, is difficult. We have reached the point in the tree where we begin to succumb to the force of gravity, and if we do not begin to be pulled upward by some other force, we will not go anywhere. We have no clear goal pulling us forward. And we are lost in repetitive thoughts that think themselves through us, creating the same feelings and the same desires over and over again, creating our lives for us in reaction to the world. And we are merely aware that our thoughts are staticy, or that our feelings are dramatic, or that our instincts are overpowering, and we don't really have much control over their expression of themselves within us. And since they are now manifesting themselves *within* us instead of *through* us, even just going through the motions of living is difficult and burdensome.

We are filled with frustration and anger regarding the present, because we don't like where we are and what we are doing. We are filled with shame and regret regarding the past, because we don't like where we were and what we did. We are filled with anxiety and fear regarding the future, because we don't like where we might be going. And this is all because we have come to identify with our instincts, or our feelings, or our thoughts. We have come to be stuck in fixation, perceiving the things in this world as the sources of what we gain from them and so holding onto them in a vain search for fulfillment. And since we are holding onto things, the result is that we are consumed with unfulfilled desires that seek fulfillment through us, driving our behavior and ruling our lives. And we don't know how far we extend into the world around us, or how we relate to the other parts of the world, or how we should be making decisions, because we are not identifying with our true essence that is choice—wherein lies the clear answers to all of these questions.

Through our reactive manifestation of our experience, we distort our view of the world from its truth and reality. This valley is marked by only partial light, which shines at severely slanted angles, casting elongated and warping shadows all around us. And so when we look at the world, we cannot perceive it as it truly is; we cannot distinguish the distorted shadows from the reality. We limit ourselves within the confines of strict definitions regarding who we are and how the world works and how we relate to that world, and we are stuck in the inertia of sameness, as our perception of the way things are tries to preserve its existence in us. The result is that we are severely limited in our experience—caught up in particular aspects of different stages, becoming personified manifestations of certain stages of development, and unable to recognize the true roles that those stages have. We have very little concept of creation, because all of the creation—all of the definition of our lives—in which we engage is *reactive*—we do *not* willfully create our lives, and this is why living seems so stressful, so difficult.

We look at the world through our physical senses in a reactive sense—in an endlessly self-reflective, repetitive sense—so that we do not truly see through our eyes or hear through our ears, etc. We manifest our experiences *within* ourselves, rather than outside ourselves, and so we are caught up in a world that is *not* the world outside of us—we are caught up in a world of our own reactive manifestation. And our self-conscious, self-involved, self-oriented, and self-focused reality *becomes* our reality as we fight to maintain a stagnant and unchanging view of ourselves and of the people and the environment and the world around us, continually creating a tension between our world and the reality. And *this* is why living requires so much energy and is so difficult, because we are using all of our energy to fight against the natural changing flow of things as the world develops in its manifestation from moment to moment—we are using all of our energy to resist the way things actually are in the present moment. As we can learn from the corrupted versions of the dominant positive experiences, or from the receiving stages as main personality type fixations, we reactively manifest experience within ourselves, and we repeat and hold onto this experience in its defined form, thereby corrupting it from its original form like a pond corrupts the fresh rainwater that it receives by holding onto it—corrupting the experience of *life*, of *living, itself*, from its original form—and we therefore don't truly experience the experience as it has been shared with us.

The only way we can ever get out of this valley is by learning to become aware of what is actually arising in the present moment—within us, and especially outside of us. We need to learn to stop repeating and holding onto our experiences and, instead, we need to let them pass without reactively manifesting them within ourselves. We need to learn to look out of our physical senses at the world and truly perceive the world as it is, rather than as it looks through the warped, subjective lens that we have created for ourselves. We need to recognize that we are *not* our thoughts or our feelings or our instincts, and that *nothing* that we gain from *anything* within this world actually comes from the manifestation through which we get it. Fulfillment comes from staying with the rise and fall of things in the present moment, and not from lingering with our attention on things that are not in the present moment. We need to overcome the inertia of sameness and allow things to manifest as they truly are—as they are constantly changing. We must learn to obtain fulfillment from the Source, through the world, by allowing the world to flow through us—by sharing all that we receive.

Our ascent of the next hill as we move out of the valley is our ascent of the hill of enlightenment—a hill whose top is illuminated completely in light, where we can see everything as it truly is, understanding everything in its true form. This is where we allow the pull of some goal—a goal that is part of the overall goal of attaining self-awareness—to draw us forward, keeping us always progressing. We allow the pull of evaporation from above to draw us up the tree; we allow the pull of self-awareness to naturally electrify and intensify our experience as we come to intimately connect with all things in this world, drawing fulfillment from the Source through them, as we are compelled forward by upward development, as self-awareness builds upon itself. Life is enjoyable; it simply flows through us, and we flow through it, and we are grateful for it. And we recognize that *we* are in control of it. *We* create our experience from moment to moment. For we come to identify with our essence of choice, itself, and we choose our experiences and our lives as we wish them to be, constantly defining and shaping them in *willful response* to the world—rather than in *mindless reaction* to the world—from moment to moment. As we can learn from the positive versions of the dominant positive experiences, or from the sharing stages as main personality type fixations, we create and share our experience with the world outside of us, thereby making ourselves capable of receiving more of the material of existence, itself, for us to define and shape and share.

Instead of an inward-oriented *self-consciousness* that results from manifesting our experiences *within* ourselves, we manifest an outward-oriented *self-awareness* that results from creating our experiences and manifesting them in the world *outside* ourselves. We are aware of all things as they rise into existence and fall out of existence—from our thoughts and feelings and inclinations within us, to our speech and actions and the world outside us. Our internal and external experiences are illuminated with the clarity of their reality as being created by *us*, by our essence, by choice. And we allow our intuition to guide us as we create our lives, understanding the control we have over the world, understanding who we are and our relation to the world, understanding how we should be making decisions. For we are choice, and we create our world through the way we actualize our essence, and we glean fulfillment from the Source *through* that world, and when we are exercising our essence, our intuition provides guidance as to which choices we should be making.

Although our entire lives are the manifestation of this paradigm of allowing, receiving, sharing (or hill of ignorance, valley below, hill of enlightenment), once we descend from our very-young-childhood hill of ignorance—atop of which we merely allow the world to be manifested through us—our ascent of the overall hill of enlightenment is marked by a series of repetitions of this paradigm. And so we learn to share a bit, ascending what is a hill of enlightenment relative to the last hill, and then we begin to allow again, and then we hold onto things and repeat them and fixate, and the small hill of enlightenment that we have ascended proves to be a hill of ignorance relative to the next valley of fixation (of reactive receiving) and the next hill of enlightenment (of willful sharing). For we progress a little further each time before we lapse in our upward progression by ceasing to willfully define and share our experience with awareness and by, instead, merely allowing our lives to be defined for us—as we drift into our thoughts and feelings and inclinations about what is happening in the present (instead of simply experiencing what is happening directly). And then this self-reflection becomes repetitive and we come to fixate upon things, holding onto them and corrupting them from their original and pure form—*reactively* receiving them and manifesting them *within* ourselves. And then we need to learn to become aware and to define our experience and share what we receive—to allow what we receive to pass so that we can receive more self-aware existence in the forms that we willfully give to it, so that we can receive fulfillment and progress upward—once again.

We experience, we self-reflect, and then we figure out and understand. And, as we apply our understanding in the form of self-awareness, we define a new experience for ourselves and experience once again. We begin each new stage of experience by experiencing the present moment as it is—with self-awareness. Then we begin to lapse into our thoughts and feelings and inclinations regarding our experience (becoming unclear about where we end and the world begins, and so becoming concerned with defining our boundaries and thereby preserving our existence as separate from the world that we are experiencing). This turns into repetitive self-reflection and re-membering—or *re-creating*—(looking to the past, to what has already happened, to see how we relate to the other parts of the world—how we fit into the world—and becoming concerned with defining who we are in relation to that world) and holding onto and fixating. And eventually this repetitive self-reflection yields figuring out (looking to the future, to what might happen if we make one decision or another) and then understanding, which can be applied to experience in the form of self-awareness and intuition-guided shaping of our experience once again.

Whenever our defining and shaping of our world becomes mere allowing the world to manifest through us, we begin the pattern anew. But, like we saw with the end of the sleep cycle, we can, at the end of the overall day, progress upward through the overall tree of life paradigm so that we settle around thought and choice (as these are manifested in this world of manifestation). We can progress to a point where we live most of the moments of our progressing lives in the sharing stage in a lot of respects, moving through the stages without falling into endless self-reflection and fixation, but rather only contained self-reflection that allows us to learn from the past so that we can better shape the future. And so we can live in self-awareness (as it is experienced within this world), experiencing, reflecting, and learning from that experience, and progressing forward with self-awareness, guided by our intuition in the defining and shaping of our next experiences.

Tracing the Path of Manifestation, and of Creation, in Abstract

In this way, we progress through the paradigm, and through life, and through several lifetimes, toward self-awareness—toward the goal of developing the higher levels of our souls that correspond to the upper worlds, toward transcendence of the tree in the tree setup, transcendence of the multiverse in both its potential and actual forms. And we can realize here that when we reach choice, we cannot truly experience the Source's experience for, within choice, we merely allow the Source's experience to flow through us. (In order to understand what follows here, we must remember that the path of creation is the reverse of the path of manifestation, and so, in the process of creation downward, we progress from sharing to receiving to allowing.) We only begin to experience the Source's experience within sharing thought, where we can define it in a form that we can receive in receiving thought. And then, as the progression of all things in downward creation occurs, we ultimately begin to reflect upon the experience that we have defined and received, recreating it and holding onto it and fixating upon it in its defined form (for we cannot actually *experience* anything anywhere in the overall world *except* in defined form, since the Source's experience only remains undefined in choice, and we can only allow it to flow through us there without our experiencing it). And by holding onto it in its defined form and thus fixating upon it, we prevent ourselves from receiving more of it and we progress through the process of the creation of the world downward, increasing our fixation through continued self-reflection—through the repetition or recreation of choice, sharing thought, and receiving thought, in allowing thought and the feeling stages and the instinctual stages and finally in manifestation, where we are atop the hill of allowing—where no fixation is actively occurring, but where the result of all fixation is allowed to manifest.

We create downward from choice from atop the highest hill of enlightenment by allowing the Source to create the world through us and by consequently reaching sharing thought, where we begin to create willfully ourselves (overall sharing stage). Then we fixate and fall into the deepest valley—the world of feeling and instinct—where we give rise to repetitive self-reflection (overall receiving stage). Then, in manifestation, we end up allowing all of this fixation to manifest through us (overall allowing stage). And then we manifest upward (with repetitions of all three stages—of both hills and the valley in between—in reverse order, from allowing to receiving to sharing) toward choice once again through the increasingly willful exercise of choice in defining and shaping the development of the world's and our experience. And we must remember: Ignorance is bliss, just as enlightenment is. It is merely that, with one, the world is defined for us and is allowed to manifest through us without our true understanding of what is happening, and with the other, we willfully define our world with complete understanding. And, in fact, they are merely different sides of the same hill.

The progression of manifestation from allowing to receiving to sharing, and back to allowing to repeat the cycle again, is all the result of, and is the path of, our movement in relation to the Source (as is the progression of creation from sharing to receiving to allowing, and back to sharing to repeat the creative cycle again). Like the earth moves in relation to the sun, orbiting it, we move in relation to the Source, and our orbit is traced out by this path from hill of allowing to valley of fixated reception to hill of sharing. In our elliptical orbit, we speed away from the sun down the hill of ignorance, allowing ourselves to be thrown away from the source of our life energy and the illumination of our awareness and into space. We get lost in reflection upon our own thoughts and feelings and instincts—our own experience of the sun's energy—and we lose sight of the sun's energy as it is in its true form as the sun shrinks in our skies. We gradually slow down as the sun begins to pull us back, and we slowly curve around in our valley of fixation—fixation upon the energy that we have already received, in the form that we have received it. And we have grown far from the sun, and we can feel the effects of the lack of its constantly renewing energy, and we are not as illuminated by its light and warmth, by the light of self-aware existence, as we reach aphelion—the furthest point from the sun in our orbit. At this point, we begin to feel the effects of our being pulled toward the sun by its gravitational force, and as the pull of the sun becomes greater than our inertial patterns, we move toward the sun instead of continuing to move away from it, and we gradually move toward it faster and faster.

But we cannot quite reach it, even as we try to, because our clinging to our own inertial movement—our own inertial momentum—prevents us from heading directly toward the ultimate goal that draws us to it. And so the closer we grow to our goal, the less directly we move toward it, so that it seems as though it is harder to get just as much nearer to it the closer we are to it, even as its pull becomes greater—even as the pull of illuminated existence builds upon itself in our experience. However, if we were to head straight toward the sun, we would fall into it and be overcome by its energy, and we would be annihilated, becoming nothing but a part of its fiery glow, nothing but an ember in the flames. And so we whip around it, reaching perihelion—our closest point to it at the peak of the hill of sharing—all the while maintaining our separation and distinction from the sun. And here, at this very same point—our closest point to it—we begin to speed away from the sun again, our distance from it growing as we begin to allow ourselves to be thrown back out into the blackness of self-reflective space, beginning our progression through the cycle anew.

Like the earth moves around the sun, we move in relation to the Source, and we progress through our cyclical orbit, again and again. Every universe does this, and every individual does this, although the orbits are more elliptical for some universes, and for some individuals, than for others. Some of us have very circular orbits, remaining close to the same distance from the sun all of the way around—not descending very deep valleys, but also not ascending very high hills. And some of us are thrown quite far out into space, like a comet on its highly elliptical trajectory, but this very same path takes us very close to the sun, just as it takes us very far from it, and we repeat this over and over again, being thrown far away from the source of life energy, and being drawn tremendously close to it, and being thrown far away again, becoming ever more consciously aware of our lack of life energy and of self-awareness each time we are thrown back out into self-reflection. We ought to work to stabilize such orbits, to make them less elliptical, just as we ought to tighten our circular orbits so that we are closer to the Source all of the way around, for the goal of all of existence is to grow closer to that Source of existence, and to remain as close to It as we can, to exist as fully illuminated by the light of self-aware existence as we can as consistently as we can (while still being us).

(Notice that, from the perspective of the timelessness and general indefinitiveness of choice and the higher thought stages, our orbit of the Source is more like that of an electron around the nucleus of an atom than that of a planet around the sun. For, from this perspective, we are, in essence, *everywhere* in our orbital—and, in fact, everywhere in every orbital, every stage—at once; we are like an electron cloud around the nucleus that we orbit—around the Source. And we can move, in stages, closer to, or further away from, that nucleus—like electrons can move into different orbitals with a loss or gain of energy—and we are attracted to that nucleus—like the negatively charged electron is attracted to the positively charged nucleus—but we keep on orbiting it, rather than falling into it. If we are thrown too far away from that nucleus, we cease to be part of the atom that is the existing world. And it is highly unlikely that we would fall all the way into that nucleus, but if we were to do so, we would cease to be ourselves, distinct from that nucleus.)

We all define our own orbits. The Source determines that we must orbit It or cease to exist (for if we were to move too far from the Source, we would not have enough self-aware existence to exist, and so we would cease to be), and It created us to experience the light of self-aware existence that It experiences always. This is the Source's say in the defining of our existence. But *we* determine, with the language that we use, the shape of our orbit, and the specific course that it takes—that *we* take. *We* determine whether we grow closer to the Source overall, or further away, or whether we remain stagnant, repeating the same course over and over again without change, without progress toward greater self-aware existence.

We can learn from this that we cannot remain in the world of choice forever, for we must continue in our orbit, progressing onward in our manifestation, from allowing to receiving to sharing, and to allowing once again—for when we are pulled as close as we can be to the sun in our orbit of our existence as *us*, separate from the *sun*, we begin to be thrown away from the sun at that very same point. And we cannot remain in the world of choice forever because when we merely allow the world to be manifested through us, we cannot truly experience what the Source experiences, for we cannot truly create and define and share the world ourselves.

With regard to the process of manifestation upward (which is what we see reflected in the orbit of the earth, repeating itself over and over again), it is actually from the world of manifestation, where we are capable of defining our world to the largest degree (for this physical world is extensively defined in its nature and is more defined than any other part of the overall world), that we are capable of learning what it is like to be the Source of all that is. For the world of manifestation is the part of the overall world where the greatest degree of freedom is given to us in defining our world. It is here where we can truly choose how we define our world—as creative agents in ourselves who have choices and are capable of deciding amongst them, who are capable of using language to define and shape our experiences—rather than merely allowing the world to be created through us by the Source.

In this world of manifestation, we are capable of choosing between allowing the *world* to create and manifest *itself* and preserve the existence of its experience through us—through our reaction to it and thereby our recreation of it—and allowing the *Source* to create and manifest *Its* experience in, and to share *Its* experience with, the world through us—all along a spectrum from the extreme of one to the extreme of the other. Except we actually have much more freedom of choice even than this because of the fact that we can choose the specific definition that we give to our experience—the specific language that we use—either way, although we can choose our language much more freely when we are willfully allowing the Source to create through us than when we are mindlessly allowing the world to create through us. And so (in the process of manifestation) it is only *here*, in this *physical world*, where we can truly come to experientially understand what the Source experiences.

But when we truly come to understand this, we come to allow the Source to create the world through us, and then we forget what it is like to be creative agents in ourselves—to create the world of our own volition, through our own choice—and thus our hill of enlightenment becomes a hill of ignorance as we no longer directly experience the experience of being a self-aware creative agent in oneself (and so choice becomes manifestation—sharing becomes allowing—in our repetitive process of manifestation upward).

Only the Source, being the Source of Its own experience, never lapses in Its self-awareness—Its experiential understanding of what it is like to create the world with awareness that It is creating the world—and in Its self-aware inclination to create and share the world. Only the Source experiences self-awareness in the purest form—completely undefined, unlimited, beyond the bounds of language, without any delineation or form upon which It might fixate. In the world of language, we cannot share without defining. And when we define, we are at risk of getting caught up in the definition—of perceiving the delineated form of what we receive as being the source of what we receive from it—and of paying attention to *this* rather than to the experience (that we are defining), itself.

(By the way, it is the inclination to share the experience that we have received that guides us in the world of choice—in the downward process of creation—as well. We may fixate on our defined thought and begin to be inclined to work with others toward a common goal of the sharing of this experience—as multiple things are brought into existence through definition in the feeling stages—and then come to be inclined to preserve the existence of the world so that it can become capable of receiving the experience, but this all begins with the inclination to share the experience, which cannot be accomplished without the creation—and the maintained existence—of the physical world.)

And so, in the downward process of creation, we progress from allowing the Source's experience to be manifested through us in choice, to defining and sharing what we receive in sharing thought, to receiving in receiving thought, to thinking about our definition—our understanding—of the Source's experience, rather than simply experiencing the Source's experience as it is, and thereby allowing the world to manifest through us, in allowing thought. And then this defined thought to which we have given our attention manifests and defines a feeling, which we receive in our experience and allow to be manifested through us. And then this defined feeling to which we have given our attention manifests and defines an inclination, which we receive in our experience and allow to be manifested through us. And then this defined inclination to which we have given our attention is allowed to be manifested in the world of manifestation as a reiteration of all of the above in reverse order—in the order in which we experience the progression of our lives—as the world of manifestation reflects the actualization, and thereby the connection to, each of the stages above it in that order.

It might be realized that if we correlate the allowing stage with manifestation, the receiving stage with the world of feeling and instinct, and the sharing stage with the thought worlds and choice, then we must question how (in the upward process of manifestation) we can fixate on the higher thought stages or aspects of them. This might be questioned anyway, considering that the higher thought stages—namely sharing thought and receiving thought—are separate from the world of feeling and instinct (as well as from the world of manifestation), and so they would seem to be things upon which we cannot fixate within this world. However, it is important to recognize that we do not truly fixate on any of the stages as they are in their overall, original forms, separate from representations or reflections of them in the world of manifestation. Nearly all of our fixation within our existence in this physical world is actually upon defined *manifestations* of the different stages of the tree of life paradigm, *as they exist within the world of manifestation*, and is not on the different stages, themselves.

Even in the afterlife within the world of feeling and instinct, this is mostly the case, although there we might be able to fixate upon the manifestations as they exist within the stages of allowing thought, allowing feeling, and allowing instinct directly as well, prior to their manifestation in the world of manifestation. And we might even be able to do this to an extent within physical life also; when we fixate upon our thoughts or feelings or instincts, we might be fixating on the manifestations within the corresponding allowing stages directly to an extent—considering we truly are manipulating these elements as they exist in their potential forms within the world of feeling and instinct—even as we are fixating upon their manifestations as thoughts and feelings and instincts within this physical world. But other than this possibility that fixation upon our thoughts and feelings and instincts is fixation upon manifestations within the allowing stages, fixation upon pretty much everything is fixation upon manifestations of the other stages as they exist within the world of manifestation.

The other very important thing to realize is that the progression from allowing to receiving to sharing is gradual, forming a continuous spectrum from one stage to the next. So while the entire world of feeling and instinct (through which the manifestation of the universe traces its path upward) exists between the two hilltops, we can refer to the beginning stage of the universe as the allowing stage, the middle stage as the receiving stage, and the end stage as the sharing stage (depending upon which stage is dominant during that period of time) and there is a continuous progression down one hill, through the valley, and up the other hill—a progression marked by the increasing light of awareness from near-complete darkness to near-complete light. And we must remember that the very top of the hill of ignorance *is* the very top of the hill of enlightenment; it is merely that it is a hill of enlightenment as we approach it and it is a hill of ignorance as we fall from it down the other side of it (it is the choice of the *next* moment as we approach it and it the manifestation of *this* moment once we reach it, making it so that we never seem actually to reach choice, similarly to the way physical matter and energy can never truly reach a singularity, or to the way we can never truly reach the horizon).

Self-Reflection on the Path

In order to understand this a bit better, we must remember that the entire world as we know it, along with all of its contents, is a reflection of—is the result of repetitive reflection upon—the higher stages. This is what it means to be between the two hilltops; it is to be lost in thoughts and feelings and instincts, never fully experiencing the self-aware existence that is being defined by these things.

First, we allow things to happen, but we drift off in our thoughts and feelings and inclinations regarding what is being allowed to happen through us and around us as we let the universe experience and try to preserve itself through us—and so we have already begun the process of self-reflection, which in the universe manifested as the reflection of the thought stages in the spatial framework, and the reflection of the thought stages in the fundamental forces, and the combined reflection of the thought stages and the rest of the stages in time and gravity, and the reflection of the instinctual stages in matter and energy and in the inertially inclined physical movements of matter and energy, all of which occurred as the result of the world of manifestation's allowing the above stages to be manifested through it. Then, we begin to reactively receive, but we drift off in repetitive self-reflection as we try to figure out who we are in relation to everything else, making it so that what we are receiving is not actually what is being shared—and so the process of self-reflection continues, gradually coming to encompass more and more of the paradigm upward in its repetition, which in the universe manifested as the arising and propagating and evolving of life, and as everything that life manifested (and manifests). Then, we begin to define and share what we receive, making decisions about what we will receive so that we can receive what we actually want, and sharing what we receive so that we make room to receive new things—and so we truly still continue the process of self-reflection here, ever learning how better to make decisions by looking to the consequences that we can predict might result from making one choice or another based upon our experience in the past, which in the universe manifests as the shaping of the environment and so forth in guiding the evolution of life toward intelligence and self-awareness and the capacity to make decisions.

So, we see that self-reflection (reflection of the higher stages) marks the entire existence of the universe in potential form within the world of feeling and instinct (it actually marks the entire existence of the world of feeling and instinct, with the entire multiverse of universes in potential form, all of which is then allowed to actualize in the world of manifestation). And yet there are still transitions from allowing to receiving to sharing. We can fixate at any point along the way, but the very top of the hill of enlightenment is marked by the self-aware exercise of choice (and therefore relative lack of fixation) in directly experiencing what is happening. And this, of course, transitions into the allowing that is at the same hilltop, which is marked by the beginning of drifting from direct experience into thoughts and feelings and inclinations regarding the experience (the beginning of fixation).

The very top of the hill is choice, and a new manifestation. For we are always progressing from bottom up, manifesting from manifestation upward to choice. And every time we are just about to reach choice (sharing, atop the hill of enlightenment), we transition into manifestation (allowing, atop the hill of ignorance), beginning to manifest from the bottom up once again, self-reflecting increasingly until we encompass enough of the paradigm that we begin to figure out and understand, at which point we apply this understanding in the form of self-awareness as we approach the top of the next hill of enlightenment. We are like the water, ever moving up the tree, evaporating, and condensing and moving up the tree again. (Remember, we are tracing the path of manifestation, alone, here—the path that goes from allowing to receiving to sharing—and not the path of creation, and once we manifest all of the way up to choice, we begin manifesting up from the bottom—from manifestation—once again; once we reach the stage of sharing, we transition into allowing once again.)

We might think of this in the following way: Choice and manifestation are the hilltops, and everything in between is the progression from allowing to receiving to sharing—from the instinctual stages to the feeling stages to the thought stages (as these are actualized upward, the manifestation of which is reflected in the world of manifestation). In accordance with this, we can consider all of the three-stage patterns of the tree of life paradigm (all of those patterns that we have previously encountered) as being able to be contained within the world of feeling and instinct, such that the first stage corresponds with the instinctual stages, the second stage corresponds with the feeling stages, and the third stage corresponds with allowing thought—although also with the thought stages in general in the sense that the third stage is what allows the transition into self-awareness, in the sense that it is the third stage that most completely contains the potential for the actualization of self-awareness. This is basically how we have considered the three-stage patterns up to this point, and we can see now that it is justifiable because manifestation and choice are really the extremes; manifestation and choice are the very tops of the hills.

And so we can consider the descent of the hill of allowing as being part of the allowing stage, and we can consider the ascent of the hill of sharing as being part of the sharing stage, even as these are, in our experience within this world, actually part of the world of feeling and instinct—which in its entirety is the valley between the two hilltops, and is thus receiving relative to those two extremes that mark the very limits of the spectrum of development. Therefore, in essence, the paradigm of development that is the entire tree of life dictates the progression from hilltop to hilltop—the transition from the first stage of development to the third stage, which opens up into self-awareness and the consequent beginning at the first stage anew.

The hilltops are a very fuzzy transition from choice to manifestation—from sharing to allowing—like the twilight of dusk between day and night. We do not even realize the moment when we slip from one to the other, although we do realize afterward that we are no longer sharing (and ascending a hill of enlightenment) but are, rather, allowing (and descending a hill of ignorance). And when we realize this—when this comes into the light of our awareness—we then need to figure out and bring awareness to where we went wrong, and stop our descent into repetitive self-reflecting and increasingly holding onto what we receive, and work on ascending the next hill through defining and sharing (sharing with others and with the world, which in many cases simply entails letting pass) with awareness what we receive.

We begin by allowing the world to sense (to see and hear and physically feel) and to experience (to think and feel and be inclined) through us, at which point we are not truly sensing or experiencing ourselves, for we have no awareness of what we are sensing or experiencing (we are in darkness). We gradually transition to reactively receiving and manifesting within ourselves what we sense and experience in a way that becomes increasingly distorted the more we repeat and hold onto things and the further we get from the original things themselves (our memory of any experience is never the same as the experience itself, and it becomes increasingly distorted the more we repeat it with the guidance of our increasingly unfulfilled desires). And we further gradually transition to deciding how we shall define what we receive and then to actually defining and sharing what we receive, so that we define or create what we sense and experience and actually sense and experience it with awareness that we are doing so (our sensing and experiencing take place in the light of awareness).

Understanding the Path and Our Aim in Traveling It

From this perspective, we see that we can parse the tree of life into the three stages according to worlds. For even as choice is allowing relative to sharing thought, which is sharing relative to receiving thought (making for allowing, followed by sharing, followed by receiving), all three of these upper worlds are definitely sharing relative to the rest (think of the decision to unite, the father, and the mother, all in relation to the child). And then the world of feeling and instinct (which, remember, includes allowing thought, the feeling stages, and the instinct stages) is receiving relative to the above worlds (think of the womb in which the embryo develops as the embryo receives from the mother), and then the world of manifestation is allowing relative to all of the previous worlds (think of the outside world relative to the womb and the father and the mother—the outside world merely allows the child to be born into it, to be manifested through it). And so, parsing the tree of life in this way, we get sharing (the worlds of choice, sharing thought, and receiving thought), receiving (the world of feeling and instinct), and then allowing (the world of manifestation).

This way of framing this situation is significant because it puts our situation in a new light. For, here, the physical world merely allows all things to manifest within (or, rather, *through*) it (acting like the arena in which the interactions of all things above it manifest and play out—an arena which, itself, is part of the manifestation) without sensing or experiencing anything itself. Then, the world of feeling and instinct is where all of the self-reflection of receiving and holding onto occurs (where reactive manifestation and holding onto—which leads to fixation ultimately in the world of manifestation—occurs as we progress through all of the tripartite patterns of development that correspond with the instinct, feeling, and thought stages—for allowing thought, our only real form of thought in this world, is here to account for the thought stages) and this world is therefore the valley that marks our progression but is where we get stuck and where living is difficult. And the worlds of choice, sharing thought, and receiving thought are where the most significant sharing occurs in the overall world (where things are defined and allowed to pass so that more can be received). And the manifestation of the world progresses upward toward the actualization of each of these stages, so that we go from allowing, to receiving, to sharing, while the world is created downward from sharing, to receiving, to allowing. And while we live physically within the arena of the world of manifestation, the world of actuality in the present—this is where our physical lives play out—we truly live in the inner world of feeling and instinct that is this actual world in potential, in the process of development and formation in the womb.

[We can actually combine, here, several concepts that we have previously encountered. Choice and the thought worlds are sharing, the world of feeling and instinct is receiving, and the world of manifestation is allowing. In the tree setup, the world of feeling and instinct is the tree, itself, and the world of manifestation is the inner tubing of the tree through which the liquid water passes upward. We can now see clearly that creation outside of the tree (day) primarily consists of sharing, while manifestation inside the tree (night) primarily consists of allowing and receiving. This makes night female (receiving) in relation to day, and it thus makes day male (sharing) in relation to night. Also, in this light, we can see that we can speak of manifesting (or allowing to manifest) and receiving (or receiving and manifesting) together in contrast, or in opposition, to creating or sharing or to both creating and sharing together.]

We see in the idea that manifestation and choice (possibly along with sharing thought and receiving thought) are the hilltops that we truly do gradually transition from manifestation to choice, and we can get stuck at any point along the way down one hill, in the valley, or up the next hill. The only place where we can't get stuck in fixation is at the top of the hill, for any fixation that occurs there causes us to descend the hill (and it is fixation upon things other than the stage of choice that causes us to get stuck and descend). We also see here that in the receiving stage (in the world of feeling and instinct to which this stage corresponds)—at which point we are in the valley due to repetitive self-reflecting and holding onto, and thereby corrupting, what we receive—we are the most stagnated, repeating experience and not truly figuring out or, rather, *understanding* anything from it, and so not progressing forward at all when it comes to our progression through life, and through parts of our lives, from one hill to the next. It is easy to get stuck in the valley, even as it is difficult to live while we are stuck there. (And it is hard to remain at the top of the hill of enlightenment, even as it is easy to live while we are there.)

This makes sense for a lot of reasons. The more we repeat things, the deeper we wear the ruts of our patterns and the harder it is to get out of these patterns. Also, the entire purpose of life and of all of physical existence (in potential and actual form, from the stage of allowing thought all the way down to manifestation in the overall, original tree of life) is truly to figure out who we are and how we relate to the world and, ultimately, to the Source, so that we can learn to receive from the Source what the Source is actually sharing with us (in its true form). And *self-reflection* is how we do this—it is how we accomplish this purpose—even as self-reflection leads us away from direct experience and into fixation (in physicality in the world of manifestation). We must learn to experience, and to choose how we define what we experience, and to share and let go of what we experience so that we can experience more, all with self-awareness. And we can only learn to do this through self-reflection—so that we can gain experiential understanding and apply this, in the form of self-awareness, to our next experience.

As we learn to apply self-awareness to the way we live, we do not get caught up in repetitive self-reflection as much. For we have already learned that self-reflection need only occur to an extent, and that we need not fixate more than this, and that fixation actually removes us from experiencing life as it truly is—in the form that the Source is sharing it with us—and so self-reflecting more than is necessary for us to learn from past experience is actually antithetical to its purpose and aim, which is to make us more capable of directly receiving the experience in the form in which it is being shared with us.

We ideally learn, in this way, to spend most of our time *not* stuck in the valleys of fixated stagnation, but rather *actively and willfully progressing* and ascending the overall hill of enlightenment. We ideally learn to spend most of our time *not* merely trying to figure out how to secure enough resources to maintain our existence in the world, or how far we extend into that world, but *knowing* that the *Source* of all that we receive and all that we require in order to continue to exist is infinite, and that the only boundaries that exist between us and the rest of the world are those that *we define*—that *we choose*—for ourselves; *not* merely trying to figure out who we are and how we relate to (and fit in with) the other parts of the world and the Source, but *understanding* that our common essence (an essence that all parts of the world share) is *choice*, and that we must receive from the Source via the world and allow all things that we receive to pass; *not* merely figuring out how to decide in order to best connect with other aspects of the world, but *deciding—choosing—*in accordance with the guidance of our *intuition*, and intimately connecting with all things in the intense light of awareness so that we can receive more self-aware existence via them from the Source. Thus, we ideally learn to spend most of our time in the sharing stage relative to the rest of the stages (as the stages manifest within our lives).

And so we come to spend most of our time *experiencing* and *understanding*—and therefore *experiencing with self-awareness*—rather than spending most of our time *self-reflecting* (where we are removed from direct awareness of experience), for we self-reflect merely to the extent that is required to learn from our experience how we relate to the world and to others and to the Source. And we spend most of our time *applying* what we learn in the form of *self-aware engagement* with our experience—defining and sharing, and thereby fully receiving in a purer form, self-aware existence and, thus, the experience of what it is to be like the Source.

The Individual's Path toward Self-Awareness

The inclination of the "I", prior to being self-aware, is to identify with the language that it is using to describe its experience—to identify either mostly with the language that is in its thoughts (its own defined thoughts, its reactively received thoughts, or its allowed thoughts), or mostly with the language that is in its feelings (its own defined feelings, its reactively received feelings, or its allowed feelings), or mostly with the language that is in its instincts and speech and actions (its own defined instincts, its reactively received instincts, or its allowed instincts). When the "I" defines itself in this way, it creates a system of beliefs (patterns of thought), in the form of a personality of boundaries and obstacles for itself, and it limits itself to this personality—to this definition that is much more limited than its essence actually is—and it ultimately creates experiences for itself that manifest and confirm these limitations.

Interacting with the world and with other "I"'s in this way—which essentially entails viewing itself and the world and other "I"'s as the source of the things that they have—serves to uphold the limiting identity that the "I" is continually creating for itself, because when the "I" identifies with the language that it is using, in this way, then this identification determines the types of language that the "I" will continue to use—for they will be the same types of language that it has been using. It is this inertia—this continuing to exist as the "I" is existing, this holding onto and maintaining the "I"'s existence as it is—that

makes the "I" like a pond and prevents the "I" from changing its language to understand and receive more accurately the
language by which the Source is sharing Its experience with
it—that makes the "I" incapable of receiving existence and
experience in the form in which the Source is sharing these
things.

Further, when the "I" is identifying with its language in
this way, then it reacts to the world mindlessly, for whatever
happens in the "I"'s experience will determine the language
that the "I" uses to describe its experience—a mere combination of the external experience and the identified-with previous
language (which the "I" seeks to maintain) will produce the
next language and, thereby, the next experience. Also, when
the "I" is identifying with its language in this way, it looks
out at the world through a very warped lens. For the world
out there is not stagnant and unchanging as the "I" makes its
language—in habitual patterns of thought and feeling and desire and speech and action. The world out there is constantly
changing—evolving toward a closer reflection of the Source.
And the "I" must learn to change with it—not *in mindless reaction* to what happens in the world, but *in mindful response* to what
happens in the world.

What happens out there is a manifestation of the combination of the language that the "I" uses and the language that the Source uses, and if the "I" is not willfully
choosing its language with self-awareness, then it is fighting against that manifestation, wishing for it to be a certain
way and focusing on its not being that way—which only
brings about more of the world's being exactly as the "I"
doesn't want it to be, because it is on language regarding
this that the "I" is giving its attention and energy, as if to
tell the Source, "This. This is what I want. You see what
I'm thinking about. You see what I'm feeling. You see
what I'm focusing my attention and energy on—*this* is what

I want You to give existence to; *this* is what I want You to give me more of."

And the "I" lives in its own world—in its thoughts about what might happen in the future, in its feelings regarding what happened in the past, and in its instincts regarding what it wishes the present were. And the "I" is filled with anxiety and fear about the future, and with shame and regret regarding the past, and with anger and frustration concerning the present. And the "I" is unfulfilled. Because the "I" does not really exist where existence is. Because existence is in the present; only the present—as it is—exists. Only this moment is fulfilled, and only in this moment can fulfillment be found.

The "I" must learn to increase its awareness enough to realize what it is thinking and feeling and desiring and saying and doing *in the present moment*. And it must learn to monitor its thoughts—what language it is using to describe and further shape its experience—by monitoring its feelings. For the feelings that the "I" experiences are the first thing created by the language that the "I" is choosing to use in its thoughts. The feelings are the first indication of what the "I" is bringing into its future experience with the language that it is using. If the "I" feels good, then it is bringing good things into the world with the language to which it is giving its attention in its thoughts. If the "I" feels bad, then it is bringing bad things into the world with the language to which it is giving its attention in its thoughts.

So, if the "I" notices itself feeling bad, then it must ask itself, "What am I thinking that is making me feel this way?" And then it must change the language that it is using in its thoughts and shift its attention away from where it was and to something new and better—to what the "I" truly wants. Further, the "I" must not focus on the wanting, but rather on the thing itself, for wherever the "I" is focusing its attention and energy, it is as if it is pointing its finger and saying to the

Source, "That's it. That's what I want you to give me. That's what I want you to give existence to in my next experience of the world."

If the "I" learns to bring awareness to the present moment as it is—to live where it has the ability to choose and experience and describe its experience and make changes—and it comes to identify with its *ability to choose* the language that it is using (and therefore to choose what it is thinking and what it is feeling and what it is inclined to say and do and what it actually says and does), then the "I" will be well on its way toward the ultimate goal of existing with self-awareness, for self-awareness builds upon itself such that, once it is cultivated, it grows, faster and faster. There are, of course, always dips in the overall upward progression, but as long as the "I" uses these dips to learn from, and to learn better what it should be doing, then the dips will become part of what allows the overall upward progression. Once the "I" learns to recognize its ability to choose the language that it uses to describe and share and create its experience, then it must learn to *exercise* this ability—changing the language that it uses in its thoughts so that it creates the experiences that it truly desires and brings itself into a fuller and more fulfilled existence.

Ultimately, when the "I" becomes self-aware enough to use language consciously and willfully and proactively to describe and share and shape its experience, then the "I" begins to recognize exactly how thought and feeling and inclination and speech and action are supposed to be used. The "I" comes to realize that it has had these tools all along and it just didn't know how to use them. The way it expresses language in its thoughts creates its feelings, and these feelings create its inclinations, which guide it in its speech and actions. So, when the "I" is self-aware, the "I" can choose (ultimately in accordance with the guidance of its intuition, the sense of choice) the language of its thoughts to set goals—to set destinations for itself—whose fulfillment lies in the future, and it can learn from the past to do this (all of this—including the entire process that follows) better and better. Then, it can monitor its feelings to make sure that it is feeling good—that it is focusing on things that it actually wants to be bringing into its physical experience of the world. And it can allow itself to be guided by its intuition (a higher form of instincts, or desires, or inclinations, that stems from the "I"'s essence and that is always guiding the "I" toward greater awareness of its essence—toward greater self-awareness) toward speech and actions (and ultimately toward thoughts and feelings) that will bring the "I" to the realization and fulfillment of its goals within the (and will bring the "I" closer to the) overall goal of attaining an ever-greater capacity to use language to shape and share its experience and to bring itself and others toward greater self-awareness.

The Source, being beyond language, is capable of choosing whether It uses language to describe and share Its existence and experience or not, and It is also capable of choosing what language It uses to describe Its existence and experience and to share Its existence and experience if It chooses to describe it (as mere written words) and if It chooses to share it (to breathe existence into the written words by speaking them). In the physical world of manifestation, the "I" is not capable of choosing whether it uses language or not, for the "I", in this physical world, is surrounded by the manifestation of language and is always inherently shaping this manifestation, always using language—both to describe its experience and to share its experience—as long as it exists, merely by existing. But the "I" within this physical world *does* have the capacity for choice—it has the ability to choose what language it uses to describe its experience (in its thoughts and feelings) and what language it uses to share its experience (in its speech and actions).

Desire (which compels us merely to try to maintain our physical existence, in one way or another—sometimes in ways that are antithetical to this aim)—or (in its higher form as it stems from the "I"'s essence) intuition (which guides us toward self-awareness)—is the interface, or intermediary, between the "I"'s internal use of language (or description of experience) and the "I"'s external use of language (or sharing of experience). The language of thought and feeling does not need to manifest in speech and action by necessity, a bit like the Source's written language doesn't need to be spoken aloud by necessity, but the language of thought and feeling is what signals the directions of desire or the guidance of intuition. (To be more precise, it is actually our *choices*, themselves, that signal the guidance of intuition, for intuition comes prior to thoughts and feelings, guiding us even in *these*—in our defining of these—and not merely guiding us in our speech and actions.) And the "I" will be guided right toward the kind of experience described by the language to which it is giving its attention in its thoughts and feelings.

So, essentially, beyond the ability to choose the language that it uses in general, the greatest capacity for the "I" to choose lies in the capacity for the "I" to choose whether the language of its thoughts and feelings manifests itself in the "I"'s speech and actions, and whether the "I" allows itself to be guided by its desires (which don't stem from its essence, and which direct it away from self-awareness and into mindless reactive patterns of behavior, and doubt, and negativity, and stress, and *lack* of awareness and acceptance of the present as it is) or by its intuition (which stems from the "I"'s essence, and directs the "I" toward self-awareness, and mindful response and growth and change, and proactive behaviors, and positivity, and awareness and acceptance of the present as it is—for the "I" must accept the present as it is in order to live in it fully, and thereby to exist fully, and to exercise the ability to choose and make decisions and shape and share experience via the language that the "I" uses).

When the "I" follows its intuition, allowing itself to be guided by this direction that stems from its essence and, ultimately, from the guidance of the Source toward Its ultimate goal for the world, then the "I" is truly part of something larger than itself, striving for the fulfillment of the greatest of all possible goals. For every "I" in this world has the same essence, and it is via this essence—the capacity for self-awareness—that the Source guides the world toward the fulfillment of the purpose for which It created the world—to receive Its experience of being self-aware existence. And so, when the "I" follows its intuition, it watches as the world that it forms in its language takes shape, realizing itself in the "I"'s experience. And it watches the world with the fullest sense of existence as every interaction with every other "I" and with every thing becomes filled with the light of intense awareness. And it watches as every interaction becomes part of the path toward the fulfillment of every "I"'s goals on the path toward the fulfillment of the ultimate goal. And so the "I" guides the world—as part of the brain of this giant organism—toward an understanding of what the Source has always been trying to communicate to us, toward an understanding of the reason that the Source brought forth the world in the first place, toward an experiential understanding of what it is to be the Source of all that is.

3372192

Made in the USA